INTERNATIONAL ECONOM

'Bretton Woods' has become shorthand for the post-war international financial and economic framework. Mindful of the historic 1944 conference and its legacy for the discipline of international economic law, the American Society of International Law's International Economic Law Group (IELG) chose Bretton Woods as the venue for a landmark scholarly meeting. In November of 2006, a diverse group of academics and practitioners gathered to reflect on the past, present and future of international economic law. They sought to survey and advance three particular areas of endeavour: research and scholarship, teaching, and practice/service. This book represents an edited collection of some of the exceptional papers presented at the conference.

International Economic Law: The State and Future of the Discipline is organised into three parts, each covering one of the three pillars in the discipline of international economic law: research and scholarship; teaching; and practice/service. It begins with an assessment of the state and future of research in the field, including chapters on questions such as: what is international economic law? Is it a branch of international law or of economic law? How do fields outside of law, such as economics and international relations, relate to international economic law? How do research methodologies influence policy outcomes? The next part looks at the state and future of teaching in the subject. Chapters cover topics such as: how should international economic law be taught, and when and to whom? Should it be taught in different ways in different places? Is the training provided in the law schools suitable for future academics, government officials, or practitioners? How might regional shortcomings in academic resources be addressed? The final part of the book focuses on the state and future of international economic law practice in the Bretton Woods era, including institutional reform. The contributors consider issues such as: what is the nature of international economic law practice? What are the needs of practitioners in government, private practice, international and non-governmental organisations? How can pro-bono service in the field be encouraged? Finally, how have the Bretton Woods institutions adapted to these and other challenges—and how might they better respond in the future?

This book will be of interest to lawyers, economists and other professionals throughout the world—whether in the private, public, academic or non-governmental sectors—seeking both fresh insights and expert assessments in this expanding field. Indeed, the book itself promises to play a role in the next phase of the development of international economic law.

International Economic Law

The State and Future of the Discipline

Edited by
Colin B Picker
Isabella D Bunn
and
Douglas W Arner

OXFORD AND PORTLAND, OREGON
2008

Published in North America (US and Canada) by
Hart Publishing
c/o International Specialized Book Services
920 NE 58th Avenue, Suite 300
Portland, OR 97213-3786
USA
Tel: +1 503 287 3093 or toll-free: (1) 800 944 6190
Fax: +1 503 280 8832
E-mail: orders@isbs.com
Website: http://www.isbs.com

© The editors and contributors jointly and severally 2008

The editors and contributors have asserted their right under the Copyright, Designs and Patents Act 1988, to be identified as the authors of this work.

All rights reserved. No part of this publication may be reproduced, stored in a retrieval system, or transmitted, in any form or by any means, without the prior permission of Hart Publishing, or as expressly permitted by law or under the terms agreed with the appropriate reprographic rights organisation. Enquiries concerning reproduction which may not be covered by the above should be addressed to Hart Publishing at the address below.

Hart Publishing, 16C Worcester Place, OX1 2JW
Telephone: +44 (0)1865 517530 Fax: +44 (0)1865 510710
E-mail: mail@hartpub.co.uk
Website: http://www.hartpub.co.uk

British Library Cataloguing in Publication Data
Data Available

ISBN: 978-1-84113-755-1

Typeset by Compuscript Ltd, Shannon, Ireland
Printed and bound in Great Britain by
TJ International Ltd, Padstow, Cornwall

Acknowledgments

The editors wish to thank all of the authors who submitted chapters for this book, as well as the other individuals who contributed to the success of the American Society of International Law's International Economic Law Group's conference at Bretton Woods, including: Padideh Ala'i (American University, Washington College of Law, Washington, DC); Perry S Bechky (University of Connecticut School of Law, Hartford, Connecticut); Marc Benitah (Département des Sciences Juridiques, Université du Québec à Montréal, Montréal, Québec); Chad P Bown (Brandeis University, Department of Economics, Waltham, Massachusetts); Chi Carmody (University of Western Ontario School of Law, London, Ontario); Barnali Choudhury (Universität Zürich Rechtswissenschaftliche, Zürich, Switzerland); Kevin Gray (Trade Law Bureau, Department of Foreign Affairs & Trade, Ottawa, Ontario); David Hall (Franklin Pierce Law Center, Concord, New Hampshire); Craig L Jackson (Texas Southern University, Thurgood Marshall School of Law, Houston, Texas); David Kinley (University of Sidney School of Law, Sidney, New South Wales, Australia); Kyung Kwak (International Monetary Fund, Legal Department, Washington, DC); Rafael Leal-Arcas (University of London, Queen Mary College, London); Georges LeBel (Département des Sciences Juridiques, Université du Québec à Montréal, Montréal, Québec); Karl M Meessen (Friedrich Schiller Universität Jena, Düsseldorf, Germany); Ziyad Motala (Howard University School of Law, Washington, DC); Junji Nakagawa (University of Tokyo, Institute of Social Science, Tokyo, Japan); Jide Nzelibe (Northwestern University School of Law, Chicago, Illinois); Chantal Thomas (Cornell Law School, Ithaca, New York); Todd Weiler (Naftaclaims.com, Ontario, Canada); Stephen Zamora (University of Houston Law Center, Houston, Texas); and Galina Zukova (Riga Graduate School of Law, Riga, Latvia).

A further note of thanks to Joseph Patton of the American Society of International Law, Washington, DC, for his valuable administrative support, and to Shaun Darby and Jennifer Berhorst, law students at the University of Missouri at Kansas City School of Law, for their editorial assistance.

We also appreciate the conference support provided by the ASIL, Aspen Publishers, Baker & McKenzie LLP, University of Missouri at Kansas City School of Law and Wolters-Kluwer Law & Business.

We are especially grateful to the members and past leaders of the International Economic Law Group, whose years of contributions in international economic law teaching, scholarship and service provided the foundation for this project.

Finally, we would like to thank Richard Hart and the editorial staff at Hart Publishing in Oxford for their support and professionalism in producing this volume.

Colin B Picker
Isabella D Bunn
Douglas W Arner

Contents

Acknowledgements.. v
List of Journal Abbreviations... xi
Editors and Contributors xv

1 The State and Future of International Economic Law 1
  Isabella D Bunn & Colin B Picker

I THE STATE & FUTURE OF INTERNATIONAL
  ECONOMIC LAW RESEARCH... 13

2 At the End of the Yellow Brick Road: International
  Economic Law Research in Times of Uncertainty............................ 15
  Tomer Broude

3 A New Legal Realism: Method in International
  Economic Law Scholarship... 29
  Gregory Shaffer

4 International Economic Law Research: A Taxonomy....................... 43
  Joel P Trachtman

5 Opportunism and the WTO: Corporations, Academics
  and 'Member States'.. 53
  Sara Dillon

6 Some Sociological Perspectives on International Institutions
  and the Trading System 73
  Andrew T F Lang

7 Law of the Global Economy: In Need of a
  New Methodological Approach?.. 89
  Federico Ortino and Matteo Ortino

8 Of Foxes and Hedgehogs: Some Thoughts about the Relationship
  Between WTO Law and General International Law...................... 107
  Emmanuel Voyiakis

9 Different Scholarships, the Same World: Interdisciplinary
   Research on IEL 121
   Chen-Yu Wang

II THE STATE & FUTURE OF INTERNATIONAL
    ECONOMIC LAW TEACHING 133

10 International Economic Law in US Law Schools: Evaluating
    Its Pedagogy and Identifying Future Challenges 135
    Karen E Bravo

11 Venutian Scholarship in a Martian Landscape: Celebrating and
    Reflecting on Women in International Economic
    Law Teaching and Scholarship 157
    Tracey Epps & Rose Ann MacGillivray

12 An Essay on Teaching International Economic Law from
    a Corporate Perspective 171
    Franklin A Gevurtz

13 New Agendas for International Economic Law Teaching in India:
    Including an Agenda in Support of Reform 185
    Seema Sapra

14 Shifting Paradigms of Parochialism:
    Lessons for Legal Education 207
    Elizabeth Trujillo

15 Corporate Social Responsibility of Multinational Enterprises
    and the International Business Law Curriculum 219
    Constance Z Wagner

III THE STATE & FUTURE OF INTERNATIONAL
     ECONOMIC LAW PRACTICE IN THE BRETTON
     WOODS ERA 235

16 The Future of International Economic Law Practice 237
    Amelia Porges

17 The Developing Discipline of International Financial Law 245
    Douglas W Arner

Contents ix

18 Investment Treaty Arbitral Decisions as *Jurisprudence Constante* 265
    Andrea K Bjorklund

19 The Role of Law and Lawyers in Vietnam's WTO Accession 281
    David A Gantz

20 Exercising Quasi-Judicial Review Through a World Bank
    Appellate Body 297
    Rumu Sarkar

21 Jurisdiction to Prescribe and the IMF 313
    Andreas F Lowenfeld

Index 331

List of Journal Abbreviations

Am Econ Rev—American Economic Review
Am J Comp L—American Journal of Comparative Law
Am J Int'l L—American Journal of International Law
Am J Soc—American Journal of Sociology
Am Q—American Quarterly
Am Rev Pol Sci—American Review of Political Science
Am Soc'y Int'l L Proc—Proceedings of the American Society of International Law
Am U J Int'l L & Pol'y—American University Journal of International Law and Policy
Am U Int'l L Rev—American University International Law Review
Arb Int'l—Arbitration International
Ariz J Int'l & Comp L—Arizona Journal of International and Comparative Law
BC Int'l & Comp L Rev—Boston College International and Comparative Law Review
Berkeley J Int'l L—Berkeley Journal of International Law
Brit YB Int'l L—British Yearbook of International Law
Buff Hum Rts L Rev—Buffalo Human Rights Law Review
Cardozo L Rev—Cardozo Law Review
Chi-Kent L Rev—Chicago-Kent Law Review
Colum J Envtl L—Columbia Journal of Environmental Law
Colum J Eur L—Columbia Journal of European Law
Colum L Rev—Columbia Law Review
Colum J Transnat'l L—Columbia Journal of Transnational Law
Cornell Int'l LJ—Cornell International Law Journal
Dep't St Bull—Department of State Bulletin
Duke LJ—Duke Law Journal
E Asian Executive Rep—East Asian Executive Reports
Eur J Int'l L—European Journal of International Law
Feminist Econ—Feminist Economics
Fin YB Int'l L—Finnish Yearbook of International Law
Fordham Int'l LJ—Fordham International Law Journal
Foreign Aff—Foreign Affairs
Geo J Int'l L—Georgetown Journal of International Law
Geo LJ—Georgetown Law Journal
Harv Envtl L Rev—Harvard Environmental Law Review
Harv Int'l LJ—Harvard International Law Journal

Harv Int'l Rev—Harvard International Review
Harv L Rev—Harvard Law Review
Harv J L & Gender—Harvard Journal of Law and Gender
Hong Kong LJ—Hong Kong Law Journal
Hum Rts L Rev—Human Rights Law Review
Hum Rts Q—Human Rights Quarterly
ILSA J Int'l & Comp L—ILSA Journal of International and Comparative Law
Int'l & Comp LQ—International and Comparative Law Quarterly
Int'l Lawyer—The International Lawyer
Int'l Org—International Organization
Int'l Stud Q—International Studies Quarterly
J Compar Econ—Journal of Comparative Economics
J Econ Hist—Journal of Economic History
J Econ Literature—Journal of Economic Literature
J Eur Pub Pol'y—Journal of European Public Policy
J Int'l & Comp L—Journal of International and Comparative Law
J Int'l Arb—Journal of International Arbitration
J Int'l Bnkg Reg—Journal of International Banking Regulation
J Intl Econ L—Journal of International Economic Law
J Int'l L & Int'l Rel—Journal of International Law and International Relations
J Interdisc Int'l Rel—Journal of Interdisciplinary International Relations
J L & Soc Challenges—Journal of Law and Social Challenges
J Legal Educ—Journal of Legal Education
J World Trade—Journal of World Trade
J World Invest & Trade –Journal of World Investment and Trade
J World Trade & Inv—Journal of World Trade and Investment
L & Bus Rev Am—Law and Business Review of the Americas
La L Rev—Louisiana Law Review
Law & Contemp Probs—Law and Contemporary Problems
Law & Pol'y Int'l Bus—Law and Policy in International Business
Law & Soc Inquiry—Law and Social Inquiry
Law & Soc Rev—Law and Society Review
Loy U Chi Int'l L Rev—Loyola University Chicago International Law Review
Mich J Int'l L—Michigan Journal of International Law
Mich L Rev—Michigan Law Review
Minn J Global Trade—Minnesota Journal of Global Trade
Minn L Rev—Minnesota Law Review
Mod L Rev—Modern Law Review
Monthly Lab Rev—Monthly Labor Review
NC J Int'l Com Reg—North Carolina Journal of International Commercial Regulation

Nordic J Int'l L—Nordic Journal of International Law
Nw J Int'l L & Bus—Northwestern Journal of International Law and Business
NYU J Int'l L & Pol—New York University Journal of International Law and Politics
Open Econ Rev—Open Economies Review
Or L Rev—Oregon Law Review
Penn St Int'l L Rev—Penn State International Law Review
Policy Rev—Policy Review
Pub Admin—Public Administration
Rec des Cours—Recueil des Cours, Académie de Droit International de la Haye
S Cal L Rev—Southern California Law Review
San Diego L Rev—San Diego Law Review
Stan L Rev—Stanford Law Review
Stetson L Rev—Stetson Law Review
Syracuse J Int'l L & Com—Syracuse Journal of International Law and Commerce
S Tex L Rev—South Texas Law Review
Tex Int'l LJ—Texas International Law Journal
Transnat'l Disp Mgmt—Transnational Dispute Management
Tul J Int'l & Comp L—Tulane Journal of International and Comparative Law
U Ill L Rev—University of Illinois Law Review
U Miami Inter-Am L Rev—University of Miami Inter-American Law Review
U of Chi L & Econ—University of Chicago Law and Economics
U Pa J Int'l Econ L—University of Pennsylvania Journal of International Economic Law
UC Davis L Rev—University of California at Davis Law Review
U Chi L Rev—University of Chicago Law Review
Urb Law—Urban Lawyer
Va J Int'l L—Virginia Journal of International Law
Wis Int'l LJ—Wisconsin International Law Journal
Wis L Rev—Wisconsin Law Review
Wm & Mary Envtl L & Pol'y Rev—William & Mary Environmental Law and Policy Review
World Trade Rev—World Trade Review
Yale LJ—Yale Law Journal

Editors and Contributors

EDITORS

COLIN B PICKER, AB (Bowdoin College), JD (Yale), is the Daniel L Brenner/UMKC Scholar & Professor of Law at the University of Missouri Kansas City School of Law. His research interests include international and comparative law. Professor Picker is currently co-chair of the Founding Committee of the Society of International Economic Law, as well as a former co-chair with Isabella Bunn of the ASIL's International Economic Law Group.

ISABELLA D BUNN, BSFS, MA, JD, MPhil, PhD, is affiliated with Regent's Park College, University of Oxford, where she specialises in ethical aspects of international economic law. She also holds a professorial Chair of Ethics at the Florida Institute of Technology College of Business. Dr Bunn has prior experience as a legal adviser in the public and private sectors. Together with Colin Picker, she served as co-chair of the ASIL's International Economic Law Group and of the conference at Bretton Woods.

DOUGLAS W ARNER is Director of the Asian Institute of International Financial Law and Associate Professor at the Faculty of Law of the University of Hong Kong. In addition, at HKU, he is Director of the LLM (Corporate & Financial Law) Programme, a member of the Board of Management of the East Asian Economic Law and Policy Programme, and co-Director of the joint Duke-HKU Asia America Institute in Transnational Law. Dr Arner is author, co-author or editor of 8 books and over 50 articles, chapters and reports on economic and financial law, regulation and development.

CONTRIBUTORS

ANDREA K BJORKLUND, BA, MA, JD, is a professor at the University of California, Davis, School of Law, where she teaches courses in international arbitration and litigation, international trade, international investment, public international law, conflict of laws and contracts. Professor Bjorklund's research focuses on investor-state arbitration, and she has written on denial of justice, the state of necessity defence, and the differences between appeal and annulment of arbitral awards, among other topics.

KAREN E BRAVO, BA, JD, LLM, is assistant professor of law at Indiana University School of Law, Indianapolis, where she teaches and researches public and private international law, including regional trading arrangements, sovereignty, democratisation, human trafficking and labour liberalisation. She served as a Co-Rapporteur for the Workshop on the Future of Teaching International Economic Law at the Bretton Woods Conference.

TOMER BROUDE, BA (Int. Rel), LLB, SJD, is Lecturer at the Hebrew University of Jerusalem Faculty of Law and Department of International Relations. He is currently Co-Chair of the American Society of International Law International Economic Law Interest Group (with Amy Porges) and a member of the International Law Association's Committee on the International Law of Sustainable Development.

SARA DILLON is Professor of Law at Suffolk University Law School in Boston, where she teaches international law subjects, including international trade law and European Union law. She previously taught in the Law Faculty at University College Dublin for seven years. She holds a PhD from Stanford University and a JD from Columbia University in New York.

TRACEY EPPS, BA/LLB (Hons) (Auckland), LLM (Tor), SJD (Tor), is a lecturer at the Faculty of Law at the University of Otago in New Zealand. Her research interests revolve around international trade and investment.

DAVID A GANTZ, AB, JD, SJM, is Samuel M Fegtly Professor of Law and Director of the International Trade and Business Law Program at the University of Arizona, James E Rogers College of Law, where he teaches in the areas of international trade and investment law. He served earlier in the Office of the Legal Adviser, US Department of State, and practised international trade law in Washington, DC.

FRANKLIN A GEVURTZ, BS, JD, is a Distinguished Professor and Scholar at the University of the Pacific, McGeorge School of Law, and the Director of the Pacific McGeorge Institute for Global Business. He has written books and articles in the area of business and corporate law, recently including the book, *Global Issues in Corporate Law* which is part of a series of books (for which Professor Gevurtz serves as series editor) designed to facilitate the introduction of international and comparative law issues in core law school courses.

ANDREW TF LANG, BA, LLB, PhD, is a member of the Department of Law at the London School of Economics and Social and Political Sciences. His research is in the field of public international law, specialising in international economic law, and focusing at present on the relations between law and knowledge in institutions of international economic governance. He is, together with Colin Picker, co-chair of the Founding Committee of the Society of International Economic Law.

ANDREAS F LOWENFELD is Rubin Professor of International Law at New York University Law School, where he has been on the faculty since 1967. He has taught, practised, and written in nearly all aspects of international law for more than five decades. He is the author of numerous publications in the area of International Economic Law, including a major treatise on the subject. He is an elected member of the Institut de Droit International and of the International Academy of Comparative Law, and has twice been a lecturer at The Hague Academy of International Law. Prior to becoming a professor, he worked in private law practice and at the Office of the Legal Adviser, US Department of State. Professor Lowenfeld is a graduate of Harvard College and Harvard Law School.

ROSE ANN MacGILLIVRAY is a doctoral candidate in the Faculty of Law at the University of Toronto and a fellow of the Centre for Innovation Law and Policy. Her area of research is parallel importation. She has 25 years of experience in teaching business law courses at business schools in Canada. She was also a visiting fellow at Nanyang Business School in Singapore.

FEDERICO ORTINO is a Lecturer in International Economic Law at King's College London. He is co-rapporteur to the ILA Committee on the Law of Foreign Investment. Previous positions include: Fellow at the British Institute of International and Comparative Law; Adjunct Professor at the University of Trento; Emile Noel Fellow at the NYU Jean Monnet Center; Legal Officer at UNCTAD. Dr Ortino holds a law degree from the University of Florence, a master of laws from Georgetown University Law Center and a doctorate from the European University Institute, Florence.

MATTEO ORTINO is Associate Professor at the Faculty of Laws, University of Verona. He holds degrees in political science and in law from the University of Florence, and a doctorate from the University of London.

AMELIA PORGES, AB, MPP, JD, practises international trade and investment law at Sidley Austin LLP in Washington DC, drawing on her experience at USTR and the GATT Secretariat litigating cases and advising on negotiations. Her current interests focus on trade in digital content. She also teaches WTO law at Johns Hopkins University.

SEEMA SAPRA is Director, Trade & Policy at Amarchand Mangaldas, a leading law firm in India. She holds an LLB from University of Delhi and an LLM from the University of Leicester. She has been a visiting fellow at Georgetown University Law Centre, where she worked for the *Journal of*

International Economic Law. She is completing a PhD from Kings College London on the meaning of development in the context of the World Trade Organization.

RUMU SARKAR, BA, JD, LLM, PhD, serves as Senior Legal Adviser to CALIBRE Systems, a defence consulting group based in Alexandria, Virginia. She has prior experience in private and government practice. She is a Visiting Researcher and an Adjunct Law Professor at the Georgetown University Law Center, with interests in government administration and litigation, commercial legal reform, and international business transactions.

GREGORY SHAFFER is Wing-Tat Lee Chair at Loyola University Chicago and in 2008 will become the James L Krusemark Chair at the University of Minnesota Law School. His publications include *Defending Interests: Public-Private Partnerships in WTO Litigation* (Brookings), *Transatlantic Governance in the Global Economy* (Rowman & Littlefield), *When Cooperation Fails: The Law and Politics of Genetically Modified Foods* (OUP) and over 50 articles and book chapters on international trade law, global governance and globalisation's impact on domestic regulation.

JOEL P TRACHTMAN is Professor of International Law at The Fletcher School of Law and Diplomacy at Tufts University. His research interests include international economic law, focusing on international trade law and the application of social scientific techniques to international legal research. Professor Trachtman has prior experience in the private practice of international commercial law in New York and Hong Kong. He graduated in 1980 from Harvard Law School where he served as editor-in-chief of the *Harvard International Law Journal*.

ELIZABETH TRUJILLO is associate professor at Suffolk University Law School in Boston. Currently, she writes and lectures in the areas of international trade and its impact on domestic regulatory structures and transnational processes. Professor Trujillo teaches Contracts, Domestic and International Sales, and NAFTA. Prior to her academic career, she worked for UNESCO in Paris, France, and in private practice.

EMMANUEL VOYIAKIS, LLB (Thrace), LLM (LSE), PhD (UCL), is a lecturer at Brunel Law School, Brunel University, UK. He conducts research on the theory of public international law, especially the relationship between different branches of international law, and private law.

CONSTANCE Z WAGNER, BA, JD, LLM, is Associate Professor of Law at Saint Louis University School of Law and is affiliated with the School of Law's Center for International and Comparative Law. She teaches and writes in the areas of international economic law, corporate law, corporate social responsibility and financial regulation. Prior to entering academia, she practised corporate law in New York City.

CHEN-YU WANG is a professor at the Chinese Culture University in Taiwan. His academic background includes studies at the American University and Harvard University.

1

The State and Future of International Economic Law

ISABELLA D BUNN & COLIN B PICKER

I. A RETURN TO BRETTON WOODS

The Conference at Bretton Woods [in 1944] erected a signpost—a signpost pointing down a highway broad enough for all men to walk in step and side by side. If they will set out together, there is nothing on earth that need stop them.[1]

FOR THE INTERNATIONAL lawyer, many place-names hold an echo of an important treaty or milestone in global politics: Versailles, Geneva, Yalta, Kyoto, Rome. For the international economic lawyer, no place name holds greater resonance than Bretton Woods. To us, Bretton Woods represents more than just the location of a war-time conference at which representatives of 44 countries founded the World Bank and the International Monetary Fund. It is short-hand for the post-war international financial and economic framework. More recently, perhaps, the name has become a lightning rod for critiques about the adequacy of such a system in the face of increased economic globalisation, unprecedented financial crises, and the social consequences of its institutional policies. But still, Bretton Woods carries a remarkable mystique.

When the prospect of holding a scholarly conference at Bretton Woods was raised at a 2005 meeting of the American Society of International Law's International Economic Law Group (IELG) in Washington, the attention of the group suddenly galvanised. There was a general sense of excitement, despite some concerns about costs, travel logistics and bad weather. But where was Bretton Woods, exactly? We had vague impressions of a legendary Victorian-style resort in the mountains of New Hampshire. The chance to visit this place that had profoundly shaped our work, whether in

---

[1] A Van Dormael, *Bretton Woods: Birth of a Monetary System* (Holmes & Meier Publishing, 1978) 222 (quoting 'Proceedings and Documents of United Nations Monetary and Financial Conference', Bretton Woods NH, 1–22 Jul, 1944 (Washington DC: Dep't of State 1948) ('Proceedings') 1224–8).

academia, private practice, advocacy groups, or governmental and international organisations, proved irresistible.

Over the following months, we reflected on a theme for the conference centring on the past, present and future of international economic law. We also wanted to survey and advance three particular areas of endeavour: research and scholarship, teaching, and practice/service. We identified these as the pillars of our discipline. Just as the seminal Bretton Woods conference led to the development of three pillars in the international economic system—the World Bank, International Monetary Fund, and later the General Agreement on Tariffs and Trade (now World Trade Organization)—so our own conference focused on three pillars in the discipline of international economic law.

A call for papers was drafted by the conference planning committee, and dispatched to various scholars, legal practitioners, government officials and international organisation representatives. We were impressed by the range and diversity of the submissions—both geographically and intellectually. We also began the process of making practical arrangements for group transportation, lodging, meals and social activities. A busy extended weekend program was soon finalised.

The conference was held from 9–12 November 2006, in the historic setting of the Mount Washington Hotel. We were mindful of this 'return to Bretton Woods,' of revisiting a venue associated with the establishment of the post-war international economic framework. But our aim was to be forward looking, with the conference title being *International Economic Law—The State and Future of the Discipline*. We were graced with fine autumn weather, extraordinary food and ambience, but most importantly, the presence of scholars and practitioners of 16 different nationalities. This book is a selection of papers presented at the conference, edited by Colin Picker and Isabella Bunn (the then co-chairs of the IELG and the conference), as well as Douglas Arner.

II. THE AMERICAN SOCIETY OF INTERNATIONAL LAW AND THE INTERNATIONAL ECONOMIC LAW GROUP

The American Society of International Law (ASIL) was founded over 100 years ago. Its broad mission is to foster the study of international law and to promote the maintenance of international relations on the basis of law and justice. Many of the Society's activities at the membership level take place through a variety of 'interest groups.' The International Economic Law Group was formed over 20 years ago, and is typically credited with being both the largest and the most successful of all the ASIL interest groups. Its objectives are as follows:

> The International Economic Law Interest Group promotes academic interest, discussion, research and publication on subjects broadly related to the

transnational movement and regulation of goods, services, persons and capital. International law topics include trade law, economic integration law, private law, business regulation, financial law, tax law, intellectual property law and the role of law in development. The group is interested in diverse interdisciplinary explorations of public and private international and municipal law, and is particularly interested in promoting the work and interests of new practitioners and scholars in the field. In addition to sponsoring panels at the ASIL Annual Meeting and co-sponsoring conferences, the group also holds annual or bi-annual conferences, following an open Call for Papers sent to group members. All IELG conferences are organized with the objective of addressing pressing and important issues in international economic law, including the role and development of the multilateral trading system and particularly the World Trade Organization. Research generated by these conferences have regularly been published as symposia in law review journals, and are often considered some of the most influential and cutting-edge scholarship in the field.[2]

We owe a great debt to the leadership of the IELG over the last two decades, including, among many others, Jeffrey Lang, Ted Kassinger, Keith Highet, John Jackson, Gary Horlick, Steve Zamora, Jeff Dunoff, Cherie Taylor, Jeff Atik, Craig Jackson, Frank Garcia, Joel Trachtman, Ron Brand, Joel Paul, Willajeanne McLean, Padideh Ala'i, and Todd Weiler. We were pleased that several previous chairs and co-chairs of the group were able to join us at Bretton Woods.

Foremost on the IELG's list of accomplishments is the series of conferences it has organised over the years. Papers presented at these conferences have often been published in the form of a law review compendium or as an edited collection of articles in a book.[3] The range of themes has included:

— Teaching international economic law
— Interdisciplinary approaches to international economic law
— The phenomenon of trade linkages

---

[2] See www.asil.org.
[3] The first IELG conference, in 1992, was devoted to teaching international economic law. The second IELG conference, 'Interdisciplinary Approaches to International Economic Law', was published in (1995) 10 *Am U J Int'l L & Pol'y* 595. The third conference, 'Institutions for International Economic Integration', was published in (1997) 17 *Nw J Int'L & Bus* 351. The fourth conference, 'Linkage as Phenomenon: An Interdisciplinary Approach', was published in (1998) 19 *U Pa J Int'l Econ L* 209 and (1998) 19 *U Pa J Int'l Econ L* 709. The fifth conference, 'Interfaces: From International Trade to International Economic Law', was published in (2000) 15 *Am U Int'l L Rev* 1231. The sixth conference, 'International Economic Conflict and Resolution', marked the first time the IELG held a conference outside of Washington—in Houston, Texas. The conference proceedings produced two law review volumes, (2002) 42 *S Tex L Rev* 1187 (Opening Session) and (2002) 22 *Nw J Int'l L & Bus* 311 (Plenary Sessions). Selected papers from the seventh conference, 'Interrelationships: International Economic Law and Developing Countries', were published in (2004) 27 *BC Int'l & Comp L Rev* 187. Papers from the eighth IELG conference were published in book form in Padideh Ala'i, Tomer Broude, & Colin B Picker (eds), as *Trade as the Guarantor of Peace, Liberty, and Security? Critical, Historical and Empirical Perspectives* (American Society of International Law, 2006).

4 *Isabella D Bunn & Colin B Picker*

— Economic conflict and resolution
— The relationship between international economic law and developing countries
— The role of trade with respect to peace, liberty, and security

Thus, this Bretton Woods conference continued a distinguished tradition of memorable events in the field of international economic law.

III. ORGANISATION OF THE BOOK

This book—*International Economic Law: The State and Future of the Discipline*—is organised into three sections, each covering one of the three pillars in the discipline of international economic law: research and scholarship; teaching; and practice/service.

A. Research and Scholarship

The book begins with a consideration of the state and future of research in the field of international economic law. The participants at our Bretton Woods conference considered a wide variety of fundamental issues associated with research in the field, including: What exactly is international economic law? Is it a branch of international law or of economic law? How do fields outside of law, such as economics and international relations, relate to international economic law? What role do national and regional legal systems play? What is the place of various actors in the process—governments, regional authorities, intergovernmental organisations, non-governmental organisations, corporations, and private parties—and how are their concerns addressed? How does research methodology influence policy outcomes?

From our setting in the White Mountains of New Hampshire, we were quickly taken to the Land of Oz, as Tomer Broude asked what we may find *At the End of the Yellow Brick Road: International Economic Law Research in Times of Uncertainty.* In today's complex global economic, social and political environment, the field of international economic law research is confronted with a double challenge. On one hand, if we strictly adhere to our expertise as interpreters and engineers of the law, our scholarship may become too narrowly 'legal' to be relevant to the major substantive debates of our times. On the other hand, if we wish to engage effectively in these debates, we must adopt theories and methods of other, non-legal disciplines, perhaps even to the point of assimilation. Thus, the diversity of research methodologies in international economic law runs the risk of irrelevance or redundancy. With allegorical reference to the heroes of Oz, Broude offers insights on how to avoid intellectual fragmentation.

Greg Shaffer examines *A New Legal Realism: Method in International Economic Law Scholarship*. His Chapter begins with a typology and brief assessment of four varieties of international economic law scholarship: formalist/doctrinal, normative/activist, theoretical/analytical, and empirical. Shaffer notes some of the strengths and limitations of each approach, and explores the relationship between them. He argues that, while we may engage in different varieties of scholarship at different times, a new legal realist empirical approach provides important insights that are currently being overlooked in scholarship in the field of international economic law.

Joel Trachtman takes us through *International Economic Law Research: A Taxonomy*, describing several types of research in terms of theory and empiricism, showing the balance between these two components, and suggesting the general strengths and weaknesses of each of these strategies. He enlivens the discussion by commenting on how his own reflections and research have evolved as a result of his greater attention to questions of methodology.

Sara Dillon warns scholars against complacency in a critique entitled *Opportunism and the WTO: Corporations, Academics and 'Member States'*. Dillon challenges the foundations of much of the legal commentary about the WTO, questioning how academics provide intellectual justification for the WTO and its law. She also underscores what she sees as the opportunism of transnational corporations in seeking enhanced profits through trade negotiations, as well as the opportunism of WTO members in using the forum as a stage for demonstrating strategic abilities. Overall, she urges international economic law scholarship to be less abstract, and more responsive to the complexities of global governance and the diversity of interests that it needs to serve.

Andrew Lang offers *Some Sociological Perspectives on International Institutions and the Trading System*. He reflects on how the international trade regime influences the trade policy choices of WTO members. Within the field of international economic law, trade lawyers tend to focus on the regulatory function of the WTO, treating the trade regime as essentially a set of rules guiding and constraining the behaviour of governments. But within the discipline of sociology, researchers examine how institutional environments influence actor behaviour in a variety of ways. Lang's aim is threefold: to describe some of the insights of sociological institutionalists; to show how these insights can contribute to a better understanding of the role of the WTO in international political life; and to offer reasons why such insights are relevant to trade lawyers.

In *Law of the Global Economy: In Need of a New Methodological Approach?* Federico Ortino and Matteo Ortino maintain that a comprehensive understanding of the law affecting the global economy can only be gained by considering international economic law as a branch of economic law. They critique the old paradigms and methodologies of public international law, urging a new methodological approach that cuts across the boundaries between *legal systems* (eg national, regional, international and trans-national) and across those between traditional *fields of law* (eg constitutional, commercial and procedural law).

Emmanuel Voyiakis challenges us to consider big and little things in *Of Foxes and Hedgehogs: Some Thoughts About the Relationship Between WTO Law and General International Law*. The WTO system may feature a complex internal structure and sophistication, but is it truly more separate from general international law than any other treaty arrangement? Voyiakis outlines what he considers the real issues in the debate between those who think of WTO law as a 'self-contained' regime and those that do not. He presents separatism as a coherent and plausible account of WTO law and its relationship with general international law.

The section on research concludes with Chen-Yu Wang, drawing on his international experience within the legal academy, in *Different Scholarships, the Same World: Interdisciplinary Research on IEL*. He notes that to better understand international economic law and policy, scholars focus on three academic fields: international law, international relations theory, and international economics. Chen-Yu Wang explores linkages between these fields and their methodologies as a means of enhancing interdisciplinary collaboration.

B. Teaching

The next section of the book considers another key pillar of activity in our field: the state and future of teaching international economic law. The participants at our Bretton Woods conference considered a variety of fundamental issues associated with pedagogy, including: How should International Economic Law be taught, and when and to whom? Should it be taught in different ways in different places? Is the training provided in the law schools suitable for future academics, government officials, or practitioners? What is the right balance of theory versus practice? What is the proper role of case law? Should we be concerned about places where the subject is not being taught, or where academic resources are clearly insufficient?

Karen Bravo conducted extensive empirical research to present *International Economic Law in U.S. Law Schools: Evaluating Its Pedagogy and Identifying Future Challenges*. She was assisted in this effort by both Steve Zamora and Craig Jackson, with the aim of improving our understanding of how and where the field is being taught within the United States. The charts and graphs they developed help illustrate their findings. By assessing 'where we are,' Bravo encourages reflections on 'where we should be.'

Tracey Epps and Rose Ann MacGillivray worked together on *Venutian Scholarship in a Martian Landscape: Celebrating and Reflecting on Women in International Economic Law.* The aims of their project were to highlight the contributions of women to the field of international economic law teaching and scholarship; to quantify the current representation of women in international economic law teaching and scholarship; and to reflect upon women's experiences and perspectives in order to see how they might be harnessed to strengthen the discipline. Drawing on little-known literature, as well as on empirical research and interviews, Epps and MacGillivray provide fresh insights into our field.

Frank Gevurtz presents *An Essay on Teaching International Economic Law from a Corporate Perspective.* He reviews basic elements within traditional domestic corporate law, such as choice of law, limited liability and management obligations. But he relates these elements to how businesses pursue free trade and regulatory arbitrage. He suggests that the degree to which corporate law is pertinent to international economic law is underestimated.

Seema Sapra, in *New Agendas for International Economic Law Teaching in India: Including an Agenda in Support of Reform,* compiles an insider's view of the content of IEL teaching in this burgeoning economy. She also assesses the future direction of legal education and research in India, noting the potential importance of IEL in supporting the objectives and outcomes of the nation's process of transformation.

A creative transborder law program provides a unique opportunity for Elizabeth Trujillo to identify *Shifting Paradigms of Parochialism: Lessons for Legal Education.* Her related teaching experience in the United States and Mexico may serve as a model for similar endeavours. Her work also provides insights into individual and group identity; for example, through her descriptions of student moot North American Free Trade Area negotiations.

Addressing a topic of increasing importance in global business operations, Constance Wagner presents *Corporate Social Responsibility of Multinational Enterprises and the International Business Law Curriculum.* She reviews key issues which arise from both domestic regulation and international initiatives, including efforts to address problems such as environmental sustainability and the protection of human rights. Wagner notes the lack of attention to the subject within law schools, and identifies areas where such teaching might be incorporated.

C. Practice/Service

The final section of the book focuses on the legacy of the location of our conference: the state and future of the operation of international economic law in the Bretton Woods Era. The participants at our Bretton Woods conference thus considered topics such as: What is the practice of international economic law? Who are the practitioners? What is the role of non-lawyers?

What are the needs of practitioners in government, private practice, international and non-governmental organisations? How do these needs vary in different cities, regions, countries? How can pro-bono service in the field be encouraged? How can the profession respond to the needs of areas with little expertise in the subject? Finally, how have the Bretton Woods institutions adapted to these and other challenges—and how might they better respond in the future?

Amy Porges draws on her extensive government, academic and private practice experiences to help identify trends in *The Future of International Economic Law Practice*. Her insights are wide ranging and thoughtful. For example, she notes that with the global expansion of trade and investment, a new range of parties needs advice in the negotiation of agreements and the settlement of disputes.

Douglas Arner, based in Hong Kong, looks at *The Developing Discipline of International Financial Law*. He observes that after decades of evolution, international financial law focuses not only on the Bretton Woods institutions and the Bank for International Settlements, but also on an ever-increasing number of international financial organisations of varying levels of formality that are involved in the development, implementation and monitoring of international financial standards. After a review of both historical and current initiatives in this area, Arner suggests that the system should be re-designed to meet the challenges of financial globalisation, focusing on the twin objectives of financial stability and financial development.

In *Investment Treaty Arbitral Decisions as 'Jurisprudence Constante'*, Andrea Bjorklund focuses on an increasingly important area of legal practice involving both the public and private sectors. Although decisions by arbitral tribunals in investment treaty cases do not have formal precedential status, she argues that such decisions do provide some guidance to later tribunals about the scope of state obligations. Over time, an accretion of decisions will likely develop a *jurisprudence constante*—a 'persisting jurisprudence' that serves to unify and stabilise judicial activity.

Next, David Gantz examines *The Role of Law and Lawyers in Vietnam's WTO Accession*, providing insight into the history and influence of international legal services in a transition economy. Lawyers in both government and private practice from many nations have contributed not only to various legal reforms in Vietnam, but to the rise of a professional cadre of local lawyers with increasing expertise in international economic law.

Rumu Sarkar speculates on how efforts toward greater accountability at the World Bank might lead to an expansion in international jurisprudence, in *Exercising Quasi-Judicial Review Through a World Bank Appellate Body*. She considers the World Bank Inspection Panel as a means of improving the operation and viability of the Bretton Woods institutions.

Finally, as a capstone to the other contributions in this book, Andreas Lowenfeld presents *Jurisdiction to Prescribe and the IMF.* Lowenfeld sets out to test whether jurisdictional guidelines can be developed for the International Monetary Fund (perhaps along the lines of the Restatement of the Foreign Relations Law of the United States), as it finds itself involved in matters that are essentially, but not exclusively, within the domestic jurisdiction of member states. Given the Professor's decades of distinguished scholarship and writing in the field of international economic law, the participants of the IELG Bretton Woods conference were particularly delighted that he could join us.

These are the 20 Chapters which support the three pillars of our discipline in the areas of research and scholarship, teaching, and practice/service. We should also note that in addition to the written submissions which form this book, a number of other papers and reports were presented at the IELG conference at Bretton Woods. We engaged in lively discussion and debate, developing answers to many of the questions posed and raising new questions which may perhaps be the subject of future conferences.

IV. THE SOCIETY OF INTERNATIONAL ECONOMIC LAW

The Bretton Woods conference provided the opportunity for formal and informal discussions about the state and future of international economic law, as well as the organisations and networks that foster our discipline. The IELG provides a superb example of such an organisation and what it can accomplish, especially under the auspices of a long-established and respected institution such as the ASIL. But, at the same time, the participants emphasised the increased globalisation of international economic law research, teaching and practice. This was coupled with a perceived need to support the establishment of similar organisations within a diverse range of countries, and to promote international cooperation among the field's scholars and academic institutions and societies. There was particular awareness of the challenges posed in countries which may lack relevant academic resources, and of the need to encourage meaningful academic collaboration in emerging economies.

To this end, during the business session of the conference, some initial ideas were presented for the formation of a new organisation to promote international economic law on a more far-reaching basis. Those ideas were further energised by many creative suggestions. For example, one participant noted the importance of coordinating efforts and facilitating local conferences; another commented on the possibilities for pro bono services by the field's academics.

The result of these discussions was a planning meeting to found a global international economic law organisation, held in May 2007 at the London School of Economics. The participants forged an ambitious agenda which covered the organisation's objectives and activities, governance structure, membership, budget and financing, and future plans. Supporting documentation was developed by members of the Founding Committee, many of whom attended the Bretton Woods conference and had then volunteered to be of service. Substantive and procedural guidance was offered by members of a newly-formed Founding Executive Council, which includes many senior figures in the field. At the London meeting, the group decided to call the new organisation the *Society of International Economic Law*.

A preliminary description is as follows:[4]

> The Society of International Economic Law is a new organisation aimed at academics and academically-minded practitioners and officials in the field of International Economic Law. The aim of the organisation is to foster co-ordination, collaboration and debate between IEL scholars and practitioners/officials and national or regional IEL organisations around the world. Additionally, it will seek to support and nurture the growth of research and teaching in the field of international economic law in parts of the world presently lacking those resources. The SIEL will be genuinely global in its reach and as inclusive as possible in terms of the expertise and interests of participants—broadly covering the many disciplines encompassed by IEL.

As this book goes to press, plans are being made for a major inaugural conference to be held in Geneva, Switzerland, in July 2008. The Graduate Institute of International Studies in Geneva (*l'Institut universitaire de hautes études internationales, HEI*) will serve as host. To be sure, many of the questions raised at the Bretton Woods event will continue to feature in the scholarly and organisational aspects of this conference. The IELG will continue to play a vital role in the activities of the SIEL. For more information about the SIEL conference and the benefits of SIEL membership, see http://www.sielnet.org/.

We are pleased that this book *International Economic Law: The State and Future of the Discipline*, forms part of the legacy that will influence the future of the discipline.

We trust that the friendships and professional contacts that emerged from those few days at the Bretton Woods resort will deepen over the years. With the emergence of the Society of International Economic Law, we hope to advance a new collaborative network for international economic law research, teaching and scholarship. In time, this new group may help inform public policy and facilitate practice in the field.

It is right and fitting that this introduction to a book that is itself part of the next phase in the development of international economic law, should

---

[4] See the website http://www.sielnet.org/.

conclude with Lord Keynes' closing remarks at the end of that deeply influential conference at Bretton Woods in 1944:

> [W]e have perhaps accomplished here in Bretton Woods something more significant than what is embodied in this Final Act. We have shown that a concourse of 44 nations are actually able to work together at a constructive task in amity and unbroken concord. Few believed it possible. If we can continue in a larger task as we have begun in this limited task, there is hope for the world. At any rate we shall now disperse to our several homes with new friendships sealed and new intimacies formed. We have been learning to work together. If we can so continue, this nightmare, in which most of us here present have spent too much of our lives, will be over. The brotherhood of man will have become more than a phrase.[5]

---

[5] Van Dormael, above n 1, at 2 (quoting the Proceedings at 1240–2).

Part I

The State & Future of International Economic Law Research

2

At the End of the Yellow Brick Road: International Economic Law Research in Times of Uncertainty

TOMER BROUDE

I. OPENING CREDITS

IN THIS CHAPTER, I would like to raise several interconnected thoughts about the state and future of International Economic Law research. These thoughts reflect the fact that we live and work in a formative period. Consider the diversity of contemporary International Economic Law research. Thirty or even 15 years ago, only a few researchers focused on the field, most of them forming a rather closed and like-minded community of insiders. In contrast, today we are blessed with a global abundance of International Economic Law research,[1] with scholars approaching the field from a variety of theoretical and methodological directions. The breadth of that research is well-presented in the typologies suggested by Gregory Shaffer[2] and Joel Trachtman[3] (both of whom have also demonstrated such diversity in their own work). International Economic Law was an area where non-specialists once feared (or did not bother) to tread; today, though there is still an obvious, even increasing, need for specialisation, the field is an accepted and significant part of the international law mainstream.

While each of us holds a preferred personal approach to scholarship, perhaps disdaining others,[4] few would dispute that this diversity is a good

---

[1] On the exponential growth in International Economic Law research in the last few decades, see DF Vagts, 'International Economic Law and the American Journal of International Law' (2006) 100 *Am J Int'l L* 769.

[2] See GC Shaffer, 'A New Legal Realism: Method in International Economic Law Scholarship', Ch 3 in this volume.

[3] See JP Trachtman, 'International Economic Law Research: A Taxonomy', Ch 4 in this volume.

[4] Myself, I have not yet settled on a methodological preference, and perhaps never will, having dabbled in formalism, institutional theory, public choice, critical legal studies, as well as sociological and other approaches to law and legal questions.

thing. Thus, while arguing for a 'New Legal Realist' approach, Shaffer acknowledges that 'all [...] scholarly modes discussed have their value and often blur in practice';[5] and although wary of the irresponsible employment of research methods outside their suitable contexts, Trachtman notes that 'each research method has a domain in which it is illuminating'.[6]

I will be advocating conclusions similar to these (although Shaffer and Trachtman both at least imply a qualitative hierarchy between research approaches, while I do not), but on the way I will problematise these typologies and the diversity they reflect. For in today's complex global economic, social and political environment, this diversity poses International Economic Law research with strategic difficulties. One is the threat of *irrelevance* or *redundancy*. The second, not unrelated to the first, is the threat of *intellectual fragmentation*. I will explore these problems through a narrative that unfolds along the following points.

First, International Economic Law, as a corpus of law (or rather, as a set of loosely interrelated corpora of law, for under the general appellation 'International Economic Law' we should include many areas of international economic activity whose international legal regulation differs in intensity and depth, such as trade, investment, aid, monetary policy, labour migration and development),[7] has for over half a century been underpinned by a coherent set of analytical and instrumental concepts. I refer in particular to the liberal economic theory that has justified and informed the establishment and evolution of International Economic Law within the constraints of pragmatic political possibility, from Bretton Woods to Doha, and beyond.

Second, the liberal and pragmatic assumptions that have guided International Economic law are increasingly beset with uncertainty, stemming from dilemmas in the study and practice of economics as well as from political disagreement and social discontent. This uncertainty can be found in the numerous forms of mounting criticism of the pragmatic-liberal tradition, many simply emotive, but many others enjoying high degrees of academic validity.

Third, to the extent that this contemporary environment of uncertainty lies beyond the proper domain of International Economic Law research (if only because it is more clearly associated with economic theory, political economy and global society), the field of International Economic Law research is posed with a double challenge of both interlocutory relevance and disciplinary necessity. On one hand, if we strictly adhere to our expertise as interpreters and engineers of the law, our scholarship may become

---

[5] See Shaffer, above n 2.
[6] See Trachtman, above n 3.
[7] Compare Vagts, above n 1, at 769.

too narrowly 'legal' to be relevant to the major substantive debates of these uncertain times. On the other hand, if we wish to engage effectively in these debates, we must adopt theories and methods of other, non-legal disciplines, perhaps to the point of complete assimilation and redundancy.

Fourth, within this almost dialectical challenge, there is nevertheless room, and need, for all research approaches.

In developing these thoughts I will make free and figurative use of the wonderful imagery of Oz,[8] and in particular will refer to the 'yellow brick road', which has controversially been interpreted as an allegory for the gold standard and for political populism,[9] thus establishing its relevance in international economic affairs. Moreover, the present chapter's perspective is distinctly different, making selective metaphoric use of the story in ways that were surely not envisaged by L Frank Baum when he wrote it at the end of the 19th century. In this narrative, the yellow brick road depicts the theoretical conventions of international economics that have guided International Economic Law research through an increasingly complicated world. To be sure, the graphic richness of 'The Wonderful Wizard of Oz' is such that a research allegory could have been far more comprehensively pursued, but our space is limited, and the chapter's ideas sufficiently compact to be conveyed with only auxiliary recourse to the Oz analogy.

II. KANSAS (IN SEPIA BLACK-AND-WHITE)

My point of departure is not devoid of controversy, nor is it entirely necessary for my cumulative arguments, but I will mark it out anyway, because I believe it is both true and apposite. In it, I refer to the paradigmatic roots of International Economic Law and its scholarship. Conceding the nature of these roots and their overwhelming importance to research in our field is key to any critical assessment of the future.

My claim is that International Economic Law research, like Dorothy in Victor Fleming's cinematographic interpretation of Baum's Kansas[10] grew up in a black-and-white world. That is, 'International Economic Law', as a field of legal prescription, was founded on and designed in accordance with a coherent, internally stable underlying theory, based on two particular subscriptions—one intellectual, the other pragmatic—that from the outset provided scholarship with a clear cut exploratory scope and a relatively uncomplicated framework of analysis.

Intellectually, International Economic Law is firmly rooted in Ricardian-Smithian traditions of liberal economic theories of market economics and

---

[8] LF Baum, *The Wonderful Wizard Of Oz* (GM Hill, 1900).
[9] HM Littlefield, 'The Wizard of Oz: Parable on Populism' (1964) 16 *Am Q* 47.
[10] *The Wizard of Oz* (Metro-Goldwyn-Mayer, 1939).

international free trade[11] Arguably, this is the legal field's entire raison d'être, if not its *mode opératoire*. The field's utility and objective is the full (or rather optimal) attainment of these traditions' goals of welfare maximisation, through international legal regulation. There seems to be little need to linger much on this point.

However, the implications for International Economic Law research should be stated clearly. Since 'International Economic Law' is almost exclusively a liberal project, most (though not all) International Economic Law*yers*, and more importantly, International Economic Law *scholars*, have traditionally been, and most still are, almost by definition *advocates*, not merely jurists. Though I may claim that my own International Economic Law writing has taken a critical stance, I have surely more often than not been, in effect, an agent of liberal economic arguments. We are advocates of universal economic liberalism if we critique antidumping laws as essentially protectionist;[12] if we consider the role of international trade dispute settlement in maintaining peaceful political relations;[13] and even if we consider how non-economic values can be preserved with minimal injury to trade.[14] In any of these cases, and most others, we are arguing well within the liberal paradigm.

This is, however, only half the story. International Economic Law is far from perfectly liberal. Pragmatically, it is not so much a translation of liberal economic theory into legal terms than a continued expression of Keynesian allowances for limited public and national manipulations of trade, be they in the movement of goods, services or currency, accounting for mercantilist reflexes and their political legitimacy—more 'political economy' than economics.[15] If the philosophy of liberal free trade is, as an expression of moral utilitarianism, a kind of ideal theory, the theory that underlies the multilateral international economic legal system is rather what Rawls has called 'non-ideal theory'.[16] It is this combination of ideal theory

---

[11] See MJ Trebilcock & R Howse, *The Regulation of International Trade* (Routledge, 2005) 1–6.

[12] See T Broude, 'An Antidumping "To Be or Not to Be": A New Agenda for Research and Reform' 37 *J World Trade* 305 (2003).

[13] See T Broude, 'Between Pax Mercatoria and Pax Europea: How Trade Dispute Procedures Serve the EC's Regional Hegemony' in P Ala'i, T Broude and CB Picker, (eds), *Trade as the Guarantor of Peace, Liberty and Security? Critical, Historical and Empirical Perspectives* (ASIL, 2006).

[14] See T Broude, 'Taking "Trade and Culture" Seriously: Geographical Indications and Cultural Protection in WTO Law' (2005) 26 *U Pa J Int'l Econ L* 623.

[15] See BM Hoekman & MM Kostecki, *The Political Economy of the World Trading System: The WTO and Beyond*, 2nd edn (Oxford University Press, 2001).

[16] Non-ideal theory 'looks for policies and courses of action that are morally permissible and politically possible as well as likely to be effective'; see, eg, J Rawls, *The Law of Peoples; with, The Idea of Public Reason Revisited* 89, 2nd edn (Harvard University Press, 2001). See also M Phillips, 'Reflections on the Transition from Ideal to Non-Ideal Theory' (1985) 19 *Noûs* 551.

and pragmatism that consistently brings about the policy compromises that John H Jackson has referred to as the 'fourth-best option'[17] (the very phrase implying that unbridled liberal economics would be the first best option), that are so familiar to students of international trade law and all other areas of International Economic Law.

When viewed from this black-and-white perspective, as foundational myths in which this theoretical-practical mix turned into rules, 1940s Bretton Woods, Havana and Geneva are to International Economic Law what 1640s Westfalen, Münster and Osnabrück are to International Public Law. For these are not only physical locations, but shorthand for political bargains on international policy transformed into long-standing international legal arrangements.

All of this is vaguely reminiscent of Ruggie's 'embedded liberalism'.[18] In the context of scholarship, reference to Jackson and his highly influential Michigan school is, however, more representative of International Economic Law research's basic drive: the straightforward and sensible conversion of liberal ideas into hard-nosed practical formulas.[19] Pragmatic liberalism is as 'embedded' in our research as it is in our economies, societies and polities. Deep down, even after we have graduated to and from other schools and adopted fancier theories, we would feel most comfortable going home to black-and-white Kansas (that is, like this volume's conference venue, to Bretton Woods; or academically, to Jackson's Michigan) and its primordial simplicity and clarity.

III. OVER THE RAINBOW: FOLLOWING THE YELLOW BRICK ROAD

In *The Wonderful Wizard of Oz*, a tornado brutally thrusts Dorothy and her faithful dog, Toto, from the comfort of her black-and-white world, over the rainbow to the Technicolor© land of Oz. This land is far more complex and indeed more dangerous than Kansas, with wicked witches from the east and the west, good-hearted but weak witches from north and south, poppy fields that threaten to gently anesthetise and winged monkeys that can wreak havoc at will. Dorothy's immersion in Baum's fantasy land is allegorical of foundational International Economic Law's encounter with post-war reality. Bretton Woods' test was not in its creation but in weathering the political ups-and-downs of the following decades—the cold war,

---

[17] See JH Jackson, *The World Trading System: Law and Policy of International Relations*, 2nd edn (MIT Press, 1997) 5.

[18] JG Ruggie, 'International Regimes, Transactions and Change: Embedded Liberalism in the Postwar Economic Order' (1982) 36 *Int'l Org* 379; and JG Ruggie, 'Taking Embedded Liberalism Global: The Corporate Connection', in D Held & M Koenig-Archibugi (eds), *Taming Globalization: Frontiers of Governance* (Cambridge Polity Press, 2003) 93.

[19] Generally in conformity with the answer to Trachtman's rhetorical question, 'what good is research?' (Trachtman, above n 3).

decolonisation, the rise of Japan and the European Community as trading powers, and the energy crisis of the 1970s. Like Westphalia, Bretton Woods is not a particular point in time but a code-word for an extended historical continuum of international policy 'muddling through'.[20]

There is, however, a striking difference between the general political international legal regime and the economic one. International Public Law, as Martti Koskenniemi has taught us, has forever been subjected to the contrasting criticisms of moral utopianism, on one hand, and apologetic inconsequence, on the other hand.[21] In contrast, International Economic Law has somehow managed to strike a balance and find a middle ground between its own 'utopia'—the utilitarian morality of welfare maximisation through liberal economics—and its 'apology'—the sufferance of targeted protectionism and national economic manipulations through internationally agreed legal disciplines.

How did International Economic Law succeed in walking the line between liberal utopia and mercantilist apologetics, through decades of economic and political turmoil? It did so because International Economic Law (unlike most other areas of law in general and international law in particular) was predicated upon a pre-existing, rational, non-legal, scientific theory. As such it is the product not only of political compromise, but of bona fide scientific research in the field of economics. International Economic Law is 'Economic', not only because it deals, *ratione materiae*, with economic transactions and their regulation by states (on a par with 'international *maritime* law', or 'international *aviation* law'), but because it purports—or at least has done so for decades—to be *the legal expression and practical transduction of economic theory*, the body of international rules that enables the discipline of economics to transform itself from theory to practice.

Liberal economic analysis has been the yellow brick road that has guided International Economic Law research. We have followed it because our law is economic, and we wish to see it legitimated by economic science (and indeed, by empirical research). It is what ties us to our scholarly roots. It makes us confident that however lost we may be, we are on the road back to Kansas, no matter which difficulties may arise along the way.

To be sure, there has never been universal consensus on the theoretical underpinnings of liberal economics. While what we now call 'International Economic Law' developed, the socialist-communist paradigm presented an alternative system of 'international economic law'.[22] Indeed, the Bretton

---

[20] On evolutionary incrementalism rather than revolutionary progress in policy-making, see CE Lindblom, 'The Science of Muddling Through' (1959) 19 *Pub Admin* 59.

[21] See M Koskenniemi, *From Apology to Utopia: The Structure of International Legal Argument* (Cambridge University Press, re-issued edn 2005) (1989).

[22] Eg, the planned coordination of the COMECON.

Woods system was established as the fissure between the competing international socio-economic theories and political systems started to deepen at the outset of the cold war. But this only pronounced the guiding nature of International Economic Law's yellow brick road, having started where the wicked witch of the East fell, with her ruby red slippers.[23]

IV. BEYOND THE EMERALD CITY...

And today, can we still rely on the yellow brick road of pragmatic-liberal theory for guidance in our research? Ought we? Pursuing the Oz allegory, my proposition is that we have now reached the point where the yellow brick road ends at the gates of the Emerald City, the point from which the story's heroes must continue their journey without a clearly defined road,[24] relying more on their independent faculties and group efforts to make progress. The liberal underpinnings of International Economic Law, at their current stage of development, have increasingly become revealed as either inconclusive or erroneous, as incapable of providing policy guidance as coherently as in the past, and at times simply irrelevant to new areas and dilemmas of regulation. The following are some (non-exhaustive) and necessarily simplified examples of the difficulties we face as International Economic Law scholars seeking guidance from our traditional policy sources, when approaching not only cutting-edge but even seemingly mundane questions of International Economic Law.

A. Does the Multilateral Trading System Promote International Trade?

Of course it does. Liberal theory tells us that it does (and should). Yet this has become a point of contention among economists in the wake of a provocative paper by Andrew Rose arguing that the international trade patterns of GATT/WTO members are hardly different from those of non-members.[25] Effective economic and methodological responses have since been produced.[26] I may subscribe to the latter, but in doing so I am not applying my professional judgment as a jurist, but rather my non-professional personal intuition, or bias. After all, if the multilateral trading system has no effect on trade, what good do I accomplish, as a trade lawyer, teacher and scholar?

---

[23] In Baum's *Oz*, the slippers were silver; the colour film depicted them as ruby.
[24] Baum, above n 8, at 140, 168.
[25] AK Rose, 'Do We Really Know that the WTO Increases Trade?' (2004) 94 *Am Econ Rev* 98. This has been followed by similarly heretic papers, such as AK Rose, 'Do WTO Members have More Liberal Trade Policy?' (2004) 63 *J Intl Econ L* 209; and AK Rose, 'Does the WTO Make Trade More Stable?' (2005)16 *Open Econ Rev* 7.
[26] See A Subramanian & Shang-Jin Wei, *The WTO Promotes Trade, Strongly but Unevenly* (CEPR Discussion Paper No 5122, 2005).

B. Does the Existing Multilateral Trading System Promote Development?

Joseph Stiglitz, for one, says it doesn't (but not that it can't, if it is properly designed).[27] Of course we might ask what we mean by 'development', and argue that the concept doesn't even belong in the pragmatic-liberal paradigm.[28] But if an Economics Nobel Prize laureate is so critical of the international economic system in general, the staunchly legalised multilateral trading system in particular, who are we as legal scholars to argue? Which professional toolbox do we open to examine the system that we legal scholars construct, maintain and critique?

C. What are Trade Agreements for?

We believe that we know what they are for. We argue that they allow governments to lower barriers to international trade—pragmatic liberalism at work. Yet some economists say that trade agreements restrain terms-of-trade manipulation instead. These are quite different, if not contradictory functions.[29] In fact, there are a number of theories relating to the purpose and effect of trade agreements, but they are often contradictory or exclusive. For example, where does the idea that trade agreements are meant to provide traders with certainty and predictability—a concept so dear to jurists[30]—fit into the other ideas? As legal academics, if we don't quite know the object of an agreement between parties, on what basis can we apply it and criticise it?

D. What are Investment Protection Treaties for?

With our feet on the yellow brick road, we think that we know the answer to this all too well. Investment protection treaties (or Bilateral Investment Treaties (BITs)) signal to private investors that their investments will not be subjected to discrimination or to arbitrary expropriation, and so on this basis corporations are encouraged to make their investments in BIT-protected jurisdictions.[31] However, practitioners and academics alike

---

[27] See JE Stiglitz & A Charlton, *Fair Trade for All: How Trade Can Promote Development* (Oxford University Press, 2005).

[28] I have discussed aspects of this problem, from a critical perspective, in T Broude, 'The Rule(s) of Trade and the Rhetos of Development: Reflection on the Functional and Aspirational Legitimacy of the WTO' (2006) 27 *Colum J Transnat'l L*.

[29] For a detailed discussion see DE Regan, 'What are Trade Agreements for?—Two Conflicting Stories Told by Economists, with a Lesson for Lawyers' (2006) 9 *J Intl Econ L* 951.

[30] See WTO Panel Report, *United States—Sections 301–310 of the Trade Act of 1974*, WT/DS152/R, 5.71 et seq (22 Dec, 1999).

[31] For survey and positive theoretical analysis, see AO Sykes, 'Public vs. Private Enforcement of International Economic Law: Of Standing and Remedy' *U of Chi L & Econ* (Olin Working

have pointed out that BITs do not independently increase levels of Foreign Direct Investment,[32] and indeed, the main effect of BITs is to influence the supply-side structuring of investments so that they will pass through investment-protected source countries. This means that BITs have very little effect on investment in capital-scarce countries, or on investment decisions in general. So, why are there so many BITs? Why do states bother to execute them?

E. How should Regional Trade Agreements be Regulated?

'Substantially all trade', barriers to trade no 'higher or more restrictive than the general incidence of the duties' etc–surely these Article XXIV GATT questions involve legal definition and interpretation that can be hammered out in dispute settlement, or specified by the WTO Committee on Regional Trade Agreements? Conservative economists decry the damage done to the multilateral trading system by regional trade agreements,[33] and yet they continue to proliferate like a band of winged monkeys in Oz,[34] and there is indeed a wealth of contrasting evidence and opinion on the economic effects of regional trade agreements.[35] In the regionalism-multilateralism debate, we lawyers can take sides and suggest helpful compromise formulas, but we have little to contribute to the economic debate itself.

F. How should International Labour Mobility be Regulated?

In liberal economic terms, the movement of labour should be liberalised just like the movement of goods, services and capital, an extension of the yellow brick road. The expected welfare gains are huge;[36] but the distributional

---

Paper No 235), available at http://papers.ssrn.com/sol3/papers.cfm?abstract_id=671801 (Feb 2005).

[32] See, eg, KP Gallagher & MBL Birch, 'Do Investment Agreements Attract Investment?—Evidence from Latin America' (2006) 7 *J World Trade & Inv* 961.

[33] Most outspokenly by members of the Consultative Board to WTO Director-General Supachai Panitchpakdi, see *The Future of the WTO: Addressing Institutional Challenges in the New Millennium*, 19 (2004), available at, http://www.wto.org/English/thewto_e/10anniv_e/future_wto_e.pdf.

[34] See J Crawford & RV Fiorentino, *The Changing Landscape of Regional Trade Agreements* (WTO Discussion Paper No 8), available at http://www.wto.org/english/res_e/booksp_e/discussion_papers8_e.pdf (2005).

[35] For a survey and discussion of literature, see A Panagariya, 'Preferential Trade Liberalization: The Traditional Theory and New Developments' (2000) 38 *J Econ Literature* 287.

[36] See LA Winters, 'The Economic Implications of Liberalizing Mode 4 Trade', in A Mattoo & A Carzaniga (eds), *Moving People to Deliver Services* (Oxford University Press and the World Bank, 2003) 59.

effects are murky,[37] the social impact even more so. Only political resistance seems clear. Liberalism is not so 'embedded' when it comes to labour migration. What is our value-added, as International Economic Lawyers engaging in this debate?

These are only some of the significant policy dilemmas we are posed with today. In each of them, current economic and political research does not provide us with clear answers upon which we might suggest legal constructs or critique. The yellow brick road seems to have eroded under our feet.

V. BETWEEN PROFESSOR MARVEL AND OZ, THE TERRIBLE, OR FROM IRRELEVANCE TO REDUNDANCY

So, if one accepts that what has preserved International Economic Law's stable position between utopia and apology is the yellow brick road of pragmatic liberal theory, where does International Economic Law scholarship stand if its yellow brick road has indeed reached its end, or rather, if we have simply outrun it?

What characterises the problems listed in the previous section is that their proper legal element is constrained, in the sense that the uncertainty associated with their solutions lies not in legal construction or interpretation but in distinctly extra-legal questions, of the empirical or scientific nature that one expects should be answered by the social sciences and their rigorous methods. International labour mobility regulation policy may involve some limited legal issues as *lex lata*,[38] but it is mainly an area that involves a cluster of political, social, moral and economic problems whose resolution is necessary to inform *lex ferenda*. No form of legal analysis of the WTO agreements can answer the riddles posed by Rose or Stiglitz. Indeed, a comprehensive survey of the uncharted territories surrounding our current knowledge reveals, perhaps unsurprisingly, terrain that needs 'blue-collar' research—economic, political, sociological, empirical and theoretical scholarship, not white-collar lawyering. What can legal research contribute to these puzzles? As long as debates rage in economic, political and philosophical circles, shouldn't the jurists keep silent—*inter armes silent leges*?[39] This question highlights the predicament of International Economic Law research, that must navigate not only between utopia and apology, but also between irrelevance and redundancy.

Consider the risk of irrelevance: if our scholarship remains focused primarily on doctrinal analyses and legal technicalities regarding

---

[37] But see HF Chang, 'The Economic Impact of International Labor Migration: Recent Estimates and Policy Implications' 16 *Temp Pol & Civ Rts L Rev* (forthcoming 2007).

[38] See S Charnovitz, 'Trade Law Norms on International Migration', in TA Aleinikoff & V Chetail (eds), *Migration and International Legal Norms* (TMC Asser Press, 2003) 241.

[39] In times of war, the laws are silent.

International Economic Law as the executioner of policies premised on traditionally dominant economic and political theories, then arguably it has little to contribute to social debates that relate to the validity of these self-same theories. Academically, it cannot add to our understanding of the real world, and in practice, it cannot add to the evolution of an International Economic Law based on more realistically complex policy preferences and arguments.

I will give an example, again from my own writing: a deliberately, self-consciously decontextualised analysis of the rule-exception-right distinction in WTO dispute settlement.[40] Highly critical of the *EC-Biotech* panel report on grounds of logic and consistency,[41] it makes no claim to normative contribution to the structuring of the relation between human health and trade. And had it attempted to, it would have had little to rest upon, in disciplinary and methodological terms. I refer to this article not to belittle it but because there is much more of this traditional genre (and much worse): ostrich-like, self-centred, technical and legalistic.[42] My point here is that however this kind of lawyerly scholarship may be useful in the legal realm, it does not seem helpful in making any progress in tackling the kind of substantive questions mentioned in the previous section. It renders scholarship in our field irrelevant to the larger debates of international economic affairs. It teaches us little of value that we could not know otherwise, and what it attempts to teach us—we have no method for verifying.[43] In Ozian terms, much of legal research is like Professor Marvel, the traveling fake that Dorothy encounters in the second scene of the cinema version,[44] a quack with a crystal ball who when peering into it fools Dorothy into believing that he actually sees her Aunt Em and her homestead, when in fact all he has done is to listen to the information she has already shared with him about herself.

Of course this threat of irrelevance is not existential. People will still listen to us when we practice these core forms of legal scholarship, for the same reasons that people have always listened to lawyers, for better or for worse (and to some extent, for the same reasons that Dorothy

---

[40] T Broude, 'Genetically Modified Rules: The Awkward Rule Exception Right and EC-Biotech' (2007) 6 (2) *World Trade Rev*.

[41] WTO Panel Report, *European Communities—Measures Affecting the Approval and Marketing of Biotech Products*, WT/DS291, 292, 293/R (29 Sep, 2006).

[42] In my own defence, I resorted to legal formalism only in order to expose some of its internal inconsistencies as manifested in WTO jurisprudence.

[43] The scholarship that is most endangered in this sense lies in the first 4 categories in Trachtman's taxonomy: doctrinal description, common law-based search for consistency, description juxtaposed with unsupported prescription, and critical intellectualism; and in Shaffer's first three: traditional legal interpretation; normative advocacy; and theoretical exposition.

[44] His wagon bearing the sign: 'PROFESSOR MARVEL, ACCLAIMED BY THE CROWNED HEADS OF EUROPE—Let Him Read Your PAST - PRESENT and FUTURE in His Crystal'.

listened to Professor Marvel, a combination of authority and pretence). And lawyers, if not laws, rarely keep silent. But if we examine ourselves critically, and compare our methods to those of other disciplines, we may rightfully develop an inferiority complex. The threat of irrelevance comes from within, from our own sense that our scholarship is empty if it cannot conform to the methodological rigor of the social sciences. This elicits the urge to abandon International Economic *Legal* scholarship. If we sense that our legal erudition rings hollow, we boldly venture into non-legal areas of research, be they economics, political science, sociology or philosophy, determined to gain more insight about the effects of the law and to formulate meaningful policy recommendations. To enable the empire of law to partake in our age's intellectual 'great game' of globalisation—the quest for an international social and economic order that is both efficient and just—it seems that we must emigrate from it. Both Shaffer and Trachtman deliver an important message in this respect, urging us to engage more intensively with reality through empirically-substantiated research.

Ay, there's the rub. Paradoxically, if we stray too far into non-legal methodologies of research, our scholarship is no longer legal, and we are no longer jurists. Once we ourselves engage in empirical research in the political economy of trade, for example, or analyse political resistance to immigration, we are no longer travelers on the yellow brick road; we are bricklayers: economists, sociologists, philosophers. We solve our fear of irrelevance, but the legal field of scholarship risks lapsing into redundancy, losing its necessity. We are no longer Professor Marvel, having transformed into Oz, the Great and Terrible,[45] exuding a new confidence, even omnipotence. We have but one weakness. Our power is not our own, but the power of others; it is not of law, but of other disciplines. Like the Wizard of Oz, we are one curtain-pull away from the discovery that no one really needs us. We may not be quacks, but we might be humbugs.

VI. 'IF I ONLY HAD A ...': THE COMPLEMENTARITY OF BRAIN, HEART, NERVE AND HOME

Taken at face value, this exposition—itself admittedly devoid of any scientific method beyond rhetorical argumentation—presents a rather bleak picture. International Economic Law research emerges as lacking any independent value. Moreover, I see in this state of affairs the additional threat of intellectual fragmentation. Faced with the looming questions of globalisation, and with what seems to be an ill-stocked arsenal of legal methods, we may

---

[45] In the film, both Professor Marvel and the Wizard of Oz were played by the same actor, Frank Morgan.

turn on each other, wasting precious energy on the preliminary question, which tool or weapon would be most effective in our efforts. Taxonomies are easily turned into self-proclaimed hierarchies.

In the limited space remaining at my disposal, I will argue against this conclusion, both descriptively and normatively. And in so doing, I hope to reaffirm some of our faith in International Economic Law research, however pursued (that is, as long as it is well-executed). Each of the valid, alternative, methodological streams of modern International Economic Law research has weaknesses that must be taken into account in adjusting to the prevailing conditions of uncertainty. And at the same time, each stream has strengths that nevertheless ensure its role in the future of International Economic Law research. If each of these is harnessed to suitable subjects and strategies, they can, indeed, make a contribution to law and to policy, as well as to the progressive reduction of the uncertainties that envelop the field from without. At the same time this scholarly field's uniqueness can be maintained, our common denominator as those who engage in International Economic *Law* research.

In *The Wonderful Wizard of Oz*, the four heroes (the Scarecrow, the Tin Woodman, the Cowardly Lion, and Dorothy herself), turn to the Wizard to receive what they each feel they are most lacking: brain, heart, courage and home, respectfully. Yet it is not the Wizard who grants them these assets; rather, in their adventures the reader or viewer discovers, incredibly, that they already possess the keys to what they most desired—the lion emerges as naturally brave, the scarecrow as quite intelligent. And they accomplish this by working together, their qualities complementing their colleagues' weaknesses. Similarly, each of the existing approaches to International Economic Law research has scope for significant contribution to our knowledge. This is not in spite of the disappearance of the yellow brick road, but because of its disappearance. It is not despite our differences, but because of them. Here is my typology of International Economic Law research.

The *Scarecrows*, intuitively smart even though they habitually doubt the adequacy of their own *brain*. They pursue theoretical exposition, and engage in salon social sciences. They may be naïve theorisers, but we need them to conceptualise potential solutions to problems, as lawyers are trained to. We need Scarecrows because they provide us with testable theoretical hypotheses, correct or incorrect. These can always be examined later. But where would we be without ideas?

The *Tin Woodmen*, compassionate and just, although seemingly devoid of *heart*: they pursue their own ideas of justice, morality and criticism, incessantly questioning those of others, and unabashedly exercising normative advocacy. They are often unpersuasive in the face of reality, or simply wrong. But we need Tin Woodmen in order to question the moral outcomes, intrinsic or consequential, of our analyses and of International Economic Law. Again, lawyers have advantages in these areas.

The *Cowardly Lion*—so afraid of every squeak of reality that he is the only one with enough *courage* to rush into it head on. He needs the constant assurance of empirical observation. Few have the nerve to confront reality so meticulously. We need such Lions to combine deep legal understandings with rigorous examinations of real behavior and consequences. Much of practical legal work, in commerce or in court, is extensive fact-finding, and so empiricists, too, exercise a legal tradition. Highly sensitive, they are our eyes and ears and our collectors of much needed evidence.

And finally, *Dorothy*, our bedrock of legal interpretative traditions, Dorothy is our *home*, the way things once were. Without her and the doctrinal scholarship she represents, we all lose our professional and scholarly legal identity. She represents our foremost comparative advantage—to present to our non-legal counterparts what the law is and what it might be. Our efforts as scarecrows, woodmen and lions are worthless if not built upon a firm understanding of the law.

Our challenge, now, is to combine the strengths of each of our representative heroes and streams, to maintain all of relevance, necessity and specific identity. This requires integration, not fragmentation. In our interactions with each other, and our inter-disciplinary work, there is need for all our respective approaches to International Economic Law research, or as Dorothy exclaimed upon her return to Kansas:

> Home! And this is my room—and you're all here! And I'm not going to leave here ever, ever again, because I love you all! And—Oh, Auntie Em—there's no place like home![46]

---

[46] *See The Wizard of Oz*, above n 10, script by N Langley et al—available at http://www.imsdb.com/scripts/Wizard-of-Oz,-The.html (last visited 13 Jun, 2007).

3

A New Legal Realism: Method in International Economic Law Scholarship

GREGORY SHAFFER

THIS CHAPTER BEGINS with a typology and brief assessment of four varieties of international economic law scholarship: formalist/doctrinal, normative/activist, theoretical/analytical, and empirical. It notes some of the strengths and limitations of each of these, and explores the relationship between them. The Chapter argues that, while we may engage, at different times, in all four varieties of scholarship, a new legal realist empirical approach provides important insights that are currently being missed in scholarship in the international economic law field.

The Chapter then stresses the importance of empirical work from what it terms a 'new legal realist' orientation in international economic law. This new legal realist approach to scholarship calls, in particular, for the use of qualitative methods to understand how international law is made and received, at least as a complement to quantitative analyses. It is wary not only of normative prescriptions based on abstract principles, but also of purely deductive theoretical models for examining legal change without examining institutions in operation. The Chapter situates 'new legal realism' in relation to the original legal realist movement in the United States. A larger work-in-progress addresses its relation to the predominant theoretical perspectives on international law that have emerged.

I. FOUR CATEGORIES OF INTERNATIONAL LAW SCHOLARSHIP

Scholarship in international economic law can be divided into four broad categories: traditional legal interpretation (also known as legal formalism, textualism or doctrinal work); normative advocacy (including through formal interpretation); theoretical exposition (which often takes the form of analytic frameworks); and empirical analysis (which varies in its approach and rigor). Of course, in practice there is not always a clear divide between these categories. Good empirical work is conducted under some sort of organising theoretical or analytic framework. The questions posed are typically shaped by some sort of normative concern with normative implications. Theoretical and analytic frameworks are built from prior observation and inductive or intuitive understandings. Much doctrinal work is likewise informed by, and infused with, normative theory and purpose. Yet the categories are nonetheless helpful for understanding tendencies in scholarship that are different in kind, and, in particular, to see what can be further developed in international economic law scholarship.

A. Doctrinal Work/Legal Formalism

Although doctrinal analysis has often been debunked for its formalist nature, it arguably remains the predominant form of legal scholarship, reflecting the comparative advantage of legal scholars over philosophers and social scientists. Most practitioners of law—judges, national and international civil servants, and lawyers who need to decide cases or advise and represent clients in respect of actual disputes—likely find this conventional approach to be the most useful, although legal realist insights are arguably just as important 'for attorneys who must advise clients what to do' in light of how law operates in practice.[1] Law's legitimacy is grounded in its formal, quasi-'scientific' character, so that legal scholars may play a more effective role in debates over the legal interpretation of treaty provisions and case law when their scholarship retains its formal analytic nature. This strategy is particularly important at the international level where judicial bodies' legitimacy is more likely to be put in question.

Academic scholarship that is predominantly doctrinal in character can be quite influential. Directly or indirectly, it can be used as a form of amicus curiae brief to shape the understanding of judges, and it may be cited by them in legitimisation of a legal ruling that has important consequences for many communities. Perhaps even more pervasively, it can affect how a broad community of scholars and decision-makers (including judges) see legal provisions whose interpretation has significant effects, provisions which could be linguistically ambiguous, but have only one 'normal' meaning within a particular 'interpretive community.'

---

[1] B Leiter, 'American Legal Realism', in M Golding & W Edmundson (eds), *The Blackwell Guide to the Philosophy of Law and Legal Theory* (Blackwell, 2005) 50.

B. Normative Advocacy

A second form of scholarship, often linked with the first (and sometimes with the third), takes an explicitly normative bent. North American law academics have been socialised in graduate school (unlike their counterparts in other disciplines) to be advocates, whether they believe they are attempting to *win* for their clients in an adversarial proceeding, or to deploy law altruistically as activists to make the world a better place. Most legal academics, and especially those who are most successful within academic hierarchies, arguably see themselves as *actors* in the world, engaged in struggles to advance principles and norms, and thus see their work as more than doctrinal or theoretical 'scholarship.'

Authors writing in a normative vein typically advance a particular normative goal and then address how the institution, treaty or case law needs to be reformed, revised or interpreted to advance that normative goal. The goal could be resource allocation efficiency (as epitomised in the basic norm of international trade economics, the theory of comparative advantage), or it could be a particular social goal, such as sustainable development, the protection of labour and other human rights, equality, fairness, due process, transparency and participation. Critical scholars, taking from post-modern discourse theory, find any engagement with legal analysis to have a normative dimension, whether or not the author is self-conscious of it. The distinction of normative scholarship is that it *explicitly* aims to be transformative, while traditional legal formalist scholarship aims to be objective, purporting to describe law in neutral terms.

Yet, from a new legal realist perspective, research should not be predetermined by a normative slant, for the very process of inquiry can lead to new understandings of perspectives and priorities of affected constituencies, and the contexts and dynamics in which any policy proposal will play out. Scholars should thus be open to changing their normative prescriptions in light of what they learn of the social and political context and power dynamics in which any proposal will unfold.[2]

C. Theoretical Exposition

A third form of scholarship, one that receives the most attention in the premier US law reviews, takes, or purports to take, a theoretical orientation. In many cases, the scholarship does not constitute theory in a positivist sense in which theory signifies the making of propositions (or axioms) that can be tested and refuted, but rather puts forward a positive or normative analytic framework for understanding law.

---

[2] See eg B Garth, 'Rebuilding International Law after the September 11 Attack: Contrasting Agendas of High Priests and Legal Realists' (2006) 4 *Loy U Chi Intl'l Rev* 3.

Theories (or analytic frameworks) vary greatly and form a central part of the competitive field in legal scholarship. Important examples of theoretically-oriented scholarship that can be applied to the international economic law context include the following: functionalist problem-solving theories (such as those assessing international trade as a public good, or those addressing international regulatory cooperation as a means to handle cross-border concerns); public choice theory's conception of the political economy of international trade relations (in which government authorities respond to producer interest groups and pursue mercantilist trade negotiating positions); rational choice game theoretic explanations of trade policy (viewing multilateral trade regimes as a means to resolve a prisoner's dilemma); the New Haven School's policy-oriented approach (seeing international law as a process of authoritative decision-making of politically-relevant actors); revisionist or structural realist theories about power and the limits of law (sometimes taking a conservative policy bent to accommodate the powerful); liberal theories about the importance of states' democratic characteristics and the role of non-state actors; various constructivist theories about the influence of norms (such as of fairness) and the role of process (as per the legal process schools); theories taking more of a sociological bent; and critical theories of the power of discourse in legitimating substantive law choices, in creating professional identities and in advancing and reconstituting hierarchy.

Theory and analytic frameworks are of course essential in providing lenses to see and understand complexity and to address policy choices, such as through regime design. However, they implicitly have a normative dimension in structuring what we look for and what we see. For this reason, the new legal realist approach advanced here prefers to avoid strong theory, wary of how strong theory can shape what we regard and, in this way, predetermine outcomes. Rather, such an approach prefers more open analytic frameworks that permit for predispositions to be unsettled in the face of inevitably conflicting perceptions and priorities of constituencies from around the world.[3]

In many cases, theory is put forward as a lens for the reader, but it is not applied empirically. As Dunoff and Trachtman write:

> While law and economics is rich in theory, it exalts empiricism (in which it is surprisingly poor). In fact, we are critical of a law and economics that has immodestly been willing to prescribe solely on the basis of theory.[4]

---

[3] See, eg, G Shaffer, 'Power, Governance and the WTO: A Comparative Institutional Approach', in M Barnett & R Duvall (eds), *Power in Global Governance* (Cambridge University Press, 2005) (applying a comparative institutional analytic approach).

[4] J Dunoff & J Trachtman, 'The Law and Economics of Humanitarian Law Violations in Internal Conflict' (1999) 93 *Am J Int'l L* 394, 394.

Similarly, Goodman and Jinks write regarding their sociological 'acculturation' perspective:

> Further empirical research is required to illustrate more concretely how states are acculturated... Our conceptual analysis of the mechanisms of social influence, for expositional clarity, is pitched at a fairly high level of abstraction.[5]

Theories and analyses based on 'seat-of-the-pants' empiricism can be problematic, and even treacherous, where they do not take account of particular social contexts and power dynamics.

The explanation for the predominance of theoretical over empirical work in the field is likely two-fold. First, legal academics note that they are not trained in empirical work unlike their colleagues in other disciplines, and thus it makes more sense for them to create theoretical frameworks regarding law that build from the empirical work of other disciplines, or that others might use when engaged in empirical work. Another more critical explanation, adopted by some in the socio-legal field, is that the structure of competition within the legal academic profession has discouraged scholars from the time-consuming (and for many, boring) work of dirtying their hands in going out and investigating underlying facts. As Lawrence Friedman wrote two decades ago:

> research itself—hard, grubby research—is less honored among scholars than 'theory' or 'model-building'; this tends to drain talent from the work of building up, and critically examining, a concrete body of knowledge.[6]

In either case, the result is that much (if not most) legal scholarship is not backed by original empirical investigation of the divergent social contexts and power dynamics in which the law that is being investigated is made, interpreted and received.

D. Empirical Approaches

These tendencies bring us to a fourth variety of scholarship, empiricism, including (but not limited to) new legal realist scholarship described below. There is a small but increasing amount of international economic law scholarship that takes an empirical approach, whether the focus is historical or contemporary. A pioneering figure for this approach in international economic law was Bob Hudec, whose data bases and studies of GATT dispute settlement form the groundwork for analysis of international trade dispute settlement in not only law, but also in economics and political science. Hudec went to Geneva frequently to obtain a better understanding

---

[5] R Goodman & D Jinks, 'International Law and State Socialization: Conceptual, Empirical, and Normative Challenges' (2005) 54 *Duke LJ* 983, 984.
[6] L Friedman, 'The Law and Society Movement' (1986) 38 *Stan L Rev* 763, 766.

of what lay beneath the surface of GATT disputes and decisions, at a time when the trade regime was much less transparent than it is today.

Empirical work itself is conventionally divided into two forms—quantitative and qualitative—each of which has its attributes and deficiencies, thus involving tradeoffs. Some scholars, in turn, combine quantitative and qualitative methods to check and test their suppositions and findings under each method.

Quantitative work on international economic law has become increasingly rigorous, much of it conducted by those outside of the discipline, or in collabourations between legal scholars and those from other disciplines. For those concerned about their lack of competence to 'do it yourself,' collabourations can be an enriching way to proceed, although a number of scholars are proceeding on their own. This scholarship's strength lies in the use of more refined data collection techniques and control variables to help to determine the relevance of different factors in explaining international economic law developments. Economists and political scientists, deploying sophisticated mathematical models and multi-variate regressions, are at the forefront of this research. The power of quantitative methods is their ability to test perceptions in a rigorous manner, especially as regards policy choices, against actual data.

This scholarship's major weakness is that its analysis relies on numbers and assumptions that reduce complex social dynamics to defined variables in order to test theoretical propositions, raising an initial question about the quality of the data, followed by questions concerning the inferences that can be made from it. In addition, the models are static, so they fail to capture dynamic and recursive processes of interaction on account of social, political and institutional context. In some cases, researchers attempting to distinguish themselves may mine the data until they find what appear to be counter-intuitive, non-conventional inferences, which may make for original scholarly claims in the academic market, but, in light of the weaknesses of the data, may be of little value, or even harmful, if actually followed.

Qualitative work can offer the advantage of paying closer attention to social context and dynamics, as it typically involves field work, such as to the sites of decision-making. Important work in this area from a socio-legal perspective that builds from interviews and that is theoretically grounded includes John Braithwaite and Peter Drahos' *Global Business Regulation*, Yves Dezalay and Bryant Garth's *Dealing in Virtue*, and Terry Halliday's new series of articles on the diffusion of global bankruptcy norms.[7] Much

---

[7] J Braithwaite & P Drahos, *Global Business Regulation* (Cambridge University Press, 2000); Y Dezalay & B Garth, *Dealing in Virtue: International Commercial Arbitration and the Construction of a Transnational Legal Order* (University of Chicago Press, 1996); see, eg, T Halliday & B Carruthers, 'The Recursivity of Law: Global Norm-Making and National Law-Making in the Globalization of Corporate Insolvency Regimes' (2006) 112 *Am J Soc* 1135;

of my work has taken a qualitative methodological approach, whether to assess the dynamics of WTO trade litigation,[8] the politics of trade-environment legal debates,[9] the definition and application of WTO 'technical assistance,'[10] the addition of a parliamentary dimension to the WTO,[11] or the export of regulatory policy and approaches abroad.[12]

Much (though by no means all) of this qualitative work is based on structured elite interviews. One potential weakness of this work is that it reflects the subjective perspectives of those interviewed (elites or otherwise). In addition, legal academics unschooled in qualitative methods are particularly susceptible to the charge of simply engaging in scattered interviews that confirm their normative inclinations, so that interviewing serves to 'build a case' in the context of ongoing policy debates in which they see themselves as 'actors.' There are nonetheless techniques that help to control for these biases, such as that of triangulation in which the researcher 'compares different kinds of data from different sources to see whether they corroborate each other.'[13] The researcher can, for example, interview those who have opposing interests in respect of the issue at stake, and who come from different backgrounds, using the same set of questions.

A third critique is that the findings from qualitative work tend to be less generalisable because they are context-specific, so that they are of less relevance to those who must make policy for the future. Yet what these studies can lose in terms of 'parsimony,' also makes them more reliable in terms of examining how social context matters, and how plugging in abstract models based on simplifying assumptions can go horribly wrong in law and social policy. As Garth writes, 'systematic interviews bring insights that simply cannot be gained by other methods.'[14] As Laura Beth Nielsen points

---

and B Carruthers & T Halliday, 'Negotiating Globalization: Global Scripts and Intermediation in the Construction of Asian Insolvency Regimes', (2006) 31 *Law & Soc Inquiry* 521.

[8] G Shaffer, *Defending Interests: Public Private Partnerships in WTO. Litigation* (Brookings Institution Press, 2003); and G Shaffer, 'What's New in EU Dispute Settlement? Judicialization, Public-Private Networks and the WTO Legal Order' (2006) 13:6 *J Eur Pub Pol'y* 832.

[9] G Shaffer, 'The World Trade Organization under Challenge: Democracy and the Law and Politics of the WTO's Treatment of Trade and Environment Matters' (2001) 25 *Harv Envt'l L Rev* 1.

[10] G Shaffer, 'Can WTO Technical Assistance and Capacity Building Serve Developing Countries?' (2005) 23 *Wis Int'l LJ* 643.

[11] G Shaffer, 'Parliamentary Oversight of WTO Rule-Making: the Political and Normative Contexts' 7 *J Int'l Econ L* 629, 654 (2004).

[12] G Shaffer, 'Managing US-EU Trade Relations through Mutual Recognition and Safe Harbor Agreements: "New" and "Global" Approaches to Transatlantic Economic Governance?' (2002) 9 *Colum J Eur L* 29, 77.

[13] See C Seal (ed), *Researching Society and Culture* (SAGE Publications Ltd, 2000) (1998) 231 (referencing generally the chapters on qualitative interviewing and ethnography). See also G King, R Keohane & S Verba, *Designing Social Inquiry: Scientific Inference in Qualitative Research* (Princeton University Press, 1994) 23–8 (commenting on improving data quality).

[14] B Garth, 'Introduction: Taking New Legal Realism to Transnational Issues and Institutions' (2006) 31 *Law and Soc Inquiry* 939.

out, it is often qualitative work that generates theory that quantitative work can test.[15]

The interviewer who approaches his subject in an open and objective manner is often, if not always, surprised by how wrong the initial research assumptions were, whether one be a right-of-centre law and economics scholar or a left-of-centre critical legal studies scholar. This point is a key methodological one for ethnographers in the field of anthropology, including those who are otherwise quite distinct, ranging from the material and functional orientation of Bronislaw Malinowski to the symbolic anthropology of Clifford Geertz.

From my own experience, leaving one's office and venturing into the field often transforms one's core conceptions and perceptions of one's subject of study. As a novice academic, for example, when I obtained a National Science Foundation grant to examine the political economy of trade-environment issues and went to Geneva with a conventional conception (within the US academic context) that the WTO was trade-biased and needed 'to balance' competing environmental norms and objectives, I soon learned how much more complex were the issues. Interviews turned into lectures from developing country representatives and groups about how my questions reflected a northern bias. I learned about how environmental issues, and thus the trade–environment debate, was constructed (and being constructed) differently by US and European representatives, NGOs and academics than by their developing country counterparts, with the Americans and Europeans having the advantage of the resources and status that US and European universities bring, greater access to Western media and learned journals, and so forth. I learned how the term 'environment' has vastly different meanings to stakeholders in developing countries where it is much more difficult to separate the concept from that of 'development' because people's livelihoods are more intimately connected on a day-to-day basis with the environment.[16] My assumptions and expectations were upset by the experience of weeks of interviewing and discussing the issues with people coming from a much broader range of experience and priorities than I could study on Westlaw or meet at US academic conferences. Ever since then, that experience has had a transformative impact on all of my scholarship. Whether it has been through interviewing regulators, parliamentarians and their staffers, technical assistance providers and recipients, private and government trade lawyers, civil society advocates, or international organisation secretariat members, my initial predispositions (inevitable no matter

---

[15] LB Neilsen, *Qualitative is Empirical Too! Law and Organizations* (23 Oct, 2006), Empirical Legal Studies Blog available http://www.elsblog.org/the_empirical_legal_studi/2006/10/selznick.html.

[16] See Shaffer, above n 9, 61–8.

how neutral and unassuming I try to be) have always been challenged and transformed.

In sum, legal scholarship will be enriched if more of it is grounded in empirical study of the actors, institutions and processes that give rise to international law, and international law's reception and effects within the world. Scholars can combine empirical methods, including through collabourative projects and checking one's work against others' empirical findings. It is in this way that legal scholarship can contribute greatly to informing ongoing debates and strategies for legal and institutional reform.

II. A NEW LEGAL REALIST APPROACH

The scholarship advocated in this Chapter can be conceptualised as a *new legal realism*.[17] Legal realism refers to a scholarly movement, particularly active in the 1920s and 1930s that responded to what it viewed as formalist legal scholarship and the conservative social policies that legal formalism tended to support.[18] Legal realists argued, among other matters, for the need to study the context in which law is made, operates and has effects before making any proposition about what a law means or should do. Llewellyn called for 'the temporary divorce of Is and Ought for purposes of study.'[19]

As does any scholarly analytic approach, new legal realism has its divisions along a spectrum, and in particular among those who rely more on traditional social science research tools, and those who exhibit a relatively greater critical skepticism of the use of those tools in practice, on the one hand, and those who orient their work more on pragmatic policy questions than on apolitical social science investigation, on the other. What, in my view, is nonetheless 'new' in new legal realism is, first and most importantly, that it actually engages in empirical work, unlike most of the legal realists themselves.[20] While the legal realists called for greater empirical work, so that the practice (and thus meaning) of law would be better understood, they were less accomplished in practicing what they preached. In this sense,

---

[17] See also H Erlanger, B Garth, J Larson, E Mertz, V Nourse & D Wilkins, 'New Legal Realism Symposium: Is it Time for a New Legal Realism?' (2005) 2005 *Wis L Rev* 335; and 'Symposium: New Legal Realism' (2006) 31:4 *Law & Soc Inquiry* 795.

[18] See Leiter, above n 1; and W Fisher, M Horwitz & T Reed (eds), *American Legal Realism* (Oxford University Press, 1993).

[19] K Llewellyn, 'Some Realism about Realism: Responding to Dean Pound', (1931) 44 *Harv L Rev* 1222, 1236–7.

[20] See, eg S Macaulay, 'The New Versus the Old Legal Realism: Things Ain't What They Used to Be' (2005) 2005 *Wis L Rev* 365, 375–6 ('The classic realists talked about doing empirical research, but relatively little was accomplished'); Leiter, above n 1, 51 ('For most of the Realists, however, the commitment to "science" and "scientific method" was more a matter of rhetoric and metaphor, than actual scholarly practice').

they have much in common with those international law theorists today who call for empiricism, but who rarely engage in it in any sustained way. New legal realism, in contrast, builds from the socio-legal tradition of 'law and society' to engage in actual empirical work.[21]

Second, new legal realism takes into account critical, epistemological challenges to legal constructions of 'fact' and 'law.' Critical legal theories have made us more skeptical of presentations of legal doctrine, as well as of 'fact.' We are more aware that presentations of 'fact' reflect, to varying extents, a subjective, normative element that is socially constructed, even in the very framing of the questions posed, and that these presentations, in turn, play into social dynamics with their dimensions of hierarchy and power.[22] Ought and Is are not so simple to disentangle.

New legal realism, however, is relatively better positioned to show how presentations of law and fact are shaped. Given that academics in the United States, in particular, are well-placed to participate in international policy debates because they write from the centre of global power (economically, militarily, linguistically, and in terms of the relative status of US universities), their presentation of 'law' and of 'fact' (whether they write in a formalist, normative, empirical or other vein) is more likely to have an impact on a broader policy community's perceptions and understandings. This international law 'community' makes decisions that affect others' livelihoods and lives, and in particular those who are more marginalised, in large part because the perspectives and priorities of those who are marginalised are less likely to be heard by those making the decisions. The very process of engaging in field work, however, inevitably pushes us beyond our initial assumptions, so that we too listen to other voices and perspectives, something particularly important in the field of international law research.

A new legal realist approach does not abandon empiricism for postmodern musing, but, at its core, stresses the importance of empirically-informed analyses of the contexts in which law is made and operates. A new legal realist approach maintains that while 'social science' is never entirely 'correct,' it is the best way for us to proceed toward a better understanding of the world in which law operates. A new legal realist approach calls for the integration of different empirical methods and framings, quantitative

---

[21] See L Friedman, 'The Law and Society Movement', (1986) 38 *Stan L Rev* 763; and B Garth & J Sterling, 'From Legal Realism to Law and Society: Reshaping Law for the Last Stages of the Social Activist State', (1998) 32 *Law & Soc'y Rev* 409.

[22] See, eg, D Trubek & J Esser, 'Critical Empiricism in American Legal Studies: Paradox, Program or Pandora's Box?' (1989) 14 *Law & Soc Inquiry* 3 (rejecting 'universal scientism'); B Whitford, 'Critical Empiricism', (1989) 14 *Law & Soc Inquiry* 61 (noting that the goal is to increase the chances of accuracy); and RW Gordon, 'Critical Legal Histories' (1984) 36 *Stan L Rev* 575.

and qualitative, as complements toward a better understanding of law's practice.[23] It contends that the story one conveys from empirical work will always be partial, so that scholars should be careful to provide appropriate caveats to their analyses and conclusions. It argues that researchers (and readers) need to be constantly on guard for biases that reflect their own social and national backgrounds and contexts. In other words, what it takes from more critical perspectives is to engage in a closer examination of potential biases in the service of relatively more objective empirical study.

A new legal realist approach takes both a top-down and a bottom-up approach in terms of how international economic law is made and how it is received. It combines them to have a better understanding of international law and its impact. It looks at the role of individuals, groups and states in the law's making; and it looks at the effects of international economic law among and within states and society, how it is translated, transplanted and resisted. From such study, one can see the ways in which the national/local and international/transnational are linked, the ways in which they reciprocally inform and affect each other.[24]

A new legal realist analysis will often distinguish itself through the inclusion of qualitative field work. It stresses the particular importance of thicker description built from sustained observation and intensive interviewing over time. Although not exclusively, it sometimes takes an inductive approach, building from observation as opposed to testing theory deductively through using explanatory and control variables to make assessments. Such an inductive, empirical approach recognises that not all riddles will be 'solved' through a model, but rather that understanding and outcomes are shaped dynamically through social and political *inter-action* in which law is both an impetus and an effect. In this way, it can better address the *recursive qualities* of law—the way law and legal actors interact and reciprocally affect each other in the process,[25] issues that are of significant importance in international economic law in a world characterised by diverse interests, norms, perspectives and priorities. In this way, new legal realist scholarship

---

[23] See also E Mertz, 'Challenging Translations: New Legal Realist Methods' (2005) 2005 Wis L Rev 482, 483–4 ('Ethnography and participant observation, as well as qualitative interviewing techniques, take their place alongside experimental and quantitative methods—not as rivals or competitors, but as necessary tools for those seeking a more rigorous picture of law's impact').

[24] For two international research collaborations addressing the impact of international and transnational networks within states, see M Zurn, S Liebfried, B Zangel & B Peters, *Transformations of the State?*, available http://www.staatlichkeit.uni-bremen.de/; and G Shaffer & D Chalmers, *Transnational Transformations of the State*, available http://www.luc.edu/law/faculty/docs/shaffer/transnatl_transf_state.pdf.

[25] See A McEvoy, 'A New Legal Realism for Legal Studies' (2005) 2005 Wis L Rev 433, 443–8. Historical studies are particularly valuable in this respect, such as the historical material in J Braithwaite & P Drahos, *Global Business Regulation* (Cambridge University Press, 2000).

can better address the dynamic, recursive interaction of law, method and social practice, as part of broader dialogic processes.[26]

To give an example, as applied to WTO law, a new legal realist perspective maintains that the law is not some essentialist (formal) 'thing' that can be understood by academics independently from its application, from its practice, from its life in the world. WTO law does not exist in a separate, autonomous sphere—such as in the treaty texts or in the Appellate Body's adopted decisions—but operates within particular legal cultures in which these texts and decisions play a part. These legal cultures include the interaction of the WTO judicial process with those who bring arguments to it, on the one hand, and the national institutions and 'civil society' to whom the judicial decisions are addressed, on the other. It is national institutions who must translate the legal decisions into practice, and, by 'implementing' them, give those decisions *effect*. Since the United States is the most active participant in the WTO legal process as complainant, defendant and third party, the United States and its constituencies play a significant role in the construction of WTO law. Much international economic law analyses, in particular, fails to take account of how the targets of international legal decisions (states, and in particular powerful states, and indirectly corporate and civil society constituencies) influence both the legal decisions themselves and their implementation in practice—what they mean in the world.

Terry Halliday's work on global bankruptcy law offers an excellent example of scholarship conducted in a new legal realist manner. Halliday has developed an empirical project regarding the interaction between international institutions, transnational networks and national law making in the field of bankruptcy in Asia. Halliday has attended international meetings organised by the IMF, the World Bank and UNCITRAL as an observer and interviewed representatives of those institutions and national representatives from government, law and business in a variety of Asian countries, including China, Korea and Indonesia. From this field work, he has developed theory in an inductive, new legal realist mode. In an article with Carruthers, for example, he develops a theory of how:

> the globalization of bankruptcy law has proceeded through three cycles: (1) at the national level through recursive cycles of law-making; (2) at the global level through iterative cycles of norm-making; and (3) at the nexus of the two.[27]

---

[26] For an example of feminist legal scholars drawing on empirical research in a new legal realist vein, see eg, J Halley, P Kotiswaran, H Shamir & C Thomas, 'From the International to the Local in Feminist Legal Responses to Rape, Prostitution/Sex Work, and Sex Trafficking: Four Studies in Contemporary Governance Feminism' (2006) 29 *Harv LJ & Gender* 335 (taking a consequentialist approach examining the background conditions in which legal prescription will have effects. Halley, for example, writes of how 'the *legal instrumentality* of rape in humanitarian law... may well have very different *effects in the world* than anticipated, I think, by the feminists who promoted them').'

[27] T Halliday & B Carruthers, 'The Recursivity of Law: Global Norm-Making and National Law-Making in the Globalization of Corporate Insolvency Regimes' (2006) 112 *Am J Soc* 1135.

Halliday and Carruthers show how bankruptcy law prescribed at the international level is resisted at the local level, in particular by corporate debtors, resulting in failed reforms, triggering new recursive law reform efforts. They note how strategies at the international level change in response to these national experiences, including through shifting primary norm-making among international institutions, such as from the IMF, World Bank, OECD, regional development banks, to UNICITRAL, the latter being considered more 'legitimate' and thus potentially more effective. These institutions bring together not only representatives from states and international institutions, but also interested professionals, such as bankruptcy lawyers and accountants. Halliday and Carruthers address the different types of mechanisms used for different countries, with coercive measures being relatively more effective in Indonesia (such as IMF loan conditionality) than in Korea, which is more likely to require persuasion to effect legal change, and in China, in which change is more likely to occur through Chinese modeling of reforms based on others' practices. They address how law's indeterminacy, internal contradictions, struggles over problem-definition, and the impact of different players participating in the law-making and law implementation modes, contribute to these recursive and iterative cycles. In other words, in the new legal realist mode advocated in this chapter, Halliday and Carothers address how repeated interactions among actors, institutions and legal forms at the national, transnational and international levels affect legal and social change in dynamic ways.

III. CONCLUSION

There is no single 'correct' approach to legal scholarship, and this Chapter's purpose is not to call for a universal 'new legal realist' approach. Rather, the Chapter recognises that all four scholarly modes discussed have their value and often blur in practice. As regards doctrinal analysis, when we engage with actual legal texts for the purpose of persuading judges, we need to use our formalist, interpretive skills to be persuasive. We use a different language to fit the situational context, cognisant of the audience to which we speak if we are to communicate effectively. As regards normative advocacy, most of us are in this profession because of a commitment to contribute to public policy. As regards theory and analytic frameworks, our work will have little resonance for the future if we do not provide coherent and useful theoretical and analytic frameworks to understand how law operates in the world, including the institutional choices that political, judicial and administrative decision-makers face.

The second part of this Chapter nonetheless calls for greater attention to be paid to empirical work conducted from a 'new legal realist' vantage. The Chapter notes two aspects of new legal realism: an empirical commitment at its core, and its taking seriously critical challenges to such empiricism. Although more quantitative and qualitative empirical work is emerging, the total is small in light of the international economic law work being published, work that can have significant effects on how the legal community prioritises the creation of new international economic law and interprets existing international economic law, without being informed of how such law operates in the world, especially for under-represented communities. Through empirical inquiry, our predispositions, as researchers, are often called into question, helping us to look outside predominant normative frames that are informed by where we live and work, or at least make us more aware of their impact. Such an approach is crucial for a better social 'science' perspective, and is particularly important in the realm of international economic law in a world characterised by considerable diversity of perspectives, priorities, and abilities for affected constituencies to be heard.

4

International Economic Law Research: A Taxonomy

JOEL P TRACHTMAN

INTRODUCTION

ALL RESEARCH—ALL knowledge—in international economic law or elsewhere, is composed of elements of theory and empiricism, of deduction and induction, of insight and proof. Theory and empiricism are both good, but they are called for in different ways, and in different combinations. The critical question is what do we justifiably find plausible in connection with particular elements of international public policy discourse?

The combination and quality of theory and empiricism that is acceptable will vary depending on the analytical tools and data that are available to us. In research, as in other areas, we are rationally ignorant. But the obverse of rational ignorance is rational knowledge: we have to recognise where it may be useful to expend research resources. International economic law is a policy science, and we must strive to train its research resources on important issues, not on unimportant ones. In our research economising, we also should recognise where our collective knowledge of a particular problem is adequate. One of the pathologies of international economic law research, as of other law research, is to cover ground that has already been covered. Greater understanding of, and agreement on, research methodology will allow us to form a consensus that certain issues are adequately known, and to go on to unknown issues.

I will describe several types of research in terms of theory and empiricism, showing the balance between these two components, and suggesting the generalised strengths and weaknesses of each of these strategies. Lawyers generally are good at one type of empiricism: we are expert at describing what courts and legislatures have done. The selection of subjects for study, and of elements for emphasis, is based on an implicit theory, but it is only by making this theory explicit that it can be assessed.

Many of us lack the tools of consequentialist social science empiricism, which are most importantly used to assess the social effects of rules. But if we are unable to use the best tools available to assess the social effects of rules, then our engagement with the discussion of the normative attractiveness of rules is limited to expression of an opinion about the attractiveness of the social effects described by others. Each of us, as citizens, is entitled to such an opinion, but our status as scholars entitles these opinions to no greater deference than the opinions of other citizens.

Stanley Fish recently said it as follows, speaking of teaching:

> college and university teachers should not take it upon themselves to cure the ills of the world, but should instead do the job they are trained and paid to do—the job, first, of introducing students to areas of knowledge they were not acquainted with before, and second, of equipping those same students with the analytic skills that will enable them to assess and evaluate the materials they are asked to read ... [T]he moment an instructor tries to do something more, he or she has crossed a line and ventured into territory that belongs properly to some other enterprise.[1]

It is as true of research as of teaching.

In a liberal model, these approaches to research are not mere strategies, to be deployed to convince others of a position that already accords with one's normative prior commitments. They are not to be deployed to convince, but to illuminate. For honest people, however, a side effect of illumination is persuasion. If you show me that a minimum wage hurts poor people, I will not advocate one.

Each research method has a domain in which it is illuminating. Outside that domain, it may be misleading. So, the taxonomy I will present is designed to assist in aligning research contexts with research methods.

I. WHAT IS GOOD RESEARCH?

A. Theory and Methodology

Traditional American legal scholarship did not comprehend the social scientific role of theory. Traditional legal scholars often took 'theory' as a reference to prior political commitment, and many eschewed it for this reason. Yet theory in the social scientific sense is quite distinct. Theory is distilled from experience, and represents an educated guess as to likely causal relationships. Social science theory serves to suggest hypotheses,[2] with the implicit requirement of testing: nothing could be further from

---

[1] S Fish, *Always Academicize: My Response to the Responses*, http://fish.blogs.nytimes.com/ (last visited 5 Nov, 2006).

[2] KW Abbott, 'Elements of a Joint Discipline' (1992) *1992 Proc Am Soc'y Intl L* 167, at 169. ('Theory suggests elements to emphasize, relationships to explore, and other ways to bring coherence to a mass of facts. Of necessity, lawyers use such frames of reference, but they often do so unconsciously.')

prior commitment. There are two kernels of truth in the traditional legal scholar's understanding. First, in accordance with rational ignorance, some hypotheses are not tested empirically. Second, especially in economic analysis of law, there is far too great a willingness to prescribe based on theory alone.

When I first arrived as a newly appointed assistant professor at the Fletcher School of Law and Diplomacy in 1989, there was an ongoing school-wide discussion of theory and methodology. A senior colleague, a political scientist, asked me to tell him about the theory and methodology of international law. I did not understand at the time that this question would beset me for the next 17 years.

I had just come from nine years of Wall Street practice. Probably the smartest answer I could have given at that time was that I did not know. As Mark Twain supposedly said, 'it ain't what we don't know that hurts us, it's what we know that ain't so.' I might add that what we purport to know that ain't so is even worse. But I was embarrassed to admit this fundamental ignorance, and did not wish to truncate my academic career.

A better informed answer would have been, and still is, that there is no agreement on the theory and methodology of international law. This lack of consensus challenges the very legitimacy of international law as an academic field. Sure, it's a subject, and sure, it exists, but if it lacks theoretical and methodological underpinnings, it is not a *discipline* of inquiry. Furthermore, this lack of consensus on what counts as research in this field makes it difficult to evaluate applicants for academic jobs or promotion. Without transparent consensus standards, there is room for mischief.

Even worse, and this is my main concern, without consensus standards on how we do research—on how we know things—it is hard to form consensus on what we should do on public policy. So, for me, there has been no higher priority than figuring out what is research.

The rest of my discussion will centre around six candidates for the role of methodology in international economic law research. These six candidates are (i) doctrinal description, (ii) common law-based search for consistency, (iii) description juxtaposed with unsupported prescription, (iv) critical intellectualism, (v) public choice, and (vi) empirical consequentialism. I will take the liberty of illustrating some of these methodologies with references to my own work.

(i) Doctrinal Description: The Scholarship of Practice

So, how did I answer at that meeting in 1989, when asked to explain the theoretical and methodological underpinnings of international law? I resisted the impulse to say that we didn't need any damn theoretical and methodological underpinnings—that the law is the law. This response, however, would have reflected my legal education, which was a practitioner's education, and not an academic researcher's education.

But indeed, given my nine years as a practicing lawyer—mostly in the corporate field—I knew that the only things practitioners like me needed were tools of identification and of interpretation. We would find the law and argue about what the law is. Because practicing lawyers need not often argue about what the law *should be*, but are more concerned with what the law *is*, theory and methodology are unimportant. That is, unless you take the extreme natural law position that the law is what it should be, as opposed to the extreme positive law position that it should be what it is.

This type of pure practical description is largely bibliographical in nature, to the extent that it places a premium on simply telling what the law is—on finding it out. Langdell's famous comment that the lawyer's laboratory is the library might be understood as a primitive pre-social science commentary on the state of research in law.[3] No scientist regards looking things up in the library as research.

Of course, practicing lawyers do important things beyond description of legal rules. They also predict what authoritative decision-makers will do in particular cases. This involves an integrative multifactor assessment, based only in part on jurisprudence. Of course, any text is incomplete in its ability to categorise complex reality. Furthermore, law expresses a variety of values without always anticipating the myriad ways that these values can come into conflict with one another. So there is always room for interpretation, and argument about interpretation and priority.

However, for the legal scholar, doctrine is a major component of empiricism. Recorded doctrine allows us to test hypotheses not about the social effects of law, but about the behaviour of legal institutions. This focus of empiricism is important to the practicing lawyer: for example, do poor countries litigate more or less frequently than wealthy countries, controlling for the value of their trade? Do they win more or less? In our field, Chad Bown and Bernard Hoekman, Marc Busch and Eric Reinhardt, Andrew Guzman and Beth Simmons, Petros Mavroidis, Hakan Nordstrom and Henrik Horn, and others, have engaged in this type of empiricism.

Importantly, information about the behaviour of legal institutions cannot alone tell us anything about legal reform: about what the law should be. The other major component of empiricism, explored by the 'Brandeis briefs' and by law and economics, is the empirical analysis of the actual social effects of law, as opposed to the Langdellian focus on cases and empirical analysis of the behaviour of courts in order to predict future behaviour of courts.

---

[3] The Centennial History of the Harvard Law School 1817–1917, at 97 (Harvard Law School Association, 1918) ('The Library is to us what the laboratory is to the chemist or the physicist and what the museum is to the naturalist').

Descriptive legal scholarship can also be understood as a source of data for social science-oriented scholarship. For example, social science-oriented scholarship may seek to relate differences in outcomes to the distinction between civil law and common law systems.[4] However, good traditional comparative law scholarship might respond that the distinction between civil law and common law hides great diversity in the characteristics that the social science scholarship theorises is causing different outcomes.[5] By challenging the plausibility of the underlying theory that generated the hypothesis, they may cast doubt on the inferences drawn from the data. For example, in 2002, Gabrielle Marceau and I wrote a paper that was designed to provide a guide through the WTO law disciplining domestic regulation.[6] We felt it necessary to describe the different disciplines contained in the GATT, SPS, and TBT Agreements, to compare these different disciplines, and to suggest some bases for determining their respective domains of applicability.

(ii) Common Law Consistency: The Hobgoblin of Small Minds or the Cornerstone of the Rule of Law?

What I did tell my senior colleague in 1989 is that the methodology of law is consistency. This is demonstrably false: one peculiarly legal value is consistency, but a value is not a methodology. Furthermore, in formal terms, the drive for consistency is a common law goal, holding that we examine cases to determine whether their ratio decidendi are consistent with one another. We might even extend this to statutory or regulatory law. Indeed, consistency is a critical strategy for those who have nothing to say about values: for liberals.

But a concern for consistency is also at the core of liberal values, insofar as consistency is an attribute of governmental regularity and fair treatment. A liberal perspective says that you can treat me poorly as long as you are willing to treat everyone else equally poorly.

Of course, while the common law process can be understood as a search merely for consistency, it also has a certain interstitially creative, and normative, outlook. Ironically, this arises from inconsistency. That is, there is an argument that the common law process is efficient, or just, or otherwise normatively attractive, because it is a mechanism for choosing (and rejecting) legal rules over time on the basis of these normative perspectives. Researchers can help to 'guide' this jurisprudence, or at least point out the choices. But how do they determine which jurisprudential path is superior?

---

[4] See, eg, S Djankov, E Glaeser, R La Porta, F Lopez-de-Silanes & A Shleifer, 'The New Comparative Economics' (2003) 31 *J Compar Econ* 595.
[5] See D Vagts, 'Comparative Company Law—The New Wave', in R Schweizer & U Gasser (eds), *Festschrift fur Jean Nicolas Druey zum 65 Geburtstag* (Schultless, 2002).
[6] G Marceau & JP Trachtman, 'TBT, SPS, and GATT: A Map of the WTO Law of Domestic Regulation' (2002) 36 *J of World Trade* 811.

Consistency analysis can help to identify or prohibit discrimination. Furthermore, even from a purely welfare-oriented standpoint, consistency analysis can at least point out errors of inconsistency—where value tradeoffs are made differently in different circumstances. Consistency analysis can therefore enhance the rigor of policy choice.

Amy Porges and I wrote a paper in memory of Bob Hudec,[7] extending to post-*Japan-Alcoholic Beverages*[8] jurisprudence Hudec's attempt to show that WTO panels charged with examining de facto discrimination will turn to the aim and effects test, because aim and effects are the only sensible parameters to consider in these cases. We wanted to show that, despite what the Appellate Body had said, it seemed to act in accordance with the aim and effects test. Our consistency-based analysis was deployed to try to show how, despite the Appellate Body's statements, it was ineluctably drawn to aim and effects.

(iii) Description Plus Prescription

Those who describe often find it difficult to resist criticising the object of their description. And once they claim that there is a problem, it is difficult to resist the next step of offering a solution to the problem. Yet, in the real world, it is not always clear what is and what is not a problem. And the solutions are even less clear. Over the years, my work has sometimes been criticised for failing to take a stand. I am asked, 'what is your position?' My response is often that I have not done enough work to be able to support a position—my efforts often developed a way to think about questions but avoided developing the data required to actually answer the questions. Furthermore, my perspective is informed by the Coasean insight that not all imperfections are worth perfecting: the transaction costs of correction may exceed the benefits. My perspective is also informed by normative individualism, which holds that one person's problem is likely to be another person's right. Moreover, all states of the world are imperfect, so simply identifying the imperfection does not necessarily indicate that a change in policy is desirable.

(iv) Critical Intellectualism: Nihilism and the Perfect as the Enemy of the Good

There are three heirs to the American legal realist movement. These are critical legal studies, public choice, and empirical consequentialism.[9]

---

[7] A Porges & JP Trachtman, 'Robert Hudec and Domestic Regulation: The Resurrection of "Aim and Effects"' (2003) 37 *J of World Trade*.

[8] *Japan—Alcoholic Beverages*, WT/DS8/AB/R, WT/DS10/AB/R, WT/DS11/AB/R (1996).

[9] At the Bretton Woods conference, Greg Shaffer pointed out to me that there is a fourth heir, law and society studies.

While the field of critical legal studies purports to look for deep political and sociological determinants of legal rules, and often challenges settled understandings and normative complacency, it has no particular methodology. Rather, it is better understood as a source of insight and conjecture, and in its naive nihilist form as a rejection of methodology.[10] Yet it is an heir to legal realism as it interrogates settled understandings for political and distributive consequences. It is an heir to legal realism as it points out doctrinal and normative contradictions. It might be understood as a kind of pre-theorising. It burns down the existing structures to permit new growth. It destroys existing paradigms in order to pave the way for new models. Yet it does not help us to know which new models will be good, and it tends toward a permanent revolutionary stance that critiques everything.

(v) Legal Realist Public Choice: Assuming Law is a Mask for Desire and Exposing Law as a Mask for Desire

Public choice scholarship applies social scientific methods to the analysis of governmental action, using the assumption that individuals engage in rational preference-maximising behaviour, even when they are government officials. This theoretical perspective, closely aligned with economics and with the field of law and economics, provides a source of hypotheses regarding the behaviour of government officials. In trade, it has been the source of a theory that explains governmental biases toward protectionism. Alan Sykes has actively applied public choice theory to international economic law issues. This approach is consistent with the use of public choice theory in economics in general, and in international economics in particular.

(vi) Empirical Consequentialism: Rigorous Learning from Experience and the Contribution of Statistical Significance to World Peace and Justice

Empirical methods are concerned with causal inference: to what extent does a particular rule affect a particular policy outcome? For example, we may ask whether entry into a human rights treaty enhances a state's human rights performance.[11] If there were no other causes of a state's human rights performance, this would be relatively easy to determine ex post. Look at the condition before and after the entry into the human rights treaty.

Yet good social science is filled with pitfalls, and good empiricists know that there is always room for judgment and debate. But there is also broad consensus regarding what kinds of data are statistically significant, and

---

[10] See M Koskeniemmi, 'Letter to the Editors of the Symposium' (1999) 93 *Am J Int'l L* 351.
[11] See O Hathaway, *Do Human Rights Treaties Make a Difference?* (2002) 111 *Yale LJ* 1935.

what methods are appropriate to deal with problems such as determining the direction of causation. The plural of anecdote is indeed 'data,' but we have a social consensus on what inferences can be drawn from data, whereas social scientists recognise that there are great dangers in drawing inferences from anecdotes.

Social science operates in the world of consequentialism. Positive economic analysis of legal rules examines the consequences of particular legal rules, while normative analysis suggests how better to achieve certain consequences deemed desirable. Normative individualism rejects the possibility that a researcher, or anyone else, can posit the preferences of others. In any event, law and economics, like all social science, operates in the domain of plausible inference regarding cause and effect. It seeks to connect independent variables like legal rules with dependent variables; that is, with consequences.

In a sense, traditional legal scholarship may be approached in the same way as social science theory. That is, both traditional legal scholarship and social science theory should be understood as sources of testable hypotheses, despite the fact that these hypotheses were rarely tested in traditional legal scholarship. The question, in a Lakatosian sense, is which body of scholarship is more consistently productive of interesting and testable hypotheses. This is a kind of meta-question that cannot itself be answered empirically, but is answered based on the experience of, and plausibility to, researchers.

However, law and economics theory, based on an open system social science consensus, seems to have greater claims to plausibility than more eclectic traditional legal scholarship. It is based on assumptions about human behaviour that have been tested in many other contexts and in which useful hypotheses have been derived. It forms a branch of a broader research program that has been subjected to greater scrutiny and discipline. Often, of course, good traditional legal scholarship operates in a way that conforms to social science perspectives on plausibility: like Molière's Monsieur Jourdain in *Le Bourgeois Gentilhomme*, traditional legal scholars often speak social science without knowing it. But self-conscious social science is able to expose its underlying values and assumptions. The legal realists early valued empirical work, but much of it was descriptive, rather than analytical.[12]

International discourse regarding law will be enhanced by the development of an internationally-agreed paradigm of theory and methodology, as already exists in the physical sciences and the more advanced social

---

[12] See TS Ulen, 'A Nobel Prize in Legal Science: Theory, Empirical Work, and the Scientific Method in the Study of Law' (2002) 2002 *U Ill L Rev* 875. See also JH Schlegel, *American Legal Realism and Empirical Social Science* (University of North Carolina Press, 1995).

sciences.[13] This discourse, addressing harmonisation, recognition and even enforcement of foreign law, could be improved if there were a common language of justification of law, as well as a common understanding of the assessment of distributive outcomes.[14]

It is now almost a cliché for law and economics scholars to criticise themselves for working on theory, and failing to test their theories empirically. And indeed, as a new generation of empirically-skilled scholars comes on line, one would expect the empirics gap to be filled. But we must recognise that there are dangers to over-emphasising theory to the exclusion of empirics. Working on theory alone can be intellectually lazy, and can lead to errors, where important variables are ignored because we fail to see their importance. More importantly, if we make public policy proposals based on theory, without adequate empirical support, we risk not just errors but the danger of research products that support a particular distributive or ideological prior commitment. It is in this way that research becomes a cloak for domination

This category of armchair social science includes most of the work that I have done that is not simply descriptive. I am currently completing a book-length project on economic analysis of international law that can only be described as armchair social science. This work is subject to the criticism that I have just described, but either theory must precede empiricism or empiricism must precede theory. It is now time for some empiricism. While I have engaged in a few econometrics-based projects with colleagues skilled in empirical methods, these have not yet borne publishable fruit.

II. WHAT GOOD IS RESEARCH?

For me, good research is nearly always normatively good. Good research illuminates the consequences of policy choices and therefore allows people to make better policy choices. Of course, bad research conforms to the computer science principle of garbage in, garbage out. Policy choice that relies on bad research is likely to be bad policy choice. Illumination almost always leads to better policy.

---

[13] For an optimistic view of the influence of empiricism, see JO McGinnis, 'Age of the Empirical' (Jun–Jul 2006) No 137 *Policy Rev*. McGinnis argues that 'our future politics is more likely to forge consensus than that of the past, because we are on the cusp of a golden age of social science empiricism that will help bring a greater measure of agreement on the consequences of public policy.'
[14] Ulen, above n 12.

5

Opportunism and the WTO: Corporations, Academics and 'Member States'

SARA DILLON

I. INTRODUCTION: MULTILATERAL AND MULTIFACETED OPPORTUNISM

THE OBJECTIVE IN this Chapter will be to offer a theory of opportunism for analysing the WTO, including a perspective on WTO scholarship and its special role in facilitating the opportunism that characterises the WTO generally. Much scholarly writing about the WTO and its 'law', it will be argued, does far more to obscure its true nature than to reveal it.

The first and foundational form of opportunism is that of certain (private) transnational actors who provided the political impetus for the creation of the body to begin with. In particular, these are the transnational corporate interests able to enjoy enhanced profits as a result of the freer flow of goods and services worldwide. The needs of these interests were clearly reflected in the drafting of the Uruguay Round agreements[1], seen as a whole. A second form of opportunism is reflected in the writing of those academics who provide intellectual justification and support for the WTO; professional support of a kind required by all systems that allocate power and influence. Last, but perhaps most important, is the opportunism of the nation states (WTO 'members') that rely on the ultimately misleading state-to-state characteristic of the WTO to demonstrate strategic abilities in the

---

[1] WTO, The Uruguay Round, http://www.wto.org/english/thewto_e/whatis_e/tif_e/fact5_e.htm (noting the dramatic Uruguay Round retrospective provided on the WTO's own website: 'It took seven and a half years, almost twice the original schedule. By the end, 123 countries were taking part. It covered almost all trade, from toothbrushes to pleasure boats, from banking to telecommunications, from the genes of wild rice to AIDS treatments. It was quite simply the largest trade negotiation ever, and most probably the largest negotiation of any kind in history.').

course of disputes and general negotiation. In this sense, the WTO provides a stage for the acting out of national know-how.[2]

It is the fact of the content of the basic WTO laws—and what these laws established politically—that must be our principal concern. (More simply put, what did these laws as a totality set out to achieve?) Despite the often-made claims, post-1995 'trade law' is not in fact about comparative advantage of nation states. This cannot be emphasised enough. Rather, it is about the needs of transnational business as it seeks to influence or pre-empt certain distributions of wealth and power within nation states. It is most truly 'about' mobility of manufacturing, access to inexpensive labour and favourable tax regimes, and thus about diminishing the role of organised labour and regulatory oversight within developed states. The legal events of 1995 created a system worthy of the ambitions of these key actors—transnational business, academics and nation states.

A. Constitutional (As Opposed to Greedy) Moments: How it Started

1995 was a major 'Constitutional moment', to borrow Trachtman's phrase, as the World Trade Organization was created.[3] One may be tired of hearing about that watershed time, but it actually bears ongoing analysis. The new WTO gained enormous attention, predictably enough, given its international legal innovations.[4] 1995 was also a time before the 'permanent state of war' in which we are now living, so its impact value was more pronounced. Over the past few years, economic law issues have been pushed to the background, but these are bound to re-emerge with renewed force.[5]

Global trade regulation became a branch of public international law with genuine enforcement 'penalties' in the form of self-help trade sanctions.

---

[2] One sees this form of opportunism in the litigation and high profile negotiating strategy of countries like Brazil; as well as in the eagerness of other countries from widely different ideological 'zones' to join the WTO, such as Saudi Arabia, Vietnam, and (still pending) Russia. The WTO's status as a significantly different kind of international forum has made it attractive as a stage for self-display on a variety of political levels.

[3] JP Trachtman, 'Changing the Rules: Constitutional Moments of the WTO' (Summer 2004) 26 *Harv Int'l Rev* 44.

[4] See PC Reed, Process, 'Compliance and Implementation Issues in WTO Dispute Resolution Settlement' (1997) 91 *Am Soc'y Int'l L Proc* 277, at 277–8. In these proceedings, John Jackson is quoted as saying that 'we are looking at what I think is probably the most rigorous model of treaty implementation, treaty effectiveness and compliance in the legalistic or jurisprudential sense. It is an extraordinary model in many ways.' He also states that 'the scope and substance of the agreements under the WTO and Uruguay Round results is enormous. I have said on several occasions that there is no government, even the most powerful government, that really knows what it has gotten into.'

[5] See J Harding, *Clamour Against Capitalism Stilled*, Financial Times, 10 Oct, 2001, at 8 (concluding a month earlier the anti-globlisation movement was preparing its biggest protest ever. Robbed of momentum on 11 Sep, it must now reinvent itself).

The WTO's creators did not go quite so far as to make an international organisation with powers to directly assess penalties and fines against sovereign states. Yet the nature of the financial penalty paid by 'losers' in litigation had an unmistakably 'real' quality poorly understood by the general public.[6] This enforceability represented, quite obviously, the wishes of the main constituency in the creation of the WTO system—business powerful enough to take advantage of new possibilities for transnational reach. As WTO law remained formally part of the state to state system of international law, this enhancement of transnational corporate power never had to be mentioned at all in polite society; only by choice, as it were. By street protesters, for instance, who played a prominent part in raising awareness of the WTO's unique international characteristics.[7]

Looking back on the very late 1990s, and probably through September 2001, it is clear that there was a high water mark for passionate views on the WTO and its new brand of trade law. There was the startling combination of the new subject matter and the Dispute Settlement Understanding (DSU); the opining of the now much fetishised Appellate Body. There were outpourings of praise and condemnation, not just on the part of the specialised legal cadre. This was something new, audacious, and ambitious. This was international law ostensibly operating according to the give and take of 'national interests'; but in fact sustained by a complex range of moneyed interests.

B. Intellectual Reactions: Global Debate in the WTO's Early Years

Two poles of speculation dominated discussion during the 'initial period' of the WTO. Some maintained that this newly judicialised system was the fulfillment of the Bretton Woods ideal—some contemporary version of Rob Howse's notion of the original GATT's embedded liberalism.[8] A disparate band of optimists saw the WTO as a step along the road to a genuine international rule of law, especially in light of its all-important enhanced

---

[6] Since it is virtually unheard of for an international tribunal hearing a state to state dispute to order the payment of penalties against the losing party, it is likely that the general public does not fully grasp the significance of news stories announcing that the 'world trade body' has handed down a ruling.

[7] Journalist James Harding in 2001 said 'the new wave of political activism has coalesced around the simple idea that capitalism has gone too far ... [t]he activists see the WTO as the corporate world's tool to turn more high streets into homogenous shopping malls, to engineer the privatization of more public services, to annul environmental protection laws in the name of free trade and to open more countries to the whimsical forces of Wall Street. With the WTO, they have handed [them] a huge target'. J Harding, *Globalisation's children strike back*, Financial Times, 10 Sep, 2001.

[8] JE Alvarez & R Howse, 'The Boundaries of the WTO: From Politics to Technocracy—and Back Again: The Fate of the Multilateral Trading Regime' (2002) 96 *Am J Int'l L* 94, 96–98.

enforcement mechanism.[9] (Even today, Director-General Pascal Lamy is the ambassador for this point of view, that global governance is the ultimate goal in this project.[10]) At the opposite end of the debate spectrum, the WTO had attributed to it the power to subvert and trample national regulatory and social value, and even biodiversity itself, through the legal acting out of international corporate greed.[11]

This discussion was inspired by the creation of the WTO, but in fact the WTO *disputes* from the first, failed to provide an opportunity for the clash of these opposing views. The early WTO cases, while somewhat interesting, never actually embodied the raw confrontation between the public interest and unfettered free trade that might have been expected. The early 'political' cases—Indian Pharmaceuticals being noteworthy[12]—were suggestive of larger social oppositions, but ultimately some of that tension dissipated—first in the fog of an Appellate Body sensitive to political division and providing increasingly 'nuanced' decisions.[13] Then in the early years of our new millennium there were diversionary tactics such as the Doha 'pharmaceutical' agreement[14]—which seems not to have done much good for anyone. Perhaps most important of all, as the 'war on terror'

---

[9] For this notion in its most basic form, see M Moore, 'The WTO, Looking Ahead' (2000) 24 *Fordham Int'l LJ* 1, at 2–3 (writing under the heading 'The Rule of Law as a Cornerstone of the WTO', 'One of the key achievements of the Uruguay Round was the establishment of the WTO as the permanent institution to oversee the multilateral trade agreements and the forum for further multilateral trade negotiations, thereby bringing the multilateral trading system officially into the universe of legally constituted intergovernmental organizations.... [O]ne of the essential functions of the WTO is to ensure that the rule of law, not force or power, presides over the conditions of international trade. In the WTO, as elsewhere, the rule of law is of fundamental importance in guaranteeing the effectiveness of negotiated results.').

[10] P Lamy, Address at the London School of Economics, *Harnessing Globalisation: Do We Need Cosmopolitics?* (1 Feb, 2000) (transcript available at http://trade-info.cec.eu.int/doclib/docs/2004/october/tradoc_119391.pdf). A hybrid luminary such as Lamy struggles to translate EU speak into global speak, where it is on less hospitable terrain, and where, by definition, there is far less control possible over the concrete implementation of integrationist ideals.

[11] See Harding, above n 5.

[12] See *US v India: Patent Protection for Pharmaceutical and Agricultural Chemical Products*, Report of the Panel, 5 Sep, 1997 (WT/DS50/R) and *US v India: Patent Protection for Pharmaceutical and Agricultural Chemical Products*, Report of the Appellate Body, 19 Dec, 1997 (WT/DS50/AB/R). On the contextual issues, see DK Tomar, 'A Look Into the WTO Pharmaceutical Dispute Between the United States and India' (1999) 17 *Wis Int'l LJ* 579.

[13] Notably *Malaysia, Thailand, India and Pakistan v US: Import Prohibition of Certain Shrimp and Shrimp Products*, Report of the Appellate Body, 12 Oct, 1998 (WT/DS58/AB/R) [hereinafter *Shrimp Turtle*] and *US v European Communities: Measures Concerning Meat and Meat Products*, Report of the Appellate Body, 16 Jan, 1998 (WT/DS26, 48/AB/R) [hereinafter *Beef Hormones*]. See also R Howse, 'The Appellate Body Rulings in the Shrimp/Turtle Case: A New Legal Baseline for the Trade and Environment Debate', (2002) 27 *Colum J Envtl L* 491 (commenting on the nuanced nature of the AB's approach in *Shrimp Turtle*).

[14] See *Implementation of Paragraph 6 of the Doha Declaration on the TRIPS Agreement and Public Health*, Decision of the General Council of 30 August 2003, WT/L/540, available at http://www.wto.org/english/tratop_e/trips_e/implem_para6_e.htm (concluding WTO efforts to deal with the criticism surrounding the pharmaceutical patent question led to protracted negotiations on the problems of developing world access to life saving medications. In fact, the

took centre stage from all political points of view the trade issues were left, unfortunately, to trade specialists

C. The Second Era of WTO Packaging

In the 'second WTO period', after 2001, much of this heated debate died away.

One can identify a turning away from the question of WTO 'legitimacy'— ie on what basis, by what authority, could the WTO decide cases that lay trade and non trade values side by side? Why was trade regulation made so unusually enforceable, when other issues of more direct concern to the world's people, have been dealt with in the form of soft law? While the political and economic underpinnings of the WTO are in many ways obvious and even crude, recent years have seen a number of earnest attempts to account for this disparity (trade law gets enforcement powers, whereas other international law areas do not), while leaving the WTO in its place of enhanced power and status.[15] Over the past five years, we have seen a striking, but perhaps not surprising, professional acceptance of the 1995 system, and the development of a cult of the Appellate Body. The legitimacy debate was all too soon passé. Wading through the many articles on the jurisprudence of the Appellate Body became a challenge to one's stamina.[16] The contextual political questions came to be seen as soft ball, irrelevant even. The 'hard stuff' was hyper textual, fortuitously favoured by both the Appellate Body and a devoted band of scholars. When the trade bloggers did venture into deeper waters, their discourse was often embarrassingly simplistic, along the lines of *The WTO does recognise non trade values and can accommodate concerns about human development.* Or, *WTO law is compatible with a theory of international justice.* A good deal of WTO scholarship, by its unseemly technical focus on dispute-generated jurisprudence, has undoubtedly assisted in obscuring the true origins of the system created.

---

result bought the organisation time until the sense of political urgency dissipated. The actual agreement on exportation of generic drugs from developing countries to least developed countries proved largely symbolic in nature.).

[15] As for attempts (ultimately fanciful, I believe) to account for the WTO's particular place in the international legal order, see CR Kelly, 'Power, Linkage and Accommodation: The WTO as an International Actor and Its Influence on Other Actors and Regimes' (2006) 24 *Berkeley J Int'l L* 79, at 80; and CR Kelly, 'Enmeshment as a Theory of Compliance' (2005) 37 *NYU J Int'l L & Pol* 303, at 303.
[16] See M Oesch, 'Standards of Review in WTO Dispute Resolution' (2003) 6 *J Int'l Econ L* 635; and D Zang, 'Textualism in GATT/WTO Jurisprudence: Lessons for the Constitutionalization Debate' (2006) 33 *Syracuse J Int'l L & Com* 393 (outlining countless examples of discussions of the AB's jurisprudential approach).

D. What of the 'Trade and' Debate?

The creation of the WTO attaches itself naturally and logically to issues of global justice. Yet certain specialised writing on WTO-related matters took on a peculiar 'maybe someday' quality. It was as if law professors were waiting for 'somebody' to bring about a transformation in the direction of a more complex global governance, or to transform non-economic soft law (pertaining to justice and rights) into hard law to better justify the existence of the WTO as a humane institution. But the implication was that if these mystical events did not occur, that would be okay too—since the WTO was doing its own job rather nicely.

I think in this regard of Steve Charnovits's 'optimistic scenario' in *The World Trade Organization in 2020*, in which he writes:

> The legitimacy crisis faced by the WTO in its early years was overcome through enlightened leadership and the adoption of important constitutional changes. Although free trade remains unpopular in many countries, the diatribes and street protests against the WTO stopped after the creation of [the?] WTO Parliamentary Assembly in 2007.[17]

In the same piece, under the heading of 'Justice', he continues:

> Although much criticized in its early years, the Appellate Body survived and received greater respect in the WTO's second decade. When the Appellate Body's name was changed to the International Court of Economic Justice (ICEJ), as had been proposed by Joseph Weiler, the WTO dropped the fig leaf of gaining formal approval of panel decision by the DSB. Over time, the contributions to trade jurisprudence by the original seven members of the Appellate Body was widely celebrated.[18]

This new genre of *trade sci fi* has the appeal of ignoring the fact that in the real world, there is no international political push towards complex global governance; and no indication, despite Professor Weiler's musing (as described by Professor Charnovitz, above), that the WTO has any aspirations towards duplicating the long-standing ambitions of the EU—ambitions that are truly complex, and that do not merely use and abuse notions of 'fairness' as a cover for expanded business opportunities.

In similar vein, Professor Trachtman in the essay I have already referred to, *Changing the Rules: Constitutional Moments of the WTO*, states:

> .... Criticizing the WTO for excluding environmental protection without examining the broader environmental regime misses an important dimension. Even more saliently, blaming the WTO for the persistence of poverty is

---

[17] S Charnovitz, 'The World Trade Organization in 2020' (2005) 1 *J Int'l L & Int'l Rel* 167, at 182.
[18] Ibid at 186.

merely attacking a straw man. It might also miss the opportunity to attack the real problem, for which the WTO might not be responsible, but perhaps can address.[19]

He goes on to say that the rules against protectionism at the WTO are 'in the aggregate beneficial.'[20] 'If they were not, why would states adhere to the WTO? Why would states like China struggle to accede?'[21] He then demonstrates a *waiting for Godot*-like tendency to dream about some future WTO that is better, more embedded as it were—saying that 'The WTO will not soon embody the kinds of human rights protections that domestic societies *hope for*,' and explains that the state can provide these protections.[22] But the WTO might become involved in 'linkages' in the future, in instances when states do not provides those benefits.[23] After all, he says, 'the EU's evolution has required delicate negotiations to insert human rights norms,' and 'so too will the WTO's evolution require human rights-type guidelines.'[24]

I could provide further examples, but note that this pie in the sky view of a future WTO—more complex in its motivations, intentions and ambitions than the current one, more integrated into 'other' constitutional structures and norms, all this having occurred through some unidentified agency—is troublesome. If the goal of complex global governance, including meaningful concepts of fairness, is worth speculating on, surely it is worth asking for rather more directly. I fully understand that this might involve WTO scholars in an unseemly form of what might be considered 'advocacy,' and detract from the technical virtuosity that is so highly favoured in certain circles.

Yet the *trade sci fi* approach places 'scholarship' into some kind of passive, even paralysed mode—where to appreciate the present is enough—but to wait for some force to create an international trade regime that more fully links to 'justice' is also set out as a worthy intellectual activity. In this way, one gets credit for imagining a nicer future with measurable benefits, while continuing to derive professional status from being a WTO expert.

E. Trade Law on the Law School Menu

At some point in time, global trade regulation became a 'discipline'; a branch of law. I would like to consider the question of how it found its

---

[19] Trachtman, above n 3, at 44.
[20] Ibid.
[21] Ibid.
[22] Ibid at 46.
[23] Ibid.
[24] Ibid.

way to law school, and thus came to be considered a coherent field of law to be studied. Prior to 1995, we see Robert Hudec toiling away, not completely on his own, but largely so in terms of defining a subject matter: international trade law.[25] Hudec was busy with his citrus fruit and oilseeds during a time when the line between political choice and free trade rules was moveable.[26]

But it is interesting to ponder how trade law entered the law school curriculum, a sure sign that either significant money or a myth of justice is on offer. While post-Constitutional moment trade rules have a minor myth of justice element, we have seen that this genre of writing tends towards the sci fi. The real reason that, after 1995, we are no longer in the realm of an upper class elective for economics majors, but rather a branch of 'law', is because of the existence of disputes (with winners and losers), and thus an adjudicating tribunal, as well as the all-important financial consequences.

This post-1995 law, interestingly, had all the trappings of public international law, but with a hard-edged difference: as well as a difference from mere (ie, conceptually trivial) private transnational law, international business transactions ('IBT'), where the questions are more or less about which party makes a few million more or less, WTO law attracted many with its unique blend of global governance at the service of private transnational actors. The principal factors in this transformation from 'Hudec's law' to law school mainstream, as mentioned, were the creation of a fixed tribunal—whose rulings had moneyed consequences for the losers. Into that cauldron of legal decisions and money, rushed, very predictably, legal academics.

For every legal discipline, there must be a supporting cadre of specialised chattering classes, and for this purpose, there was the eager and active production of 'trade law scholarship'. To say that most trade law scholarship strikes me as self-referential, hyper technical, stifling, off the point or banal as the topic at hand dictates, these flaws are not arbitrary or coincidental. It seems to me that this turgid quality is dictated by the fact that WTO law sets in stone a certain fixed political view, thus leaving relatively few subjects to discuss at any level of sophistication.[27] This is a prisoner's dilemma of an intellectual sort.

---

[25] JP Trachtman, 'Robert E. Hudec (1934–2003)' (2003) 97 *Am J Int'l Law* 311; R Blackhurst & P Mavoidis, 'A Tribute to Robert E. Hudec' (2005) *World Trade Review*, 4:1, 3–5.

[26] Professor Hudec identified the GATT as a legal system worthy of academic attention in his seminal book, Robert E Hudec, *The GATT Legal System and World Trade Diplomacy* (Praeger, 1975). Also see RE Hudec, 'A Statistical Profile of GATT Dispute Settlement Cases: 1948–1989' (1993) 2 *Minn J Global Trade* 1; and RE Hudec, *Enforcing International Trade Law: The Evolution of the Modern GATT Legal System*, (Lexis Law Publishing, 1993).

[27] In this regard, I still value the insightful article by David Driesen on the over-definition of 'free trade' made by WTO law. D Driesen, *'What is Free Trade?: The Real Issue Lurking Behind the Trade and Environment Debate'* (2001) 41 *Va J Int'l L* 279.

In other words, where the underlying target of analysis is by its nature not contestable, unless the writer is extremely imaginative, most suggestions for law reform read like science fiction, as already indicated. It is safer to stick with the *technique*, a zone in which one is at least known as a specialist. William Davey's division of WTO disputes into two sets (roughly 1995-2000 and 2000-2005)[28] seems useful to me in ways not discussed or perhaps even contemplated by Davey. In the first five years, not only were the disputes more politically charged—and more hotly anticipated—but scholars seemed to feel greater compulsion to flounder around in the legitimacy debate. In more recent years, technique has come to dominate in a manner that could be seen as escapist, realist, or opportunist—but rarely, in my view, enlightening for any larger purpose than the production of scholarship in the service of a 'set' system.

To return to Bob Hudec and the world before 1995—the fact that national acceptance of rulings was more or less 'voluntary' back then meant that the line between trade doctrine, as reflected in the GATT rules, and political viewpoint or sovereign views on certain regulatory values was to a far greater extent contestable. The interpretative line between these zones was to some degree fluid. The competitive impulse, the global market impulse, was set in a context of non-global (for want of a better term, national) political forces. As a point of interest, Professor Hudec spent a good deal of his time in his last years talking about how the old system worked quite well, and achieved reasonable rates of compliance in the absence of the DSU-based system.[29]

The effect of the 'constitutional moment' that created the WTO (judicialisation, enforceable international law) was to draw a far more rigid line, whereby a certain neo liberal or market-only view became indistinguishable from the law itself, Yeats' dancer and the dance.[30] Legal analysis or scholarship would naturally derive from that set-in-stone format. At its worst, one could argue that there has been a fetishising of the doctrine of competition, and the legitimising of a kind of econo-patriarchy.

By contrast, the EU drew and continues to draw a completely different set of lines, with the market at the service of other values. The market is utilised and recognised, but it is a shifting space, sometimes taking up

---

[28] WJ Davey, 'The WTO Dispute Settlement System: The First Ten Years' (2005) 8 *J Int'l Econ L* 17.
[29] See RE Hudec, 'The New WTO Dispute Settlement Procedure: An Overview of the First Three Years' (1999) 8 *Minn J Global Trade* 1.
[30] While I fear Yeats would oppose inclusion in such a discussion, I refer to his poem Among School Children, wherein he writes:

O chestnut-tree, great-rooted blossomer,
Are you the leaf, the blossom or the bole?
O body swayed to music, O brightening glance,
How can we know the dancer from the dance?

greater and sometimes lesser space in the entire 'project'. The energy of the market is acknowledged and legally protected, but its proponents must deal with counter-forces. Annoyance over the rather more neo-liberal character of the composition of the latest European Commission, and the prospect of chillier economic winds were apparently motivating factors in French rejection of the European Constitution, or Constitutional Treaty. (Note also in this regard the recent flap over the EU services directive.)

F. Where the WTO is Probably Not Going

It is clear to me by now, although it took a while, that the WTO is not in fact a kind of halfway house on the roads to enlightened global governance. It is small wonder that some of the writing on 'trade and' matters—the social clause, environmental swords and shields—has somewhat faded away, leaving the field to those with the stamina to engage in the 'contact sport' of WTO studies—what about zeroing, will the peace clause yield—with the comforting touchstone of Article 31 of the Vienna Convention just there to lend credibility. The 'trade and' debate was a very sterile one, a bit different from the *trade sci fi* I have discussed, but in its way built on a fantasy. This fantasy led to attempts to analogise WTO law to other branches of law that might be touched and shaken up by criticism, whether mild or scathing.

Just as WTO law is itself essentially non human, or inhuman—perhaps even anti-human, its trade scholarship has developed a correspondingly frozen rhetorical style.[31]

As for the panel and Appellate Body rulings, they are, even compared to almost any other branch of legal discourse, dense, hyper-textual, and quite resistant to any contamination of social or political context, as if their authors were aliens and in fact did not even really 'know' human language—but had learned how to express in linguistic form from a course at some celestial Berlitzschule. The WTO lingo is more obsessive than doctrinaire, because its political underpinnings must be hidden. When I saw on a specialist trade law blog that someone found the recent GMO panel report[32] too long, and was essentially crying out for mercy in having to read the thing, I knew to how extreme a pass things had come.

Legal scholarship represents a process of mobilisation. The legal clustering effect—disputes, lawyers, money and resulting academic production—provides a scholarship to buoy the image of the underlying object of

---

[31] At one of the first international trade conferences I ever attended in the US, back in the late 1990s, I was advised by a prominent trade scholar never to use the word 'feel' when discussing trade law matters!

[32] Comment made on the International Economic Law and Policy Blog, found at http://worldtradelaw.typepad.com/ielpblog, referring to the panel report in *EC—Biotech Products ('GMOs')*, WT/Ds291/R, 29 Sep 2006.

regard. In both the WTO disputes and related scholarship, the dense and technocratic diction in fact tends to lack philosophical complexity. As indicated above, one is only too likely to hear such inanities as 'It would be nice if this system led to prosperity for more people.'

Into this scholarly fortress, scarcely a whiff of critical legal studies, feminism or post modernism has arrived. There may be rare exceptions, but the overwhelming impression is of safe, reliable academic hands on this great treasure chest of WTO-related trade law. Just as the underlying law enshrines a neo-liberal glorification of competition—so too WTO-related scholarship seems over time increasingly a contact sport, where the last one standing at the end not just of one but of all the Appellate Body reports is the winner. Needless to say, those disinclined to compete for that honour must be presumed to be many.

II. TRADE-RELATED OPPORTUNISM, IN PHASES

A. Step One: Corporate Opportunism

This Chapter presents the argument that the WTO is a site for the allocation of power, wealth and influence, and so in that sense, its specific subject matter is secondary. Nevertheless, at the moment of its creation, it did matter what the WTO was 'about': making the world more accessible to business and investment. (The WTO did not effect this all by itself—the WTO gave coherence and as such acted as symbol or summing up of the post-colonial dream giving way to the neo liberal bargain.)[33] It is a fact that no other branch of international law could have been truly 'judicialised' so easily, so quickly, so utterly. We can hardly imagine the major human rights conventions being set to this tune: an across-the-board human rights court—with consequences in money terms for violators, for instance. Despite the recent development of post-conflict war crimes tribunals, human rights treaties are notorious for their general lack of enforceability.[34]

It appears that in 1995, based on a convergence of forces, transnational business interests came to be represented in a branch of public international law. While preserving the myth of a legal system that places obligations on 'nations,' in fact the system was designed in large part to make manufacturing

---

[33] On the failed New International Economic Order of the 1970s, see AA Shalakany, 'Arbitration and the Third World: A Plea for Reassessing Bias Under the Specter of Neo-liberalism' (2000) 41 *Harv Int'l LJ* 419, at 419–20.

[34] Whatever one's view of the degree of state compliance with such treaty commitments, it is clear that enforcement mechanisms in the human rights context are weak. For an overview of commitment and compliance issues in international human rights treaties generally, including a discussion of optional protocols allowing for individual petitions to treaty bodies, see OA Hathaway, 'The Cost of Commitment' (2003) 55 *Stan L Rev* 1821.

even more mobile than it already was. Member countries also came to be divided into 'strategic blocks', similarly designed to mask the fact that *nations* or *members* never had anything like monolithic 'trade interests' that were pursued on behalf of the 'people of the nation'. Despite the many GATT and WTO disputes that reference the 'trade rights' of participating nations, trade rights are not the property of the nation states, but of those who reside within them and have the 'relevant' transnational abilities.

What became WTO law in 1995 was a fairly straightforward set of items on the wish lists of transnational business; foremost among these, as mentioned, enhancing access to cheap manufacturing locales and cheap labour. Let me demonstrate what a fraudulent presentation it is to speak of nations and their rights with a simple example. It makes little sense to describe China as 'joining the WTO,' when a huge percentage of products coming from China are from companies originally set up and active in countries that 'approved' the accession of China. Nations are in fact trading with themselves; or certain actors have managed, via trading rules imposed on 'nations,' to alter the relative position of states and international markets.

This national/de-national or anti-national mix (at once privileging and whittling away the nation state) might work or find justification in a complex, multi-motivated system like the EU—but it is politically suspect when it happens at global level. This is especially so given the fact that the WTO facilitates backpedaling on basic characteristics of the twentieth century social or welfare state.[35] The new trade laws did not just 'unleash' market forces onto a complex global environment—they moved these forces about—and in the process redistributed wealth, power, prestige and influence.[36]

It should be taken as a willful failure, that so much of mainstream WTO—related trade law scholarship consistently misses the connection between the drive towards enforceable international trade laws and the history of the modern nation state, particularly the development of labour rights within states. More advantageous relations between business and labour (from the point of view of business) is so clearly a major part of the global free trade agenda; far more relevant than an ongoing struggle between nations. This more advantageous position for transnational

---

[35] See, eg, among many other possibilities D Goulet, 'Changing Development Debates Under Globalization: The Evolving Nature of Development in the Light of Globalization' (2004) 6 *J L & Soc Challenges* 1, at 11 (writing that 'globalization has also exacted a high price in the form of new and large inequities, the dilution of effective national sovereignty, and multiple insecurities. Among threats to human security arising from globalization the UNDP lists: economic insecurity, job and income insecurity, health insecurity, cultural insecurity, personal insecurity, environmental insecurity, political and community insecurity.').

[36] Issues of distribution tend to be kept out of sight in all areas of legal analysis, not just analysis of trade rules. But here the gap between reality and discourse is particularly striking.

business can be seen as a prime motivator for the creation of our current international trade laws, symbolised by mobility but not a complex 'free movement.'[37]

B. Step Two: the Outpouring of Scholars—What to Say After You Say Violation?

There are many well-known witticisms about scholarship in the former Soviet Union: medical students discussing anatomy by way of Marx and Lenin; or literature during the Chinese Cultural Revolution—boy meets tractor. We chuckle over these apparent intellectual anomalies, not recognising the fact of a similar phenomenon in our scholarly midst. Most of the dispute-related WTO scholarship one reads not only has no basis in a larger reality, no empirical check (such as, is this system achieving some desirable set of economic goals?); it barely seems to have any link with interesting theory. While apparently difficult, it often appears merely abstract and escapist.

Just as the decisions of the panels and Appellate Body elevate what amounts to the application of a set of rules with fairly crude motivations, so too WTO-related trade scholarship relies on a woefully convoluted manner of addressing issues that are not in themselves that complicated—the rhetoric, in other words, is more complex than the underlying legal-conceptual structure. One could take this paradox to indicate that the hard edges of the economic system require that the scholarship that legitimises it remain in safe hands. The safe hands idea is useful in all kinds of contexts—but especially here—where insiders seem not to see the humour in the endless and endlessly hair splitting 'jurisprudence' that provides the target of 'analysis'.

As indicated in the discussion of *trade sci fi* above, there is actually little point in talking about WTO 'law reform' in any fundamental way—since there is slight chance that any organised political forces could successfully array themselves around reform in the name of equalisation—cohesion—and so forth. Newly leftist countries may take up the challenge of trade agreements for the benefit of the general population, but there is no chance whatsoever that the major trading countries will accept enforcement mechanisms for non-trade values.

The WTO accession process will never come to be based on rigorous pre-accession cohesion, with years of advance preparation in the form of

---

[37] The EU concept of free movement, whether of goods, workers, capital or services, is embedded in countless other integrationist impulses, relating to such areas as the environment, the international rule of law, and so forth. There is no need here to fully describe the European idea of 'free movement,' but it bears no relationship to the crude mobility of production that GATT/WTO rules have achieved.

wealth transfers. This is what the EU does; but the idea of its happening on the 'global' stage is at this point in time preposterous. In the North American context, the proposed US-Mexican 'fence' is only a dramatic example of the crude link between 'free trade doctrine' and opportunism by transnational business actors, in that the labouring classes of a NAFTA 'trade partner' can be legally and without great outcry bottled up where they belong.

Discussion of such matters is treated as out of place among serious trade law scholars. On the other hand, though, writing in great technical detail about a system whose rights and wrongs one does not attempt to assess has rather nasty historical precedent in scholarly support for the powerful. Many questionable assertions of power have been supported by highly technical academic analyses. Instead of dialectical materialism, we are instead preoccupied with the Appellate Body. If we touch on justice at all, it generally has to be kept within very safe parameters. From the scholarly point of view, it does not seem to matter what WTO law is in the larger sense 'about'—as long as there are professional opportunities attached.

C. Step Three: the Opportunism of Participating States—It's the Global Forum, Stupid

A further and related feature of global trade law is that just as it attracts a mobilised legal profession to its service, so too does the nation state fall into line where there are opportunities for strategising and promoting the national profile. Countries like Brazil and India come readily to mind as having taken the vehicle of the WTO and used it to great strategic advantage.[38] Although under great pressure recently as the Doha Round has faltered, the WTO as a symbolic forum continues to act as a magnet for national strategic behavior: Brazil has proven to be an arch-strategist in its WTO dealings, within and without litigation; Saudi Arabia and Vietnam have 'joined,' erasing mountains of complex history; Russia discusses its own possible entry with high awareness as to the symbolic value of such a move.

As mentioned above, WTO law promotes and demotes the national simultaneously. (This is in a different way true of the EU, as well.) As

---

[38] See BL Jacobs, 'Brazil's Agricultural Trade War: Success and Failure on the Southern Route to Antarctica' (2005)36 *U Miami Inter-Am L Rev* 167. Also note the role played by India and Brazil during and following Cancun, see A Hurrell, 'A New Politics of Confrontation? Brazil and India in Multilateral Trade Negotiations' (2006) 20 *J Interdisc Int'l Rel* 415. See also G Shaffer, M Ratton Sanchez & B Rosenberg, *Brazil's Response to the Judicialized WTO Regime: Strengthening the State through Diffusing Expertise* (ICTSD working paper, forthcoming 2007), available at http://www.ictsd.org/issarea/dsu/resources/Brazil_paper.pdf.

explained, the world trading system is clever in that it gives the appearance of encouraging states to pursue their 'national interests' in the forum, obscuring the fact that there is no one national interest, thereby flattening out internal divisions and disparities. This means that the pursuit of strategic high profile at the WTO gives pleasure to governments and elites, while generally not agitating the masses. One can assume that the general populace principally hears that the 'national economic interest' is being pursued.[39]

Analogies to previous economic empires are appropriate here. For regional leaders, being a good team player in the friendship of Soviet peoples, for example, was important. Learning the techniques of discourse and orientation are significant when it comes to systems that apportion power and influence. After the establishment of the system, actual content is largely a matter of indifference, especially when there is no mechanism for negotiating fundamental changes to that system. Such issues as effects (does the law achieve something measurable?) and propriety (is this sound/ethical/good/desirable?) cease to be matters of discussion when law and its politics are indistinguishable—the dancer and the dance metaphor cited above.

Within monarchies, how to do well at the imperial court was a serious matter; how to curry favour at the seat of empire; how to show oneself to advantage in order to accrue personal benefits. It is not entirely without interest in this regard that Brazil and other countries show themselves to great advantage by hiring the most expensive DC lawyers available to pursue 'strategic' disputes.[40] In this sense, the discussions of 'NAFTA at ten

---

[39] It would be interesting to examine fully the manner in which newer leftist governments in several Latin American countries invoke the idea of trade either to demonstrate their market or leftist credentials. The message often seems to be, 'Don't worry, we support free trade', perhaps as a means of staving off international ostracism, while at the same time pursuing a vigorous alternative trade agenda, as per Venezuela's sponsorship of the 'other' regional free trade agreement. On this latter point, see *Leftist Trio Seals Americas Pact*, BBC News, 29 Apr, 2006, available at http://news.bbc.co.uk/2/hi/americas/4959008.stm (stating that 'The left wing leaders of Bolivia, Cuba and Venezuela have signed a three way trade agreement aimed at countering US influence in Latin America... . The deal aims to reduce or eliminate tariffs between the three countries. But apart from this, it is very unlike conventional trade agreements... . Participants have vowed to work towards the eradication of illiteracy and the expansion of employment.').

[40] Note a recent South American conference entitled *South American Dialogue on WTO Dispute Settlement and Sustainable Development*, in June 2006, available at http://www.ictsd.org/dlogue/2006-06-22/2006-06-22-desc.htm. Topics included 'Using the DSU system strategically to influence negotiations' and 'Economic gains for developing countries from use of the DSU system.' Numerous DC lawyers and American academics participated. See also C Davis and S Blodgett Bermeo, *Who files? Developing Country Participation in GATT/WTO* (Princeton University, 2006); and R Abbott, *Are Developing Countries Deterred from using the WTO Dispute Settlement System? Participation of Developing Coutres in the DSM in the years 1995–2005* (ECIPE Working Paper, No 01/2007, 2007) (stating 'that the vast majority of the developing country cases were launched just by five members.').

years old' during 2004[41] were quite revealing, as it was apparent that the general effects of NAFTA, a subset of contemporary trade law, were, well, a kind of wash at best, and a disaster in some sectors.[42] Yet this 'empirical' discussion did not seem to be taken by scholars as an intellectual referendum on NAFTA. It did not create a pause or a recoiling from obsessive focus on NAFTA-related 'investment disputes' and the like, since this is the technical bread and butter of NAFTA studies. And such reflections do not appear to alter the behaviour of states in their pursuit of strategic advantage within the new forum for self-display.

III. CHANGING THE WHO AND THE WHAT OF WTO LAW

A. Corporations, Scholars, States

In sum, then, at the initial stage, we have a clear motivation for the creation of enforceable trade law, as this reflects the will of transnational business. In the next phases, we have a general (scholarly and state-based) indifference to the good or bad of the subject matter, and to questions that consider the observable effects of all this new trade law. The EU has these game-like properties, but also has some elasticity to respond to the wishes of a broad range of people who actually know about the rules and expect something of what the rules produce. Results must be delivered or the system will be altered, by a process of demand inputs. A significant function of WTO-related scholarship appears to be to keep 'trade law' obscure. Certainly the panel and Appellate Body decisions are written in a manner that indicates no expectation that a general reader, even an educated one, could or would follow.[43] And in fact, readers don't need to follow, as they are not being asked anything. This may be why when trade commentators have to discuss something that has to do with the non-trade world, they often sound either simplistic or out of their element.

Speaking way back in the days of the 'legitimacy debate', Larry Summers was interviewed for the film 'Commanding Heights', and stated that it was

---

[41] See C Terbeek, 'Love in the Time of Free Trade: NAFTA's Economic Effects Ten Years Later' (2004) 12 *Tul J Int'l & Comp L* 487; JC Moreno-Brid et al, 'NAFTA and the Mexican Economy: A Look Back on a Ten-Year Relationship' (2005) 20 *NCJ Int'l Com Reg* 997, at 1018 (stating '[t]he fundamental constraints on Mexico's long-term economic growth have not been alleviated ... [s]ome have actually become more binding. NAFTA's positive impact may have by now reached a point of exhaustion and the Agreement should be revamped.').

[42] See D Papademetriou, J Audley, S Polaski, & S Vaughan, *NAFTA's Promise and Reality: Lessons from Mexico for the Hemisphere*, Carnegie Endowment Report, Nov 2003 (A report published by the Carnegie Endowment for International Peace on the occasion of NAFTA's 10th anniversary pointed out that the most detrimental effects in terms of unemployment occurred within Mexico's agricultural sector).

[43] It seems to me that all the panel and AB reports suffer from this bizarre quality of impenetrability, such that singling out one or two would be unilluminating. It is a question of systemic style.

too bad that in trade discussions, what the losers lost was so apparent—ie, a job lost—whereas the fact that someone could buy a child more toys for Christmas because of free trade was a kind of invisible benefit. He lamented the fact that this ability to buy extra toys might not get attributed to free trade at all.[44] The spectacle of Mr Summers attempting to draw equivalence between these two issues shows the absurdity of much trade theory from the point of view of people most affected by its operation. His comments reveal the degree to which states are constrained, once locked into WTO techno-ideology, Article XX exceptions included, should they wish to pursue such goals as the re-creation of a large middle class, a reduction in consumerism, or a fundamental response to the urgent matter of global warming.

Indeed, the real environmental issues of our time have absolutely nothing to do with GATT Article XX , and of course never did. The endless and fruitless debate over how broadly Article XX could be invoked to justify trade restrictions was completely irrelevant to the grave problems of global environmental degradation. (The Article XX debate was a sideshow along the lines of, 'How much power does the national legislature still have on rare occasions when its action is challenged before a GATT (later WTO) panel?') The real questions have to do with contemporary consumerism and sustainability, soon to greet us in serious form as our temperatures continue to rise.[45] Note the recent World Wildlife Federation report to the effect that we would require several 'worlds' to support the commercial lifestyle we are collectively pursuing. But 'real' trade scholars seem not to spend time on fluffy issues like that—they have better things to do.

What the WTO accomplished was not conceptually grandiose, and it was relatively easy to pull off in political terms because of the culmination of commercial interests it represented. Environmental and human rights controls are correspondingly hard to bring into the hard law realm because they do not have such interests behind them. The WTO is not a precursor to global governance or the international rule of law—or if it is, there is little concrete sign of that occurring. Global trade law and its constructed world, academic and empirical, is no more intrinsically valid and no less

---

[44] Interview with Lawrence Summers, Past President of Harvard University (21 Apr, 2001) (Transcript available at: http://www.pbs.org/wgbh/commandingheights/shared/minitextlo/int_lawrencesummers.html#1).

[45] See 'Landmark Climate Report Issues Strong Warning on Global Warming', *Bridges Weekly Trade News Digest*, 7 Feb, 2007, available at http://www.ictsd.org/weekly/07-02-07/story5.htm (noting that 'A group of the world's top climate scientists has issued its strongest ever warning that human activity is to blame for climate change, and that global temperatures and extreme weather phenomena will increase unless greenhouse gas emissions are substantially reduced.'). It is interesting that global trade liberalisation is largely responsible for the fact that China and India are developing global carbon 'footprints' to rival that of the world's largest offender, the United States. Both countries issued statements in the wake of the UN report to the effect that their rights to develop (ie, to continue to emit greenhouse gases) should not be interfered with.

self-interested than were systems based on religion and/or feudalism—or the Union of Soviet Socialist Republics.

B. What Abstraction and Escapism Miss

I am resigned to not getting my wishes (complex global governance based on the needs of a wide array of interests), and it is nonsensical to earnestly advocate for what will almost certainly not occur. But the glaring misfit between the thinking of WTO scholars and the effects and implications of global trade regulation is a very serious matter. The original proposal for this Chapter was based on reading the introduction to Catharine MacKinnon's *Women's Lives, Men's Laws*[46]—borrowing a small segment of this work for use in the WTO context. In her introduction, MacKinnon denounces the intensely abstract nature of so much legal analysis—writing that:

> some judges and legal commentators seem genuinely to believe they are called upon to apply their minds neutrally to abstract legal questions. While the attempt may rein in their biases to some extent, it more surely conceals them, even from themselves, and permits unconscious commitments on substance, which tend to favor the status quo and established interests, to control.[47]

I can think of no more abstract branch of law than global trade regulation, especially that touching on WTO matters—and no more abstract scholarship—whether practice-oriented or supposedly theoretical. MacKinnon states, bravely, that:

> Legal theory ... should analyze the legal issues in terms of the real issues, and strive to move law so that the real issues *are* the legal issues. Legal scholarship should accordingly analyze the real life behind the legal curtains and how the back story and the window dressing interact. Apart from being more democratic and honest, this could help women a lot, and other members of socially disadvantaged groups as well.[48]

She continues:

> Because confronting reality directly is not abstract, this approach has not qualified as a legal theory worthy of the name ... Reality gets one dirty and involved, and talking about it requires knowing something about the world, which is harder than knowing something about the law of that aspect of the world.[49]

Applying this to recent trends in global trade scholarship, it seems to me that a high level of abstraction and insularity is key to being considered the

---

[46] C MacKinnon, *Women's Lives, Men's Laws* (Belknap Press, 2005).
[47] Ibid at 6.
[48] Ibid.
[49] Ibid.

'right sort' for being taken seriously in the trade law world. Trade scholars are the safest of safe hands. The more abstract the legal atmosphere, the more likely it is that those of a reality orientation will conclude that the subject matter is not for them. And from the point of view of mainstream trade scholarship, these people are not much missed.

C. Will the WTO and its Law Survive? Ask Pascal

To win people over to the international trade changes in the offing during the mid 1990s, Peter Sutherland[50]—that ultimate right person at the right time and place—talked about the billions and zillions to be generated and unleashed and set free by the creation of the then brand new WTO.[51] Whether that actually occurred or not, seems to be of little interest now. We now hear frequently that liberalisation of agricultural trade will unleash vast amounts of economic potential, this time to reconfigure the balance between developing and developed countries. The hidden reality and concealed drama, as before, has to do with lost jobs and global hierarchies and labour rights, not merely with protectionist devices.

It will be something to see what happens to the WTO under the leadership of Pascal Lamy, as he continues to attempt the impossible: to make the WTO appear to be EU-like, which it is not.[52] I am assuming that with all the system momentum generated over the past 10 years, the WTO will reconstitute itself and survive. But one should not underestimate the resistance of those who dislike what the WTO represents in terms of a model

---

[50] Former GATT/WTO Director General 1993–95, see http://www.wto.org/English/thewto_e/dg_e/ps_e.htm.

[51] See P Sutherland, *Freer Trade, Freer Choice—How the Uruguay Round Result Helps Consumers*, Address to the Consumers for World Trade Award Dinner (21 Jun, 1994) available at http://www.wto.org/gatt_docs/English/SULPDF/91790185.pdf ('On the world scale, a provisional estimate by the GATT Secretariat puts the global value of the improvements in market access at an extra $755 billion-worth of trade annually by 2002 ... Some estimates put the overall gains to the US economy as high as $100-200 billion a year once the Uruguay Round results are fully implemented.'); and P Sutherland, *A New Framework for International Economic Relations*, Third Annual Hayek Memorial Lecture (16 Jun, 1994) available at http://www.wto.org/gatt_docs/English/SULPDF/91790168.pdf ('Very conservative estimates point to annual income gains of around $250 billion from the market access part of the Round, that is, from the reduction in tariffs and the removal of non-tariff barriers on merchandize trade alone.').

[52] Monsieur Lamy's most recent venture into the EU-WTO zone is seen in remarks he made at the 24th session of the Governing Council/Global Ministerial Environmental Forum in Nairobi, *Globalization and the Environment in a Reformed UN: Charting a Sustainable Development Path* (5 Feb, 2007), available at http://www.wto.org/english/news_e/sppl_e/sppl54_e.htm ('The Doha Round of trade negotiations contains a promise for the environment. A promise to allow for a more efficient allocation of resources—including natural ones—on a global scale through a continued reduction of obstacles to trade (tariffs and subsidies). But it also includes a promise to ensure greater harmony between the WTO and MEAs: a promise to tear down the barriers that stand in the way of trade in clean technologies and services; as well

72 Sara Dillon

for enforceable international law. (These are political types who may support the economic goals of transnational business, but distrust any form of enforcement-oriented international rules.) At this rate, in any case, we are not moving in the direction of global governance. That would require a discussion of underlying reality. Some early writing, including my own, speculating on how the very fact of the WTO could act as a springboard for other non-trade areas of enforceable or judicialised international law now seems hopelessly naïve, buried under several tons of legal and academic abstraction.

---

as a promise to reduce the environmentally harmful agricultural subsidies that are leading to overproduction and harmful fisheries subsidies which are encouraging over-fishing and depleting the world's fish stock. The WTO needs the engagement of the environmental community in these negotiations.'). In Lamy's vision, the WTO is in fact an environmental hero. Ibid.

6

Some Sociological Perspectives on International Institutions and the Trading System

ANDREW TF LANG

BY WHAT MECHANISMS do the international trade regime influence the trade policy choices of its Members? Trade lawyers pay most attention to the *regulative*[1] function of the WTO, and treat the international trade regime as essentially a set of rules guiding and constraining the behaviour of governments. In this model, the mechanisms by which the trade regime influences governmental behaviour are largely coercive, and the effectiveness of the regime depends primarily on the clarity, enforceability and (to some extent) legitimacy of its rules. But institutionalists within the discipline of sociology have taught us that institutional environments influence actor behaviour in other, perhaps more subtle, ways. In this Chapter, my aim is threefold: to set out some of the insights of sociological institutionalists; to make the claim that these insights can help us more fully to understand the role of the WTO in international political life; and to offer reasons why such insights are of relevance for those specifically interested in WTO law.[2]

I. THE DISSEMINATION OF POLICY NORMS AND POLICY BELIEFS

A. The Core Processes

Institutional theorists within sociology remind us, first of all, that institutions embody not just regulative, but also *normative* systems. The decisions of political actors, just like those of other kinds of actors, are shaped by

---

[1] WR Scott, *Institutions and Organizations*, 2nd edn, (Sage, 2001) 51.
[2] This Chapter is therefore following very much in the footsteps of Philip Nichols: see PM Nichols, 'Forgotten Linkages-Historical Institutionalism and Sociological Institutionalism and Analysis of the World Trade Organization' (1998) 19 *U Pa J Int'l Econ L* 461.

prevailing beliefs about how it is appropriate to behave, and the kinds of goals it is appropriate to pursue. 'Much of the behaviour we observe in political institutions,' March and Olsen observe, 'reflects the routine way in which people do what they are supposed to do.'[3] Part of the function of institutions, on this view, is to define and pass on precisely these norms and routines. Institutions, in other words, are not just regulative systems, but also 'social environments,'[4] which constitute particular policy-making communities, and in which a variety of social pressures are brought to bear, so that participants come over time to share a particular set of normative beliefs characteristic of that community. International institutions such as the WTO work not just by laying down enforceable rules of behaviour, but also by diffusing social and policy norms among elite policy-makers. They do not simply prohibit the pursuit of policies which states might otherwise perceive to be in their interests, they are a venue in which, through social interaction, states (or their representatives) come to perceive their interests in new ways.

There is already a wide variety of literature exploring the way international institutions contribute to processes of normative diffusion, much of which has been carried out by so-called 'constructivist' international relations scholars. In the present context, it is worth drawing attention to only two different lines of enquiry. First, some scholars have focussed on defining and illustrating the precise microprocesses by which governmental representatives come to be socialised into a particular normative or ideological framework. Some of these microprocesses centre on the notion of 'persuasion'[5]: in this model, governmental representatives come to new beliefs about appropriate policy choices through rational argumentation, conscious deliberation, and 'thinking harder', as well as more coercive processes such as shaming, back-patting, and so on. Risse, for example, has explored these processes at work in the post-Cold War transformation of Europe,[6] and in the work of the human rights regime.[7] Others have concentrated on less conscious forms of socialisation. Goodman and Jinks, for example, distinguish persuasion from 'acculturation,' by which they mean the various implicit processes of 'mimicry, identification and status maximisation' through which members of a community come to take on

---

[3] JG March & JP Olsen, *Rediscovering Institutions: the Organizational Basis of Politics* (Free Press, 1989) 21.
[4] AI Johnston, 'Treating International Institutions as Social Environments' 45 *Int'l Stud Q* 487.
[5] See, eg, J Brunnée & SJ Toope, 'Persuasion and Enforcement: Explaining Compliance with International Law' (2002) 13 *Fin YB Int'l L* 273.
[6] T Risse, '"Let's Argue!": Communicative Action in World Politics' (2000) 54 *Int'l Org* 1.
[7] T Risse et al (eds), *The Power of Human Rights: International Norms and Domestic Change* (Cambridge University Press, 1999).

its normative orientation. Johnston's notion of 'social influence' is similar.[8] There are, in addition, other mechanisms which are perhaps less often explored. Discursive processes by which particular normative positions are legitimated, and which construct social roles for state representatives to take on and internalise are one example.[9] The role that organisational routines play in habituating participants into particular ways of thinking, talking and acting, may be another.

Second, other scholars have focussed on *macro*historical processes of normative diffusion, through which policy norms are globally disseminated and become embedded in domestic political processes.[10] For example, Finnemore has explored the connection between norms promoted by UNESCO and the establishment of science bureaucracies by a number of states.[11] Risse, Ropp and Sikkink's 'spiral model' of the internalisation and domestic institutionalisation of human rights norms is another example.[12] There is also a large array of literature within the 'world polity' tradition emphasising the ways in which states come to formally resemble one another through the global dissemination of cultural 'scripts' and norms which teach governments what it means to be and act like a modern state.[13]

While these writers (and many others) use different concepts and focus on different stages in processes of normative diffusion, common to all of them is an interest in the role of 'culture,' 'ideas' and 'ideology' in policy-making processes—and, more specifically, in the role of international institutions in generating, authorising, disseminating, legitimating and operationalising these ideas.

B. The Relevance of These Processes to Our Understanding of the Trade Regime

Does this view of international institutions as 'normative systems'—or 'social environments'—help us to understand the operation and efficacy of the international trade regime? In my view, there is a strong argument that it does. There are essentially two stages to this argument.

The first is the simple claim that norms, ideas and ideology represent a significant causal factor in the production and evolution of trade policy.

---

[8] Johnston, above n 4.
[9] AS Yee, 'The Causal Effects of Ideas on Policies' (1996) 50 *Int'l Org* 69.
[10] Johnston, above n 4, at 11.
[11] M Finnemore, *National Interests in International Society* (Cornell University Press, 1996).
[12] Risse, above note 7.
[13] GM Thomas et al, *Institutional Structure: Constituting State, Society, and the Individual* (Sage, 1987); R Goodman & D Jinks, 'Toward an Institutional Theory of Sovereignty' (2003) 55 *Stan L Rev* 1749, at 1757.

Although not widely discussed among trade lawyers, this claim has received relatively widespread support among political scientists and historians interested in the historical evolution of trade policy.[14] Kindleberger, for example, identifies ideology as one of the most important factors behind the spread of free trade policy throughout Europe as a whole in the third quarter of the 19th century.[15] Krueger makes a similar case in respect of the 'rush to free trade' among numerous developing countries during the 1980s and surrounding decades.[16] Goldstein, too, has argued that it is the ideas of policy-makers that matter most, and has shown how, by being embedded in durable institutions, these ideas can continue to shape and inform policy-making processes, as well as the normative inclinations of policy-makers, long after their initial architects have left office.[17]

The second claim is that the international trade regime has played an important role in generating, legitimating and disseminating the kinds of ideas which have shaped and underpinned trade policy in the postwar economic order. Clearly there is a need for further research before a fully persuasive case can be made either way in respect of this claim. But, in the spirit of offering a set of hypotheses on which to base this research, let me provide some brief and preliminary reflections on how I see these processes operating in the trade regime, and how they have changed over time.

There is little doubt that, in the early years of the GATT, processes of normative socialisation were understood to be a fundamental part of the regime's operation. In an often quoted paragraph, Weiler has written that:

> a very dominant feature of the GATT was its self-referential and even communitarian ethos explicable in constructivist terms. The GATT successfully managed a relative insulation from the 'outside' world of international relations and established among its practitioners a closely knit environment revolving round a certain set of shared normative values (of free trade) and shared institutional (and personal) ambitions situated in a matrix of long-term first-name contacts and friendly personal relationships.[18] [footnote omitted]

---

[14] Indeed, 'ideas' and 'ideology' explanations regularly feature as one among about 4 standard explanatory variables for the evolution of trade policy, see, eg, HV Milner, 'The Political Economy of International Trade' (1999) 2 *Am Rev Pol Sci* 91; PA Gourevich, 'International Trade, Domestic Coalitions, and Liberty: Comparative Responses to the Crisis of 1873–1896', in JA Frieden & DA Lake (eds), *International Political Economy: Perspectives on Global Power and Wealth* (St Martin's Press, 2000).

[15] CP Kindleberger, 'The Rise of Free Trade in Western Europe, 1820–1875' (1975) 35 *J Econ Hist* 20.

[16] AO Krueger, 'Trade Policy and Economic Development: How We Learn' (1997) 87 *Am Econ Rev* 1.

[17] J Goldstein, *Ideas, Interests, and American Trade Policy* (Cornell University Press, 1993). See also Yee, above n 9, at 21 for a nice survey of some of the literature on how institutions mediate the role of ideas in policy-making (outside the trade context).

[18] JHH Weiler, 'The Rule of Lawyers and the Ethos of Diplomats—Reflections on the Internal and External Legitimacy of WTO Dispute Settlement' (2001) 35 *J World Trade* 191, at 194.

Weiler's words echo similar sentiments expressed both before and since by other well-placed commentators.[19] The GATT, it appears, was initially a form of Slaughterian 'transgovernmental network,'[20] a close-knit community of like-minded representatives, cultivating a sense of detachment from ideological fault-lines, and maintaining amongst themselves a set of powerful normative beliefs in the desirability of 'free trade.' It was therefore crucial to the effectiveness of the regime that it insulated elite trade policy-makers—not only (as Weiler suggests) from the 'outside world of international relations,' but also to a large extent from the cut and thrust of domestic political debate.[21]

Aside from this initial communitarian 'ethos,' there are other interesting institutional features of the GATT/WTO regime which are explicable by reference to its 'socialisation function.' As Wilkinson has noted, for example, it is a distinctive feature of the GATT that it seems always to be punctuated by regular crises, and appears to be never more than a few unsuccessful meetings away from fears of total collapse.[22] In fact, this regular sense of crisis has less to do with fluctuating commitments to free trade among elite policy-makers, and more to do with precisely the opposite. The everpresent immediacy of potential crises helps precisely in these socialisation processes: it is after all in part the fear of collapse engendered by such 'crises' that helps to maintain momentum in favour of free trade, and sustain a normative commitment to it. That is to say, the trade regime in part has helped to build a relatively strong normative consensus in favour of the liberal trade project by continuing to make immediate to policy-makers the potential for, and the potential consequences of, its breakdown.

While dense interpersonal connections and relative insulation from explicit political debate were among the most important socialising tools in the early years of the GATT, over time a number of different factors seem to have undermined and put pressure on these mechanisms. For one thing, the expanded membership of the GATT, and later the WTO, inevitably tended to dissolve the 'close-knit community' which formed in the decades

---

[19] See, eg, RE Hudec, *Enforcing International Trade Law: the Evolution of the Modern GATT Legal System* (Butterworth Legal Publishers, 1993); JE Alarez & R Howse, 'From Politics to Technocracy-and Back Again: The Fate of the Multilateral Trading Regime' (2002) 96 *Am J Int'l L* 94.

[20] AM Slaughter, *A New World Order* (Princeton University Press, 2004).

[21] On the importance of the 'insulation' of policy-makers, and its systematic influence on trade policy-making, see R Rogowski, 'Trade and the Variety of Democratic Institutions' (1987) 41 *Int'l Org* 203; S Haggard & SB Webb, *Voting for Reform: Democracy, Political Liberalization, and Economic Adjustment* at 13 (World Bank Publications, 1994); S Haggard & RR Kaufman, *The Political Economy of Democratic Transitions* (Princeton University Press, 1995) 378; HV Milner, 'The Political Economy of International Trade' (1999) 2 *Am Rev Pol Sci* 91.

[22] R Wilkinson, 'The WTO in Crisis—Exploring the Dimensions of Institutional Inertia' (2001) 35 *J World Trade* 397; and see generally R Wilkinson, *The WTO, Crisis and the Governance of Global Trade* (Routledge, 2006).

immediately after the war. The rapid expansion of developing country members of the GATT, and their constitution as a distinct (and dissatisfied) subgroup within the international trade community, had a similar effect. For a period through the 1960s and 70s—and again more recently—these countries have acted as a powerful source of 'counter-regime' normativity, which has tended at least partially to undermine the belief in mutual and reciprocal benefit which was always the normative cornerstone of the GATT. Furthermore, in more recent years, increasing public awareness of the activities of the WTO, as well as growing public disillusion with 'top-down,' expert-driven policy consensuses, have also put sustained pressure on traditional modes and forms of socialisation and ideological persuasion at work within the trade regime. Finally, as explained further below, the legalisation of trade relations, in the period leading up to and since the creation of the WTO, has also tended to erode the kinds of close, interpersonal social relations characteristic of trade politics in the early GATT years.

The result is that the ways in which the present trade regime carries out its 'normative work' looks very different from the early years. One consequence, perhaps, has actually been a reduced emphasis on this kind of work. It seems fair to say that processes of deep socialisation and normative persuasion feature less prominently now than they used to, particularly when compared to the attention and resources devoted to the regulative and coercive aspects of the WTO's operation. To some extent, in fact, the 'consensus-building' aspect of the trade regime's operation has been farmed out to the Secretariat, which now often plays the role of public advocate and defender of 'free trade values', as well as to other international organisations such as the OECD and G8.[23] But this does not tell the whole story. Another consequence has been that these processes of socialisation have moved to different venues, and come to take different forms. In part, they have been embedded in formal institutional processes. The Trade Policy Review Mechanism (TPRM) is one example: this is a process by which many elements of each Member's economic policies are subject to periodic scrutiny from other Members, who offer non-binding suggestion and critique on the overall nature, direction, and orientation of their economic programs. Whatever other functions the TPRM performs, it is clear that it provides a venue for persuasion and ideological diffusion, for 'teaching' Members norms of appropriate behaviour. Another obvious example is the recent, and still embryonic, development of technical assistance programs. Particularly when it comes in the form of seminars and training for domestic policy-makers, 'technical assistance' can of course be understood in part as an institutionalised form of socialisation, in which new inductees to the community are again taught roles and behavioural norms. Furthermore,

---

[23] My thanks to the editors for drawing my attention to this point.

it may be that some parts of the Committee system operate presently as 'below-the-radar' sites of normative consensus-building and persuasion. This may be particularly true of committees such as the SPS Committee, which self-consciously aim to bring together networks of like-minded regulators to discuss and elaborate norms of behaviour of particular relevance to the trade regime.[24] If so, it seems that the trade regime has perhaps come to resemble an overlapping patchwork of different and sometimes conflicting normative communities, rather than the 'closely knit environment' of the early years.

II. THE GENERATION OF COLLECTIVE REPRESENTATIONS AND SHARED MEANINGS

A. The Core Processes

So far I have suggested that sociological institutionalism usefully draws our attention to the distinction between the regulatory and normative aspects of institutions, and helps us to think more concretely about the relationship between the two. But this is still an incomplete picture. One of the most distinctive contributions of sociologists is their attention to the *cognitive-cultural*[25] dimension of institutions—a dimension which is distinguishable in principle from both its regulative and normative counterparts.

Policy-makers (like all individuals) are influenced not only by their material interests and normative commitments, but also by the cognitive frameworks that they use to interpret and understand the world. Policy-makers do not simply respond mechanically to external events, they 'first interpret them and then shape their response' in light of the meanings that they assign to these external events.[26] We should not understand these processes of sense-making as an alternative, independent set of factors influencing policy-making. Rather, interpretative frameworks structure and inform the ways in which other factors such as material conditions and normative commitments 'translate into specific courses of action.'[27] In Suchman and Edelman's words, 'tacit cognitive assumptions are often prior to—and determinate of—both cost-benefit analysis and moral reasoning.'[28]

It follows that, in order to understand why policy is what it is, and why policy makers make the choices that they do, we need to explore the

---

[24] See generally J Scott, *The Agreement on the Application of Sanitary and Phytosanitary Measures* (forthcoming 2007).
[25] Scott, above n 1, at 57.
[26] Ibid at 14.
[27] M Moschella, 'A New Role for the IMF in an Era of Globalized Finance: Testing the Idea of an Orderly Liberalization', 7 (2006) (unpublished paper, on file with author).
[28] MC Suchman & LB Edelman, 'Legal Rational Myths: The New Institutionalism and the Law and Society Tradition' (1996) 21 *Law & Soc. Inquiry* 903, at 915.

meanings and interpretive frameworks that mediate their action. From this perspective, what is of interest is the means that such policy-makers have of classifying and constructing the world, the ways they make sense of their environment, and thereby enable meaningful policy action. What is of interest, moreover, is how these interpretative frameworks—'symbolic structures,' 'systems of meaning,' 'cognitive frames' and 'schema'—are generated and disseminated.

In order to understand how these general observations relate to the study of institutions like the trade regime, it is useful to draw briefly on sociological accounts of the 'objectification' of meaning systems. Within Berger and Luckmann's influential model, the first stage of this process involves the 'production, in social interaction, of symbolic structures whose meaning comes to be shared by the participants' of a social order.[29] During the second stage, these shared meanings come to take on an external reality of their own. They become authorised ways of knowing the world: they confront actors as a 'social fact,' are perceived as expressive of the world as it is, and take on the appearance of commonsense. And it is at this second stage that 'institutions' are relevant. Sociologists working within this framework see institutions as venues within which these common frameworks of meaning are authorised and given a kind of objective existence. The particular contribution of sociologists, that is to say, has been to draw attention to the ways in which institutions act as carriers of authorised cognitive schema, and as repositories of symbolic resources which participants use to make sense of the world.

Barnett and Finnemore are probably the scholars who have done most to apply this perspective to the analysis of international institutions.[30] They see international organisations primarily as bureaucracies, and argue that one of the most important sources of bureaucratic power is the ability to produce authoritative ways of knowing the social world. Barnett and Finnemore's term for this—'social construction power'—recalls, among other thing, Scott's notion of 'cultural–cognitive control,' defined as the ability to determine the nature of social problems, and 'how these problems are to be categorized and processed'[31] They disaggregate this into the power to *classify* (to invent and apply meaningful social categories), and the power to *fix meanings* (that is, the ability to make particular situations meaningful to relevant actors).[32] They show, for example, how the ability

---

[29] PL Berger & T Luckmann, *The Social Construction of Reality: A Treatise in the Sociology of Knowledge* (Doubleday, 1966) 60. See also Scott, above n 1, at 40.

[30] MN Barnett & M Finnemore, 'The Politics, Power, and Pathologies of International Organizations' (1999) 53 *Int'l Org* 699 [Barnett & Finnemore, 'Politics']; MN Barnett & M Finnemore, *Rules for the World: International Organizations in Global Politics* (Cornell University Press, 2004) [Barnett & Finnemore, *Rules*].

[31] Scott, above n 1, at xii.

[32] Barnett & Finnemore, *Rules*, above n 30, at 31.

of the UNHCR to define and redefine the category of 'refugee' has had crucial real-world consequences for the people affected by their classifications. Similarly, they note (drawing on the work of Escobar[33]) that the World Bank is a key venue for the authoritative definition of the notion of development. The power to define the social meaning of development is crucial, they suggest, because it:

> determines not only what constitutes the activity (what development is) but also who (or what) is considered powerful and privileged, that is, who gets to do the developing ... and who is the object of development.[34]

B. The Relevance of These Processes to Our Understanding of the Trade Regime

Do these insights provide useful ways of thinking about the trade regime and how it affects the world? Does the trade regime exercise 'social construction' power? The decisions of trade policy-makers are, of course, just as dependent on interpretation and 'sense-making' as those of any other decision-maker. Can the trade regime be said to shape the symbolic landscape in which trade policy-makers find themselves, and influence the systems of meaning which they use to understand and act in the world? Does the trade regime provide a venue for generating authoritative ways of knowing the world, and does it help to institutionalise and objectify certain collective representations which structure trade policy-making? Again, I think it does. There are many possible illustrations, but for clarity I will confine myself to one, which closely tracks the work of Barnett and Finnemore described above.

In much the same way as the UNHCR—to use the illustration mentioned above—authoritatively classifies particular people as 'refugees' (or 'internally displaced people,' or whatever), the trade regime similarly provides an area in which particular kinds of governmental measure are authoritatively classified as a 'trade barrier,' or as an 'interference' with trade. This process is not to be confused with the interpretive process of determining lawful and unlawful measures through the application of particular provisions of trade law. What I am talking about are the *conceptual* processes by which certain categories of acts are classified as potential impediments to trade, and therefore the proper subject of trade disputes.

This is most easily explained by briefly recounting some of the historical evolution of the concept of 'trade barrier' since the early days of the GATT. The most profound change in the concept occurred during the period

---

[33] See generally A Escobar, *Encountering Development: the Making and Unmaking of the Third World* (1994).
[34] Barnett & Finnemore, 'Politics', above n 30, at 711.

between the beginning of the Tokyo Round and the conclusion of the Uruguay Round—roughly from the mid-1970s to the early 1990s. As has often been noted, this was a period during which the trade regime turned its attention from traditional border barriers (tariffs and quantitative restrictions), and began to create new categories of prohibited domestic regulation under the broad rubric of 'behind-the-border' barriers to trade. This focus on domestic regulation was a product of a number of factors. In the United States, perceptions of declining global competitiveness, and the move in domestic politics away from industrial policy and towards supply-side 'Reaganomics,' combined with the rise to prominence of public choice theory which emphasised risks of 'regulatory capture,' all led to an increased inclination to view certain kinds of foreign domestic regulation with suspicion, and to interpret it as a disguised trade barrier and an illegitimate attempt to secure an unfair advantage in international trade. These perceptions crystallised during the late 1980s in part as a result of very public high profile trade disputes during the period with Japan (in respect of domestic industrial policy and market structure generally), and with the European Union (particularly in respect of food safety standards and hormone-treated beef).

Other forces also led to the creation of new categories of 'trade barrier' at much the same time. First, in developing countries, the widespread move towards market-oriented economic systems, and away from interventionist development policies, permitted many to reconceive certain ('outdated') development policies—including subsidy programs, local content requirements, and so on—as impediments to international trade. Second, as Drake and Nicolaidis have documented, the creation of a new conceptual category of 'trade in services' during these decades also necessarily involved the reconstruction of particular kinds of domestic regulatory measures—licencing requirements, joint venture requirements, even public service obligations—as 'barriers' to trade in services.

It is important to keep in mind that all the different measures which were thereby newly constructed as 'trade barriers' are not self-evidently so: they are perfectly amenable to being 'known' in different ways. For example, the difficulty that American firms faced in penetrating Japanese markets could have been (and in some circles was) interpreted as a firm-level problem, relating to the inability of American firms to adapt to new environments and learn new ways of doing business. The 'problem,' in other words, might have been constructed as relating to the 'fit' between firms and their institutional environment, rather than as stemming fundamentally from collusion between the Japanese government and firms to erect barriers to market entry. Similarly, a variety of subsidy programs in developing countries could have been (and, again, were for some time) seen as regulatory corrections to domestic market distortions—and, in accordance with the theory of the second-best, as therefore preferable, *less* trade-restrictive means of regulating markets than tariffs or quantitative restrictions. Moreover, those measures which were constructed as barriers to trade in services could just as easily be understood within an *investment* framework as raising issues of expropriation or discrimination against foreign investment. And finally, food safety regulation might have been understood—as it is by numerous economic sociologists—not as a potential barrier to trade, but rather as providing the necessary facilitating infrastructure for trade, as the part of the institutional frameworks which enable the creation of global markets.[35]

The point of this brief story, however, is simply that all of these measures now strike us as self-evidently posing potential obstacles to international trade—and that the trade regime has played an important role in that outcome. To return to the language used earlier, these classifications—by which certain measures are constructed as trade barriers—have been institutionalised through and by the international trade regime, and now confront trade policy-makers with the force of commonsense, and the potentially false cloak of objective reality. Everything about the trade regime—its activities, organisational narratives, laws, discursive practices—combine to create particular habits of thinking among trade policy-makers, and a particular cognitive environment in which it simply 'makes sense' to see (say) government procurement practices or food safety regulations as potential impediments to trade. To say that this power to classify influences the choices of trade policy-makers, is not, of course, to say that it determines those choices. Once particular Japanese market structures and practices are constructed as trade barriers, for example, it does not mean that they will inevitably be prohibited by the trade regime. But what it does mean is that such measures will now come under the scrutiny of trading partners and of the trade regime more generally, and that the debate will come naturally to be about the extent, nature and basis of any potential restrictions on those measures.

III. RELEVANCE FOR LAWYERS

Even if we accept the arguments put forward so far, there is a legitimate question whether the processes described are of particular relevance to trade lawyers. Let me offer a number of reasons why, in my view, the kinds of insights set out above provide interesting and productive lines of enquiry for trade lawyers.

First, it has long been recognised that legal rules command greater levels of compliance where they correspond with pre-existing norms and value

---

[35] See N Fligstein, 'The Political and Economic Sociology of International Economic Arrangements', in NJ Smelser & R Swedberg (eds), *The Handbook of Economic Sociology* (Princeton University Press, 2005).

commitments in the regulated polity, or where they are internalised over time as rational, reasonable and mutually beneficial.[36] Indeed, in my view, one of the great lessons from 60 years of experience with international trade law is that trade rules cannot be effective in the long run in the absence of a broad and lasting consensus that their strictures are necessary for sustaining an international economic order which is broadly in the interests of all participants.[37] A number of incidents in the history of GATT/WTO dispute settlement illustrate well the need for this kind of normative consensus.[38] To the extent, then, that international trade lawyers are interested in compliance with trade law, we need also to have a close eye on the processes by which WTO Members become persuaded that these legal disciplines—and liberal trade policies generally—are in their interest.

Second, and conversely, there is a real possibility that the legal dispute settlement machinery of the WTO may undermine or work against a variety of normative and socialising pressures which have historically been at work within the trade regime. The benefits of the WTO's formal dispute settlement machinery are clear and well understood by trade lawyers. But it is not so well recognised that formalised dispute settlement can have both positive and negative effects on compliance. We know from the domestic context that the creation of formalised rules governing transactions and institutionalised dispute settlement procedures is often part of a broader reconstitution of social relations. This has been described as a process of 'disembedding' social relations, or a disintegration of social relations based on trust, dense interpersonal communications, strong social ties and shared

---

[36] This basic point has been made by many commentators, eg, TM Franck, *The Power of Legitimacy Among Nations* (Oxford University Press, 1990); J Brunnée & SJ Toope, 'International Law and Constructivism: Elements of an Interactional Theory of International Law' (2000) 39 *Colum J Transnat'l L* 19, 51; R Goodman & D Jinks, 'How to Influence States: Socialization and International Human Rights Law' (2004) 54 *Duke LJ* 632.

[37] The experience over the first decades of the GATT with regional trade agreements, agriculture, and (later) with so-called Voluntary Export Restraints surely suggests that without such a consensus, it will usually be a relatively simple matter to find a way around even tightly drafted legal rules. This is not, it should be noted, the lesson that is typically drawn. It is more usual to suggest that the history of the GATT teaches us that international trade commitments cannot be effective without a binding and enforceable dispute resolution: eg, J Pauwelyn, 'The Transformation of World Trade' (2005) 104 *Mich L Rev* 1. No doubt there is some truth to both accounts.

[38] There are at least 3 obvious and interesting examples of these incidents. The first is the history of the DISC (later FSC) case, recounted in Hudec, above n 19, at 99—a history which, to my mind, illustrates as much as anything the difficulty of ensuring compliance with trade law where the WTO is seen by regulators to be over-extending itself, into regulatory fields which are not within its core perceived competence. The second and third examples (which teach the same lesson) are the post-ruling histories of the Hormones and Varietals disputes, see D Wuger, 'Never Ending Story: The Implementation Phase in the Dispute between the EC and the United States on Hormone-Treated Beef' (2002) 33 *Law & Pol'y Int'l Bus* 777, and JP Whitlock, 'Japan—Measures Affecting Agricultural Products: Lessons for Future SPS and Agricultural Trade Disputes' (2002) 33 *Law & Pol'y Int'l Bus* 741, at 761.

normative commitments. As a consequence of such transformations, social pressures to resolve disputes in particular ways—appealing as they often do to values such as concern for the 'system' or the 'community' as a whole, or allegiance to shared norms—can become less effective. To the extent that this accurately describes what has occurred in the trade regime over the past two decades or so, there may be some cause for concern. Indeed, concerns of this type have already surfaced among constructivists interested in the role of 'legalization' in world politics. Finnemore and Toope, for example, have noted that judicialisation may lead to reduced levels of adherence to the 'spirit' of the law, in part by encouraging aggressive legal argumentative strategies, and fostering an environment in which compliance with legal formalities is understood as all that is required of participants in the regime.[39]

Third, and perhaps most importantly, it is wrong to conceptualise law and legal practice as separate from, or independent of, the normative and cognitive processes at work within the trade regime. Normative processes of persuasion and socialisation are not 'extra-legal': law is part of, and involved in, such processes. The work of a number of legal commentators has already made this clear. For example, Tarullo—in an article which resembles in some respects some of the more recent 'world polity' scholarship referred to above[40]—was one of the first to observe that the discursive and cognitive structure of international trade law, functions to define and communicate particular, historically specific notions of what constitutes a normal trading nation.[41] Kennedy has since made a similar claim about the role of international trade law in generating prevailing ideas of what a modern liberal trading nation looks like.[42] (In addition, of course, the converse is also true: prevailing ideas of what economic liberalism means deeply structure and influence the interpretation and application of international trade law.) At a different level, Koh's work on so-called 'transnational legal processes' captures many of the mechanisms by which legal practice involves the internalisation of norms and a redefinition of interests

---

[39] M Finnemore & SJ Toope, 'Alternatives to "Legalization": Richer Views of Law and Politics' (2001) 55 *Int'l Org* 743, at 753. See also J Brunnée & SJ Toope, 'International Law and Constructivism: Elements of an Interactional Theory of International Law' (2000) 39 *Colum J Transnat'l L* 51; J Goldstein & LL Martin, 'Legalization, Trade Liberalization, and Domestic Politics: A Cautionary Note' (2000) 54 *Int'l Org* 603; EL Lutz & K Sikkink, 'International Human Rights Law and Practice in Latin America' (2000) 54 *Int'l Org* 633; LR Helfer, 'Overlegalizing Human Rights: International Relations Theory and the Commonwealth Caribbean Backlash against Human Rights Regimes' (2002) 102 *Colum L Rev* 1832; Goodman & Jinks, above n 36.

[40] Slaughter, above n 20.

[41] DK Tarullo, 'Logic, Myth, and the International Economic Order' (1985) 26 *Harv Int'l LJ* 533.

[42] D Kennedy, 'Turning to Market Democracy: A Tale of Two Architectures' (1991) 32 *Harv Int'l LJ* 373.

and identities.[43] Similarly, Brunée and Toope, through their concept of an 'interactional theory of international law,' seek to demonstrate the 'persuasive power of law,'[44] and the constitutive ability of legal practice to generate and articulate shared normative expectations.

On the cognitive side, lawyers might think creatively about the ways in which trade law is involved in the processes by which our knowledge of the trading system is constructed. Do legal processes help to produce and authorise particular ways of knowing the world? Suchman and Edelman, for example, have suggested that law exerts pressure on actors:

> primarily ... by creating the cognitive building blocks for new [practices], rather than by applying substantive penalties in strict accordance with specific sovereign edicts.[45]

They suggest that law helps to shape the common frameworks of meaning circulating among social actors, in part because such actors tend to incorporate legal categories into their cognitive schema.[46] Or is it more accurate to think of legal processes as providing *occasions for* collective sense-making? This would seem particularly relevant in respect of those rules which are ambiguous and indeterminate in some significant sense. The General Agreement on Trade in Services is arguably a good example of this. The negotiations which led to that agreement were noteworthy primarily because they led effectively to the creation and entrenchment of a new collective concept ('trade in services'), which was defined in the course of negotiations, and which has since deeply structured our thinking about policy interventions into the services sector. The rules which were created—prohibiting discrimination, market access barriers and unnecessary trade restrictions—remain ill-defined and ambiguous, and have led (in the context of the Working Party on GATS Rules, and the Working Party on Domestic Regulation) to considerable discursive and conceptual work, attempting to operationalise those rules and define their appropriate meaning in respect of particular situations. The point is a general one: lawyers have a special interest in processes of normative socialisation and knowledge production within the trade regime, because law and the legal system is one of the most important venues in which such processes occur.

Fourth and finally, it is commonly noted that lawyers have a degree of interest and expertise in questions of institutional design.[47] The research

---

[43] HH Koh, 'Why Do Nations Obey International Law?' (1997) 106 *Yale LJ* 2599.
[44] Brunée & Toope, above n 39, at 38.
[45] MC Suchman & LB Edelman, 'Legal Rational Myths: The New Intitutionalism and the Law and Society Tradition' (1996) 21 *Law & Soc. Inquiry* 903, 930.
[46] Ibid at 936.
[47] See, eg, JP Trachtman, 'Legal Aspects of a Poverty Agenda at the WTO: Trade Law and "Global Apartheid"' (2003) 6 *J Int'l Econ L* 3.

agenda outlined above holds interest for trade lawyers, then, to the extent that it raises issues concerning the kinds of institutional features which encourage, impede or influence processes of socialisation. This strand of the research agenda is normative, rather than positive: instead of simply describing the actual operation of socialisation processes within the trade regime, the aim here is to design an institutional structure to shape and channel those processes in desirable ways. Clearly, different people will have different views of what is 'desirable.' For my part, it strikes me that the fundamental focus should be on creating a more *open* normative environment. Rather than simply teaching and disseminating policy orthodoxies in a 'top-down' fashion, it may be better to design the trade regime as an environment which facilitates ongoing policy learning and consensus-building, a venue for the production and exchange of innovative policy learning.[48] And rather than reproducing a policy consensus shaped largely through centrally-defined and expert-driven knowledge, it may be better to encourage 'bottom-up' participatory processes of knowledge-sharing and policy experimentation. Finally, rather than building support for free trade through 'education' and the strategic marshalling of constituencies behind a predetermined policy agenda, it may be better to create forums within the trade regime for open dialogue, deliberation and consensus-building about the nature and purpose of the liberal trade project in contemporary circumstances. In terms of the particular institutional configurations which may support this kind of normative agenda, we might look for inspiration to the literature on organisational learning,[49] as well as to that on 'new approaches to governance' developed in the context of study of the European Union.[50]

IV. CONCLUSION

Attention to the insights of sociological institutionalism promises to expand our understanding of how the trade regime affects social and political outcomes. One of the most important insights of this literature is that institutions tend to play as much of a positive, *enabling* role for policy-makers, as they do a negative, constraining one. The trade regime, we are reminded, works

---

[48] On the potential of the WTO as a site of learning, see, eg, B Hoekman, 'Operationalizing the Concept of Policy Space in the WTO: Beyond Special and Differential Treatment' (2005) 8 *J Int'l Econ L* 405; R Cooney & ATF Lang, 'Taking Uncertainty Seriously: Adaptive Governance, Alien Invasive Species and the WTO' *Eur J Int'l L* (forthcoming 2007).
[49] For a useful general introduction, see M Dierkes et al (eds), *Handbook of Organizational Learning and Knowledge* (Oxford University Press, 2001).
[50] G De Burca & J Scott (eds), *Law and New Governance in the EU and the US* (Hart Publishing 2006). See also O Lobel, 'The Renew Deal: The Fall of Regulation and the Rise of Governance in Contemporary Legal Thought' (2004) 89 *Minn L Rev* 342.

not simply through the implementation and coercive enforcement of binding rules, but through processes of socialisation and normative diffusion, as well as through the creation and 'institutionalization' of collective meanings. Exploration of these key insights—and how the WTO's legal system interacts with, and is involved in, such processes—promises to create productive new research possibilities for international trade lawyers.

7

Law of the Global Economy: In Need of a New Methodological Approach?

FEDERICO ORTINO AND MATTEO ORTINO[*]

INTRODUCTION

THE INTERCONNECTED PHENOMENA of the IT revolution and globalisation of markets—a development that cannot be factually contested—have given rise to fundamental methodological questions for the study of international economic law (IEL); that is, the study of the legal rules regulating economic actors and activities that cross or have impacts across the boundaries of a single legal and economic system, and thus operate in or impact the global economic system.

The starting question of this chapter is whether IEL should also be understood as a branch of economic law, and not only as a branch of international law. This Chapter argues that only by considering IEL as a branch of economic law can a comprehensive view be gained, and thus also acquire a proper understanding, of the law affecting the global economy. But this perspective needs a 'new' methodological approach, one that cuts across the boundaries between *legal systems* (eg national, regional, international and trans-national) and across those between traditional *fields of law* (eg constitutional, commercial and procedural law). The international law methodological approach, premised on the old paradigm of the Nation-state, lacks the necessary comprehensiveness to achieve a truly comprehensive understanding of the global economy. International law fails in this regard because it is limited through its focus on 'its' sources of law, omitting other

---

[*] The authors gratefully acknowledge Dr Larisa Dragomir's helpful insights on Basel and EC prudential regulation. All errors are the authors' sole responsibility. Although this Chapter was jointly drafted and its findings and conclusions are fully shared by the authors, Sections I (A, B), II (A, B) (with respective subsections) are attributed to M Ortino, while the rest of the Chapter to F Ortino.

rules that can be as much, and sometimes more, relevant to the regulation of the global economy.

This is certainly neither a novel nor revolutionary argument. More than fifty years ago, for instance, G Erler submitted that the definition of IEL should not be founded on the origin of the norms but on the object of the norms: cross-border economic transactions.[1] This means that national norms regarding transnational economic relations, as well as rules of private and public law concerning the ordering of cross-border economic relations, should also be included in the study of IEL. In his opinion, all these groups of norms relating to the same economic activities and facts can only be understood in relation to each other. In the same line of thought, in one of the leading recent texts on IEL, the authors emphasise that one of their goals is:

> to look at the legal principles and processes as they affect decisions regarding international economic relations, whether the decisions be those of private citizens or enterprises, or government officials. Thus there is an integration of national regulation and international law, to a lesser extent private transaction law [...]. For example, United States constitutional and regulatory rules have an intimate and weighty connection and influence on the international rules of the WTO. One must study both to fully understand how they operate, because they interact.[2]

The methodological approach promoted by commentators such as the ones cited above can be referred to as the 'Economic Law' approach. Although it may not be scholars' prevailing approach to the topic today, the methodological implications of globalisation have been the subject of some debate.[3]

Within such a debate, this Chapter attempts to sketch some of the salient features of the suggested, more comprehensive, methodological Economic Law approach to the study of the law of the global economy, highlighting both the shortcomings of the traditional methodology and the advantages of the 'new' methodology. Section I sets out a few basic theoretical

---

[1] G Erler, *Grundprobleme des internationalen Wirtschaftsrechts* (Verlag Otto Schwartz & Co, 1956), at 9–19, 38.

[2] JH Jackson, WJ Davey & AO Sykes, *Legal Problems of International Economic Relations: Cases, Materials, and Texts on the National and International Regulation of Transnational Economic Relations*, 4th edn (West, 2002) at iv. According to the authors, the law of international transactions has 3 components: private law of the transaction, national government regulation of the transaction and international law. Ibid at 2–3. See also D Carreau & P Juillard, *Droit International Economique*, 4th edn (Dalloz-Sirey, 1998); EU Petersmann, *Constitutional Functions and Constitutional Problems of International Economic Law: International and Domestic Foreign Trade Law and Foreign Trade Policy in the United States, the European Community and Switzerland* (University of Fribourg Press, 1991).

[3] See PT Muchlinski, 'Globalisation and Legal Research' (2003) 37 *Int'l Lawyer* 221; B Kingsbury, N Krisch & RB Stewart, 'The Emergence of Global Administrative Law' (*Institute for International Law and Justice Working Paper*, 2004); S Ortino, *The Nomos of the Earth* (International Culture Research Network, 2002); K Matthias Meessen, *Economic Law in Globalizing Markets* (Kluwer Law International, 2004); GE Frug and DJ Barron, 'International Local Government Law' (2006) 38 *Urb Law* 1.

underpinnings of the Economic Law methodological approach, while section II focuses on three case studies (the private law regulation of cross-border commercial transactions, the prudential regulation of cross-border banking activities and the international law of foreign investment) to show a few reasons justifying the more comprehensive Economic Law approach.

I. THE ECONOMIC LAW METHODOLOGICAL APPROACH

A. International Law

International law is defined by its sources, not by its object. Traditionally, international law consists of legal rules deriving from certain sources, involving certain methods or procedures and actors.[4] A rule stemming from a process other than those sources falls outside the international legal system. The main sources of international law are custom and treaty. The only two law-makers under international law are States and, to a much less extent, international organisations. Under international law no other subject may make legal rules; not even in the widest sense of the concept of source of law, as it is the case of (national and transnational) contracts, which can be understood as a source of rules governing relations between the contracting parties. In the international legal system, there are no legal rules outside those originating from the action and will of States (and international organisations) through certain procedures or methods.

International law is not, instead, defined by its object; that is, by the legal relationships which it governs.[5] The most common definition of international law is based on the type of legal relations regulated by it. International law is often defined as the law governing the relations between States or as the law governing the relations between the various international law subjects. It is possible to generally state that international law deals with part of the *conduct* of international law subjects (States, international organisations, individuals, etc) and with some of their *relations* inter se. For example, it might govern how States must protect their own environment, and how States must act vis-à-vis each other during a war. Not all conduct of international law subjects nor all aspects of their relations are governed by international law. International law rules might

---

[4] On the doctrine of sources, see O Schachter, 'International Law in Theory and in Practice' (1982) *Rec des Cours*, Vol 178, at 60–1. On the definition of international law, see RMM Wallace, *International Law* (Sweet and Maxwell, 2005) 1–2. On sources of law, see VD Degan, *Sources of International Law* (Martinus Nijhoff Publishers, 1997); and G Teubner, *Global Law Without a State* (Dartmouth Publishing, 1997).

[5] It is interesting to emphasise how traditionally federal constitutions granted to the federal state broad competence in international matters. However, from the 1990s onward the new or amended federal constitutions had to distinguish between those competences granted to the federal state and those granted (ex novo) to the sub-federal entities. See S Ortino, M ŽZagar & V Mastny, *The Changing Faces of Federalism* (Manchester University Press, 2005).

not govern the way individual States organise their political institutions, nor the way they tax foreign corporations.

However, while the above statements broadly describe the object of international law, they fail to pin-point its defining characteristic, that is the element that makes the international legal system a discrete legal system. As noted, that element is, instead, to be found only in its sources of law. Since the relations between the various international law subjects can *also* be governed by rules other than international law rules, the regulation of such relations is not what distinguishes international law from the other 'laws'. Relations between States or between a State and an international organisation can be subject to rules other than international law rules. Take two States that, acting as private law subjects, decide to conclude a private law contract. The ensuing contractual relation is governed (at least predominantly) by legal rules other than international law rules. How a State conducts itself vis-à-vis other States can also be governed by legal rules unilaterally laid down by the former State (eg a State may be prohibited by its constitution to enter into a military agreement with other States). Moreover, rules pertaining to relations between States and individuals do not, for the most part, involve international law.

(i) International Economic Law as a Branch of International law

The definition of IEL understood as a branch of international law necessarily follows from the above definition of international law. IEL consists of international law rules dealing with some of the *economic conduct* of international law subjects, and with some of their *economic relations* inter se.

IEL in this sense only looks at such economic conduct and relations *as are governed by international law*. The boundaries of this legal discipline are strictly defined by the sources of the relevant legal rules. For this reason it can also be referred to as 'international law of the economy'. Rules that are not recognised as international law rules are not covered by this discipline, notwithstanding their possible economic impact. In other words, aspects (activities, actors, etc) of the international economy that are not covered by international legal rules fall outside 'international law of the economy'. For these reasons, IEL as a branch of international law is not sufficiently inclusive to be a suitable approach to understanding the legal aspects of the international economy.

B. Economic law

Economic law is an autonomous field of law encompassing all legal rules relevant to the establishment and functioning of an *economic system*.[6]

---

[6] The economic law method has found its most fertile academic ground in Germany since the first half of the 20th century (for the latest German academic contribution to the discipline at hand, see KM Meessen, *Economic Law in Globalizing Markets* (Kluwer Law International, 2004)).

An economic system can be defined as the collection of actions of, and interactions between, economic institutions, within a given space, that determines the contents of economic decisions such as what to produce, what to exchange, in what quantities, and who receives the benefit of this production and exchange.[7] Economic institutions' actions and interactions are governed or influenced by various types of 'laws'.

Among the most important economic institutions are households, governments *lato sensu*,[8] and enterprises. Each economic institution has its own set of objectives and goals. Households aim at maximising their own utility, in terms of material income, satisfaction from leisure, etc. The goals that governments choose to pursue may vary a great deal, ranging from economic growth to the protection of the environment, from assisting to the poorest part of the population to military security. The most common objective pursued by economic enterprises is profit maximisation.

Economic institutions' actions and interactions are governed or influenced by different kinds of 'laws'. There are *economic laws* such as the 'law' whereby marginal cost can decrease in situations of economies of scale; *formal laws*, providing for legal rules; and *informal laws*, such as non-legally binding customs and practices influencing economic behaviours.

Governed or influenced by these sets of 'laws', economic institutions act and react to one another, each in the pursuit of its own set of goals. Collectively these actions and reactions shape the economic system.

As the answers to the above economic questions vary a great deal in time and space, so do the types of economic systems. These can be classified according to a wide range of overlapping criteria. One of the most important distinctions is between 'centrally planned systems' and 'market systems'. Another useful classification can be made according to an economic system's geo-political boundaries. Using this criterion, it is possible to distinguish between a national, a regional and a global economic system.[9] Every State (eg France, South Africa, Japan) constitutes a separate economic system. The best known regional economic system is represented

---

[7] On the subject see HS Gardner, *Comparative Economic Systems*, 2nd edn (Dryden Press, 1998) 4; and DA Kennett, *A New View of Comparative Economic Systems* (Harcourt College Publishers, 2001) 5–10.

[8] The term 'government' is used here to refer not only to national and sub-federal governments, but also to supranational authorities (eg EU institutions) and international authorities (eg WTO institutions).

[9] The three above-mentioned categories do not exhaust the types of economic systems that can be distinguished according to their geo-political boundaries. Other types include intra-national and infra-national economic systems. The former case is where there is more than one economic system inside the geo-political boundaries of a single nation state. Infra-national economic systems are to be found in those economic areas encompassing part of the territories of different nation states.

by the European Union. The global[10] economic system is increasingly shaped by the political agenda of 'public' institutions like the World Trade Organization (WTO) and by the cross-border activities of private actors such as transnational enterprises and consumers.

National, regional and global economic systems are discrete categories of economic systems, even though they all are, to some extent, interdependent. As regards their differences, the three types of economic systems differ, or may differ, in various ways, with respect to, for example, the type, number and actions of economic institutions, and the rules governing them. In the global economic system there are *types* of economic institutions (eg international economic organisations, such as the WTO) that do not exist in national economic systems. The *goals* pursued by the same economic institution can be different in different economic systems: for instance governments may be liberal within national or regional boundaries but protectionist in the international economic system.[11] The *legal rules* governing the actions and interactions of institutions change, at least partially, from one type of economic system to another. For example, as opposed to firms operating within national borders, firms active globally may rely on *lex mercatoria* instead of national law rules, or may be subject to a multiple set of national rules. Similarly, in the context of an international or regional economic system and its legal obligations, individual national governments usually find themselves more restricted in their policies than they are in the exclusive context of their own national economic systems (for instance with regard to the treatment of foreign firms as opposed to domestic firms).

Economic law studies what and how legal rules affect/shape economic systems. In other words, it analyses rules in relation to their *impact* on economic systems. Economic-law analysis can start by identifying what kinds of economic system-related goals are pursued by rule-makers (States, international organisations, corporations, etc). It can be assumed that, within market-oriented economic systems, economic efficiency is among the fundamental goals. It follows that, relying on the law-and-economics methodology, one of the main tasks of economic-law analysis is to assess *if* and

---

[10] The vocabulary of 'global' is preferable to that of 'international' because the latter term still takes the nation-state as its reference point. The term 'international economic system' can be wrongly taken to imply that world economic relations are organised (only or predominantly) in terms of country units and governed (only or predominantly) by state governments. 'International' exchanges occur between country units, while "global" transactions occur within a planetary unit. Whereas international relations are inter-territorial relations, global relations are trans- and sometimes supra-territorial relations.' See JA Scholte, *Globalization: A Critical Introduction*, 2nd edn (Palgrave, 2005) 65.

[11] Or the same government may pursue different economic policies in different geo-political contexts. The British government in the 1960s and 1970s, eg, held welfare-oriented economic policies at home, while adopting a largely hands off, laissez-faire approach in its administration of Hong Kong.

how the rules relevant to a given economic system actually contribute to the efficient functioning of such a system (positive analysis), and eventually to identify what elements should be amended/added to achieve that outcome (normative analysis). Overall this assessment involves a systematisation of the relevant rules, in order to determine whether all the various elements form a coherent whole, effectively functional to the given policy objective.

Economic efficiency, however, is just but one goal among many others, of an economic and non-economic character. As regards rules that do not pursue economic efficiency, the economic-law approach aims at, inter alia, assessing these rules' impacts on the functioning of the economic system and at highlighting and evaluating the legal instruments employed to reconcile or to balance the competing goals (eg fair competition versus social interests; economic growth versus environmental protection).[12]

From the above it should be clear that economic law is a discipline that necessarily cuts across the boundaries between traditional *fields of law* and those between *legal systems*. Rules that are part of traditional fields of law (eg constitutional law, company law, contract law, tax law, private international law, procedural law, etc) also form part of economic law if, and to the extent that, they are relevant to the establishment and functioning of an economic system. Moreover, the sources of these latter rules may be located within various legal systems: of a national, trans-national, regional, supranational or international nature. For example, a rule contributing to the shape of a given national economic system may have emerged at the international level.

(i) International Economic Law as a Branch of Economic Law

IEL is the branch of economic law that studies the legal rules affecting the global economic system. The end purpose of such analysis is to evaluate the relevant rules in light of their impact on the establishment and functioning of the global economic system. The distinctive characteristic of this field of law is that it analyses the rules—any rules—in relation to their impact on the global economic system; that is, the rules—any rules—that are relevant to the existence and operation of the global economic system.

Unlike the 'international law of the economy', this branch of economic law is not defined by its legal sources but rather by its object: the global economic system. Hence, the expression 'law of the global economy' can also be used to refer to the field of law that applies the economic law approach to the global economic system.

From the above it follows that this branch of economic law encompasses a vast area of rules. It overlaps with a number of other legal fields of research as it deals with regulations that are also studied by other specialists.

---

[12] KM Meessen, above n 6, at 20.

The law of the global economy overlaps, in particular, with international (economic) law when, and to the extent that, the former addresses international law rules governing international economic relations. However, the overlap is only partial. As noted, the 'international law of the economy' only addresses aspects (ie, activities, actors, etc) of the economy regulated by international law rules. Aspects of the economic system that are not governed by international law rules fall outside the scope of this branch of international law. The 'law of the global economy', on the other hand, does not limit itself to rules originating from international law sources. The establishment and functioning of the global economic system is also influenced by types of rules (eg of a transnational or national nature and of a public or private law character) and by the action of subjects that fall outside the legal concepts of international law. The economic law approach (law of the global economy) is needed to understand more properly and completely the legal aspects of the global economic system.

II. CASE STUDIES

The proposed methodological approach to IEL advocated here is based perhaps on a very pragmatic view of the legal discipline at issue. In order to play their respective role in the global economy, all relevant stakeholders (whether States, international organisations, individuals, corporations, or NGOs) need to realise that several legal systems are already participating in the 'regulation' of the global economy. Accordingly, a comprehensive methodology is necessary to properly understand and deal with all the legal rules that are operating in the global legal and economic system(s).

There is, however, at least a further important consideration that would justify the new methodological approach. This comprehensive approach would enable a better *coordination* among the several legal systems involved in the regulation of cross border activities and actors. In particular, such coordination would take place, first of all, at the level of setting out the several (and at times conflicting) economic and non-economic objectives that may be pursued through, or affected by, the regulation of such cross border activities. Secondly, the coordination among legal systems would also take place at the implementation stage in order for the policies pursued by different stakeholders at the different levels to be actually effective and bring about the wanted results.[13]

The purpose of this section is to show, by focusing on three case studies, why the economic law methodological approach, as opposed to the international law one, is needed for a proper understanding of the legal aspects

---

[13] Muchlinski has emphasised that further research is needed to address more fully the issue of power and control over regulatory agendas at the national and international levels. Muchlinski, above n 3, at 239.

of the global economic system. The international law method is unsuitable to properly and fully understand the legal aspects of the global economic system because it only covers international law rules, whereas the global economic system is also governed by other legal rules. There are legal rules which are not part of international law, such as rules of national and transnational law, that greatly contribute to the regulation of the global economic system. As will be shown below (section A), the private law regulation of cross-border economic activities well exemplifies this point. Furthermore, in many instances the regulation of single aspects of the global economic system is jointly provided for by a variety of, and interconnecting, sets of legal rules. In order to understand the regulation of such aspects, all the relevant sources need to be examined, with a view to highlighting their interrelation, and to assessing their impact on the economic system. As will be shown below (section B), cross-border banking provides a good example of such cases. Furthermore, the comprehensive methodological approach would enable a better understanding and coordination of the several legal systems involved in the regulation of individual aspects of the global economy, such as the cross border flows of investment (section C).

A. The Private-Law Regulation of Cross-Border Economic Activities

The regulation of the global economic system comprises both public and private law rules. Public law rules govern the way States act with respect to economic activities, in the exercise of sovereign powers (to legislate, to adjudicate, to enforce; to levy taxes, to subsidise, etc). Take, for example, a rule prohibiting national public authorities from discriminating between foreign and domestic firms. Private law regulation, on the other hand, lays down the reciprocal rights and duties of parties to a private transaction. Such parties may be, for instance, individuals, companies, or States acting in a private capacity, that is, not in the exercise of sovereign powers, etc. The legal rules governing a cross-border contract between two companies well exemplify the category of private-law regulation.[14]

Both public and private law rules regulate the global economic system in that they jointly govern the actions of economic subjects—such as States and corporations—in the global economic system and, thus, shape the way such system works. These rules may have various, positive or adverse, effects on the development of the global economic system.[15] Since both

---

[14] G Van Harten, 'The Public-Private Distinction in the International Arbitration of Individual Claims Against the State' (2007) 56 *Int'l & Comp L Q* 371.
[15] Take, eg, the WTO most-favoured-nation rule (of public law), which reduces discriminatory barriers hindering international commerce; or the Unidroit principles (of private law), which are designed specifically to govern cross-border contracts (as opposed to wholly domestic contracts): by addressing the specific needs of international economic actors, such rules

private and public law rules are relevant to the functioning of the global economic system, they both need to be included in the analysis of the law of the global economic system.

For the purposes of this chapter, what needs to be focused upon here is the fact that the private law regulation of cross-border economic activities is for the most part outside the realm of international law. This provides support for the argument that the international law methodology has a too limited scope of analysis to be relied upon for the study of the law of the global economy.

Most private-law rules governing cross-border economic transactions or activities are not international law rules, as they do not originate from an international law source. The relevant private law regulation is mostly produced by domestic law and by transnational law (as will be defined below). To be sure, there are international law rules (in treaties) that provide for private law rules governing cross-border economic activities. The most common goal of these treaties is to reduce the transaction costs stemming from the existence of a plurality of different legal systems within the globalising markets. Important efforts have been made at the inter-governmental level to lay down uniform private-law regulations in the field of cross-border economic activities.[16] These international law treaties, however, only cover a limited portion of the private-law regulation governing cross-border transactions.[17] Most private law matters are not regulated by international law.

National legal systems are still the major source of law in the field of cross-border economic activities. More precisely, two sets of national law regulations usually come into play in these cases: the conflict of law (or private international law) and the substantive law regulation. Through

---

facilitate trans-border transactions. Private and public law rules may also have negative effects on the development of the global economic system. Such adverse effects may be produced, eg, by agreements among several States establishing a protectionist regime against products of third countries (eg, the agriculture policy of the EU); or by the mere existence within globalising markets of multiple national jurisdictions: the same cross-border activity or transaction may be subject to different, or even contradictory, national regulations (of public and/or private law), increasing the cost of expanding business beyond domestic borders.

[16] See, eg, the 1980 Convention on Contracts for the International Sale of Goods (Vienna Convention), prepared by the United Nations Commission on International Trade Law (UNCITRAL).

[17] International uniform-law conventions usually address very specific subject-matters only, such as specific types of contracts; and even of those subjects-matters such conventions do not provide for a complete regulation. Eg, the 1980 Vienna Convention does not govern some categories of sales of considerable importance for the international economy, such as the sales of shares and other securities, of ships and aircraft (Art 2). Excluded from the scope of the Convention are also a number of important issues concerning ordinary sales contracts, such as the validity of the contract or of any of its provisions or of any usage; the effect which the contract may have on the property in the goods sold, the liability of the seller for death or personal injury caused by the goods to the buyer or any other person (Arts 4 and 5).

the applicable set of national conflict-of-laws rules, the judge or arbitrator determines the law of which State (or States) he will apply to solve the substantive legal issue at hand. In this way most aspects of cross-border transactions are governed by national laws.

The still predominant role of national law in the private regulation of cross-border economic affairs is increasingly at odds with the development of a global market place. The international business community would benefit a great deal if it could avoid the legal fragmentation of the global market and rely on common sets of rules, applicable on a global scale. In the pursuit of that goal, and in light of the insufficient achievements made by international law-makers, the international business community is increasingly laying down its own sets of legal rules. A prominent example of this self-regulation is the new *lex mercatoria*. It is made of binding legal rules and principles originating from the usages of internationally active merchants and from the case-law of international arbitrators, as (partially) evidenced by standard-term contracts, and general principles and rules and restatements formulated by various agencies (eg the Unidroit). *Lex mercatoria* is, thus, the product of spontaneous law-making by the international business community, and not the product of national or international traditional law-making processes. In so far as it is applied instead of national laws, *lex mercatoria* enables to avoid the complexities of the conflict of laws mechanism and the diversity of national substantive laws. The rules of the new *lex mercatoria* are part of the wider 'transnational law', which encompasses the private law principles and rules governing cross-border economic activities that are neither of international nor of national law character. Other examples of transnational law are 'private' legal instruments like the Unidroit Principles and the ICC Incoterms.[18]

In sum, the fact that sources other than international law have the predominant role in the private law regulation of the global economy has important methodological consequences. As the international law methodology necessarily leaves out fundamentally important sources of private law, such as national law and transnational law, it is not sufficiently wide in scope for it to be relied upon for the study of the legal aspects of the global economic system. Hence the proposition, supported in this Chapter, to use the 'economic law methodology' instead.

B. The Prudential Regulation of Global Banking

There is a second characteristic of the law of the global economy that needs to be highlighted in order to show why international law is not the

---

[18] On the notion of 'transnational law', see PC Jessup, *Transnational Law* (Yale University Press, 1956); KB Berger, *The Practice of Transnational Law* (Kluwer Law International, 2001).

proper methodology to study this field of law, and why economic law, on the other hand, is the proper methodology. The second feature of the law of the global economic system is strictly connected to the first one, discussed above. In the preceding section we have seen how international law is not the only legal source of regulation of the global economy, and often not even the most important one. In the present section, we want to show that the application of the international law perspective in this field may not enable an adequate understanding even of the international law rules that are relevant to the regulation of the global economic system. What studies based on the international law method may fail to achieve is a comprehensive view and analysis of the effects that law (including international law) has on the functioning of the global economic system. The argument put forward here draws from the fact that a single type of cross-border economic activity, or a single component of the global economic system, is ever more often jointly governed by various and interplaying sources of law (or legal systems). Often, the impact of international law on the economic system can only be understood if international law rules are analysed in a wider legal context, that is, in a larger framework made also of other types of legal rules. Such wider analysis is what the international law method may fail to make possible. To elaborate our argument we will take the prudential regulation of global banking as an example.

The prudential regulation of cross-border banking activities is aimed at protecting financial soundness and safety in the global banking market. It is thus a fundamental component of the law of the global economic system. Prudential regulation of global banking is made up of multiple sets of rules resulting from a variety of heterogeneous and interacting sources of law. There are rules formulated at the international level (eg by the IMF, the Basel Committee on Banking Supervision, and through memoranda of understanding between national banking supervisors), at the regional level (eg the EC banking legislation) at the national level and at a private (self-regulation) level. If the purpose of one's inquiry is to examine the prudential regulation that actually governs cross-border banking, *all* the different sources must be included in the analysis.

The regulation of cross-border banking activities is made of interconnected and heterogeneous 'scales' of regulation. The single most important set of rules is laid down at the inter-governmental level by the Basel Committee on Banking Supervision (Basel Committee).[19] The Committee is composed of central bankers and prudential banking supervisors of

---

[19] On the history, activities, and the documents of the Committee, see *Bank for International Settlements*, http://www.bis.org/bcbs/index.htm (last visited 12 Jul, 2007). In the most recent literature, see MS Barr and GP Miller, 'Global Administrative Law: The View from Basel' (2006) 17 *Eur J Int'l L* 15.

13 countries.[20] The Committee's most successful regulatory achievement is a legal framework for bank capital adequacy requirements (the 1988 'Basel I' Accord, recently revised by the 'Basel II' Accord).[21] These rules, while not formally binding—they fall into the category of 'soft law' rules of international law—have been adopted on a global scale, beyond the Committee members' home states, representing one of the fundamental influences on national banking prudential legislation. Besides international law rules, the prudential regulation of global banking also consists of regional and national rules. And it is not only composed of public rules, ie top-down rules, but also relies on private rules, ie rules set out by the regulated entities themselves in the form of self-regulation.

To take the European context as an example, rules laid down by the Basel Committee are implemented at European and EU member state level. However, it would be wrong to perceive European and national banking rules as the outcome of a mere (and almost mechanical) transposition of rules from one level to another. Such a perception would lead an observer to believe that effective policy and rule-making only take place at the international level. All levels complement each other; it is not just a matter of making international rules formally effective in a (regional and/or) national legal system, or, at most, of introducing mere technical aspects of marginal importance to the regulation agreed upon at the international level. At each level, a substantial integration of the preceding regulation takes place.

The Basel Committee lays down the framework principles and general rules (even though in a very detailed manner—Basel rules fill hundreds of pages). At the European level, some policy decisions have been added (for example, the extension of the Basel rules to cross-border investment firms, and their adjustment to the specific characteristics of the EC internal market). At the national level—the only level provided with enforcement capacities—the competent authorities have used their allowed discretion to determine and specify (often in cooperation with regulated entities) the actual content of prudential rules. In other words, the national level is where supervision and enforcement of regulation, essentially decided upon elsewhere, take place. However, the distinction between regulation and supervision-enforcement is getting ever more blurred. The latter activity is ever more complex, as it entails not simply the application of pre-determined legal criteria but also a form of rule-making: the concrete determination of legal rules in light of the specific characteristics of the regulated entity.

---

[20] The Committee's members come from Belgium, Canada, France, Germany, Italy, Japan, Luxembourg, the Netherlands, Spain, Sweden, Switzerland, the United Kingdom and the United States.
[21] Basel II: International Convergence of Capital Measurement and Capital Standards: A Revised Framework—Comprehensive Version, June 2006 [Basel II (June 2006)], available at http://www.bis.org/publ/bcbs128.htm.

It is very important to note, furthermore, that the three above-mentioned levels (international, European/regional and national) do not operate in a strict time sequence. Rule making at Basel and rule making by the European authorities were proceeding in parallel, and it is uncertain who influenced whom.

Finally, self-regulation integrates top-down rules. The Basel II Accord provides that financial institutions can engage in a form of self-regulation by relying on internal risk measurements in determining capital standards.[22] International (economic) law does not include such rules, as they do not originate from any source of international law.

In sum, to have a proper understanding of the regulation as it finally stands and actually governs cross-border banking activities, the entire range of sources of law and of rules need to be included in the analysis. All levels and types of regulation are part of an integrated whole, and as such they need to be taken into account. Such type of analysis cannot follow the international law methodological approach. The more comprehensive approach of economic law has to be adopted.[23]

C. International Law of Foreign Investment

There is a growing body of international law and jurisprudence aimed at stimulating and protecting the cross border flows of investment (generally including both direct and indirect forms of investment). This is another fundamental component of the law of the global economic system.

The economic law methodological approach is better suited to address this body of law, since such rules play multiple functions—of a developmental, administrative, commercial nature—at different levels (international, national, private). Accordingly, the international law of foreign investment needs to be examined at a minimum taking into account: (1) other international (ie, intergovernmental) disciplines aimed at the economic and social development of States and (2) national and trans-national administrative and commercial disciplines.

This comprehensive methodological approach would enable a better *coordination* among the several legal systems involved in the regulation of cross border flows of investment. Subsidiarity principles could help

---

[22] Basel II (July 2006), above n 21, Pt 2—The First Pillar. The Minimum Capital Requirements. III Credit Risk—The Internal Ratings Approach.

[23] The fact that to solve a cross-border economic dispute the competent bodies (arbitrators, national courts, international dispute settlement bodies, etc) need, more often than not, to jointly apply (or at least take into account) various sources of law, strengthens the need for academic studies to adopt the comprehensive methodological approach at issue. It is very common, eg, for arbitrators to apply to the same dispute sets of legal rules of different origins: national laws, international conventions, principles of international law, usages of international trade, etc. See below Section C.

guide the levels of policy coordination. Moreover, such an approach would also improve the coordination of the several (and at times conflicting) economic and non-economic objectives that may be pursued or affected by the regulation of such cross border flows.

(i) Intergovernmental Economic and Social Development Disciplines

The promotion and protection of foreign investment has constituted, in the last few decades, one of the core objectives of economic cooperation among States. This has been premised on the belief that such cooperation would be instrumental in the economic growth and development of the home and host States. In 1959, in the first of the bilateral investment treaties (BITs) of modern times, Germany and Pakistan expressly recognised:

> that an understanding reached between the two States is likely to promote investment, encourage private industrial and financial enterprise and to increase the prosperity of both the States.[24]

Investment agreements have focused in particular on protecting foreign investors through a few basic treatment guarantees, principally against discriminatory, unfair and expropriatory conduct by host States. However, the underlying aim has always been to promote the economic growth of all the State parties involved in the form of higher standards of living, higher levels of employment, growing volume of real income, and other benefits.

Nonetheless, the economic dimension is not the exclusive dimension of investment agreements. Inasmuch as increased prosperity and economic growth constitute essential elements in furthering broader societal interests, it may be said that investment agreements also feature an underlying, albeit indirect, social dimension. Economic growth and prosperity typically may engender higher societal expectation for better quality jobs, employment protection, workers' participation in business management, corporate social responsibility, health standards and protection, etc. Even more crucially, economic growth and prosperity make available the resources necessary to meet such expectations. Thus, while economic growth is the immediate goal of investment agreements, social spillovers (whether positive or negative) are also part of the equation when assessing investment agreements' actual impact.[25]

In reflecting upon the international community's challenge of strengthening both the economic and social dimensions of international investment agreements, one cannot avoid addressing the issue of horizontal allocation of responsibilities at the multilateral level. Currently, a variety of international

---

[24] Germany-Pakistan BIT (25 Nov, 1959), available at www.unctad.org/iia.
[25] See F Ortino, 'The Social Dimension of International Investment Agreements: Drafting a New BIT/MIT Model?' (2005) 7 International Law FORUM du droit international 243.

organisations is in charge of developing policies at the multilateral level, each in a specific field: monetary policy (IMF), trade (WTO), health (WHO), labour (ILO), development (UNDP), environment (UNEP), etc. This is clearly an oversimplification of reality, as certain organisations do in fact look at relevant linkages; for example, trade and development (UNCTAD) or finance and development (World Bank). There are also formal and informal linkages between different organisations.[26] However, there seems to be a problem of excessive specialisation and lack of dialogue within the international cooperation architecture.[27] This is principally reflected in the respective 'public servants' communities that operate within these organisations, but also, and perhaps more surprisingly, in the respective 'academic' communities (just think about the trade/WTO and investment/BITs 'self-contained' communities). There is a risk that this sort of institutional isolation at the international level may represent an obstacle in the pursuit of effective economic and social development objectives. Indeed, at times such isolation may exacerbate the contraposition of values at issue, such as 'investment' or 'trade' versus 'labour' or 'environmental standards'.

Accordingly, the institutional structure at the multilateral level needs to keep apace and conform to the realities of a more complex and interrelated world. Whatever the future role of such levels of government may be, the linkages and cooperation between the various existing bodies needs to be strengthened. Equally, the research methodology in the law of the global economy needs to reflect such complexities and interrelations, if the discipline is to maintain its grip on reality.

(ii) National Administrative Disciplines and Transnational Commercial Disciplines

International investment law is intricately connected with both national administrative disciplines and transnational commercial disciplines.

One of the functions of international investment laws is to provide normative yardsticks to control the exercise of discretionary regulatory powers by States that may have an adverse impact on the flows of capital between States. The national treatment standard and the fair and equitable treatment standards, for example, may be seen as embodying, inter alia, the principle of 'administrative validity' to protect the rights of foreign investors against abuses by the State of its administrative powers. The standards that the host State has to comply with may include both 'substantive' and

---

[26] See D Ahn, 'Linkages between International Financial and Trade Institutions—IMF, World Bank and WTO' (2000) 34 *J of World Trade* 1.

[27] For a recent call for a higher level of dialogue between the human rights and development communities, see P Alston, 'Ships Passing in the Night: The Current State of the Human Rights and Development Debate Seen Through the Lens of the Millennium Development Goals' (2005) 27 *Hum Rts Q* 755.

'procedural' requirements including concepts such as proportionality, necessity, transparency, and participation.[28] Given their very general nature, it has so far been principally up to investment arbitration procedures to give meaning to these standards through applying them to disputes concerning public utility concessions, construction permits, tax refunds, environmental regulations, etc.[29] As recently noted by Van Harten and Loughlin:

> Like the members of any administrative tribunal or court, in reviewing these types of measures, arbitrators rule on the legality of state conduct, evaluate the fairness of governmental decision-making, determine the appropriate scope and content of property rights, and allocate risks and costs between business and society. This is the stuff of administrative law.[30]

The complex nature of foreign investment disputes has been directly recognised by investment arbitration tribunals. In *Occidental Exploration and Production Company v Ecuador*, for example, the Tribunal noted that the dispute at hand (concerning Ecuador's denial of a certain VAT refund to which the investor claimed it was entitled), even aside from its contractual aspects, involved:

> a number of issues arising from the legislation of Ecuador, the Andean Community legal order and international law, including of course the question of rights under the [bilateral investment treaty].[31]

At the same time, international investment disputes show how cross-border investment flows are also embedded in transnational contracts usually concluded between the foreign investor and the host government or one of its agencies. As noted by Douglas:

> investment disputes are only partly concerned with the compliance of acts attributable to a state with its treaty obligations; and the principle stated in Article 3 of the ILC Articles [on State Responsibility] only comes into play when there is actual conflict between the two legal orders—orders which nonetheless coexist

---

[28] F Ortino, 'From Non-discrimination to Reasonableness: A Paradigm Shift in International Economic Law?', (Jean Monnet Working Paper 01/05, 2005); G Bermann, 'The Principle of Proportionality' (1977–1978) 26 *Am J Comp L* 415, 416.

[29] '[...] international law has yet to identify in a comprehensive and definitive fashion precisely what regulations are considered "permissible" and "commonly accepted" as falling within the police or regulatory power of States and, thus, noncompensable. [...] It thus inevitably falls to the adjudicator to determine whether particular conduct by a state "crosses the line" that separates valid regulatory activity from expropriation.' *Saluka Investments BV v The Czech Republic*, at 263–4 (Perm Ct Arb 2006), available at http://ita.law.uvic.ca/documents/Saluka-PartialawardFinal.pdf. For an excellent analysis of several international investment disputes, see T Weiler, *International Investment Law and Arbitration: Leading Cases from the ICSID, NAFTA, Bilateral Treaties and Customary International Law* (Cameron May, 2005).

[30] G Van Harten & M Loughlin, 'Investment Treaty Arbitration as a Species of Global Administrative Law' (2006) 17 *Eur J Int'l L* 121, at 147.

[31] *Occidental Exploration and Production Company v Ecuador*, LCIA Award, ¶48 (1 July, 2004), available at www.investmentclaims.com.

in principle (and in fact), in relation to any investment situation. In other words, investment disputes are significantly concerned with issues pertaining to the existence, nature, and scope of the private interests comprising the investment. These issues go beyond the purview of international law and the rule of state responsibility just recalled. To treat international law as a self-sufficient legal order in the sphere of foreign investment is plainly untenable.[32]

The point that we want to emphasise here is that the only way to properly appreciate the administrative and commercial disciplines affecting the cross border flows of investment is to follow a more comprehensive approach which includes both national and international administrative norms, as well as national and transnational commercial norms. As noted above, this is important not just to understand whether these different norms complement, or clash with, each other but also to ensure a higher level of coordination between the several objectives pursued by these norms.

III. TENTATIVE CONCLUSION

At this stage, the only tentative (and somewhat unsatisfactory) conclusion that we can offer is a pledge to try out the methodological approach suggested in the Chapter. Following Professor Meessen's recommendation, 'Law has to be divided up by problem areas rather than by its sources';[33] the next step is to fully apply the economic law approach to a specific aspect of the global economy (starting perhaps with the case studies highlighted in this Chapter). Ultimately, the usefulness and feasibility of the suggested approach may only be determined when properly tested.

---

[32] Z Douglas, 'The Hybrid Foundations of Investment Treaty Arbitration' (2004) 74 *Brit YB Int'l L* 151, at 155.
[33] KM Meessen, above n 6, at 90.

8
Of Foxes and Hedgehogs: Some Thoughts About the Relationship Between WTO Law and General International Law

EMMANUEL VOYIAKIS[*]

THESE ARE HARD times for anyone who thinks of WTO law as a 'self-contained' regime, a system with its own separate logic and principles, which differs very much from the logic, principles and structure of general international law. In fact, the attack on this 'separatist' view has been articulated in such strong and unequivocal terms, it is difficult to avoid the impression that either separatists have no idea of how general international law works or that those separatists who studied international law in their youth might be entitled to a refund. WTO law is part of general international law and there is no other way about it. It is a body of rules based on a founding treaty and several other instruments adopted thereunder. The law of treaties, especially the law of treaty interpretation, is part of general (customary) international law. This entails that general international law itself is central to the interpretation of WTO rights and obligations. But even if WTO law must be understood to have departed from these general rules about how treaties work and how they should be interpreted, it is still operating within the confines of general international law. After all, one of the first rules about the sources of international law is that international agents can agree on specific and special rules among themselves. The WTO system may feature a complex internal structure and sophistication, but it is no more separate from general international law than any other treaty arrangement. These points are so obvious, it is astonishing that anyone could think otherwise.

---

[*] I am grateful to Stephen Allen, Chi Carmody, Rafael Leal-Arcas and Joel Trachtman, whose comments and discussion helped me to clarify several point of the original paper.

I used to think this critique of separatism devastating, but I have changed my mind. This Chapter is an effort to explain my dissatisfaction with the standard attacks on separatism and to outline what I regard as the real issues in the debate between those who think of WTO law as a 'self-contained' regime and those that do not. Although I do not propose to take a stand on that latter debate here, one of my two aims is to present separatism as a coherent and plausible account of WTO law and its relationship with general international law. The other aim is to articulate the important challenges facing its declared opponents.

My intuition is that international legal scholarship has nothing to gain from knocking down the straw man of a thesis that separatism has been presented as. I hope that clearer sight of the intuitions behind separatism will allow us to confront some much more interesting and difficult questions about the relationship between WTO and general international law and between the values that each body of rules is best interpreted as reflecting. Separatism may eventually fail as an account of WTO law, but our understanding of *why* it fails will be obscure until we have confronted the deep and important insights that lie at its heart.

The Chapter falls into three parts. Part I explains why the standard critiques of separatism, echoed in the recent work in the context of the International Law Commission's study on the fragmentation of international law and much academic writing, misunderstand the separatist thesis and obscure the real issues at stake. Part II offers an account of separatism as the general thesis that the values and interests promoted by WTO rules need not be identical with the values and interests promoted by general international law. It then shows why this account draws some support from the structure of the WTO system and our ordinary thinking about values and their conflicts. Part III argues that, whether or not it can succeed, separatism challenges its opponents to articulate explicitly the substantive values common to general international and WTO law. A note at the end of the Chapter will explain how this challenge relates to current debates about WTO constitutionalism and why it might be harder to meet than is commonly thought.

I. SEPARATISM AND THE FORMAL CASE AGAINST IT

Should WTO institutions appeal to legal materials outside the WTO texts and practices when interpreting the rights and duties of WTO members? In what circumstances should they do so? Do they have a discretion on the matter or are there compelling principles that require or prohibit appeal to non-WTO legal materials? As cases like *US-Shrimp Turtle* or *EC-Beef Hormones* show, these questions are important not only in theory but also in practice.[1] The view I will call 'separatism' offers a distinctive set of answers to them.

Separatism could be casually described in the following terms. Separatists believe that one can study and apply the rules and obligations that flow from the WTO treaty system without having to engage in questions about customary international law, general principles of international law and the like. This is not to say that they believe that WTO rules are always crystal clear and in no need of interpretation. Rather, their claim is that they can find all the legal materials and interpretive tools they need to resolve such problems within the context of the texts and practices of the WTO. That is also the sense in which they regard the WTO as a 'self-contained regime'.

The case against separatism—which I will sparingly refer to as 'integrationism'—has so far been dominated by two arguments. The first argument draws attention to the fact that the practice of WTO institutions has clearly shown an intention to incorporate general international law into the proper understanding of WTO rights and obligations ('the argument from practice'). In other words, WTO institutions have themselves recognised that the proper interpretation of WTO rights and obligations requires the use of legal materials outside the WTO system. The second argument emphasises the idea that, as a species of law, WTO law must derive its validity and binding force from a more fundamental set of rules, namely certain rules of general international law ('the formal argument'). The formal argument is much more potent and sweeping than the argument from practice. It claims that even if WTO institutions had comprehensively declared the WTO system to be 'self-contained', such declarations could not possibly cast doubt on the dependence of WTO rights and obligations on some more fundamental rights and obligations found in general international law, because that dependence is entailed by the very form of WTO rights and obligations as *legal* rights and obligations. Let me take each argument in turn.

It should be quite clear that the argument from practice has at best probative and at worst only derivative value. For every statement to the effect that WTO law 'should not be read in clinical isolation from public international law'[2], one will find some evidence for the view that the drafters

---

[1] Appellate Body Report, *US—Standards for Reformulated and Conventional Gasoline*, WT/DS2/AB/R (29 Apr, 1996) [*US—Standards*]; Appellate Body Report, *EC—Measures Concerning Meat and Meat Products (Hormones)*, WT/DS48/AB/R (16 Jan, 1998); Appellate Body Report, *US—Import Prohibition of Certain Shrimp and Shrimp Products*, WT/DS58/AB/R (6 Nov, 1998).

[2] *US—Standards* above n 1, at 17; G Marceau, 'A Call for Coherence in International Law: Praises for the Prohibition Against "Clinical Isolation" in WTO Dispute Settlement' (1999) 33 *J of World Trade* 110; JH Jackson, 'Fragmentation or Unification Among International Institutions: The World Trade Organization' (1999) 31 *NYU J of Int'l L & Pol* 824, 828–9. For a general overview of the use of general international law in WTO dispute settlement see D Palmeter & PC Mavroides, 'The WTO Legal System: Sources of Law' (1998) 92 *Am J Int'l L* 398.

of GATT were not even remotely concerned with public international law when they designed their trading system.[3] A recent study by Lindroos and Mehling argues that, at any rate, the balance of the evidence is not overwhelming one way or the other.[4] Be that as it may, the argument from practice is hardly conclusive for another reason: any evidence from the practice of WTO institutions can only be interpreted against the background of assumptions about whether separatism is correct or false. For example, convinced integrationists will interpret the *US—Reformulated Gasoline* dictum as saying that it is in principle *impossible* to separate WTO law from general international law. Convinced separatists, on the other hand, will read the same passage as saying that it is sometimes *expedient* for WTO lawyers to look to general international law for interpretive purposes, even though they do not have to. The point is that these camps do not disagree just on which side has more evidence of WTO practice in support, but also about what the available evidence actually tells us.[5] So I will leave the argument from practice to one side.

The formal argument presents separatism with a much more difficult test. In fact, the formal argument is often considered to be not just strong but positively crushing: if it stands up to scrutiny, then separatism cannot even get off the ground as a theory of the relationship between WTO and general international law.

The formal argument has found favour with several theorists, but perhaps its most famous exposition to date can be found in the recent work of the designated Study Group of the International Law Commission on the fragmentation of international law. The Group, chaired by Martti Koskenniemi, has considered in some depth the question of 'self-contained regimes'. The relationship between WTO and general international law has been a central feature of its discussion. Here are three extracts from the Group's reports:

> The Chairman suggested that in fact the term 'self-contained regime' was a misnomer in the sense that no set of rules ... was isolated from general law. He doubted whether such isolation was even possible: a regime can receive (or fail to

---

[3] J Pauwelyn, *Conflict of Norms in Public International Law: How WTO Law Relates to Other Rules of International Law* 538 (Cambridge University Press, 2003); R Howse, 'From Politics to Technocracy—and Back Again: The Fate of the Multilateral Trade Regime' (2002) 96 *Am J Int'l L* 98.

[4] A Lindroos & M Mehling, 'Dispelling the Chimera of "Self-Contained Regimes": International Law and the WTO' (2005) 16 *Eur J Int'l L* 857.

[5] Joost Pauwelyn says that 'it is for the party claiming that a treaty has "contracted out" of general international law to prove it', Pauwelyn, above n 3, at 213. I think that this way of putting the matter is misleading. The idea of a 'burden of proof' implies that one must be looking for proof that, when adduced, will convince advocates of all competing positions, whatever their background theory of the relationship between WTO and general international law.

receive) legally binding force ('validity') only by reference to (valid and binding) rules or principles *outside* it.[6]

There was no support in practice to the suggestion that general international law would apply to special regimes only as a result of incorporation. In fact, it was hard to see how regime-builders might agree *not* to incorporate (that is, opt out from) general principles of international law. Where would the binding nature of such an agreement emerge from?[7]

No treaty, however special its subject matter or limited the number of its parties, applies in a normative vacuum but refers back to a number of general, often unwritten principles of customary law concerning its entry into force and its interpretation and application. Moreover, the normative environment includes principles that determine the legal subjects, their basic rights and duties, and the forms through which those rights and duties are modified or extinguished.[8]

I think that the most intuitive way to understand the core of the argument is to focus on the Study Group's liberal use of spatial metaphors. The Group argues that regimes like the WTO system cannot be *self-contained*; they cannot lie *outside* international law; they cannot exist in a normative *vacuum*; their drafters cannot opt *out* of general international law and so on. These spatial metaphors are telling in that they reveal the formal nature of the Study Group's claims. What matters is not the substantive *content* of the respective rules of WTO law and general international law (indeed, the Study Group has not found it necessary to look deeply into any substantive questions of international law), but the *form*, the shape or the structure of those rules. If only we paid enough attention to matters of legal form, the Group implies, we would see enough reason to doubt that WTO law can really exist separately from general international law.

It does not take extensive acquaintance with legal theory to identify the intellectual ancestry of this view in the legal philosophy of Hans Kelsen and, by extension, Kant's philosophy of normativity.[9] Following Kant, Kelsen thought that all pure ought-statements have the same logical form and eventually derive their validity from the same source. For Kant and Kelsen, norms are never self-standing and cannot emerge from facts alone. Their authority and action-guiding nature always depends on the existence of a logically prior rule that imbues them with normative character.[10] A treaty concluded between two States is binding exactly because

---

[6] Report of the International Law Commission on its Fifty-Sixth Session, Fragmentation of International Law: Difficulties Arising from the Diversification and Expansion of International Law, ¶ 318 (2004), Martti Koskenniemi—Rapporteur.

[7] Ibid at 321.

[8] M Koskenniemi, *Study on the Function and Scope of the Lex Specialis Rule and the Question of 'Self-Contained Regimes'*, UN Doc ILC(LVI)/SG/FIL/CRD.1/Add.1 (2004) at 7.

[9] For an account of the Kantian character of Kelsen's pure theory of law, see SL Paulson, 'On the Puzzle Surrounding Hans Kelsen's Basic Norm' (2000) 13 *Ratio Juris* 58.

[10] H Kelsen, *The Pure Theory of Law*, Knight (trans), (UC Berkeley Press, 1967) 114–17; H Kelsen *Principles of International Law* (Rinehart & Company, 1952) 17–20.

international law decrees that such treaties are binding. States can opt out of a generally binding international rule exactly because international law features a rule which allows such 'opting out'. Similarly, the special legal rules of the WTO system do not derive their validity from the mere fact that States have signed up to them, but from the norm of general international law which attributes legal authority to voluntarily assumed international commitments.[11]

Kant's and Kelsen's argument entails that all ought-statements must derive their validity from the same source, the famous *Grundnorm*. Whereas Kant's general theory of normativity identifies rational will as the only self-governing entity and the source of all ought-statements, Kelsen's pure theory of law is content to leave the content of the legal *Grundnorm* open, but—and this is the important point for our discussion- it insists that there can be only one such norm. In that sense, what is sometimes called 'the unity of the legal order' becomes a matter of logical form. It follows that separatists are wrong because they are not attentive enough to the structure and form of any statement of WTO law. Were they so attentive, they would see that statements of WTO law cannot be understood as legally normative statements except on the condition that they derive their validity from the same source that validates all other rules of international law.

Despite some evidence of prevarication[12], I do not think it oversimplifies things to say that the ILC Study Group's discussion of the relationship between WTO and general international law is formalist in letter and spirit. The core of its argument is that one cannot even begin to make sense of WTO rights and obligations as *legal* in nature unless one assumes that those rights and obligations are part of the same system as rules of general international law. Kelsen would have been proud.

The question, of course, is whether the formal argument is actually good and whether it defeats separatism. To be more specific: is it true that it makes no sense to speak of WTO rights and obligations *as law* and still be a separatist? Can't we give an account of the authority of WTO rules that is reasonably independent from the authority of general international law? Is it not possible that when States created the WTO system they succeeded in creating a new 'normative order' or a new source of authority in their relations?

---

[11] For a similar argument, see GG Fitzmaurice, 'Some Problems Regarding the Formal Sources of International Law', in *Symbolae Verzijl* (M Nijhoff, 1958) 174.

[12] Eg, one passage in the 2004 ILC Report, above n 6, at 324, reads: '[The Chairman] also noted that no homogeneous, hierarchical system was realistically available to do away with problems arising from conflicting rules of legal regimes. The demands of coherence and reasonable pluralism will continue to point in different directions.' Kelsen and his followers would clearly not allow the idea of irresolvable conflicts in international law: they would say that if two rules appear to be in conflict, then one of them must be invalid. In any case, the passage appears in the context of the Committee members' discussions and is not relied upon in the Report's substantive argument against separatism.

I will present some intuitive reasons why the formal argument might sound hollow. I think that these are also the intuitions that make separatism attractive. The next section will try to explain how they can be arranged into a coherent and reasonable separatist account of the relationship between WTO and general international law.

For one thing, the idea that States and other international agents may be subject to different forms of regulation and sources of authority in their relations should not sound alien. We normally think that the authority of international law is distinct from the authority of international morality. Both law and morality have rules about how States should behave: one may allow developed States to pursue third world debts, the other may disallow it. We tend to describe such cases as cases of conflict between law and morality. Of course, the conflict may sometimes be more apparent than real: for example, perhaps international law also prohibits States from exacting third world debt. But there are many cases where the conflict seems genuine, unavoidable and irreducible.

Or take the case of regulatory bodies like the Basel Committee on Banking Supervision. The Basel Committee is not empowered to nor purports to make law, yet it has great authority over the ways States design and implement banking and securities regulation. Governments are occasionally faced with the choice of disregarding the Committee's guidelines in favour of implementing legitimate policies of, say, tighter regulatory controls. The fact that the Basel Committee guidelines are not law does not make the job of government officials any less difficult. These officials will regard themselves as torn between two genuinely different authoritative standards.

Other examples of non-legal regulation are not hard to find.[13] The issue raised by their simultaneous presence and application in international affairs is this: if international law, international morality and Basel-style guidelines register in our common experience as different sources of authority over how States ought to behave towards each other, why can't it be that international legal rules too may derive their authority from a variety of sources, rather than just from a single source? This, I want to suggest, is a concern that lies at the very heart of the separatist project.

II. SEPARATISM AS VALUE PLURALISM

Archilochus (ca 650 BC) is credited with having immortalised the following brilliant, if somewhat cryptic, saying:

The fox knows many things, the hedgehog knows one big thing.

---

[13] For discussion see AM Slaughter, 'Global Government Networks, Global Information Agencies and Disaggregated Democracy' (2003) 24 *Mich J Int'l L* 1041.

114 *Emmanuel Voyiakis*

Isaiah Berlin has put the Greek poet's words to a very good and widely appreciated metaphorical use. He has used it to describe:

> a great chasm between those who relate everything to a single central vision, one system more or less coherent or articulate, or a single, universal, organizing principle' (the 'hedgehogs') and those 'who pursue many ends, often unrelated and even contradictory, connected, if at all, only in some *de facto* way' and not in accordance with some general organizing idea (the 'foxes').[14]

The foxes and the hedgehogs that Berlin speaks of have very different intellectual outlooks. While one pursues a single all-important aim, the other pursues several ends at once. And while one seeks principled coherence, the other seeks pragmatic, case-by-case accommodation. Both regard their interests, ends and values as generating 'ought'-statements, ie as normative. However, they disagree about the source of this normativity. The hedgehogs believe that their values and interests are normative to the extent that they hang together as a coherent whole. The foxes disagree; they think that their values and interests are normative because they are *their own* values and interests, while accepting that sometimes they will stand in conflict. The hedgehogs defend their position by 'curling up' into a single solid mass with every point of their body of argument equally armed and equally exposed. The foxes defend theirs with the conviction that the art of living consists in making the best out of one's genuinely held but rarely fully coherent values and goals.

I am drawing on Berlin's metaphor for two reasons. The first is its ability to amplify the separatist view. It seems to me that, in essence, those who take a separatist view of the relationship between WTO and general international law take something quite like the foxes' outlook. Their chief intuition is that the sources of international legal authority can vary because the interests and values of international agents can and do often vary. If the point needs to be put more tightly, separatists are pluralists about the 'ought'. They hold that ought-statements, such as statements of legal rights and obligations, come in several and mutually irreducible varieties. Their reason for so thinking is that the human interests and values that exercise a normative pull over our lives are often similarly irreducible. Consider the contrasts between prudence and morality, morality and law, commitment and freedom of action, liberty and equality, personal profit and distributive justice, etc. We regard each as valuable and yet we accept that these values may sometimes generate conflicting demands. The separatist idea that general international law and WTO law may derive their validity from different and mutually independent sources is premised on a similar

---

[14] I Berlin, *The Hedgehog and the Fox* at 7 (New American Library, 1957). For a discussion of the different philosophical uses of Berlin's metaphor see S Lukes, 'An Unfashionable Fox', in R Dworkin et al (eds), *The Legacy of Isaiah Berlin* (Oxford University Press, 2001) 43.

thought: that *the values and interests reflected in WTO law may not be reducible to the values and interests reflected in other areas of international law*.[15] This is a version of a position that philosophers sometimes refer to as 'value-pluralism'.

This thought applies itself in legal argument in familiar ways. Parties in dispute settlement proceedings argue frequently that WTO institutions should not necessarily try to make WTO rights and obligations consistent with other areas of international law, such as environmental law or the law of human rights, for each of those bodies of law is designed to promote different values and interests. WTO law is primarily intended to promote States' interest in global trade and free economic relations; environmental law promotes the value of sustainable use and exploitation of natural resources; the law of human rights protects individuals against government abuses and so on. Their point is not that these values and interests are necessarily incompatible, for most of the time it is clear that they can all be pursued fruitfully and in parallel. It is, rather, that *these values and interests are appealing (reasonably) independently of each other*. If a community in which trade relations are feeble and rudimentary invented new methods of ensuring sustainable use of its natural resources, we would count that as genuine progress. If a community where trade relations are highly developed and efficient decided to curtail individual freedoms, we would count that as a loss. For all our commitment to both free trade and freedom, we would *not* say that free trade within a community is valueless except when individual freedoms are thoroughly respected. The two values may be connected in important ways, but they do not necessarily stand or fall together.

The second reason for paying close attention to the tale of the fox and the hedgehog has to do with one sense in which Berlin's metaphorical description *does not* resolve into the formalist position I outlined in the last section. Whereas the foxes in Berlin's story resemble WTO separatists quite closely, the hedgehogs Berlin speaks of are not the equivalent of Kantian philosophers and Kelsenian lawyers. Hedgehogs, you will have noticed, do not treat the unity of the legal order as a formal or conceptual matter. They regard it as a *substantive value*, as an end to be achieved or desired.

---

[15] DM McRae, 'The WTO in International Law: Tradition Continued or New Frontier?' (2000) 3 *J Intl' Econ L* 27 (drawing attention to this point by discussing the differences between dispute settlement in WTO and general international law.) Note, incidentally, the following passage in the 2004 ILC Report, above n 6, at 329, 'There is no single legislative will behind international law. Treaties and custom come about as a result of conflicting motives and objectives—they are "bargains" and "package-deals" and often result from spontaneous reactions to events in the environment.' It is quite striking that the Commission is alert to the multitude of interests behind the development of various international rules and yet does not consider this as a challenge to its formalist conception of the 'unity of the international legal order'.

116 *Emmanuel Voyiakis*

Furthermore, this is a point on which foxes and hedgehogs actually agree; they only differ as to whether the end can ever be achieved in full, so that all our values will make up a coherent unity. Hedgehogs are optimists on that front. They hold that, unless we are given some strong reason to think that the values reflected in WTO and general international law are inconsistent *in principle*, we should keep on trying to reach interpretations of these values that make sense of each one in the light of the others.[16] Foxes see things differently. They believe that there are no general guarantees of coherence in the values reflected in WTO and general international law. They hold that the value of, say, economic development through trade and other values such as environmental protection will sometimes pull in opposite directions and that one's best response to this conflict would be to seek a pragmatic accommodation that sacrifices as little of each value as possible. They would thus agree with Berlin that:

> [w]hat is clear is that values can clash. Values may easily clash within the breast of a single individual. And it does not follow that some must be true and others false ... The notion of the perfect whole, the ultimate solution in which all things coexist seems to me to be not merely unobtainable -that is a truism- but conceptually incoherent. Some among the great goods cannot live together ... We are doomed to choose and every choice may entail an irreparable loss.[17]

Notice that Berlin does not argue that our values are doomed to conflict in each and every case. His concern, rather, is to show that such conflicts cannot be erased from the picture as mistakes in rationality or as defects in one's understanding of the form of normative statements. The reason is that they are an ineliminable element of human moral experience. As Bernard Williams has put it, whenever an agent is faced with a case of conflict between values or other moral requirements:

> it must be a mistake to suppose that what we have here is a case of logical inconsistency, such that the agent could not be justified or rational in thinking that each of these moral requirements applied to him. *This is to misplace the source of the agent's trouble, in suggesting that what is wrong is his thought about the moral situation, whereas what is wrong lies in his situation itself*—something that may or may not be his fault ... In this, as elsewhere in these areas, ... theory has to be responsive to what a reflective agent feels he needs to say.[18] (emphasis added)

I do not intend to take sides on this controversy in the present context. My aim is to highlight the key intuition, shared by foxes and hedgehogs, that

---

[16] Ronald Dworkin holds this view; see R Dworkin, 'Do Liberal Values Conflict?' in Dworkin, above n 14, 73.

[17] I Berlin, 'Two Concepts of Liberty', in *Four Essays on Liberty* (Oxford University Press, 1969) 169.

[18] B Williams, 'Conflicts of Values', in *Moral Luck* (Cambridge University Press, 1981) 74–5.

conflicts between our values and the norms that these values entail are not just incidents of conceptual confusion, as Kelsen thought, but a genuine and irreducible feature of human life and practical deliberation. Whether the values reflected in WTO and general international law hang together in harmony or are doomed to clash is a substantive question calling for moral and political argument, not a matter of formal structure.

To sum up: the separatists of my description believe that the normative authority of WTO law does not necessarily have the same source as the authority of general international law. They believe that the normative force of each body of rules derives from the values and interests that these rules are meant to promote. They also believe that the values and interests reflected in WTO law differ from and are not reducible to the values and interests reflected in other areas of international law. This does not mean that these different values are doomed to clash all the time; imagination and pragmatism should defuse most instances of conflict. It does imply, however, that there is no use in pretending that these values will always dovetail or that all apparent conflicts could be resolved if only we were more attentive to their formal structure.

III. BUILDING A SUBSTANTIVE CASE AGAINST SEPARATISM

Those drawn to the version of separatism I have outlined will probably agree that many of the real issues in the debate about the relationship between WTO and general international law have remained largely untouched in contemporary legal thinking. For one thing, the ILC's formalist argument seems to misunderstand the nature of that relationship and the problems to which it gives rise. The real question is not whether Kant and Kelsen were right in claiming that all normative statements, like statements of law, must have a single source as a matter of formal truth, but to what extent WTO and general international law reflect the same or different values and how these values are interrelated.[19] The challenge facing international lawyers is not to uncover some hidden structure that unifies all international rules into an elegant whole, but to reach a deeper understanding of the substantive values that each area of international law, and WTO law in particular, is best interpreted as reflecting.[20] We should, of course, hope that these

---

[19] Joel Trachtman has argued that one of the most important challenges for the WTO system is to identify 'the extent to which broad social values are integrated with one another, and more specifically, the way in which market concerns are integrated with non-market concerns.' See J Trachtman, 'The Constitutions of the WTO' (2006) 17 *Eur J Int'l L* 623, 634.

[20] See also B Simma & D Pulkowski, 'Of Planets and the Universe: Self-Contained Regimes in International Law' 17 *Eur J Int'l L* 483 (2006). Chi Carmody has recently made an important contribution to this project, by showing why the WTO system is best seen as promoting multilateral rather than bilateral interests, see C Carmody, 'WTO Obligations as Collective' (2006) 17 *Eur J Int'l L* 419.

values turn out to dovetail in most cases and that conflicts are rare and manageable with imagination and practical wisdom. At the same time, we should recognise that reaching a satisfactory accommodation of these different values is an aim to be pursued, not a given.

It should also be clear that separatism promotes a particular perspective on current debates about the constitutional aspects of the WTO.[21] Separatism suggests that talk about the existence and content of a 'WTO constitution' is fertile not because it facilitates some sort of formal ordering of the various values reflected in WTO texts and practices, but because it forces us to confront the difficult questions about the relationship between equally pressing but imperfectly coherent moral demands on the institutions of the WTO. Its point is that constitutions may internalise these questions, but they do not resolve them.

I hope that, whether or not you are attracted to it, this version of separatism and its commitments is one that you can recognise as plausible and principled. However, I have not argued—nor does it follow from my discussion—that separatism is also a correct account of the relationship between WTO and general international law. Recall that, in its own terms, separatism would be correct only if it turns out that WTO law and general international law promote *different* substantive values. I want to close with a very brief look into a powerful argument about why this might not be the case. I believe that, whatever its other merits, this argument also incorporates the best intuitions behind the formalist position I have been criticising.

That argument could be briefly stated as follows. Even if WTO law and general international law are not necessarily parts of a single normative structure as a matter of formal truth, they do share in at least one substantive value: the value of *legality* or the rule of law.[22] Whatever their other aims, both WTO and general international law aim to promote some substantive conception of the idea that it is important for the rights and duties that international actors have towards each other to be governed by the community's past practices.

I believe that an appropriately worked out version of this rough idea would represent the best case against separatism. Legality, understood as

---

[21] DZ Cass, *The Constitutionalization of the World Trade Organization* (Oxford University Press, 2005); R Howse & Ka Nicolaides, 'Legitimacy and Global Governance: Why Constitutionalizing the WTO is a Step Too Far', in R Porter et al (eds), *Efficiency, Equity and Legitimacy: The Multilateral Trading System at the Millennium* (Brookings Institution Press, 2001) 227; EU Petersmann, *Constitutional Functions and Constitutional Problems of International Economic Law* (Westview Press, 1991).

[22] Georges Abi-Saab may have been making this point about the importance of legality in the context of the WTO when he remarked that 'without the omnipresence of a general law, a special legal subsystem may mutate into a legal Frankenstein that no longer partakes in the same basis of legitimacy.' See G Abi-Saab, 'Fragmentation or Unification: Some Concluding Remarks' (1999) 31 *NYU J Int'l L & Pol* 919.

governance on the basis of past practices, seems to be a genuine value and it would be difficult to argue that WTO law is not informed by it. Having said that, the claim that both WTO and general international law share in the value of legality might not be enough to discredit the separatist thesis altogether. In particular, the precise extent to which the WTO system must be regarded as committed to the rule of law needs to be the focus of specific research.[23] To take one example, the idea that Panel and Appellate Body reports develop their legal effects on the condition that they are accepted by the Dispute Settlement Body does not seem to be on all fours with the idea that the rights and duties of WTO members ought to be governed by their common *past* decisions, rather than depend on the political consensus of the day.[24] So although it might be true that legality plays a distinct role in the system of WTO values, it is far from clear whether that role has the central and controlling character that it does in the context of general international law. As long as this important question remains open, separatism would be guaranteed all the breathing space it needs both in practice and principle.

---

[23] J Weiler, 'The Rule of Lawyers and the Ethos of Diplomats: Reflections on the Internal and External Legitimacy of WTO Dispute Settlement' (2001) 35 *J of World Trade* 193 (noting a number of adverse consequences that an increased commitment to the rule of law might bring about in the context of the WTO).

[24] Be that as it may, it would be a mistake to think that an arrangement that lacked a strong commitment to the rule of law would thereby be unable to promote other important values. As Joseph Raz reminds us, there are many ways in which governments and governmental agencies can do good without making a claim to legal authority. See J Raz, 'The Obligation to Obey: Revision and Tradition', in J Raz *Ethics in the Public Domain*: Essays in the morality of Law and Politics (Oxford University Press, 1994) 344–5.

9

Different Scholarships, the Same World: Interdisciplinary Research on IEL

CHEN-YU WANG

I. FROM BRETTON WOODS TO THE DOHA ROUND

IN JULY 1944, as the Second World War was drawing to a close, the world's leading politicians gathered to consider how to reorganise the world economy. Representatives from 44 nations met at the Mount Washington Hotel in Bretton Woods for the United Nations Monetary and Financial Conference—popularly known as the Bretton Woods Conference. For the first time in human history, global institutions—the International Monetary Fund (IMF) and the World Bank—were established to solve global economic problems. The common view at the Conference was that the depression of the 1930s and the rise of fascism could be traced, in significant part, to the collapse of international trade and to interwar isolationist economic policies. The Conference established a system based on the free movement of goods, with the US dollar as the international currency. The Fund and the Bank were limited to managing problems related to deficits and to currency and capital shortages. The summary of agreement states:

> The nations should consult and agree on international monetary changes which affect each other. They should outlaw practices which are agreed to be harmful to world prosperity, and they should assist each other to overcome short-term exchange difficulties.

The World Bank was created to speed up post-war reconstruction, to aid political stability, and to foster peace. This was to be fulfilled through the establishment of programs for reconstruction and development.

But, even as the Bretton Woods conference created the two main institutions concerning international monetary relations and development, there was an understanding that the inter-war problems of international trade had to be resolved as well, and that international trade also needed its own institution—the International Trade Organization. There was thus an understanding of the connectedness of the different fields. In addition, at

Bretton Woods, and later in the development of the GATT, there was an understanding that economics, international relations, and international law were all vital foundations for these institutions and the fields they covered. Sadly, since then, the separate fields have generally developed isolated from each other. They have viewed the same problems, but from different perspectives. But the success of the international economic law movement since the Second World War requires that all these fields be understood and treated together. This paper concerns recent moves and pressures to end that isolation, and to bring all three fields more closely together through interdisciplinary collaboration.

II. NEW THEORETICAL APPROACH OF INTERDISCIPLINARY RESEARCH

The methodology explored in this chapter is animated by the spirit of interdisciplinary collaboration. Scholars of law, economics and international politics approach complex global issues from different views.[1] Unfortunately, the linkages among these three disciplines have not been utilised well in the past. Indeed, seeking to better understand IEL policy, scholars have typically focused on three usually separate academic fields, namely: international law, international relations theory, and international economics. This Chapter explores these segregated theories as a means of explaining what should be an interdisciplinary collaboration (Table 1).

Table 1 Interdisciplinary Research on International Law, Relations, and Economics

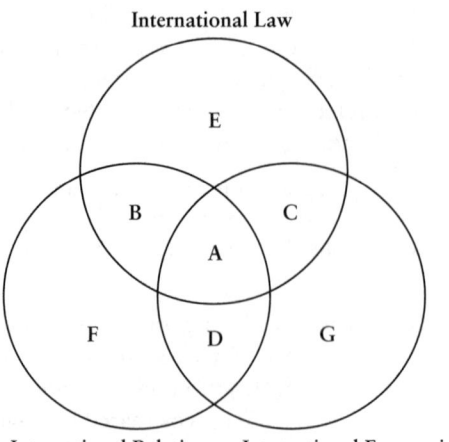

[Venn diagram with three overlapping circles labeled "International Law" (top), "International Relations" (bottom left), and "International Economics" (bottom right). Regions labeled: E (International Law only), F (International Relations only), G (International Economics only), B (Law ∩ Relations), C (Law ∩ Economics), D (Relations ∩ Economics), A (all three).]

---

[1] AM Slaughter, 'International law and International Relations Theory: A Dual Agenda' (1993) 87 *Am J Intl L* 205, at 205. As a professor Ann-Marie Slaughter has cogently argued,

Part A in the Figure is the area which will be the final focus of this Chapter. As the graph depicts, it combines the three different scholarly fields. That congruence is equally applicable to trade dispute resolution as it is to trade negotiations.

Part A + B reflects the combination of international law and international relations theory. In exploring that intersection, this Chapter examines institutionalism, international regime theory, functionalism, and economic interdependence as applied to the multilateral trading system.

Part A + C is the intersection of international law and international economics. This chapter discusses how that intersection has been applied to the IEL governing global economic activities as well as the extent to which the multilateral trading system, namely the WTO, would be better served by balancing legal enforcement with economic concerns.

Part A + D covers the overlap between international relations and international economics. Historically, the Bretton Woods system has attempted to solve international economic problems by using international relations theory.[2] But, in the past decades, international political economy became a popular analytical method, attracting the attention of significant numbers of international scholars. Furthermore, international trade exporters have also recognised that trade negotiation and litigation is not merely an amalgamation of legal issues, but contain other disciplines inside their 'soul,' most importantly the 'theory of international political economy.'

Parts E, F, and G represent the specific fields of the theories in each approach, which will not be discussed in this Chapter.

But Part A, alone, represents the confluence of all three fields, and is perhaps where the most sophisticated and effective international economic law takes place. Only through consideration and application of the methodologies and theories of the three can IEL satisfy its full potential.

A. International Law and International Relations

The relationship between international law and international politics is often too close to separate. After the Second World War, the idea of establishing the United Nations (UN), as well as the adoption of the UN Charter changed the fundamental principles of international law and international relations. Although the UN is the primary international organisation managing

---

'Just as constitutional lawyers study political theory, and political theorists inquire into the nature and substance of constitutions, so too should two disciplines that study the laws of state behavior seek to learn from one another.'

[2] S Krasner, *International Regimes* (Cornell U Press, 1983) 3–6. 'The three important debates of international relations theories are: (1) The First Debate: Idealism vs Realism, (2) The Second Debate: Scientific Behaviouralism vs Traditionalism, (3) The Third Debate: Neo-realism vs Neo-liberalism.'

international affairs, the states still rely on their hard power—sovereignty and economic policy. There were many international relations theories presented in the mid 20th century to try and explain the post-War world, and various debates advocating different theoretical approaches.[3] One of those theories, Realism, has as its key assumption that mankind is not inherently benevolent and kind, but self-centred and competitive. Realism also fundamentally assumes that the international system is anarchic, in the sense that there is no authority above states that is capable of regulating their interactions; states must arrive at relations with other states on their own, rather than being controlled by some higher controlling entity (that is, no true authoritative world government exists). Finally, it assumes that sovereign states, rather than international institutions, non-governmental organisations (NGOs), or multinational corporations, are the primary actors in international affairs. According to this theory, each state is thus a rational actor that always acts in its own self-interest, and the primary goal of each state is to ensure its own security. Realism holds that in pursuit of that security, states will attempt to amass resources, and that relations between states are determined by their relative level of power. That level of power is in turn determined by the state's capabilities, both military and economic. As a logical extension, realists do not focus on the weight of international law or international institutions, and they emphasise the capabilities of sovereignty and state power instead.

Although Realism was the main trend among international relations theories, there were lots of debates and opposition from other theoretical concerns.[4] With respect to the relationship between international law and international relations theory, the main concern was that the realists believe in the polarity of law and power, one diametrically opposes the other as the respective emblems of the domestic vs the international realm, normative aspiration vs positive description, cooperation vs conflict, soft vs hard, and idealist vs realist. They also believe that states seek only to protect their own national interest. The only relevant laws are the laws of politics, and politics is a struggle for power.[5] The realists have argued with international lawyers about the relevance of international law. At the same time, however, international legal theorists have tended to focus on the theoretical

---

[3] JS Nye, Jr, *Soft Power: The Means to Success in World Politics* (Public Affairs, 2004) 20.

[4] A Moravcsik, *Liberalism and International Relations Theory* (Harvard University Press, 1992) 42–8. The discipline of international relations was born after World War I in a haze of aspirations for the future of world government. Notable Realists scholars include Hans Morgenthau, Georg Schwarzenberger, EH Carr and George Kennan, Reinhold Niebuhr, Arnold Wolfers and Robert Strausz-Hupe. These seasoned observers of the interwar period reacted against Wilsonian liberal internationalism, which presumed that the combination of democracy and international organisation could vanquish war and power politics.

[5] HJ Morgenthau, *Politics among Nations: The Struggle for Power and Peace*, Brief Edn (McGraw-Hill, 1993) 4–5 & 25–6.

conundrum of the sources of international legal obligations—of the law being simultaneously 'of' and 'above' the state.[6]

The challenge did not just come from international legal theorists, but was also a result of the rapid changes in global economic interdependence after the Cold-War era which suggested that realism had less power in driving international affairs than previously thought. Indeed, beginning in the late 20th century, an important group of mainstream international relations theorists laid the foundation for a more fundamental attack on core realist propositions concerning the role and relevance of international institutions and international law.[7] The result was a new emphasis on the role and impact of international regimes, which focus more on the principles, norms, rules and decision-making procedures that pattern state expectations and behavior. This new approach has been exhibited in new theories—including Regime Theory,[8] which soon impacted on the study of international law. Regime theory was subsumed in international legal theory under the more general rubric of institutionalism,[9] a powerful alternative to realism. The dawning of a new era in terms of 'global governance'[10] to some extent may mean greater congruence in the areas of international law and international relations than ever before. These and other overlaps across the two methodologies should lead to a dual agenda in interdisciplinary scholarship.[11]

Overall, international legal scholars cannot ignore the growing wealth of international political circumstances and their impact on the world they seek to regulate. On the other side, as an emerging discipline, international political science long rejected the insights of international law, but as time has gone by, international political scientists have rediscovered what international lawyers never forgot, the role of principles and norms, and in the process have been adding insights of their own. This dual interdisciplinary agenda of mixing realism and liberalism offers a new hope of reaching the goals of both fields.[12] Furthermore, the sophistication engendered by such interdisciplinary collaboration will also then better serve the development of international economic law.

---

[6] Slaughter, above n 1, at 208.
[7] Ibid; cooperation theory, system theory, interdependence theory, international political economy, international regime theory, and collective security theory oppose tenets of Realism.
[8] See Krasner, above n 2. See also S Haggard & B Simmons, 'Theories of International Regimes' (1987) 41 *Intl Org* 491, 491–517.
[9] See M Hollis & S Smith, *Explaining and Understanding International Relations* (Oxford University Press, 1990).
[10] See E Mendes & O Mehmet, *Global Governance, Economy and Law: Waiting for Justice* (Routledge, 2003).
[11] Slaughter, above n 1, at 210.
[12] Ibid at 239.

B. International Law and International Economics

The linkages between international economics and international law are based on the global interdependence of international economic activities, both national and international. The causes of contemporary economic developments are numerous, and almost every conceivable type of government economic regulation must now take account of the international and global competitive implication of its activity. Often national government officials feel frustrated at their relative inability to control economic forces that vitally affect their constituents and prevent the fulfillment of official goals and promises made to those constituents.[13] These pressures are the forces that have propelled IEL to its central position in all three fields.

The term 'International Economic Law' ('IEL') was coined after the Second World War.[14] Generally, IEL governs various aspects of international economic activities, including embracing the law of economic transactions, government regulation of economic matters, and related legal relations including litigation and international institutions for economic relations. In contrast to international law, much of IEL does not regulate nation-state relations (use of force, human rights, intervention etc), but does indeed involve many questions of traditional international law, particularly treaty law.[15] There are three characteristics of IEL. First, IEL cannot be separated or compartmentalised from traditional public international law. The economic activities relating to IEL involve much state practice, which is relevant to the development of international law. Conversely, public international law has considerable relevance to the development of international economic relations and transactions. Second, the relationship of IEL to national or municipal law is particularly important, and especially the application of treaty norms to municipal law expressed through such mechanisms as self-executing treaties or direct applications.[16] Third, there is a fundamental need for interdisciplinary research and thinking for the field of IEL—the prime example being the incorporation of economic theories into IEL.[17]

---

[13] JH Jackson, 'Global Economics and IEL' (1998) 1 *J Intl Econ L* 1, 1–2.

[14] Ibid at 2.

[15] JH Jackson, 'IEL: Reflections on the "Boilerroom" of International Relations' (1995) 10 *Am U J Intl L Pol'y* 595, 595–606.

[16] See JH Jackson, 'Status of Treaties in Domestic Legal Systems: A Policy Analysis' (1993) 86 *Am J Intl L* 310, 310; See also T Cottier, 'The Relationship between World Trade Organization Law, National and Regional Law' (1998) 1 *J Intl Econ L* 83, 83–122.

[17] See Jackson, above n 13, at 10. 'Of course, "economics" is important and useful, especially for understanding the policy motivations of many of the international and national rules on the subject. In addition to economics, of course, other subjects are highly relevant. Political Science (and its intersection with economics found generally in the "public choice"' literature) is very important, as are many other disciplines, such as cultural history and anthropology, geography, etc'.

To some extent IEL can also be divided into two broad approaches which cut across most of the subjects embraced by IEL. These approaches can roughly be termed 'transactional' or 'regulatory.' Transactional IEL refers to transactions carried out in the context of international trade or other economic activities and focuses on the way mostly private entrepreneurs or other parties carry out their activity. Regulatory IEL, however, emphasises the role of government institutions (national, local or international). Although it cannot be argued that international trade transactions are the most regulated of all private economic transactions, nevertheless, most attention, traditionally, to IEL has been focused, perhaps for practical and pragmatic reasons, on transactions.[18]

The international economic system exists among states that more often than not pursue non-economic goals. Hence economic theories alone are unable to account or operate in such a non-market environment. In particular, economic theories have trouble coping with the various formal, or informal, linkages of various kinds of market failure, such as peace and national security, ie, peacemaking in the UN and human rights. This reality reflects the fact that there are broader values in IEL than just economic market-oriented values, a troubling issue for the interaction of the two fields of international law and economics. For example, in economic literature, there are generally several kinds of government responses to market failures that have been suggested—ways that governments can intervene, such as through taxes, tariffs, and subsidies. However, some of the economic theory responses to national market failure suggested in the literature cannot easily be used in such a global situation. International economic institutions, constituted and operating under international law, are thus necessary. But IEL without international relations is but a poor tool though goes a tremendous way towards serving the needs of the expanding and increasingly complex international economic order.

C. International Relations and International Economics

Although the birth of modern IEL was against the backdrop of the Second World War, the IEL movement in the GATT years tended to focus on pure economic issues, such as the reduction of tariffs. Despite such devices as GATT's Article XX General Exceptions provision, the early trade regimes tended not to be concerned with non-economic matters. The movement toward regional economic integration or regionalism, which appeared in the mid-1980s, however, differed from the prior economic integration of the 1950s and 1960s. The later regionalism and the successful multilateral trade negotiations that established the World Trade Organization

---

[18] See Jackson, above n 15, at 600.

(WTO) are not merely focused on trade and economic issues, but also include goals with non-economic purposes, such as political and security concerns.[19] Indeed, traditional economic theory cannot clearly explain the current regional economic integration. Economic theories did not provide a satisfactory explanation of economic integration. This is because economic analysis generally assumes that a political decision has been made to create a large economic entity, and that economists need only analyse the welfare consequences of that decision and concern themselves with just a few aspects of the process of economic integration.[20] The new institutionalism approach assumes that international, including regional, institutions, such as those of Western Europe, are established to overcome market failure, solve coordination problems, and/or eliminate other obstacles to economic integration. These institutions create incentives for states to cooperate and, through a variety of mechanisms, to facilitate such cooperation. Although the new institutionalism provides valuable insights, it does not consider the political reasons for regional arrangements. Bridging the gap between the fields of economics and international relations are now two new interdisciplinary approaches, neo-functionalism[21] and economic regionalism,[22] which involve international economics and international relations, that have taken efforts to explain this new style of regional economic integration.

Forces leading to an integrated economic system tend to be self-reinforcing, as each stage of economic integration encourages further integration. Neofunctionalism[23] assumes that economic and other welfare concerns have become, or at least are becoming, more important than such traditional concerns as national security and interstate rivalry. Underlying this assumption is a belief that industrialisation, modernisation, democracy, and similar forces have transformed behavior. The theory assumes as well that the experience of integration leads to redefinition of the national interest and eventual transfer of loyalty from the nation-state to emerging regional or global entities. Neofunctionalism believes that economic cooperation will lead to political integration at either the regional or global level. The core idea of neo-functionalism is that economic and technological

---

[19] R Gilpin & JM Gilpin, *The Political Economy of International Relations* 343 (Princeton University Press, 1987). Professor Gilpin indicated: 'Albert Fishlow and Stephan Haggard have made a useful distinction between market-driven and policy-driven regional integration; certainly both political and economic considerations are involved in every regional movement. However, the relative importance of economic and political factors differs in each. Whereas the movement toward integration of Western Europe has been motivated primarily by political considerations, the motivation for North American regionalism has been more mixed, and Pacific Asian regionalism has been principally but not entirely market-driven.'

[20] See J Viner, *The Customs Union Issue* (Carnegie Endowment for International Peace, 1950).

[21] Gilpin & Gilpin, above n 19, 353.

[22] Ibid at 354.

[23] Ibid at 356.

forces are driving the world toward greater political integration. Neo-institutionalism, domestic politics, and inter-governmentalism have influenced the research interests of international relations scholars in economic and political integration. Many scholars have studied the effects of various factors including the pressures of domestic economic interests and the interests of political elites on economic and political integration. Their literature emphasises the importance of the distributive consequences of integration for domestic groups and has noted that winners support integration while losers oppose it. It has also recognised that political leaders are guided by the consequences of integration for their own political survival, and domestic interests and institutions may facilitate or discourage integration. In this regard, many political scientists share a viewpoint very similar to those of economists.[24]

Another trend impacting the scholarship was that in the late 1990s, economic regionalism became an important component in the national strategies of the major economic powers as they sought to strengthen their respective domestic economies and their international competitiveness. They attempted to achieve at the regional level what they were no longer able to achieve at the national level.[25] These efforts have caused difficulties for those involved, be they economists or political scientists, in efforts to develop a general theory of regional integration. There are too many different factors involved in regional movements around the world. The differences among various regional efforts are too great to be tested by a general rule. A universal theory explaining such a diverse and wide-ranging phenomenon is undoubtedly impossible to formulate. In fact, all the recent regional economic integration involves some degrees of political motivation, making the contributions of the political scientists in their international relations work all the more relevant to the economist.

On the other hand, international relations can not ignore the underlying economics—as technical as it may sometimes be. For example, some of the other factors influencing the movement toward economic regionalism include the increasing importance of world trade competition, and the theory of strategic trade. The earlier economists approached regionalism by emphasising trade creation and diversion as consequences of regional trading arrangements. But more recently the focus has been on the importance of internal and external economies of scale that could be achieved through economic integration.[26] Nor can international law be ignored. For example, both the economists and the international relations theorists need to

---

[24] Ibid at 354–7.
[25] R Gibb & W Michalak, *Continental Trading Blocs: The Growth of Regionalism in the World Economy* (John Wiley & Sons Inc, 1994) 1.
[26] D Dinan, *Encyclopedia of the European Union* (Lynne Rienner, 1998) 153–8.

consider the legal consequences of the failure of multilateral negotiations under the WTO as another reason that countries are seeking regional trading partners. Thus, the different fields, more than ever before, have need of each other's help, for without it they can not see or understand the whole picture.

III. CONCLUSION

The methodologies explored in this Chapter, reflecting attempts to bridge often segregated fields, are animated by the spirit of interdisciplinary collaboration. Scholars of law, economics and international politics are today facing increasingly complex global issues—but from different views. The limitations of study methods in each field have made development of IEL much more difficult than would otherwise have been the case. Nonetheless, this Chapter has explored the different intersecting theories that do exist between and among international law, international relations, and international economics to try to explain the interdisciplinary collaboration used and some possible future directions for such interdisciplinary work.

Institutionally, the establishment of international IEL institutions that appeared to cover these different fields did not resolve the inherent conflicts between the fields, such as that between international law and traditional economic goals. Rather, instead, it typically fulfilled certain discrete economic, political or legal goals. Furthermore, there are risks in this international cooperation activity or international governance. Some of those risks are in the institutional fundamental principles, such as the danger of decision rules like consensus in GATT/WTO regime, which led to the lowest common denominator approach that inhibits some countries from embracing higher standards, such as those concerning product safety or environmental considerations.[27] Furthermore, while the associated trade liberalisation increases the free movement of goods or public welfare for the international society overall, there is no direct evidence showing that every state, or their people, are better off as a result. In fact, international affairs are like a series of games. Winners and losers are not merely determined from an economic perspective, but also from a political side. For example, beyond various international economics activities, the peace-keeping process and human rights protection are important elements of both international relations and economic theory.[28] Many international economic institutions, like the WTO, World Bank, and IMF, have had to construct institutions that will follow or mediate the many public interest goals such as human

---

[27] Ibid at 15.
[28] AO Sykes, 'Comparative Advantage and the Normative Economic of International Trade Policy' (1998) 1 *J Intl Econ L* 49, 49–50.

rights, environmental protection, and labour standards. However, it's still uncertain whether the relevant international economic institutions are the appropriate place to resolve these complicated public affairs issues. In a number of cases, the optimum approach would be some kind of global response, but the institution concerned may be weak, or so fraught with the potential for abuse that the institution fails to make certain decisions.[29]

From a theoretical perspective, however, consideration of institutionalism and regime theory provide a lot of advantages for these international institutions, which can reach the purpose of better regulating international economic affairs. Furthermore, when analysing the relationship between international law and international relations, realist theory may be critical. This may be the case, because the realist does not focus on the weight of international law or international institutions, instead following the capabilities of sovereignty and state power. However, rapid changes after the Cold-War era in global economic interdependence has diminished Realism's ability to explain the factors driving international affairs. As a consequence, Regime theory, soon thereafter, became a powerful alternative to Realism. The result is the possibility of a dual agenda in interdisciplinary scholarship (institutionalism and liberalism). This offers a new hope for reaching both goals in international law and politics.

Relatedly, the potential for a closer relationship between international law and international economics may be based on the interdependence of international economic activities. IEL's operation on and between states involves many questions of traditional public international law, particularly treaty law. Additionally, IEL is important to national or municipal law, and there is thus a need for interdisciplinary research focusing on IEL. Similarly, such collaboration is apparent when combining international relations and international economics. There, for example, two new interdisciplinary theories—neo-functionalism and economic regionalism—seek to explain regional economic integration. Neo-functionalism assumes that economic cooperation leads to political integration at either the regional or global level. Economic regionalism is an important component in the national strategy of major economic powers to strengthen their respective domestic economies as well as international competitiveness.

The conclusion of this Chapter, that the different fields must work more closely together, is applicable to scholars not only in the trade and investment negotiations arena, but also in the trade and investment dispute resolution one as well. Thus, all three fields should be present not only on the scholar's desk, but also at the negotiation table or standing before the hearing.

---

[29] See Jackson, above n 13, at 16. 'There are goals for the institutions that we might need and some of these goals are addressed, eg, in the WTO. It is not clear that the WTO is going to be able to succeed with respect to all these goals, however, but they deserve some though. One important goal is the concept of a rule-oriented system that provides the predictability and stability for the system for which many see a need for a variety of reasons.'

Part II

The State & Future of International Economic Law Teaching

10

International Economic Law in US Law Schools: Evaluating Its Pedagogy and Identifying Future Challenges

KAREN E BRAVO[*]

I. INTRODUCTION

US LAW SCHOOLS share with each other and with legal educational institutions worldwide the challenge of preparing students for the increasingly globalised practice of law. International economic law (IEL) encompasses a wide spectrum of subjects including trade in goods and services, financial law, economic integration, development law, business regulation and intellectual property. The expansive scope of the fields of practice and study within the discipline presents a challenge for identifying the key issues with which scholars should try to stay up to date and the relevant material that should be imparted to students.[1] Because of the breadth and depth of developments in the various fields of international economic law, it is imperative that professionals who are engaged in teaching, practicing and writing about international economic law in US law schools, and indeed elsewhere, collaborate on a uniform understanding of essential components that constitute effective teaching of this fundamental subject area.

In preparation for a seminal conference of the American Society of International Law's (ASIL) Interest Group on International Economic Law[2] held 9–11 November, 2006 at the historic Mount Washington Resort in

---

[*] I wish to thank my Co-Rapporteurs, who assisted with the survey and analysis of the data: Craig Jackson, Professor of Law, Thurgood Marshall School of Law, Texas Southern University; and Professor Stephen Zamora, Leonard B Rosenberg Professor of Law, University of Houston Law Center. I join my co-Rapporteurs in acknowledging the invaluable assistance of Ms. Taffie Jones, JD Candidate (2008), Indiana University School of Law—Indianapolis, in administering the survey and organizing the data that form the basis of this report.

[1] *Overview of International Economic Law Research*, American Society of International Law. http://www.asil.org/resource/iel1.htm#overview (last visited 8 Jan, 2007).

[2] *Overview*, American Society of International Law. http://www.asil.org/aboutasil/index.html (last visited 8 Jan, 2007).

Bretton Woods, New Hampshire,[3] the conference chairs appointed Stephen T Zamora, Craig L Jackson and Karen E Bravo, Co-Rapporteurs for the Workshop on the Future of Teaching International Economic Law.

The Bretton Woods Conference, titled 'International Economic Law—The State and Future of the Discipline' was intended to identify:

> concrete actions that may be undertaken by the Group, its members and others in the field in order to aid the development of IEL.[4]

The Co-Rapporteurs were charged by the conference chairs with fleshing out some of the critical issues or ideas relevant to teaching international economic law that would provide catalysts for future action aimed at significantly developing the discipline of teaching IEL.

A. Surveys[5]

To help define for conference participants and parties interested in the teaching of IEL the goals and approaches for future action, the Co-Rapporteurs designed and administered two surveys to (1) provide a contemporary snapshot of the teaching of IEL, (2) identify developing trends in the substantive content and pedagogy of the subject, and (3) determine the extent of a consensus, if such did indeed exist, regarding the future of the discipline.

B. Methodology

The surveys, administered via a web-based third party site, were directed to administrators of US law schools and to professors who taught IEL at US law schools.[6] The first survey was administered to the then-current Associate Deans of all member schools of the Association of American Law Schools (AALS) through invitations disseminated on the AALS Associate Dean

---

[3] Determined to rebuild a post-war international economy, delegates from 44 nations gathered at the Mount Washington Hotel in Bretton Woods, New Hampshire to sign the Bretton Woods Agreements. These agreements led to the system that would address various economic and monetary issues on an international level through the creation of the International Monetary Fund and the International Bank for Reconstruction and Development (World Bank). See AF Lowenfeld, *International Economic Law* (Oxford University Press, 2002) 502–3.

[4] *Annual conference preliminary program*, American Society of International Law. http://www.asil.org/pdfs/ielgconf0606.pdf (last visited 8 Jan, 2007).

[5] To view the full results of the 2 surveys, see http://www.indylaw.indiana.edu/instructors/Bravo/FinalIEL_ADPresentation.pdf and http://www.indylaw.indiana.edu/instructors/Bravo/FinalIEL_ProfPresentation.pdf, respectively.

[6] In addition, in an attempt to garner a comparative perspective on the issue, via the ASIL International Economic Law Interest Group listserv, the Co-Rapporteurs unsuccessfully solicited volunteers to adapt the survey for administration outside the United States.

listserv.[7] In many US law schools, the position of Associate Dean is held on a rotating basis by a senior faculty member who consequently straddles the worlds of administration and academia. The responsibilities of the typical Associate Dean of academic affairs usually include class scheduling and curricular development. As a result, the Co-Rapporteurs believed that associate deans would be most familiar with the curricular offerings of individual schools. The survey of professors of IEL was administered via direct email invitation to all professors of International Business Transactions (IBT) listed in the 2005–06 AALS Directory of Law Teachers. The Co-Rapporteurs undertook to report results without attribution in order to encourage participation and to fulfill their goal of identifying overarching similarities or differences rather than trends specific to individual schools.[8]

Since the survey of law school administrators focused on Associate Deans at AALS member schools, the surveys' findings necessarily report only on the teaching of IEL in law schools which are members of the AALS. Consequently, the survey did not gather information from non-AALS law schools or from schools with graduate programs in related disciplines, such as business, economics or foreign relations, all of which may offer courses in IEL. The decision to target self-identified professors of IBT at AALS member schools may have affected the survey findings as follows: (1) new arrivals to the legal academy, who would not have been listed in the 2005–06 Directory; (2) professors who changed their teaching assignments to include IBT since their last report to the AALS; and (3) professors who teach IEL in undergraduate or business schools or other graduate institutions were not invited to participate. In addition, professors at AALS member schools who teach in related fields, such as Trade Regulation and Public International Law, for example, were not targeted for participation in the survey.

The initial results of the surveys were tabulated and presented at the Bretton Woods Conference. However, a final round of invitations, accompanied by the raw initial data, was disseminated to the targeted associate deans and professors following the conference and additional responses were gathered until the surveys were closed at the end of the 2006 calendar year. Associate deans representing a total of 37 AALS member schools[9] and 70 individual IBT professors of a total of 581 invitees participated in their respective surveys.

The results are reported below, organised by individual survey and specific questions. The report concludes with the Author's interpretation of the raw data and a report on the concrete actions suggested by participants at the Bretton Woods Conference.

---

[7] See The Association of American Law Schools, http://www.aals.org/about.php (last visited 8 Jan, 2007).

[8] In addition, the Co-Rapporteurs, who also teach international economic law courses, abstained from participating.

[9] In some cases, more than one administrator from an individual school responded to the invitation distributed via the AALS Associate Dean listserv.

138 *Karen E Bravo*

II. SURVEY RESULTS

A. Associate Deans' Survey (44 respondents)

Associate Deans representing a diverse array of law schools in the United States participated in the survey. No single geographic area predominated, and schools throughout the reputational spectrum were represented among the 44 survey respondents. However, some common themes emerged from the results.

Geographic Regions Represented by the Law Schools of the Participating Associate Deans

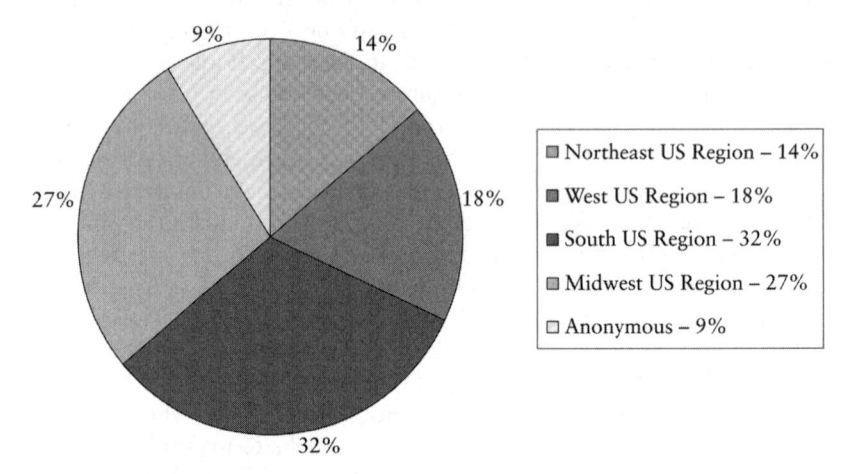

- Northeast US Region – 14%
- West US Region – 18%
- South US Region – 32%
- Midwest US Region – 27%
- Anonymous – 9%

Popularity of IEL Among JD Students[10]

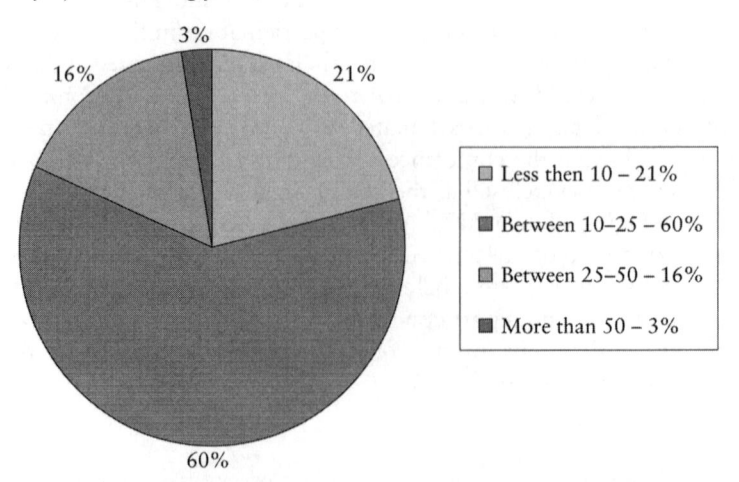

- Less then 10 – 21%
- Between 10–25 – 60%
- Between 25–50 – 16%
- More than 50 – 3%

---

[10] Participants responded to the following question: 'Approximately what percentage of your students takes at least one (1) International Economic Law course during their JD studies?'

The majority (more than 60 per cent) of the responding schools reported that between 10–25 per cent of their JD students enroll in at least one IEL course during their law school studies. 21 per cent of the respondent schools reported that less than 10 per cent of their student body enrolls in at least one IEL course, while 16 per cent of the respondent schools reported that between 25–50 per cent of their student body enrolls in at least one IEL course. In addition, three per cent of the participating law schools reported that more than 50 per cent of their JD students enroll in at least one IEL course during their law school tenure.

(i) IEL Course Offerings and their Frequency[11]

A majority of the Associate Deans who responded to the survey reported that their respective law schools offer some select IEL courses each year. However, other courses covering more specialised areas of IEL were offered only occasionally, while some survey participants reported that many courses were not currently offered at their individual institutions. The following chart indicates the frequency of the IEL course offerings at the schools represented by the respondents.

Course	Annually	Occasionally	Not Currently Offered
International Antitrust Law	2	5	34
International Business Transactions	30	9	5
International Commercial Law	7	16	19
International Economic Law	2	6	31
International Labor Law	2	3	32
International Trade Law (Law of WTO)	21	11	10
International Tax Law	12	19	9
US Customs Law (Import or Export Regulation)	4	2	34
International Banking Law	3	4	33
International Financial Law	2	8	33
International Capital Markets (International Securities Regulation)	1	3	35
Regional Trade Agreements (NAFTA or otherwise)	6	17	19

(continued)

[11] Participants responded to the following question: 'Indicate when the following International Economic Law Courses are taught.' The course choices given are included in the list reproduced in the text (*see* IEL Course Offerings and their Frequency), and the respondents were asked to choose one of the following: 'Each Year,' 'Occasionally' and 'Not Currently Offered.'

(Continued)

Course	Annually	Occasionally	Not Currently Offered
International Intellectual Property Law	19	6	17
Licensing and Technology Transfer	10	8	22
International Contracting	1	4	33
International Enforcement of Intellectual Property	4	6	29
European Economic Integration	11	13	14
Foreign Investment Law	5	4	29
Law and Economic Development	6	4	29
International Project Finance	4	1	32

(ii) Additional Coverage of IEL[12]

A number of the Associate Deans reported that their schools have incorporated some of the IEL topics into other classes, rather than offering stand-alone courses, but did not indicate the reasons for this curricular choice. Those other classes that Associate Deans considered to be IEL-related included: China Trade Simulation; Chinese Investment Law; International Insolvency; Investment and Trade Laws of the Middle East; International Financial Architecture; Stock Market Development; International Negotiations; International E-Commerce; Human Rights in the Marketplace; Islamic Law; Comparative Government Procurement; International Pharmaceutical Regulation; International Protection of Human Rights; Cross-Border Transactions in Latin America; US & EU Approaches to Regulating Chemicals; Biotechnology and Nanotechnology; and Comparative Law.

(iii) The Importance of IEL Courses to Law Schools' Curricula[13]

The varying responses offered by the respondents ranged from 'essential,' 'very important,' 'significant,' 'moderately important,' 'increasingly important,' and 'semi-important' to that 'of limited importance,' 'not important,' and 'nonexistent.' A majority of the responses indicated that the courses were either moderately or very important and/or if currently limited in importance, that courses were increasing in their significance for the schools. A small number of the participating law schools offer

---

[12] Participants responded to the following question: 'Are there any other classes on International Economic Law that were not listed above and how often are they taught?'
[13] Participants responded to the following question: 'How important is International Economic Law as an element of your curriculum?' The question was open-ended, with no pre-determined choices offered by the survey.

certificate programs (to both JD and LLM students) in IEL. Other respondents reported that their schools struggle to offer IEL courses, due to unavailability of faculty to teach these subjects or a perceived lack of clear necessity to incorporate these topics into their school's curriculum.

(iv) Adequacy of Preparation for Practice[14]

34 of 44 respondents answered this question. A significant number of the respondents affirmatively responded that the courses currently offered at their institutions do adequately prepare outgoing law students for the practice of IEL.[15] However, a number of associate deans expressed some doubts that this was the case. Some participants averred that the courses fundamentally or rudimentarily prepared students, who would later need more thorough review and instruction. Others commented that some discrete areas are likely taught more effectively than others. A lack of resources, including available faculty, was also reported in response to this question.

(v) IEL Opportunities Outside of the Classroom

(a) Moot Competitions[16]   36 of 44 respondents answered this question. 32 per cent of the respondents indicated that their institutions provide their students with access to the Willem VIS International Commercial Arbitration Moot program, 29 per cent reported that they provide access to the Jessup International Moot Court Competition, and 14 per cent provide access to the Georgetown University International Trade (WTO) Moot program.[17] Additionally, three participants indicated that their institutions offer further opportunities in the Space Law

---

[14] Participants responded to the following question: 'Do the course offerings at your law school adequately prepare your students for the practice of international economic law?'

[15] It is not clear how the responses to this question would compare with responses to questions regarding the adequacy of preparation in domestic law subjects. However, the Author believes that it would be unusual for law schools to express uncertainty regarding the adequacy of their preparation of students for the practice of strictly domestic legal fields.

[16] Participants responded to the following question: 'Does your law school participate in any extracurricular activities that generate interest in International Economic Law, such as the following?' The listed options were the Willem VIS International Commercial Arbitration Moot; Georgetown University WTO Moot; Jessup International Moot Court Competition; Niagara International Moot; Space Law Moot; Inter-American Moot Court Competition; and None.

[17] Information on the VIS, Jessup and Georgetown International Trade Moot Court Competitions are available at the following internet sites. See Willem VIS International Commercial Arbitration Moot—http://cisgw3.law.pace.edu/vis.html; http://www.cisgmoot.org/; Jessup International Moot Court Competition, http://www.ilsa.org/jessup/; Institute of International Economic Law—Georgetown University WTO Moot, http://www.law.georgetown.edu/iiel/mootcourt/about.html.

program, the Niagara Moot program, and the Inter-American Moot Court Competition.[18]

(b) Study Abroad Programs[19]   The majority of the responding schools do not offer a study abroad program that emphasises IEL. However, several Associate Deans reported that some of their institution's study abroad programs may include some IEL content. Reproduced verbatim below, the responses were as follows:

> International Commercial Arbitration in Austria, Vienna, Venice, Salzburg, Budapest;
> Economic and Human Rights Law in Innsbruck and Austria;
> Ireland, China, or Korea Summer Programs;
> International Entertainment & Media in London;
> Intellectual Property Law Centre in Munich;
> Transnational Business in Salzburg;
> NAFTA in San Diego, Mexico;
> Summer institutes in Geneva or Hong Kong;
> Introduction to EU Law, Comparative Labor & Employment Law, Introduction to Comparative Property Law in Vienna; and
> Comparative Property Law in Brazil.

(c) Internships and Other Opportunities[20]   In addition, some Associate Deans reported that their schools provide for individual student placements in internships and externships during both the academic year and summer terms. The locations included Mexico, Switzerland, The Netherlands, Brazil, Spain, and Argentina as well as other American Bar Association (ABA) approved summer program offerings. Lastly, Associate Deans provided information on their schools' LLM programs tailored towards IEL subjects.

B. Law Professors' Survey (70 Respondents)[21]

This survey differed from the Associate Deans' survey, which sought an institutional/administrator's perspective. The Law Professors' survey, in

---

[18] Information on the Manfred Lachs Space Law Moot Court Competition, Niagara International Moot Court Competition and Inter-American Human Rights Moot Court Competitions are available at the following internet sites. See Space Law Moot, http://www.spacemoot.org; Niagara International Moot, http://www.cusli.org/niagara; and Inter-American Moot, http://www.wcl.american.edu/hracademy/mcourt.

[19] Participants responded to the following question: 'Does your law school sponsor a study abroad program emphasizing International Economic Law?'

[20] Participants responded to the following question: 'Describe any programs for placing students in internships that emphasize International Economic Law (eg, at an international economic organisation, the Court of International Trade, or other institution).'

[21] The higher raw number of responses by professors of IEL (70 responses) does not represent a higher rate of responses than the 44 respondents to the Associate Deans' survey.

contrast, sought to elicit the individualised experience and perceptions of professors of IEL. As with the Associate Deans' survey, no one geographic area of the U.S predominated. Many professors of both active and Emeritus status, representing diverse law schools nationwide, participated.

(i) IEL Course Offerings[22]

IEL professors (68 respondents of 70 participants) reported that the following IEL courses were offered at their schools:

Courses	Percentage of Respondents
International Antitrust Law	2.94
International Business Transactions	13.03
International Commercial Law	4.62
International Economic Law	3.78
International Labor Law	1.47
International Trade Law (Law of WTO)	9.66
International Tax Law	9.24
US Customs Law (Import and Export Regulation)	1.26
International Banking Law	2.94
International Financial Law	3.78
International Capital Markets (International Securities Regulation)	2.52
Regional Trade Agreements (NAFTA or otherwise)	4.20
International Intellectual Property Law	6.72
Licensing and Technology Transfer	2.52
International Contracting	2.52
International Enforcement of Intellectual Property	2.10
European Economic Integration	6.51
Foreign Investment Law	2.52
Law and Economic Development	2.52
International Project Finance	2.10
Other	6.51[23]

With respect to the Associate Deans' survey, responses were received from administrators from 37 of approximately 200 AALS member schools, while only 70 of the 581 professors of IEL responded to the survey. In some instances, more than 1 Associate Dean responded from an individual school.

[22] Participants were asked to 'Select the International Economic Law courses taught at your school.'

[23] Under the category 'Other,' 0.84 % of professors indicated that International Arbitration was taught at their schools; 0.42% indicated that the following courses were taught at their school: Transnational Litigation, International Law; Globalization, and International Environmental Law; and 0.21% of professors listed International Enforcement of Intellectual Property, International Business Franchise Law, Problems of World Order, Comparative Commercial Law, International Criminal Law, International Trade Workshop/International Legal

Based on the responses, IBT, International Trade Law (Law of the WTO), International Tax Law, International Intellectual Property, and European Economic Integration are the most widely offered IEL courses in US law schools.

(ii) Professors' Own Coverage of IEL[24]

When asked about the courses that *they* teach, the IEL professors again reported IBT as the most frequently offered course—18.27 per cent of the respondents. The other courses most frequently taught by the participants include: International Trade Law (Law of WTO) (14.72 per cent), International Financial Law (7.11 per cent), IEL (6.60 per cent) and International Tax Law (6.09 per cent). Other courses taught by the respondents and the percentage of such participants who reported that they teach them are indicated in the table below.

Course	Percentage of Respondents Who Teach Course
International Antitrust Law	1.52
International Commercial Law	3.05
International Banking Law	2.03
International Capital Markets (International Securities Regulation)	2.54
Regional Trade Agreements (NAFTA or otherwise)	3.05
International Intellectual Property Law	1.52
International Contracting	0.51
International Enforcement of Intellectual Property	0.51
European Economic Integration	3.55
Foreign Investment Law	3.05
Law and Economic Development	2.54
International Project Finance	1.02

Individual participants also reported that they teach the following courses that were not listed in the survey: International Litigation and Arbitration; International E-Commerce; International Business Franchise Law; Transnational Litigation; International Legal Regimes; International Arbitration; International Environmental Law; International Sales (commercial law); International Law Process (WTO adjudication); Globalization;

Regimes, International eCommerce, Specialized Seminars, Law and Economic Development, Latin American Law, International Art Law, International Sales, Combating Corruption and Money Laundering in International Business Transactions, Comparative Contract Law, EU Competition Law, US Foreign Trade Law, and Licensing and Technology Transfer.

[24] Participants were asked to: 'Select the International Economic Law courses that you teach.'

Combating Corruption and Money Laundering in IBT; International Art Law; Corporate Social Responsibility in IBT; Comparative Contract Laws; Transnational Private Equity; International Commercial Arbitration; and specialised seminars.

(iii) Coverage of Individual IEL Subject Areas

The survey was also designed to ascertain the extent of the coverage of specific IEL topics in individual courses. Respondents were asked[25] to indicate which of the following substantive topics were covered in their IEL courses: International Economic Organizations; Trade Liberalization & Trade Law Principles; WTO Dispute Mechanisms; International Banking; International Intellectual Property Ownership & Protection; International Competition Law; International Monetary Law; Regionalism; Customs Law; Transborder Investment; CISG, Incoterms, Unidroit, and ICC; Transborder Dispute Resolution; and Transborder Regulation of Securities' Markets.

The responses yielded a snapshot of the coverage of IEL topics in each particular IEL course enumerated in the survey. Of the five most popular courses, IBT and IEL offered the broadest array of coverage of specific topics: each of the listed topic areas was checked by the respondents. However, with respect to each particular topic, the number of professors who covered the listed material varied with either a large majority or small minority of professors covering the listed subject areas.

For example, as shown in the table below, with respect to IBT, the subject areas most frequently covered were 'CISG, Incoterms, Unidroit, ICC' (29

Subject Area	Number of Professors Who Cover Subject in IBT Course	Number of Professors Who Cover Subject in IEL Course
International Economic Organizations (ie, the Bretton Woods System)	19	13
Trade Liberalization & Trade Law Principles	18	12
WTO Dispute Mechanisms	13	10
International Banking	12	5
International Intellectual Property Ownership & Protection	22	4
International Competition Law	16	3
International Monetary Law	8	8

(continued)

---

[25] Participants were asked to 'Select the International Economic Law topics that you cover in your courses.'

146 *Karen E Bravo*

(Continued)

Subject Area	Number of Professors Who Cover Subject in IBT Course	Number of Professors Who Cover Subject in IEL Course
Regionalism	9	6
Customs Law	15	4
Transborder Investment	25	7
CISG, Incoterms, Unidroit, and ICC	29	2
Transborder Dispute Resolution	25	5
Transborder Regulation of Securities' Markets	3	1

of 33 respondents), 'Transborder Investment' and 'Transborder Dispute Resolution' (each with 25 of 33 respondents), 'International Intellectual Property Ownership and Protection' (22 of 33 respondents), 'International Economic Organizations (ie the Bretton Woods System)' (19 of 33 respondents) and 'Trade Liberalization and Trade Law Principles' (18 of 33 respondents). For IEL, the subject areas most frequently covered were International Economic Organizations, Trade Liberalization and Trade Law Principles, and WTO Dispute Mechanisms.

For International Trade Law, the course ranking second with respect to the number of participants who reported that they teach it, the coverage of the specific subject areas by the 29 respondents was as follows:

Subject Area	Number of Professors Who Cover Subject in International Trade Law Course
International Economic Organizations	21
Trade Liberalization & Trade Law Principles	27
WTO Dispute Mechanisms	29
International Banking	1
International Intellectual Property Ownership & Protection	13
International Competition Law	1
International Monetary Law	0
Regionalism	17
Customs Law	14
Transborder Investment	6
CISG, Incoterms, Unidroit, and ICC	0
Transborder Dispute Resolution	5
Transborder Regulation of Securities' Markets	0

The less widely offered IEL courses do not cover as broad an array of the listed topic areas, reflecting the more specialised nature of those courses. For example, as reflected below, the four respondents who teach International Banking Law reported that they covered only the following six topics in that course: International Economic Organisations, WTO Dispute Mechanisms, International Banking, International Monetary Law, Regionalism and Transborder Investment.

Subject Area	Number of Professors Who Cover Subject in International Banking Law Course
International Economic Organizations	3
Trade Liberalization & Trade Law Principles	0
WTO Dispute Mechanisms	1
International Banking	4
International Intellectual Property Ownership & Protection	0
International Competition Law	0
International Monetary Law	3
Regionalism	1
Customs Law	0
Transborder Investment	1
CISG, Incoterms, Unidroit, and ICC	0
Transborder Dispute Resolution	0
Transborder Regulation of Securities' Markets	0

In response to a survey question[26] requesting additional subject areas that may not have been included in the list provided by the survey and reproduced above, the participants listed several in-depth content areas not offered as stand-alone courses that were also covered in some of their courses.[27]

---

[26] Participants responded to the following question: 'Are there any additional IEL topics not outlined in Questions 3 and 4 that you teach and in which courses are these concepts taught?'

[27] The responses were as follows: International Financial Crimes; the trade law crossover in International Environmental Law; taxation in IBT; CISG as introduced in basic Contracts; Foreign Corrupt Practices Act (US); OECD Anti Bribery Convention; OAS Anti Bribery Convention; EU Directives barring bribery of foreign officials; UN Convention on Corruption Bank Secrecy Act as amended by the US Patriot Act (anti-money laundering); Financial Action Task Force (OECD anti-money laundering); and EU Directives on Money Laundering; tax evasion and anti-money laundering/anti-terrorism issues in Banking law and National Security Law; Comparative Law; Export Controls and Trade Sanctions; COGSA;

(iv) Perceived Fundamental Competences

The survey also attempted to ascertain whether a consensus existed as to the IEL topics that a student should cover in order to understand fundamental issues in the field.[28] As reflected in the table below, the responses reflect a broad diversity of opinion regarding the core areas with which a student of IEL should be familiar.

Subject Area	Percentage of Respondents in Agreement
International Economic Organizations	11.43
Trade Liberalization & Trade Law Principles	12.99
Regionalism	7.01
Customs Law	4.16
WTO Dispute Mechanisms	10.13
International Banking	3.38
Transborder Investment	10.65
International Carriage & Delivery of Goods: CISG, Incoterms, Unidroit, ICC	8.83
Transborder Dispute Resolution	9.61
International Intellectual Property Ownership & Protection	6.23
Transborder Regulation of Securities Markets	2.34
International Competition Law	4.42
International Monetary Law	3.12

In addition to the topics listed in the survey, some respondents suggested that knowledge of the following topics was also required for a fundamental understanding of IEL: export controls and trade sanctions; comparative law; private and public international law; prohibitions on bribery of foreign officials; law of treaties, especially with respect to international environmental law; international tax; IBT;[29] franchise opportunities a range of international financial agreements and development issues in International Financial Law; Sustainable Development Planning in International Environmental Law; Trade & Environment, Trade & Labor, and Trade & Human Rights in International Trade Law; currency transactions—how to protect oneself with forward contracts, futures, fluctuating currencies; laws regulating Offers and Sales of Business Franchises and Business Opportunities; and Relationships between Franchisors and Franchisees—taught in International Business Franchise Law; and International Dispute Resolution through Arbitration.

[28] Participants responded to the following question: 'In your opinion, which International Economic Law topics do you think an IEL student must take in order to understand fundamental issues in the field?'

[29] The inclusion of IBT in response to this question and the next suggests some degree of confusion. While IBT is generally perceived as a gateway course in which a wide variety of topic areas are covered, at least one participant conceptualised 'IBT' itself as a topic embedded within another course.

alongside franchisor/franchisee relationships; and international business and investment arbitration.

(v) Institutional Coverage of Perceived Fundamental Competences[30]

As indicated in the table below, the coverage of topics considered fundamental by the respondents generally tracked the responding professor's expressed perception of the importance of the specific subject matter. In combination, the responses from these two questions suggest either a great deal of autonomy or buy-in on the part of IEL professors in US law schools with respect to the specific subject areas covered in their courses.

Subject Area	Institutional Coverage
International Economic Organizations	11.76
Trade Liberalization & Trade Law Principles	12.02
Regionalism	5.37
Customs Law	9.97
WTO Dispute Mechanisms	4.35
International Banking	9.72
Transborder Investment	7.93
International Carriage & Delivery of Goods: CISG, Incoterms, Unidroit, ICC	10.23
Transborder Dispute Resolution	6.39
International Intellectual Property Ownership & Protection	7.42
Transborder Regulation of Securities Markets	2.81
International Competition Law	4.09
International Monetary Law	3.32

In addition to the topics listed in the survey, some respondents identified as fundamental a number of other topics taught at their schools: international environmental law; public international law; IBT;[31] export controls and trade sanctions; international business arbitration; and franchise opportunities alongside franchisor/franchisee relationships.

(vi) Non-Traditional Pedagogical Choices[32]

As detailed in the table below, respondents reported that all of the non-traditional pedagogical methodologies listed in the survey were utilised in their courses, although in varying proportions.

---

[30] Participants responded to the following question: 'Which of the topics that you checked or wrote in above does your school cover?'
[31] See above n 29.
[32] Participants responded to the following question: 'In addition to lectures, which of the following methodologies do you use in your IEL classes?'

Methodologies	Percentage of Reported Usage
Negotiation and conduct of mock transactions	35.14
Internships	10.81
Moot court	16.22
Seminar-style discussion/dialogue	4.39
Problem solving approach and exercises	6.75
WTO case-law research	1.35
Papers	1.35
Videoconferencing	1.35
Student presentations	1.35
Documentary films	1.35
Field trips (ie, to the stock exchange)	1.35
Class debates	1.35

(vii) Suggestions for Teaching IEL in US Schools[33]

The suggestions of IEL professors responding to the survey revealed several broad themes. These included the need for earlier and more coherent introduction of students to IEL concepts; broader course offerings—including specialised subject areas; increased institutional support aimed at the better integration of IEL concepts in the core curriculum; and an increased profile highlighting the importance of IEL in light of the more globalised practice environment that awaits students.

Among the specific suggestions were: (i) that students be required to take either a public international law or IEL course earlier in their law school careers; (ii) a broader focus on the transnational or comparative perspective, rather than the current focus on US domestic law treatment of IEL issues; (iii) the introduction and integration of more IEL elements into other courses, such as intellectual property, antitrust and securities law; (iv) broader coverage in the curriculum of more specialised IEL courses, such as international banking, taxation and securities regulation; (v) greater coordination of course content by IEL faculty to avoid potential conflicts or redundancies in the subject areas covered in particular courses; (vi) greater exposure to and contact with other parts of the world; (vi) more institutional support; (vii) public relations outreach to students and institutions regarding the importance of IEL; and (viii) an increase in the course offerings of individual schools.

---

[33] Participants responded to the following two questions: 'Please describe your suggestions for changes in the teaching of IEL courses in your school?' and 'Please describe your suggestions for changes in teaching IEL courses in US law schools?'

(viii) Suggestions for Institutional Support[34]

Survey participants identified various types of institutional support that would enhance the teaching of IEL. These included: research grants for the development of new courses, including faculty's onsite research outside the United States; funding for faculty exchanges and expert speakers, including IEL practitioners and government lawyers, as well as policy makers from IEL institutions; funding for student internships with IEL institutions, such as the Bretton Woods institutions and the WTO; and increased use of available fora, such as the American Bar Association, ASIL and AALS, for the exchange of knowledge and ideas.

III. INTERPRETING THE DATA

The data arising from the two surveys yields a contemporary portrait of the teaching of IEL in US law schools, and identifies trends that will impact the development of pedagogy utilised with respect to the discipline. Survey participants among both the Associate Deans and the targeted professors expressed some frustration regarding institutional support for IEL and its place (perceived and desired) in the law school curriculum. In particular, survey participants expressed a strong strain of doubt regarding the adequacy of the preparation for practice offered by US schools to their students. Other concerns included the manner in which IEL should be, and has been, integrated into the curriculum, and the lack of available resources that might otherwise be aimed at expansion of course offerings. The need to provide more practical experiences for students and greater coordination of course content was also mentioned. Some aspects of the data are discussed below.

A. Gateway Courses

IBT and International Trade Law (Law of WTO) have emerged as the two most widely offered courses. There is a general consensus as to the content of the IBT course, in that some or all participants reported inclusion of all the suggested specific subject areas listed in the survey.[35] This wider substantive coverage would appear to be appropriate, offering law students exposure to a wide range of concepts and topics and revealing the fundamental interconnections among superficially stand-alone areas of

---

[34] Participants responded to the following question: 'What kinds of institutional support (research grants, teaching assistants, faculty exchanges, etc) do you think would be helpful for the teaching of IEL courses—and what possible sources of such support can be suggested (government, foundations, etc)?'.

[35] See Perceived Fundamental Competences, above.

law.[36] The widespread offering of International Trade Law indicates that it, too, is a gateway course. Its popularity no doubt stems from greater general awareness of the impact of multi- and bi-lateral trade negotiations and treaties on global economic relations, as well as their implications for US domestic law and economic conditions. Although not offering coverage as extensive as that provided in IBT courses, International Trade Law appears to provide a good foundation for a student's initial exploration of IEL courses dispelling, through the WTO jurisprudence and domestic trade regulation and disputes, for example, the separation of public and private international law.

B. Depth and Breadth of Expertise

US law schools, as a group, offer a wide variety of IEL courses. Participants reported that more than 20 different IEL courses are taught in US law schools. In addition, responses to the Associate Deans' survey indicated that IEL concepts are embedded in other curricular offerings.[37] Further, a diverse array of more specialised courses illustrates the range of interests of teachers of the discipline. Those specialised courses included International Antitrust, International Securities Regulation, International Licensing and Technology Transfer, Franchising, and others. Using the offering and teaching of these courses as an indicator, it is possible to identify a considerable expertise in the various IEL subject areas within the US legal academy. That pool of expertise represents a valuable resource for the continued development of the discipline of teaching IEL, one which is perhaps not fully tapped.

However, while the apparent depth and breadth of expertise may indeed exist, it is unclear whether that expertise is concentrated in and perhaps limited to particular institutions which have decided to offer curricular concentrations in the area of IEL or international law in general. Such a conclusion would be supported by Associate Dean complaints of limited faculty availability.[38] That is, IEL faculty may indeed be in short supply in a significant number of US law schools outside a circumscribed geographic and/or reputational sphere.

The interrelationships of other factors revealed by the surveys are worth exploring. As discussed above,[39] the breadth of coverage of specific subject areas within the discipline varies, depending on the more specialised

---

[36] Such as international trade law and international economic institutions, eg.
[37] See Additional Coverage of IEL, above, listing China Trade Simulation and Investment and Trade in the Middle East, among others.
[38] See Importance of IEL Courses to Law School Curricula, above.
[39] See Coverage of Individual IEL Subject Areas, above.

nature of particular courses. Also noted is the fact that the coverage of specific subject areas appeared to track the respondent professors' opinions regarding fundamental competences.[40] In combination, these factors suggest that professors of IEL have marked control in directing the substantive content of their courses. If the survey results do reveal that degree of autonomy, it highlights the power of IEL professors in the United States to direct the substantive content of their institutions' IEL offerings. This further suggests that a coordinated effort by IEL professors to standardise or harmonise IEL offerings and coverage in US law schools could effectuate concrete changes. Alternatively, the professors' responses may reflect institutional biases regarding the desired content of IEL courses, biases that they have absorbed and now hold. Whatever the reasons for the congruence in the two responses, the relative uniformity of reported beliefs about fundamental competences across institutions reflects an apparently widespread consensus regarding some aspects of the pedagogy of IEL topics in US law schools—at a minimum, with respect to the identity and substantive content of the introductory IEL courses.

C. Institutional Support and Student Participation

In light of the apparent depth and breadth of expertise among faculty, the lack of institutional support reported by both Associate Deans and faculty, as well as the relatively low student participation in IEL courses call for further investigation. The low levels of student interest[41] may be related to the low institutional support. That is, the low student participation rates may be based upon such factors as students' perception of the lack of relevance of or need for IEL in practice and/or lack of professional opportunities after graduation. Further the very names of the courses may seem daunting to students and feed into student perception of the IEL subject area as overly technical, requiring math-based skills and/or overly tedious, thus negatively affecting their rates of participation in IEL courses. In addition, in some regions of the United States, integration in the global economy may appear to be less advanced than in others, so that the geographic location of the law school that the student attends may play a role in student perceptions of the importance of the IEL subject area. Institutional support, exemplified in such factors as the placement of IEL courses in the law school's class schedule and/or lack of moot court and other experiential offerings, may interact with those student misperceptions to lower the rate of student participation in such courses. Therefore, the low participation rates may

---

[40] See Perceived Fundamental Competences and Institutional Coverage of Perceived Fundamental Competences, above.
[41] See Popularity Among JD Students, above.

be symbiotic with low rates of institutional support, since institutions may be leery of devoting resources to courses in which students appear to have little interest.

The foregoing discussion suggests that increased institutional support would stimulate student participation in IEL subject areas. Such support could include, for example, greater care directed toward the placement of IEL courses in class schedules and public relations efforts directed toward introducing students to the importance and interest of the subject area. Additionally, if IEL professors enjoy the freedom to mold their curriculum suggested by the data, the professors have the ability to design the courses they teach to maximise student interest, participation and satisfaction.

IV. CONFERENCE PROCEEDINGS

Following the Co-Rapporteurs' presentations of their findings at the Bretton Woods conference, the wider discussion centred on the following issues: (1) the place of IEL in the law school curriculum; (2) the role of practical or more experiential pedagogical methodologies in the teaching of IEL; and (3) institutional and outside support for the teaching of IEL and the discipline of IEL in general. Broad consensus emerged during the discussion of the foregoing matters, to the following effect.

A. Curricular Changes

In order to meet the challenge of preparing law students for practice in an increasingly globalised world, a more interventionist model of curricular development is recommended. Continuing a wait-and-see approach, whereby only *interested* students are exposed to IEL and/or international law would be detrimental. IEL (and public international law, more generally) including a strong comparative perspective, should be introduced earlier in students' law school training.[42] Such earlier introduction could take place on either a stand-alone basis or through greater integration of IEL and international law subjects in the core curriculum of law schools. In order to meet this goal, conference participants acknowledged that some changes in course design would be required, including the use of supplementary materials not currently utilised in core domestic law courses in US law schools. In this regard, the responses of Associate Deans summarised above under 'Additional Coverage of IEL' supra, is worthy

---

[42] There was some discussion of Harvard Law School's recent announcement that international law would be a required course in the first year for all their JD students. See Harvard Law School, http://www.law.harvard.edu/news/2006/10/06_curriculum.php (last visited 8 Jan, 2007).

of further exploration. The reported embedding of IEL concepts in alternate courses may reflect an already existing trend toward integration of IEL into the current curriculum. This reported trend may be the result of attempts to overcome limited institutional and/or faculty resources in the IEL field by the efficient use of limited resources. Under current circumstances, institutional and other resource constraints may already be leading toward the coordinated approach advocated by the conference participants and some survey respondents. The possible pre-existence of that trend does not, however, undercut the expressed need for a more directed and interventionist approach to curricular reform. It may indicate, however, that such coordination already may be occurring due to the confluence of other factors.

B. Adoption of Available Technology

As technology advances, so should the variety of pedagogical methods utilised by law professors. More concretely, attendees supported the use of video-conferencing to offer transborder courses to students within and outside the United States. The experience of being in a transborder class (even virtually) would foster cross-cultural and comparative legal understanding among students in the United States, as well as their counterparts in other countries. In furtherance of the goal of greater utilisation of available and helpful technology, attendees suggested greater coordination and integration among IEL professors and their schools to form networks both inside and outside the United States that could facilitate such transborder interactions. The participants also discussed the creation of a database of course materials that would utilise an experiential pedagogical approach.

C. Moot Court Competitions

Similarly, conference attendees agreed that participation in international moot competitions creates invaluable experiences for students. As such, additional moots and other competitions (such as arbitration and/or negotiation) specialising in IEL issues would improve students' preparation for global practice. Other experiential learning opportunities that attendees believed would foster a comparative perspective and greater understanding of IEL include: student and faculty transborder exchanges, internships outside the United States, and summer abroad programs with a focus on the practice of IEL.

Finally, in order to address these issues, the conference participants concurred with survey respondents regarding the need to seek out greater support for teaching the discipline of IEL. That is, in addition to institutional support at individual law schools, participants pointed to the AALS and ASIL as domestic US fora with influence outside the United States which could provide an interested audience for discussion of the curricular and other changes suggested above. Furthermore, IEL private practitioners attending the conference suggested that law firms and other institutions, such as corporations or IEL intergovernmental institutions, represented other potential sources of support. Finally, conference participants indicated that institutions and fora outside the United States also constitute potential avenues for deepening the opportunities for experiential learning.

V. CONCLUSION

In accordance with the charge to the Co-Rapporteurs, the information gathered by the two surveys provides a contemporary picture of the status of the teaching of IEL in US law schools, revealing trends in pedagogy, substantive content, and the types of courses offered by US law schools. The two surveys also allowed the Co-Rapporteurs and the attendees of the Bretton Woods Conference to identify concerns widely held among professors and administrators about the role and status of the discipline in their individual schools and in the United States generally, as well as the need and desire for more institutional support to improve the preparation of students.

Conference participants identified fundamental issues that should be acted upon by IEL practitioners, ASIL IEL Interest Group members, and others interested in the discipline.[43] The focus rests on the need for greater resources, both institutional and faculty; alternate teaching methods, including incorporation of video conference and other technology; and greater coordination among state and private practitioners and the academy. Further, in the Author's opinion, a fundamental next step toward enhancing the study and teaching of IEL is the administration outside the United States of a similar information gathering survey that will facilitate both a comparative perspective and a movement toward international harmonisation.

---

[43] See Curricular Changes, Adoption of Available Technology and Moot Court Competitions, above.

11

Venutian Scholarship in a Martian Landscape: Celebrating and Reflecting on Women in International Economic Law Teaching and Scholarship

TRACEY EPPS & ROSE ANN MacGILLIVRAY[*]

INTRODUCTION

To COMMEMORATE INTERNATIONAL Women's Day in 2006, the Faculty of Law at the University of Toronto paid tribute to the achievements and contributions of its women graduates. As part of the recognition of the accomplishments of the Faculty's alumni generally, 19 'trailblazers' were honoured, from the first woman barrister in Canada to women pioneers in the corporate world. The occasion was a source of inspiration for all who were present. For us, the event provoked a desire to look at the achievements and contributions of women in the field of international economic law. The conference held at Bretton Woods in November 2006 took stock of this discipline and provided a fitting opportunity to examine the past, present, and future contributions of women to the field.

The purpose of this Chapter is first, to *celebrate* the contributions of women to the field of international economic law teaching and scholarship; second, to *quantify* the current representation of women in international economic law teaching and scholarship; and third, to *reflect* upon women's experiences and perspectives in order to see how they might be harnessed to strengthen the discipline.

This Chapter is organised in two parts. Part I provides contextual background for the celebration, quantification, and reflection to follow. First, it

---

[*] We would like to acknowledge and thank the women who shared their valuable experiences and insights with us, including: Patricia Hansen, Jane Kelsey, Meredith Kolsky Lewis, Gabrielle Marceau, Sylvia Ostry, Debra Steger, Cherie Taylor, and Constance Wagner.

discusses what we mean by the term 'international economic law' and looks at the importance of the discipline, from both a domestic and a global perspective. For the purposes of this Chapter, we focus on the regulatory rather than transactional content of the subject, but from a broad interdisciplinary perspective. Second, it situates the present study in relation to feminist literature in international law more generally, and makes a case for why it is important to look at women's contributions to and participation in scholarship and teaching in international economic law in particular. In Part II, we take up the task of celebrating, quantifying, and reflecting upon women's contributions to international economic law teaching and scholarship. In the *celebration* section, we note some of the achievements of women in the discipline to date. In the *quantification* section, we provide some quantitative and semi-quantitative data regarding the representation of women in international economic law teaching and scholarship in North American academic settings. Finally, in the *reflection* section, we record qualitative research undertaken through interviews with a number of current female scholars in international economic law and international economics. The future of IEL scholarship is shaped by its present and its past. These first-hand accounts of experiences and impressions can act as an inspiration to new generations of scholars who accept the responsibility of helping to shape future law and policy.

I. DEFINING AND SITUATING THE DISCIPLINE

A. Meaning and Importance of 'International Economic Law'

The term 'international economic law' can, as Jackson notes, be used in an extremely broad sense, embracing almost all of international law in some form. Jackson divides this subject matter into two main approaches, 'transactional' and 'regulatory'.[1] Transactional international economic law refers to transactions carried out in the context of international trade or other economic activities, and focuses on the manner in which private parties conduct their activities. Regulatory international economic law, on the other hand, focuses on the role of government institutions. It is the second approach that we use as a starting point for defining the scope of international economic law for our study.

Within the regulatory approach, we adopt Jackson's definition of international economic law as law relating to the 'regulation of economic behaviour which crosses national borders' or, 'regulation of international trade and foreign investment'.[2] This may include, for example, areas such as the

---

[1] J Jackson, *The Jurisprudence of GATT and the WTO* (Cambridge University Press, 2000) 450.
[2] Ibid.

environment, human rights, and labour law as they relate to international trade law. This is consistent with our view that international economic law is inherently multidisciplinary, involving economics and political science, as well as other disciplines. Given this multidisciplinary understanding and the field's close relationship with 'public' international law more generally, we will also note recent trends in feminist scholarship in international law, as well as in economics.

B. Feminist Perspectives within International Economic Law

Feminist perspectives can introduce fresh insights, thus acting as a stimulus for growth and development of the relatively new field of international economic law scholarship. This is particularly important at a time when governments and international institutions such as the World Trade Organization (WTO) are facing increasing pressure to address concerns of stakeholders that have traditionally been overlooked in international policy-making.

Two broad approaches to feminist scholarship are evident from a review of the literature. First, feminist scholars in both international law and economics have documented how their discipline has excluded women from the production of knowledge. In other words, they have examined ways in which women's contributions have been ignored, misrepresented, and/or marginalised.[3]

Second, feminist economic scholars have worked to expose and challenge the androcentric bias inherent in economic theories, assumptions, discourse, methods, and methodologies.[4] More recently, feminist legal scholars have undertaken the same task with respect to international law. Noting the discipline's tendency to brush aside the injustices that women face around the world, they are seeking to redraw the boundaries of international law so that it responds to these injustices.[5] In an article concerning feminism and the mission of international law, Orford finds particular reason to be concerned with development of feminist scholarship in the field of international economic law. She notes the difficulties encountered by feminists in seeking to 'contest the meanings of international economic law, international trade law and collective security' and

---

[3] Charlesworth and Chinkin argue, eg, that the absence of women in the development of international law has produced a narrow and inadequate jurisprudence that has, among other things, legitimated the unequal position of women around the world rather than challenged it. See H Charlesworth & C Chinkin, *The Boundaries of International Law: A Feminist Analysis* (Manchester University Press, 2000) 1.

[4] PI Olson & Z Emani, *Engendering Economics: Conversations with Women Economists in the United States* (Routledge, 2002) 1.

[5] Charlesworth & Chinkin, above n 3, at ix.

argues that there is a need to criticise the masculinist foundations of these discourses.[6]

Outside of these observations by Orford, academic literature reveals little in the way of feminist analysis of international economic law. However, research within the non-governmental organisation (NGO) community does emphasise the critical gender dimensions to international economic law. The Center for International Development (CID) at Harvard University, for example, notes that many of the trade issues discussed by the WTO today have differential gender impacts. This is especially true in specific sectors of the economy where women tend to work, such as textiles, the informal market, and agriculture. CID notes, however, that the study of the gender impact of trade is still in its infancy.[7]

The timeliness of this Chapter is underscored by these observations of feminist scholars. Beginning the task of celebrating and quantifying women's contributions to international economic law can help ensure that such scholarship receives recognition. More importantly, it can focus attention on some of the inequities that such scholarship seeks to address. Reflecting on the experiences and views of women scholars can help us to provide constructive suggestions on how fresh perspectives can be encouraged and accepted by the discipline.

II. CELEBRATION, QUANTIFICATION, AND REFLECTION

A. Celebration

As noted, international economic law has a strong economics component and it is therefore useful to consider not only the contributions of women legal scholars but also those of economists. Contemporary research has not only documented ways in which women's achievements in the discipline of economics have been ignored, but has also begun to uncover contributions of women economists during the eighteenth, nineteenth, and early twentieth centuries.[8] Dimand writes that one reason these contributions have traditionally been overlooked in North America is that many of the women working in economics during this period did not publish in

---

[6] Anne Orford, 'Feminism, Imperialism, and the Mission of International Law', 71 *Nordic J Int'l L* 275, 285 (2002). She traces these foundations back to the seminal work of Adam Smith, *Wealth of Nations*, suggesting that his writing helped to stifle political struggle and make possible the international division of labour today; in many cases, such practices exploit women.

[7] Center for International Development, Harvard University, Global Trade Negotiations Home Page, *Gender Issues and International Trade* (2006), http://www.cid.harvard.edu/cidtrade/site/gender.html (last visited 14 Oct, 2006).

[8] Olson & Emani, above n 4, at 1. See also MA Dimand, RW Dimand & EL Forget (eds), *Women of Value: Feminist Essays on the History of Women in Economics* (Edward Elgar, 1995).

mainstream economics journals, but in periodicals such as the *Publications of the Association of Collegiate Alumnae, MacMillan's Magazine*, as well as in pamphlet form.[9] While noting that most classical histories of international economics do not cite any women, Dimand makes reference to a number of women writing in the area of trade theory. For example, he notes that Ethel Dietrich wrote four papers between 1928 and 1935 dealing with import quotas, model trade agreements, and export credit insurance, while Eleanor Lansing Dulles and Karin Koch wrote on monetary and international economics. In 1939, Marion Crawford Samuelson wrote a paper on the so-called 'Australian' case for import protection to raise the return on nationally scarce factors of production, which was cited by Paul Samuelson and in the inaugural issue of the *Journal of International Trade and Economic Development*. Dimand notes, however, that her paper has been otherwise ignored in the literature on trade theory.[10]

Dimand also brings our attention to the work of Jane Marcet. While largely ignored in the work of later economists, Jane Marcet has in recent years been hailed as 'one of the greater pioneers of adult education.'[11] In 1831 she wrote *Conversations*, a series of essays aimed at young people, particularly girls, as well as at the upper classes, for whom she tried to justify wealth in the face of growing political unease with financial inequality.[12] One of the essays in *Conversations*, entitled 'Foreign Trade: or the Wedding Gown', sought to popularise the writings of Adam Smith and David Ricardo. Dimand notes that Jane Marcet's work was well received by her contemporaries; the economist Robert Torrens, for example, stated that 'we know one female, at least, fully competent to instruct the members of our present cabinet in Political Economy'.[13] She also reportedly influenced other women, with Harriet Martineau noting that Marcet inspired her to write the popular *Illustrations of Political Economy* (1832–34).[14] Thomson argues that it took courage for Marcet to write about economics, not only because she was a woman, but also because economics had not previously been considered a 'gentlemen's subject' since it dealt with trade, and had 'been born outside the universities, without the blessing of the academic

---

[9] RW Dimand, 'The Neglect of Women's Contributions To Economics', in Dimand, Dimand & Forget, above n 8, at 1.

[10] Eg, in surveys of trade theory by J Bhagwati, J Chipman, WM Corden, and G Haberler. See Dimand, above n 9, at 14.

[11] B Polkinghorn, J Marcet (Forestwood Publications, 1993), cited in H Hollis, 'The Rhetoric of Jane Marcet's Popularizing Political Economy' (2002) 24 *Nineteenth-Century Contexts* 379, 380.

[12] Hollis, above n 11, at 380.

[13] Polkinghorn, above n 11. Cited in RW Dimand, 'The Neglect of Women's Contributions to Economics', in *Women of Value: Feminist Essays on the History of Women in Economics*, above note 8 at 13.

[14] Hollis, above n 11, at 380.

scholars'.[15] Thus, by writing about economics in a pedagogical framework, Marcet helped garner respect for both the subject of classical economics and for the political economists of the day.

Dimand refers to a post-1930 decline in women's representation in the economics profession. Yet such a lull soon came to an end, as women participated in the most significant development for international economics in the twentieth century—the Bretton Woods Conference of 1944 and the origins of the General Agreement on Trade and Tariffs (GATT). Several American women, including Alice Bourneuf, Eleanor Lansing Dulles (US Department of State), and Mabel Newcomer (an economist on the faculty at Vassar College) contributed to the drafting of the Bretton Woods documents.[16]

Currently, we are witnessing enormous contributions to international economic scholarship by women. We note the contributions of a few as a way of acknowledging all women in the field: renowned Canadian economist, Sylvia Ostry, who has held numerous influential positions including head of the Department of Economics and Statistics at the Organisation for Economic Cooperation and Development (OECD) and Canada's Deputy Minister of International Trade and Ambassador for Multilateral Trade Negotiations; Merit Janow, who in 2003 was the first woman to be appointed as a member of the WTO Appellate Body; and Canadian Debra Steger, who was the founding Director and first Chief Legal Adviser to the WTO Appellate Body from 1995–2001. These women, along with countless others who cannot be listed here, no doubt inspire the present generation of female scholars and will continue to inspire those in the future.

B. Quantification

The quantitative component of this Chapter is, to the best of our knowledge, the first attempt to take stock of the number of women engaged in international economic law teaching and scholarship. Clearly, the data provided here is only a rudimentary beginning, and as the discipline develops there will be room for studies that take, for example, a closer look at the gender balance in international economic law scholarship, compared with that of legal scholarship more generally.

We conducted research to determine a range of information. First, we surveyed North American law school websites to ascertain the number of

---

[15] D Lampen Thomson, *Adam Smith's Daughters* (Exposition Press, 1973). Cited in Hollis, above n 11, at 381.
[16] The World Bank Library Network, Celebrating the Bretton Woods Institutions: Breaking the Mold, www.worldbankimflib.org/bwf/60 (last visited 14 Oct, 2006).

women engaged in international economic law teaching and scholarship as compared to the number of men. We based our survey on the top 100 law schools listed in the US News and World Report ranking of America's Best Graduate Schools 2007[17], as well as those listed on worldtradelaw.net as having faculty with expertise in international economic law. Where available, we relied upon the 'media' sections of the schools' websites, which list faculty by area of expertise, to determine those scholars who self-identify as being engaged in international economic law teaching and scholarship. Where such a function was not available, we browsed faculty lists to determine who self-identifies as engaged in this area of teaching and research. Of the 85 law schools we examined who have faculty with expertise in international economic law, we found that 21 per cent of faculty members engaged in international economic law teaching and scholarship are female.

These initial findings mirror the results of a much more comprehensive examination of the status of women in the academic branch of economics in Canada, the United States, the United Kingdom, and China.[18] The trend in the academy from 1972 to 2004 shows that while there is progress in the representation of women in economics, this representation 'lags far behind the representation of women in the academy overall' and also shows 'a substantial decline in women's representation on successive rungs of the academic ladder.'[19] Further analysis along the same lines would be required to determine changes in the participation rate of women through the academic hierarchy in the discipline of international economic law.

Second, we surveyed enrolment numbers in international trade regulation courses between 1996 and 2006 at American and Canadian law schools to ascertain whether there is a pattern in terms of student interest in the discipline. While a number of schools have only begun to offer such courses in the last five years, our survey shows that average annual female enrolment across the schools surveyed over this period has tended to fall close to the 40 per cent mark, with a range from a low of 32 per cent to a high of 51 percent.[20] These statistics suggest a significant degree of interest among female law students in trade issues. Given that females entering law school outnumbered males for the first time in 2001,[21] female enrolment in trade

---

[17] USNews.com, America's Best Graduate Schools 2007, http://www.usnews.com/usnews/edu/grad/rankings/law/brief/lawrank_brief.php (last visited 10 Oct, 2006).

[18] JP Jacobsen, 'Exploration of the Status of Women Economists' (2006) 12 *Feminist Econ* 427.

[19] Ibid at 431.

[20] While we approached over 75 schools, we only received enrolment information from 19 schools. These figures are based on those 19.

[21] JG Baker, 'The Influx of Women into Legal Professions: An Economic Analysis' (2002) *Monthly Lab Rev* 14 (citing Marjorie Williams, 'A Woman's Place is at the Bar', Wash Post 4 Apr, 2001, at A23).

courses that tracks in the 40 per cent range does not appear to be out of line with expectations.

Our results show that the proportion of women enrolled in international economic law courses is greater than that of those engaged in scholarship. We analysed authorship of articles published in a number of leading international economic law journals to quantify the number of articles written by women compared to men. We focused on five journals specifically devoted to international economic law, expecting this would provide a representative overview of scholarship in the field. We made a number of findings.

The *Journal of International Economic Law* was first published in 1998. The journal states that it is 'dedicated to encouraging thoughtful and scholarly attention to a very broad range of subjects that concern the relation of law to international economic activity'.[22] The journal has become recognised as one of the leading publications in the field of international economic law. We found that since 1998, only 13 per cent of articles published have been authored by women, with another 5 per cent co-authored by a team which includes a woman.

The *World Trade Review* was established at the initiative of the Secretariat of the WTO. It includes articles written from economic, legal, political and inter-disciplinary perspectives on issues of relevance to the multilateral trading system. Our analysis found that since its inception in 2002, only 8 per cent of articles have been authored by women, with another 5 per cent being co-authored by a team which includes a woman.

The *Journal of International Trade Regulation*, published by Sweet and Maxwell, has a more practical focus, asking that submissions focus on a major, current theme of interest to financial lawyers and academics alike, and provide explanations in a 'fairly practical way.' Our analysis found that since this journal began in 1995, a total of 17.5 per cent of published articles have been authored by women, with a further 8 per cent being co-authored by a team which includes a woman.

The *Journal of World Trade*, published bi-monthly by Kluwer Law International, adopts a multidisciplinary approach to trade issues, focusing on law, economics and public policy. Since 1995, women have authored just under 10 per cent of the articles, with another 8 per cent co-authored by a team which includes a woman.

The *Journal of World Investment* offered its first bi-monthly publication in July 2000 and incorporated 'Trade' into its title in 2004 to become *The Journal of World Investment and Trade*. It provides a forum for debating issues of foreign direct investment, including WTO trade issues which affect

---

[22] *Journal of International Economic Law*, http://jiel.oxfordjournals.org/ (last visited 14 Oct, 2006).

investment. Since its inception, just over 10 per cent of the articles have been authored by women, plus another 4 per cent co-authored by a team which includes a woman.

While these journals are testament to the valuable contributions of women to academic scholarship, more attention could be focused on encouraging women to publish both classic and alternative approaches to international economic law scholarship. The overall publication rate by women in international economic law journals tracks behind the participation rate of women who are engaged in teaching international trade law courses. As more women are promoted through the academic ranks, and with an emphasis on mentorship programs, the publication rate by women should increase.

It is important to note that these findings do not support any inferences as to why women are under-represented in international economic law teaching and scholarship. Comprehensive empirical research could help identify root causes. This would require an investigation into two related issues: attraction and retention. Women may simply opt for other academic career choices, which is not a negative reflection on international economic law scholarship. However, if women choose other academic career paths because of the perception of a chilly environment within the discipline, corrective measures could be implemented to address any valid concerns. Retention is a separate issue. Once a woman has undertaken an academic career path in international economic law scholarship, measures that support, encourage, and promote the advancement of teaching, research, and scholarship could help to hold valued scholars within the discipline.

C. Reflection

For its qualitative component, this Chapter draws on the approach taken by Olson and Emani, who in their book, *Engendering Economics*, present the oral histories of contemporary women economists.[23] In doing so, they highlight the advantages of using oral history as an additional method of inquiry within economics. They state that 'by allowing us to ask new and qualitatively different questions, oral history allows us to challenge orthodox ways of knowing and to create new material about women'.[24] Combined with quantitative and semi-quantitative data, this approach will, in the words of Olson and Emani, begin to develop a richer

---

[23] Olson & Emani, above n 4. They hope to encourage similar oral history projects incorporating the voices, experiences, interests, and insights of various generations of women economists from around the world.

[24] Olson & Emani, above n 4, at 2.

understanding of the sociology of the discipline from the perspective of female scholars.[25]

For this study, we interviewed a number of women engaged in international economic law teaching and scholarship. Our purpose was to begin the task of developing an understanding of the sociology of international economic law as a discipline, and also to learn more about women's experiences and perspectives to ascertain how they might be harnessed to strengthen the discipline. We asked women a number of questions, focusing on two main strands: first, their perceptions of the state of the discipline and the contributions of women to it; second, the issue of a feminist-based approach to international economic law.

The women we spoke to came from different backgrounds and theoretical perspectives. Some perceived little or no difficulty in having their voices heard in policy debates around international economic issues, while others felt that the discipline is largely male-dominated and noted some related concerns. The following discussion is intended to raise points for discussion. Not all the women we spoke to would agree with the points raised by each of the others; no doubt in the wider academic community, some of the issues could provoke considerable discussion. We put these issues forward in the hope that they will promote a debate that will potentially enrich the discipline for all.

(i) On Women's Contributions

One notion shared by all the women we interviewed was the motivation to be an agent for change in their work. Each of the women talked of focusing on research that would have a real impact, and that would result in governments and international organisations developing better policy and laws.

One interviewee recollected her experiences at international law conferences in the late 1980s. She was disappointed when her female colleagues expressed surprise that she had chosen to engage in scholarship relating to international economic issues, rather than fields such as human rights. She noted that they did not seem to find international economic law relevant to women, a view she found extremely narrow considering the enormous impact of economic issues in society generally. Fortunately, our interviewee had a strong conviction that such a narrow view of international economic law is misguided. Many other women have demonstrated a similar conviction.

In a similar vein, some noted that women tend to bring a different approach to international economic law scholarship. One interviewee felt that women have a sensitivity to certain issues that men may overlook because they have fewer reasons to be oriented in that direction. This

---

[25] Ibid. Olson and Emami speak of the 'sociology of the economics profession from the perspective of women economists.'

reflects observations from the legal profession more generally. For example, it has been suggested that women's approach to dispute settlement tends to be more resolution seeking through consensus building, an approach which has been revolutionary in the family law field.[26] Similar dynamics may be applicable in the field of international economic law. One scholar we interviewed, for example, is working on a project to develop new models for trade negotiations.

Following a related theme, a number of the respondents indicated that women scholars tend to focus disproportionately on 'trade and' subjects such as trade and human rights or trade and environment. One interviewee related, for example, her anecdotal experience that male students in her classes tend to be predominantly interested in subjects such as financial services, investment and intellectual property, whereas female students tend to be less interested in these areas. It was suggested, too, that the number of women working in the 'trade and' area may be in large part due to women's previous academic and work experiences before they came to international economic law. As one woman observed, the majority of students studying economics at the undergraduate level tend to be male, while a greater proportion of women tend to have backgrounds in the humanities, taking subjects such as sociology, environmental studies, and women's studies.

Concern was expressed that some of these 'trade and' areas of international economic law scholarship may be 'ghettoised' if they become perceived as 'women's issues' or 'soft issues.' One interviewee questioned whether women working in some of the 'trade and' areas will, at the end of the day, be in a position to effect a significant impact on the WTO and governments. In this regard, there was a sense that there remains, in the higher echelons of decision making, a strong network of economists who come from a classical, orthodox academic tradition; it is difficult for scholars to break into this network if their ideas differ from those espoused by the mainstream. However, a more positive view was also expressed. As one woman explained, the agenda of trade law is broadening as a result of citizens' concerns, and the WTO is being forced to consider these 'trade and' issues. As a result, it is likely that rather than being marginalised, these issues will take centre stage in the coming years, providing a greater opportunity for women's voices to be heard.

---

[26] M Webb, *Trail Blazers*, Spring/Summer Nexus, (2006) University of Toronto Faculty of Law 61. A possible biological explanation as to why women bring different perspectives to international economic law scholarship might draw on a recent book by Louann Brizendine, entitled *The Female Brain*. Dr. Brizendine's research has found that women's brains show heightened development of communication, connection, and emotional sensitivity. 'The female brain has tremendous unique aptitudes—outstanding verbal agility, the ability to connect deeply in friendship, a nearly psychic capacity to read faces and tone of voice for emotions and states of mind, and the ability to defuse conflict. All of this is hardwired into the brains of women.' See L Brizendine, *The Female Brain* (Morgan Road Books, 2006) 8.

We discussed our findings that women tend to be under-represented in the well-known, 'mainstream' international economic law journals. One thought offered in this regard is that such journals tend to take a fairly narrow, orthodox approach to issues and are not open to alternative ideas. This was raised as a concern not only for the discipline at large, but also because a number of women scholars tend to question the classical approach. As a result, they may have difficulty having their views incorporated into the mainstream notion of what shapes international economic law. For example, it was suggested that women wishing to provide a gendered analysis of international trade issues are more likely to publish in feminist legal journals than they are in mainstream international economic law journals. This can be problematic on two counts.

First, to the extent that such ideas are omitted from the mainstream, it may be more difficult for these women to make an impact on decision-makers. As noted, the ability to make an impact was a recurring theme throughout the interviews. Yet it may be easier to have an impact on decision-making at both the governmental and inter-governmental levels if the analysis were consistent with mainstream notions of international economic law. That said, some women are taking innovative steps to make their views known to those in a position to make decisions, including by making presentations in broader academic and policy contexts.

Second, an inability to publish in the more 'mainstream' and recognised journals may have an impact on women's opportunities to gain tenure and promotion. In today's academic environment, where many universities evaluate research output and 'impact', certain journals carry more weight than others. For example, an article published in the *Harvard Law Review* will carry more weight than if the same article were to be published in *Feminist Legal Studies*. This may pose a dilemma for younger academics who must weigh their options carefully if they wish to progress through the academic ranks. There may be limited room for them to explore different perspectives.

We discussed our (by no means scientific) findings that on average, there tend to be fewer female students enrolled in international trade law courses than male students. We also noted that, in North America at least, far fewer women than men are involved in teaching and researching in the discipline. It was suggested that there may be a perception that international trade law tends to be fairly technical and quantitative, characteristics which appear to lessen the appeal of a discipline to some women. In terms of teaching, however, it was also suggested that there remains a glass ceiling in the international economic law field which, to date, relatively few women have broken through. Not all women shared this perception, however. Interestingly, it was suggested that this obstacle appears to be less of a problem for women working within the governmental rather than the academic sector (in North America at least).

(ii) On Feminist Perspectives

It was noted that there is a real dearth of feminist perspectives in international economic law, which contrasts to public international law more generally, as noted above. One woman discussed, for example, her recent experience researching a paper on mode four of trade in services as defined under the General Agreement on Trade in Services (movement of natural persons). While considering the situation of temporary migrant workers, she found that although there was some material published by gender-based NGOs, there was no academic literature on the subject, despite its huge importance in the debate on the issues. However, the work being done by NGOs might be ignored by decision-makers because its approach is outside the mainstream. In this regard, we recall the women economists of the past whose work was largely overlooked because they were not published in the usual academic venues. Are some women choosing to work outside of the legal academy—for NGOs for example—to facilitate their research, even at the risk that their findings may not have as much credibility and influence?

In terms of encouraging feminist (and other 'alternative') perspectives to be brought forward, the importance of mentoring students and young scholars was noted. It was also suggested that senior women scholars in the discipline have a key role to play in creating the intellectual space for students and young scholars to explore different perspectives. This might include mentoring of students and colleagues, as well as introducing different perspectives at conferences in order to encourage and legitimise such work. It was suggested that post-graduate supervision plays a particularly important role in this regard, as it tends to provide a 'safer' space for students to explore ideas and unorthodox theoretical perspectives. Similarly, with respect to teaching, it was suggested that the development of courses on international economic law should encompass perspectives outside of the classical orthodox economic approach. It is hoped that focusing on these kinds of steps will lead to greater acceptance of feminist perspectives in the mainstream academy.

Finally, the interviews highlighted another important issue: the virtual invisibility of feminist contributions from developing countries. In advancing the relevance of international economic law from a gendered perspective, it is vital to encourage work produced throughout the world. Given the difficulties women scholars face in many countries, colleagues in the developed world might provide opportunities by, for example, involving them in collaborative projects and conferences.

CONCLUSION

This Chapter has only begun to touch on some of the important questions surrounding the role of women in international economic law scholarship and teaching. In doing so, it has highlighted some key issues regarding international economic law scholarship in general, as well as the place within the discipline for perspectives that differ from traditional 'mainstream' views.

We also gained some practical ideas for the continued development of women's international economic law scholarship. In the classroom, for example, traditional trade law courses can introduce alternative approaches to problem-solving as a way of opening students' minds to the impact of their choices on all stakeholders. Professors can adopt formal or informal mentoring programs, granting students the intellectual space to explore various perspectives. In the publishing field, journals related to international economic law can encourage submissions reflecting feminist directions in scholarship. Academic associations and conference organisers can diversify their membership and the composition of their panels. We hope that this effort to chart Venutian scholarship in a Martian landscape will contribute to further suggestions.

Overall, developing this Chapter has provided us with an opportunity to reflect on the contributions made by women scholars in international economic law, and on how this legacy can continue and expand in the years to come. First, this Chapter celebrates those invaluable achievements. Second, quantitative research suggests the importance of attracting and retaining women in the discipline. Third, reflecting on such contributions has allowed us to see international economic law scholarship in a broad context that encompasses traditional analysis, as well as alternative approaches. With a strong foundation, new dimensions that take the discipline of international economic law in new directions can be embraced. Indeed, this is vital in stimulating debate on how international economic law scholarship can remain relevant, and make meaningful contributions to the development of international economic law and policy.

12

An Essay on Teaching International Economic Law From a Corporate Perspective

FRANKLIN A GEVURTZ

I. SOME BASIC QUESTIONS AND ANSWERS

IMPLICIT, IF NOT explicit, in the discussions in this section on teaching international economic law are questions including: What should one teach as within the scope of international economic law?[1] When should one teach international economic law?[2] And, to whom should one teach international economic law?[3] In order to give sensible answers to such questions, however, it is necessary to explore the more fundamental question of why should one teach international economic law.

It is important not to conflate the question why one should teach international economic law, with the question of whether anyone should teach international economic law (in the sense of whether the topic is important). To use a non-law related example, nuclear physics is certainly a critical enough topic that there is not much question of whether it should be taught somewhere; but one cannot answer when, to whom, or what to encompass within the instruction, unless one asks exactly what one hopes to accomplish in teaching nuclear physics. The same is true with international economic law.

---

[1] Compare T Epps & R MacGillivray, 'Venutian Scholarship in a Martian Landscape: Celebrating and Reflecting on Women in International Economic Law Teaching and Scholarship', Ch 11 in this volume (taking a narrow view of international economic law as focused largely on trade law), with CZ Wagner, 'Corporate Social Responsibility of Multinational Enterprises and the International Business Law Curriculum', Ch 15 in this volume (taking a broader view of international economic law as encompassing corporate social responsibility).

[2] Eg, A Porges, 'The Future of International Economic Law Practice', Ch 16 in this volume (discussing teaching international economic law through moot court competitions); E Trujillo, 'Shifting Paradigms of Parochialism: Lessons for Legal Education', Ch 14 in this volume (discussing teaching international economic law through a course on NAFTA).

[3] This is an implicit corollary to the question of when to teach international economic law in the 2 papers cited in n 2 above.

A narrow answer to the question of what to teach within international economic law focuses on the law governing trade between nations—including obligations created by the WTO—with a begrudging nod to rules governing international finance and other international economic law issues.[4] A narrow answer regarding when to teach international economic law tends to focus on international trade courses, and maybe courses on foreign investment and international business transactions.[5] This, in turn, means that a narrow answer regarding to whom to teach international economic law becomes that small slice of the students in a law school who sign up for electives in trade, foreign investment and/or international business transactions.[6] Underlying these answers is an often unspoken assumption as to the goal for teaching international economic law—this being to prepare students for a specialised practice in the international business and trade arena.[7]

In itself, there is nothing wrong with this unspoken goal for teaching international economic law, and the narrow answers as to when and to whom to teach international economic law, and what to address within the topic. It must be said, however, that this is a fairly unambitious goal, leading to fairly unambitious answers to the other questions. The reason is practical: the demand for lawyers specialising in international business and trade can sop up only an extremely small fraction of the graduates from the vast majority of law schools.

This, in turn, raises the question as to whether teachers of international economic law might be missing a more ambitious goal, which will lead to different answers as to when and to whom to teach international economic law, and what to include within the topic. Specifically, while the force of globalisation may only provide a limited number of opportunities for specialists in trade and international business law, the impacts of globalisation increasingly reach many traditionally domestic areas of law and practice. This, in turn, suggests that the vast majority of, if not all, law school graduates should have some exposure to the legal impacts of world trade and the globalisation of the economy, even if not to the minute details of the law governing the trading obligations of nations and other international economic law.

Once we change the goal, the practice of teaching international economic law only in specialised electives is no longer sufficient. Whether

---

[4] Eg, Epps & MacGillivray, above n 1.
[5] See, eg, K Bravo, 'International Economic Law in US Law Schools: Evaluating Its Pedagogy and Identifying Future Challenges', Ch 10 in this volume.
[6] Ibid (at 3/4 of the schools responding, less than 25% of the students take at least 1 international economic law course during their JD studies).
[7] Eg, S Sapra, 'New Agendas for International Economic Law Teaching in India: Including an Agenda in Support of Reform', Ch 13 in this volume.

this should lead to introducing international economic law through a new required course devoted to transnational topics, or through the integration of international economic law into traditionally domestically-oriented core courses, is a subject addressed elsewhere,[8] and will not be repeated here. For now, it is useful to ask what this change in goals means to the question of what topics to encompass within the scope of what one teaches as international economic law. The answer is to broaden considerably the scope of international economic law, at least as a curricular matter.

In fact, this broadening nicely corresponds to the changing nature of the discussion of trade policy. Traditionally, trade policy revolves around the tension between the benefits of free trade underlying the theory of comparative advantage and the detrimental impacts of free trade on local industry. As openly mercantilist arguments ceased to be respectable, the arguments for trade barriers increasingly became based upon notions of reciprocity, ie 'we should not open our markets to nations that do not open theirs.' In more recent years, the conversation has become considerably more complex, as discussion of another basis for restriction has come alongside the reciprocity rationale: this being the concern that free trade allows for regulatory arbitrage in which production shifts to nations with lower environmental, labour or even human rights standards, thereby potentially triggering a race to the bottom with regard to such laws. Moreover, not only may trade flows impact the sustainability of local regulations on production, local regulations on sale can impact trade flows. Thus, a requirement that genetically modified foods be so labeled may, at the same time, be one nation's legitimate exercise of consumer protection and another nation's impermissible trade barrier. As a result, trade law increasingly impacts other, heretofore domestic, fields of regulation.

Rather than attempting an overview of all the ways in which global trade impacts other traditionally domestic fields of law, and therefore legal study, the rest of this essay will focus on one example: my own field of corporate law.

II. GLOBAL TRADE AND CORPORATE LAW

Politically, arguments against free trade find it useful to have villains. The villains in traditional mercantilist or reciprocity arguments are foreigners. The xenophobic nature of casting foreigners as the villains has made such arguments less appealing in these (hopefully) more enlightened times. Indeed, the desire in some political circles to avoid casting foreigners as the villains may account for the increasing invocation of the regulatory

---

[8] See FA Gevurtz, 'Incorporating Transnational Materials into Traditional Courses' (2007) 24 *Penn St Int'l L Rev* 813.

arbitrage, as opposed to the reciprocity, concern, as the reason for opposing free trade. This, however, leads one to ask who can play the role of villains in the regulatory arbitrage rationale. The common answer is the so-called multinational corporation.

In a nutshell, the argument goes that multinational corporations—many with more resources than some nations—scour the globe in search of jurisdictions with lax labour, environmental or other regulations, in which the corporations might set up shop. Moreover, under this narrative, not only are such corporations the passive beneficiaries of lax regulatory policies, but the corporations use their economic muscle to coerce poor or corrupt governments into adopting lax regulatory regimes under threat that, if the governments do not, the multinational corporations will take their production activities elsewhere. Free trade facilitates this regulatory arbitrage by potentially denying nations the ability to deploy the leverage otherwise available by threatening to cut off access to domestic markets to corporations setting up shop in regimes with lax regulations. Under this scenario, promoting so-called corporate social responsibility, as a means to offset this detrimental impact of free trade, assumes primary importance as an element of sound trade policy.

In fact, however, stated in these broad terms, this notion of corporate social responsibility may not really be a matter of what is understood by teachers and scholars as corporate law. Corporate law does not encompass all laws, domestic or otherwise, governing corporations. If it did, then corporate law would subsume almost the entirety of at least domestic law, since most domestic laws govern corporations in much the same manner as domestic laws govern any other person or entity. Properly understood, corporate law is concerned with those laws, normally domestic, that uniquely govern the rights and obligations of shareholders, directors and officers of corporations. The need for managers of a business to act responsibly toward workers, the environment and the community in which the business operates, is not, on its face, uniquely applicable to corporate managers. If wealthy individuals scoured the globe for lax regulatory regimes, and lobbied for lax regulation as a condition for maintaining local production rather than moving elsewhere, the same concern with regulatory arbitrage would exist. Hence, the idea that business enterprises ought to behave responsibly, even beyond the minima required by law, in itself is not an issue of corporate law.

This does not mean that international regulatory arbitrage does not implicate uniquely corporate law concerns. Rather, it means we must be more subtle in considering exactly what issues arise when the business enterprise engaged in world trade is a corporation. In fact, the role of corporations, as opposed to other business enterprises, in world trade raises three particularly corporate law issues. They involve choice of law, limited liability, and management selection and obligations.

A. Choice of Law

The first difference between corporations and individuals occurs at their birth. Persons establishing a corporation have far more flexibility to pick the corporation's home state with an eye toward choice of law than do individuals have the ability to decide on their citizenship with an eye exclusively toward choice of law.

Choice of corporate law rules involve two doctrines. The first pertains to whether persons can form corporations in jurisdictions other than one(s) in which the company will conduct operations. Many continental European nations traditionally have operated under the view that corporations must be formed in the nation in which the company had its headquarters—variously called the *siege social, siege real*, or seat theory. Under this view, a nation would reject the effort to incorporate under its law if the corporate headquarters would be in another nation, and a nation in which a firm had its headquarters would refuse to recognise the firm as a corporation—meaning, for example, the firm would lack the capacity to sue in this nation's courts and its owners might face personal liability—unless the firm incorporated under this nation's, rather than another nation's, laws.[9] In contrast to the seat theory, there is an Anglo-American approach, often referred to as the incorporation doctrine. Under this increasingly ascendant view, the mere filing of a piece of paper (combined with a nominal local address) dictates the nation (or state) of incorporation.[10] What this means is that a corporation can choose the state or nation under whose laws it will exist without regard to where the company actually conducts its activities. It is as if an individual could establish citizenship by the mere act of where one files a piece of paper, without regard to where one lives and works.

What gives the incorporation doctrine choice of corporate law significance is another doctrine known as the internal affairs rule. Under this rule, the corporate laws of the state or nation of incorporation govern the company's so-called internal affairs.[11] Narrowly conceived, this rule would not allow corporations to engage in regulatory arbitrage through free trade, any more (or less) than individuals. After all, internal affairs deal with the rights and obligations of corporate shareholders, directors and officers as such. By contrast, environmental, employment and the vast majority of other laws governing any person doing business within a nation do not come within the meaning of internal affairs.[12] Hence, a corporation can no more ignore the environmental, labour or other generally applicable

---

[9] Eg, WH Roth, 'From Centros to Uberseering: Free Movement of Companies, Private International Law, and Company Law' (2003) 52 *Int'l & Comp LQ* 177, 180–5. See also Kaisha Hou *[Corporations Law]*, art 821 (Japan, 2005).
[10] Eg, Del Gen Corp Law §§ 101(a), 102(a)(2).
[11] Eg, Restatement (Second) Conflict of Laws § 302.
[12] Eg, *McDermott Inc v Lewis*, 531 A.2d 206 (Del 1987).

laws of the nation in which it does business than can any other person, simply because the corporation or other person happens to be the citizen of another nation or state.

The problem is that the precise boundary between internal affairs governed by the laws of the state or nation of incorporation, and external matters governed by the laws of the state or nation in which the corporation acts, is not always clear, and may lead courts to treat, as internal affairs, rules having external impact.[13] Indeed, as discussed in the next two sections of this Chapter, some rules traditionally considered to fall within corporate law, and hence the internal affairs rule, do impact the relations between the corporation and those outside of the company.

Before turning to that broader discussion, however, it is useful to mention a series of cases decided in the last few years by the European Court of Justice, which demonstrate the potential interplay between regional economic agreements, choice of corporate law doctrine, and regulatory arbitrage. These cases involve Articles 43 and 48 of the European Community Treaty. Article 43 prohibits, subject to certain conditions, 'restrictions on the freedom of establishment of nationals of a Member State in the territory of another Member State.' Article 48 extends this freedom of establishment to:

> companies or firms formed in accordance with the law of a Member State and having their registered office, central administration or principal place of business within the Community.

In other words, the economic integration created by the European Community Treaty goes beyond the free flow of goods between European Union member nations, and also allows individuals or corporations, who are citizens of member nations, to set up shop in other member nations.

What does this all have to do with corporate law and regulatory arbitrage? A number of European nations have provisions in their domestic corporate laws requiring the owners of private, as well as public, companies to invest a certain minimum amount of capital in the company prior to commencing business.[14] The idea is to protect creditors, who might otherwise lose money dealing with fly-by-night operations. Other European nations, notably England, require only a nominal amount of invested capital. England also follows the incorporation doctrine under which persons can form English companies by simple filing regardless of where the company actually will be headquartered or conduct operations. This state of affairs has led Danish, German and Dutch citizens to incorporate in England and then seek to have their English corporations conduct business in Denmark,

---

[13] Eg, *Abu-Nassar v Elders Futures, Inc*, 1991 WL 45062 (SDNY 1991) (court refused to decide whether the internal affairs rule governed a creditor's claim to pierce the corporate veil of a foreign company).

[14] Eg, M Lutter, 'Limited Liability Companies and Private Companies', in *XIII International Encyclopedia Of Comparative Law* (1998) 9.

Germany and the Netherlands, without complying with minimum capital rules applicable to Danish, German and Dutch corporations.

In a pair of cases,[15] the European Court of Justice held that Articles 43 and 48 of the European Community Treaty compelled recognition of corporations formed under one member nation's law, despite the fact that the headquarters, business and owners of the company were all within the nation (Denmark or Germany) that refused to recognise the corporation—thereby preventing application of the seat theory. In a third case,[16] the European Court of Justice dealt with a Dutch law, which followed the incorporation doctrine to recognise non-Dutch corporations doing all of their business in the Netherlands, but which then ignored the internal affairs rule and sought instead to apply Dutch minimum capital rules to such 'formally foreign' corporations. This too, the court ruled, violated Articles 43 and 48.

The result illustrates a potentially significant interplay between traditional domestic corporate law doctrines and international economic law, which can occur as economic treaties creating regional and even broader compacts move from simply seeking to facilitate the free flow of goods between nations, to call also for the right of enterprises to set up shop in different nations.

B. Limited Liability

The fact that corporations, like any other person, are subject to the environmental, worker protection, consumer safety, and other laws of the nations in which they conduct operations only has as much real significance as the practical ability of nations to ensure that corporations either comply with these laws or else pay the full damages resulting from non compliance. Here, however, the traditional domestic corporate law doctrine that the owners of a corporation are not personally liable for the debts of the corporation—in other words, have limited liability—can act as an important constraint on the ability of nations to ensure compliance or full compensation.

To understand the nature of the problem, it is useful to start by noting that the phrase 'multinational corporation' is typically something of a misnomer. Specifically, the typical multinational business enterprise involved in international business transactions is normally not a single corporation, but rather a group of affiliated corporations tied together in parent-subsidiary relationships. Under these circumstances, if a subsidiary

---

[15] See Case C-212/97, *Centros Ltd v Erhvervs-og Selskaabsstyrelsen*, 1999 ECR I-1459; Case C-208/00, *Uberseering BV v Nordic Construction Co Baumanagement*, 2002 ECR I-9919.

[16] See Case C-167/01, *Kamer Van Koophandel en Fabrieken voor Amsterdam v Inspire Art Ltd*, 2003 ECR I-10155.

conducts its operations in a manner that causes significant environmental damage, harms its workers through unsafe working conditions, or injures consumers by selling dangerous products, only the subsidiary's assets may be at risk to pay the damages. So long as the other affiliated corporations have limited liability, the bulk of the assets of the multinational business enterprise may be beyond reach.

A concrete example can illustrate the danger. An English multinational business enterprise engaged in mining asbestos in South Africa, and in selling the asbestos in other countries. To sell the asbestos in one former English colony, the multinational business enterprise formed a local subsidiary. The subsidiary operated in rented offices, had only four employees, and the liability insurance the subsidiary carried, if indeed it carried any at all, turned out to be woefully inadequate. After waves of lawsuits by persons suffering lung disease from coming into contact with the asbestos, the English parent corporation dissolved the local subsidiary, allowed default judgments against itself in the nation in which the subsidiary sold the asbestos, and then successfully contested jurisdiction when the injured parties attempted to enforce the judgments in English courts; all the while continuing for several more years to sell asbestos in the nation in question through a new, nominally independent, Liechtenstein corporation.

The traditional domestic corporate law tool most directly implicated in this sort of situation is the doctrine of piercing the corporate veil. Under this doctrine, courts can disregard the separate entity status of a corporation and thereby assert jurisdiction over a parent corporation (or controlling individual shareholder) based upon the activities of the controlled corporation in the state or nation, and hold the parent corporation (or controlling individual shareholder) liable for the debts of the controlled corporation. Indeed, the asbestos example above comes from reported decisions dealing with efforts to pierce the veil in order to assert jurisdiction, and to hold parent corporations liable for the subsidiaries' debts.[17] In the United States, the decision to pierce typically results from the parent corporation (or individual controlling shareholder) exercising control in such a manner as to defraud the complaining creditor(s) or otherwise abuse limited liability.[18] This illustrates how a very traditional domestic corporate law doctrine, which often comes up dealing with 'mom and pop' operations, can become critical in dealing with possible regulatory arbitrage and abuse of free trade by multinational corporations.

---

[17] See *Craig v Lake Asbestos of Quebec Ltd*, 843 F.2d 145 (3d Cir 1988); *Adams v Cape Indus*, 1989 WL 651250 (CA 1990).

[18] Eg, FA Gevurtz, 'Piercing Piercing: An Attempt to Lift the Veil of Confusion Surrounding the Doctrine of Piercing the Corporate Veil' (1997) 76 *Or L Rev* 853.

C. Management Selection and Obligations[19]

Discussions of corporate social responsibility typically focus on improving the conduct of the individuals charged with the management of corporations.[20] As explained earlier, often such discussions fail to address why protecting workers, consumers, the environment, the community, or the like is really a matter of corporate law, rather than the province of labour, consumer protection, environmental or other generally applicable laws. Sometimes, proponents of so-called corporate social responsibility seek to use corporate law rules as a means to provide additional sanctions upon corporate managers for violation of other non-corporate laws. This, however, raises the question of why not simply increase the sanctions for anyone, corporate manager or otherwise, violating generally applicable laws. At other times, proponents of so-called corporate social responsibility argue for actions by managers that go beyond the requirements of generally applicable laws. Yet, this forces one to ask why corporate managers (or corporations) must conduct themselves in a manner that goes beyond the strictures of generally applicable law.

Looking at the matter from the standpoint of international trade, a policy argument exists for pushing corporate managers to go beyond the strictures of generally applicable law. Specifically, minimal law compliance fails to address the problem of regulatory arbitrage opened up by international trade, since the nub of the problem is that businesses will set up shop in nations with the weakest regulatory schemes. Yet, there is no reason why non-corporate business enterprises cannot engage in regulatory arbitrage, just like corporations. This fact argues against a solution limited to corporate law. Instead, concerns of regulatory arbitrage might lead one to reconsider approaches to prescriptive jurisdiction or to reconsider the scope of topics appropriately addressed in trade and other international agreements.

One common argument made for imposing, as a matter of domestic corporate law doctrine, a heightened obligation of socially responsible conduct specifically on corporate managers is that this is an appropriate quid pro quo for the 'privilege' of receiving a corporate charter and thereby enjoying limited liability. Centuries ago, when the corporate charter commonly carried monopoly privileges, this argument had merit. In an era of free incorporation based upon filing a paper and paying a fee, the argument seems much less compelling. As discussed above, traditional domestic corporate law contains a doctrine to deal with the abuse of limited liability. Beyond this, the policies behind limited liability and corporate social responsibility are quite different.

---

[19] The following section elaborates on views expressed during a dinner conversation at the conference at which the papers underlying the chapters in this book were presented, proving that the exchange of ideas at conferences such as this are not limited to the formal sessions.

[20] See Wagner, above n 1.

Still, there is one fundamental fact, which corporate law must address in dealing with the conduct of corporate managers (whether through requiring socially responsible conduct or otherwise). Specifically, in running the corporation, corporate managers are controlling other peoples' property. Indeed, the agency problem created by the fact that corporate managers are controlling other peoples' property is at the heart of most of domestic corporate law, and it is within the context of this agency problem that discussion of corporate social responsibility becomes a corporate law issue.

Individual entrepreneurs have, and commonly exercise, discretion to operate their businesses in a manner that provides greater protections for workers, consumers, the environment or the community, than demanded by law. Indeed, in this context, it makes no sense to talk about requiring the entrepreneur to use his or her discretion to do more than the law requires since this would simply change what the law requires. The analysis changes, however, once we start talking about managers controlling other peoples' property. Much of the purpose of traditional domestic corporate law doctrine, as shown below, is to constrain the discretion of corporate managers, in recognition of the fact that they are dealing with other peoples' property rather than with their own. Seen in this light, issues of corporate responsibility impact four different aspects of traditional domestic corporate law doctrine.

The first aspect of traditional domestic corporate law doctrine potentially impacting corporate social responsibility involves who selects corporate managers. After all, once we recognise that managers inherently possess considerable discretion to have a corporation operate in a manner exceeding legal requirements for the protection of workers, consumers, the environment, and the like, the question of who selects the managers that will exercise this discretion assumes considerable importance. In most of the world, stockholders elect the corporation's directors, who, in turn, have the ultimate power to select and command the managers.[21] This reflects the notion that the stockholders 'own' the corporation. Yet, the conclusion that the law should consider the stockholders, by virtue of their contributing capital to the corporation through the purchase of stock, to be the exclusive owners of the corporation, is contestable. Indeed, in Germany and a number of other European nations, domestic corporate law provides the employees of the corporation with the right to elect some members of the corporate board.[22]

The notion that groups other than the stockholders have an ownership stake in the corporation (the so-called stakeholder model of corporate law)

---

[21] Eg, FA Gevurtz, 'The European Origins and Spread of the Corporate Board of Directors' (2004) 33 *Stetson L Rev* 925.

[22] Eg, Mitbestimmungsgesetz [Co-determination Act], 4 May 1976, BGBI. I; G Wirth, M Arnold & M Green, *Corporate Law in Germany* (CH Beck, 2004) 103.

also could impact how corporate managers should exercise their discretion in operating the corporation. Traditional domestic corporate law doctrine limits the discretion of corporate managers, in order to take into account that managers are not dealing with their own property, and, accordingly, must exercise their discretion in a manner consistent with fiduciary obligations to the corporation and its owners. To the extent courts conceive of the owners of the corporation solely to consist of its stockholders, and the interests of the corporation to be entirely congruent with the interests of the stockholders, then traditional domestic corporate law doctrine, rather than promoting corporate social responsibility, actually could penalise actions by managers that favour workers, consumers, the environment, or the like, over the interests of the stockholders.[23] Conversely, to the extent courts follow a stakeholder model, in which the owners of the corporation include groups other than the stockholders, then fiduciary obligations of corporate managers might call for conduct favouring workers, consumers, the environment or the like beyond the minima required by generally applicable labour, consumer protection, or environmental laws.[24] Actually, however, this discussion of to whom directors owe a fiduciary obligation turns out to be more important in the classroom than in real life; at least in the United States. This is because courts in the United States tend to apply the so-called business judgment rule in such a manner as to grant virtually unchecked discretion to corporate directors to set corporate policy in matters of so-called corporate responsibility (so long as the corporation avoids outright illegal conduct).[25]

Even if the law conceives of the stockholders to be the sole owners of the corporation, the stockholders themselves might wish managers to exercise discretion so as to operate the corporation beyond the legal minima with respect to worker, consumer, environmental and community interests. After all, there is no reason to assume, a priori, that stockholders lack any personal sense of social responsibility. This, in turn, means that domestic corporate law must address the extent to which managers must inform stockholders of the manner in which the corporation operates with respect

---

[23] Eg, *Dodge v Ford Motor Co*, 170 NW 668 (Mich 1919).

[24] While there is no authority in the United States compelling corporate directors to act in the interests of workers and other corporate stakeholders (outside of obligations toward creditors owed when the corporation is at or near insolvency), under Article 26 of the Netherlands Enterprise Councils Act, worker councils can challenge decisions by a Dutch corporation's management before a specialised court in Amsterdam. The court is empowered to block implementation of the decision if the 'entrepreneur in balancing the interests involved, could not reasonably have come to his decision.' The court has applied this standard to block corporations from closing down divisions and profitable (and even unprofitable) subsidiaries in the Netherlands. Eg, E Wymeersch, 'A Status Report on Corporate Governance in Some Continental European States', in Klaus J Hopt, et al (eds), *Comparative Corporate Governance—The State Of The Art And Emerging Research* (Oxford University Press, 1998) 1082.

[25] Eg, FA Gevurtz, 'Getting Real about Corporate Social Responsibility: A Reply to Professor Greenfield' (2002) 35 *UC Davis L Rev* 645.

to these sort of concerns, and domestic corporate law must also address the extent to which stockholders should be able to communicate to managers the stockholders' preferences in regard to such issues.[26]

Finally, even if the law views the sole obligation of corporate managers to be profit maximisation for the stockholders, compliance with generally applicable employment, environmental, or consumer protection laws would raise concerns with respect to the managers' duties to the corporation and its stockholders. The reason is because violation of generally applicable laws can expose the corporation to sanctions. Hence, traditional domestic corporate law doctrine may require managers, who decide to have the corporation violate generally applicable laws, not only to face whatever sanction the generally applicable law imposes upon individuals who violate the law, but also to reimburse the corporation for whatever fines or other consequences the corporation suffers.[27] Moreover, the fact that corporate managers are dealing with other people's property imposes an additional obligation with respect to unlawful corporate activities. Specifically, under traditional domestic corporate law doctrine, managers may have a duty to act with reasonable diligence to avoid sanctions to the corporation, not only from unlawful actions by the managers themselves, but also from unlawful actions carried out by lower level corporate employees.[28] In other words, even if the generally applicable labour, consumer protection, or environmental laws impose no affirmative duty upon any persons to monitor and discipline other persons who violate the law, traditional domestic corporate law doctrine may impose such a duty to the extent the violation of generally applicable law produces sanctions upon the corporation.

In sum, traditional domestic corporate law doctrine inevitably raises issues involving corporate social responsibility, not simply because of an ideological wish for corporations and their managers to behave better than individual entrepreneurs, but because such issues arise as a consequence of the fact that corporate managers control other peoples' property. Given the impact of corporate social responsibility on trade policy, the result is once again to suggest that domestic corporate law be considered part of international economic law.

III. CONCLUSION

In designing a survey to determine the extent to which law schools offer classes dealing with international economic law, few might think to include

---

[26] Eg, *State v Honeywell, Inc*, 191 NW2d 406 (Minn 1971).
[27] Eg, *Miller v AT&T*, 507 F.2d 759 (3rd Cir 1974); *Matsumaru v Ootsuru*, 15 Hanrei Jiho 3 (Tokyo D Ct, 1994), translated in JM Ramseyer & M Nakazato, *Japanese Law: An Economic Approach* (University of Chicago Press, 1999) 112–13.
[28] Eg, *In re Caremark, Inc Derivative Litig*, 698 A.2d 959 (Del Ch 1996).

Teaching Int'l Economic Law from a Corporate Perspective 183

a question concerning the role that might be played by a course in basic corporate law.[29] The above discussion, of the ways in which traditional domestic corporate law doctrines impact upon the ability of corporations to exploit free trade by engaging in regulatory arbitrage, suggests that this omission underestimates the degree to which corporate law is pertinent to international economic law. What is true about corporate law and international economic law is also very likely true of many other areas of the curriculum.

---

[29] Indeed, the survey by Bravo, Jackson & Zamora, Ch 10 in this volume, does not—albeit it includes more specialised courses in comparative corporate law and corporate social responsibility.

13

New Agendas for International Economic Law Teaching in India: Including an Agenda in Support of Reform

SEEMA SAPRA

'Revolutions are rare. Reform, perhaps, is even rarer'
'The way of the reformer is hard. ... his problems are more difficult than those of the revolutionary.'[1]

I. INTRODUCTION

THIS CHAPTER ARGUES that at this time of India's ongoing 'Great Transformation,' legal educators and researchers in India need to pay greater attention to international economic law (IEL), and that a renewal and perhaps some re-orientation of the approach to teaching IEL (along with the research and discourse this would generate), could provide significant contributions to and shape and support both the objectives and outcomes of 'reform' in India. New agendas for IEL teaching in India (and indeed for other developing countries also engaged in their own processes of reform and reconstruction), must it is suggested, derive from and support domestic 'reform' objectives. Throughout, this Chapter, the term 'reform' is used as shorthand to refer to the wide range of processes and interventions undertaken by actors and institutions in developing countries (including India) and which are directed at bringing about the social, economic and political transformation required for development.

This Chapter presents some initial thoughts on how we could begin to draw conceptual links between broad issues of reform in India and IEL teaching in the classroom. An important link relates to what reform means or should mean. The reform agenda for India is neither self-evident, nor

---

[1] SP Huntington, *Political Order in Changing Societies* (Yale University Press, 1968) 344.

given. It is likely to be and indeed is increasingly the object of contestation and political struggle over acceptable outcomes and structures. This Chapter suggests that the ideas first developed by Karl Polanyi in his book titled *The Great Transformation*[2] and subsequently elaborated by John Ruggie in his work on embedded liberalism[3] are useful in imagining, defining and mapping the meaning of 'reform' for India. These ideas which were developed in IEL discourse in the context of the regulation of the international and domestic economic orders, not only provide language and concepts that are useful to contestation and debate over substantive meanings and outcomes of 'reform', but they also embrace notions of meaningful societal participation in the processes of both the definition and implementation of 'reform'. Indeed, the concept of *The Great Transformation* is already being applied to the Indian context, and not only in respect of reform of economic governance but also in relation to the significant changes to the social, political and cultural fabric of the country.[4]

It is suggested that IEL teaching in India more actively engage with domestic issues arising on account of the liberalisation of India's external trade as well as the liberalisation of its domestic economy. While being relatively 'new' agendas for Indian law schools, especially in relation to an emphasis on the liberalisation of the country's domestic economy, such agendas would nevertheless still fall within conventional approaches to teaching IEL. This Chapter goes further to suggest that IEL teaching in India consider adopting even broader agendas. These can be found within reform discourses that extend beyond economic reforms into bigger questions about reform of governance in India, with corresponding implications for constitutional law, federalism, reconstructions of meanings and structures of governance, and in their broadest sense become questions about negotiating and defining the social purpose of domestic governance and of providing adequate delivery systems for such governance. IEL teaching in India cannot remain unresponsive to and outside of these wider reform discourses.

Specifically, this Chapter makes a few initial and tentative forays into imagining more concrete implications of this discussion for IEL teaching in India. First, there is a need to consider teaching IEL as part of different discourses to serve the different agendas of the broad governance reform

---

[2] K Polanyi, *The Great Transformation* (Beacon Press, 1957).
[3] See JG Ruggie, 'International Regimes, Transactions, and Change: Embedded Liberalism in the Postwar Economic Order' (1982) 36 *Int'l Org* 379.
[4] See N Kumar, *The Great Transformation: Education as the KEY to India's Split Development*, available at www.idpad.org/pdf/Nita_Kumar-Paper%2013.pdf; A Vanaik, *The Great Transformation: The Old Congress has Changed Unrecognizably*, available at http://www.tniarchives.org/detail_page.phtml?page=archives_vanaik_transformation; PB Mehta, *India: Reform and the Politics of Gradual Accommodation*, available at www.carnegieendowment.org/files/Mehta.pdf.

process. This would contribute towards the creation of a mega-discourse or a network of linked discourses that would be crucial to the appropriate framing, designing and execution of the broad reform process and agenda for the country. By packaging different reform discourses together, IEL courses could enable the creation of new knowledge, the development of new discourses, and the creation of new capacity as well as space for useful social, political, constitutional, and legal activity. Second, as part of the case for more IEL teaching, efforts are required to broaden the audience or market for IEL knowledge, and increasing 'demand' for IEL would be an important component. IEL teaching would thus facilitate stakeholder participation by making more strongly the case for its own relevance. Third, IEL teaching in India might usefully develop an inward looking focus, by engaging more with issues and problems confronting the domestic political economy. And fourth, IEL teaching and research must develop new issue linkages between competing substantive values, competing interests, and substantive outcomes and procedural mechanisms. In doing so, IEL teaching would contribute towards constructing a more inclusive redefinition of the 'problem-space' of reform in India.[5] This would, it is hoped, result in fairer and more efficient reform outcomes. (These ideas are further developed in this Chapter later. However, a more comprehensive exploration of such linkages would form part of a curriculum development program).

Also, as an initial matter, some other points need to be stated. First, any thinking about IEL teaching in India would necessarily have to take place in the larger context of an understanding of legal education in India generally, and of the constraints (but also un-explored and under-utilised possibilities) that determine the role and provision of legal education in a poor developing country like India. Second, though this Chapter addresses the 'teaching' of IEL, its arguments are based upon a broader concept of 'knowledge creation, dissemination, and use' which would, in addition to teaching, also include research, discourse, scholarship as well as the practice and application of such knowledge. Also, the suggestions made here are not made with a view to advance the cause of the discipline of IEL, but instead with the expectation that the creation, dissemination and utilisation of such disciplinary knowledge would advance other causes of national interest. Arguments for increasing the relevance of IEL teaching in India and for creating discourses that feed IEL knowledge into broader reform discourses are not narrowly conceived in the sense of ensuring that domestic law and

---

[5] I borrow the concept of 'problem-space' from David Scott, *Conscripts of Modernity: The Tragedy of Colonial Enlightenment* (Duke University Press, 2002) 2–6. He questions the limitations that a concept of problem-space brings into the context of intervention. A defined problem-space fails to question how problems get defined in the first place, why certain questions get asked and others do not.

structures remain or become compliant with IEL. Instead, it is hoped that IEL teaching would facilitate a more interactive engagement between the international regime and domestic political economy structures, so that domestic actors can more effectively use and respond to, as well as influence IEL, in order to achieve broader domestic and international objectives for India.

II. TEACHING IEL IN INDIA

Without going into a detailed account of the present state of and future prospects for legal education in India, it is nevertheless relevant to recall the constraints that any effort directed at improvement of the system must address. The more obvious constraints are inadequate financial and academic resources which limit opportunities for both teaching and research.[6] Further, the resources that do exist, tend to be located in elite institutions leading to huge differences in quality between law schools.[7] Despite difficulties, current events in India provide an opportunity for academia to reflect upon new agendas for the teaching of IEL in India. Structural changes in India have led to the development of a strong discourse on 'reform' in India in addition to the more traditional discourse on 'development.' One strand of this reform discourse extends to the reform of higher education in India and includes a sub-discourse on reform of legal education in India.[8] There is now a significant momentum in India behind efforts for the improvement of legal education.

There are almost 695 law colleges in India which offer an LLB degree approved by the Bar Council of India.[9] These 695 law colleges

---

[6] The problems include under-funded libraries; non-availability of electronic resources and in some cases even computers; and non-availability of suitable study materials including text books. In addition, inadequate remuneration fails to attract qualified and committed faculty to teaching careers, leading to low standards. See R Dhawan, 'Means, Motives and Opportunities: Reflecting on Legal Research in India' 50 Mod L Rev 725 (1987). The situation described by Dhawan by and large continues to persist today.

[7] See brief discussion on qualitative differences between the premier institutions including the new National Law Schools and the majority of the other old regional and local law schools below in this section.

[8] The Government of India has created a National Knowledge Commission, whose mandate includes the study and the making of specific recommendations for the improvement of higher education. A separate working group has been established for legal education. See their website at http://knowledgecommission.gov.in/. See also P Agarwal, *Higher Education in India: The Need for Change* (ICRIER Working Paper No 180, 2006); S Kaul, *Higher Education in India: Seizing the Opportunity* (ICRIER Working Paper No 179, 2006).

[9] The figures available are as of 1 Jan., 2006. See http://barcouncilofindia.nic.in/. At present, the Bar Council of India (acting through its Legal Education Committee) constituted under the Advocates Act, 1961 is by statute responsible for the promotion of legal education and for setting standards for such education in consultation with Universities. It is also required to undertake inspections of all universities imparting the LLB degree, and 'recognize' those universities

are affiliated to 111 different Universities. While some universities are stand-alone law schools, in other cases the number of law colleges per university ranges from 2 to 38. A revolution of sorts in Indian legal education commenced in 1987 with the creation of the first National Law School in Bangalore which developed a new five-year integrated LLB curriculum for students fresh from high school.[10] Since then, this highly successful model has been replicated across the country.[11] Such new and better resourced law schools are attracting more qualified and competent teaching and research faculty. Admission to the new premier institutions is extremely competitive with national-level entrance exams.[12] The emergence of these new law schools has coincided with a booming market for corporate legal practice. Well-paying corporate law firms have made law practice an attractive career prospect for young people. To a large extent, the momentum for legal education reform is elite-driven. This is because the lucrative opportunities for law graduates that are creating this demand for high quality legal education exist mostly in the corporate sector. As a result, legal education standards are now quite high in the new 5-year national law schools and also (though to a lesser extent) within the traditional premier national institutions. On the other hand, standards in many of the non-elite law colleges spread across India remain low. These function essentially as degree granting institutions but with little value added in terms of legal education or enhancement of career prospects.

I now turn to the specific background of IEL teaching in Indian law schools. As recently as ten years ago, teaching of international law in most law schools extended only to a general course on public international law. A few law schools offered other courses like private international law or international environmental law. Even though the Uruguay Round had been in its final stages during the author's three year LLB course (1992–1995),

---

whose LLB degree will be accepted as qualification for enrolment as an advocate. The Bar Council of India Rules on Standards of Legal Education available online at http://lawmin.nic.in/la/subord/bcipart4.htm set out very minimal requirements for recognition. These rules also list the subjects/modules that are taught for the LLB. International Economic Law as an optional module for final year students.

[10] The traditional LLB route was (and still is) a 3 year post-graduate course for students who have already acquired a 3 year graduate degree in another academic discipline. This format is still being followed at the older law schools including at the law department of the University of Delhi.

[11] The 7 National Law Schools are: National Law School of India University, Bangalore (1987); National Law Institute University, Bhopal (1998); National Academy of Legal Studies and Research, Hyderabad (1998); Hidyatullah National Law University, Raipur; Gujarat National Law University, Gandhi Nagar; National Law University, Jodhpur (1999); West Bengal National University of Juridical Sciences, Kolkata (1999).

[12] The NALSAR LLB entrance exam in 2002 was taken by 5,145 students out of which 50 were granted admission, giving a student conversion ratio of 1:103. See http://www.rccnalsar.org/admission_process.htm. Applicants use coaching institutes to prepare for these exams.

there was no classroom discussion on any aspect of it. No discussion on TRIPS ever entered our discussions in the course on intellectual property. This position has changed. Today, law schools in India are teaching a wide range of international law courses with an increasing emphasis on IEL. The National Law School of India University at Bangalore for instance offers the following international law courses as part of its LLB program: International Trade Law;[13] Conflict of Laws; Public International Law (in two parts); International Taxation; International Commercial Arbitration; Fundamentals of Corporate Finance; International Criminal Tribunals; European Law; International Aspects of Corporate Tax; and Dispute Settlement in International Trade and Investment.[14] Research centres with a focus on IEL are also being established in India.[15] International intellectual property law is another area where teaching and research in India is rapidly gaining ground.

Even though IEL can be quite broadly defined, this Chapter's suggestions mainly draw upon teaching and research on trade (WTO) and investment law issues in India. Today all the new national law schools as well as most other leading law schools offer (usually) an elective masters level course on international trade law (ITL) that covers the WTO. The curricula of these courses tend to reflect a combination of two broad approaches to teaching ITL. The first is a basic introduction to the WTO, and the law of the WTO agreements. Thus the topics covered include institutional issues, dispute settlement, GATT, TRIPS, services, the WTO agreements on Technical Barriers to Trade and Sanitary and Phytosanitary Measures, anti-dumping remedies and the regulation of subsidies. Foreign textbooks are usually used and the materials looked at are the WTO agreements and DSU reports, as well as commentaries. The second approach focuses on development and developing countries in the WTO generally. There is some discussion of the history of the developing countries association with the GATT. Topics covered include UNCTAD, the UN debates on the New International Economic Order, the right to

---

[13] The course description for this module, available on the school's website, reads: 'International sales, transportation with reference to shipping and aviation, financing and settlement of commercial disputes will be the major components of the course. Apart from the relevant Indian laws, the focus will be mainly upon the international legal conventions and Indian legal system in these four areas. In addition, the international trade regime, as reflected in the Foreign Trade (Development and Regulation) Act and other related enactments will also be discussed in detail.'

[14] For details of course outlines see http://www.nls.ac.in/academic_programmes_undergraduate_courses.html.

[15] WTO related legal research institutes and initiatives in India include the following: Ministry of Commerce Chair in WTO at the National Law School at Bangalore; Centre for WTO Studies at the Indian Institute of Foreign Trade in New Delhi; Centre for WTO Studies at National Law University, Jodhpur; and Centre for Studies in WTO Laws at West Bengal National University of Juridical Sciences.

development, Special & Differential Treatment for Developing Countries, the Generalised System of Preferences for developing countries, and perhaps a discussion of the Doha 'development' trade round at the WTO. While the first approach is doctrinal or legalistic, the second tends to be descriptive and historical.

IEL courses on offer in Indian law schools are popular, but less than 0.1 per cent of all law students in India who take a course on IEL probably go on to use their knowledge in future careers.[16] This small percentage includes students who go on to join law firms and work either on intellectual property issues or on trade remedy litigation (safeguards, anti-dumping and CVD). Governance positions in India (including positions specifically charged with making trade policy and advising on WTO matters) are still largely filled by candidates who are recruited as civil servants at the start of their careers, and not from among law students who study IEL or lawyers who practice IEL. Finally, a few students might go on to teach law and some might decide to work for an NGO. For the most part, IEL courses are thus not seen as being particularly career-friendly. They do, however, get valued for the topicality of the issues, for their perceived elitism, and for their possible usefulness as a base for further study abroad. Besides the law schools offering LLB and postgraduate degrees, another institution with a long history of teaching IEL is the Centre for International Legal Studies at the School of International Studies of the Jawaharlal Nehru University in Delhi. It does not, however, offer professional law degrees but rather offers non professional masters degrees.[17] Most doctoral research on the GATT or the WTO in India has traditionally been carried out here.

---

[16] This is an estimate by the author based upon her experience in India. The actual figure is likely to be much less than 0.1%.

[17] The MPhil/PhD in international law program has a course on IEL (that covers definition and history of international economic law; new international economic order; charter of economic rights and duties of states; 'soft law' and 'hard law'; permanent sovereignty over natural resources; transnational watercourses law; intellectual property rights; draft code of conduct on transfer of technology; draft code of conduct on transnational corporations; multilateral investment guarantee agency; trade related investment measures; international centre for settlement of investment disputes; bilateral investment protection agreements; international monetary law (IMF/World Bank); right to development), as well as a course on International Trade Law (that covers origin and history of GATT; MNF clause; national treatment clause; prohibition of quantitative restrictions; general exceptions; security exceptions; art XVIII B; code on anti-dumping; code on subsidies; agreement on agriculture; dispute settlement understanding; India and WTO dispute settlement mechanisms; trade and environment; social clause; competition policy; international commodity agreements; the common fund for commodities; international sales of goods; lex mercatoria; international commercial arbitration). See K Bravo, Chapter 10 in this volume (International Economic Law in US Law Schools: Evaluating Its Pedagogy and Identifying Future Challenges) for information on topics covered by IEL courses in US law schools.

While making the case for more, as well as more relevant, teaching of IEL in India, it should be acknowledged that law graduates when looking for work have the impression that there is a lack of demand for IEL knowledge among prospective employers in India. Indeed, during a short research visit to India for this Chapter, I asked some lawyers that were involved in WTO related legal work whether in their opinion Indian law schools were teaching enough IEL and whether there was sufficient capacity building occurring. A response received from more than one lawyer (and these were people who ought to know) was that the issue was not the availability of expertise but the availability of work. There just was not enough IEL related work going around for Indian lawyers, and that the work that there was, did not pay well either. Leaving aside anti-dumping cases in India (which pay well as the clients tend to be private industry), the number of Indian lawyers engaged in other IEL related work is miniscule. Further, these few lawyers do not work exclusively on IEL issues. Their WTO work forms a small part of their overall practice and they make their money mainly from their non-WTO practice. Given this perception of the lack of opportunities to practice trade or WTO law in India, shared by law students as well as law teachers, there does not exist in India a general sense that law schools ought to be teaching more IEL or perhaps teaching it differently.

III. NEW AGENDAS FOR IEL TEACHING IN INDIA

This Chapter argues that despite the perception that there is enough IEL teaching in India to meet the 'limited demand' for capacity in this area, there is a need not only to teach more of IEL, but more importantly to rethink why and how IEL should be taught in India. This Chapter has already suggested that new agendas for IEL teaching and indeed for legal education in general must support the national project of 'reform' and 'development'. How can IEL teaching contribute to this project of national transformation? This and the following section will explore the linkages that exist or could be constructed between the IEL classroom and IEL research activity and the Indian reform project.

An important link relates to the beneficial effects of the exchange of knowledge and ideas. Indian reform discourses could gain from importing concepts, ideas and knowledge developed within IEL discourses. In particular, the ideas in The Great Transformation and the idea of embedded liberalism could be imported from IEL and used to challenge and redefine the meaning and objectives of governance reform in India. In order to further explore what I mean by this and why this is necessary, a brief introductory discussion of these ideas and their relevance for projects of national reform follows.

The Great Transformation is Karl Polanyi's alternative narrative of the history of the economic and political order in Europe in the 19th and the 20th centuries as an account 'of the rise and fall of market society'.[18] Polanyi describes two great transformations of state–society relations over this period, with the first inevitably leading to the second (the double movement). The first transformation was 'the emergence of market society out of mercantilism'[19] (1815–1914) and required the commodification of labour. The second was 'the collapse of market society into fascism and world war'[20] and was the result of an unplanned but inevitable protectionist counter-movement to the first, as all sections of society including land, labour and capital reacted to protect 'society' itself from the ravages of an unregulated market. What is the significance of Polanyi's Great Transformation for the Indian national reform project? Commentators on The Great Transformation note that Polanyi's account demonstrated fundamental flaws and contradictions in the idea of self-regulating markets.[21] Polanyi's message was that 'a society that elevated economic motivation to absolute priority could not survive'.[22] As Joseph Stiglitz explains, the 'market' is only a part of the broader economy and that the broader economy is part of a still broader society. Economic systems or reforms 'can affect how individuals relate to one another'[23] and can sometimes have adverse consequences for 'social capital' or the social order. The lesson for Indian reformers would thus be that the establishment of a market economy must not be seen as an end in itself, but as the means to more fundamental ends.[24]

Building upon Polanyi, John Ruggie used the term embedded liberalism to describe the economic order established under the global economic regimes that emerged after the second world war. As used by international economic lawyers, this term conveys the normative agreement among developed country governments about the substantive manner in which trade liberalisation under the GATT would be balanced by attention to domestic economic security and stability by these governments, through a series of protectionist and welfare measures. The embedded liberalism

---

[18] F Block and M Somers, 'Beyond the Economistic Fallacy: The Holistic Social Science of Karl Polanyi', in T Skocpol (ed), *Vision and Method in Historical Sociology* (Cambridge University Press, 1994) 47, 53. See also F Block, 'Introduction', in *Great Transformations: Economic Ideas and Institutional Change in the Twentieth Century* (Cambridge University Press, 2000) xxii.
[19] Block and Somers, above n 18, at 53.
[20] Ibid.
[21] Block and Somers, above n 18. For Polanyi, the goal of establishing unregulated markets was a utopian experiment that was destined to fail.
[22] Block and Somers, above n 18, at 64.
[23] J Stiglitz, 'Forward', in *Great Transformations: Economic Ideas and Institutional Change in the Twentieth Century* (Cambridge University Press, 2000) x.
[24] Ibid at xv.

model of managing the global economic order worked well from 1945 till the 1970s. It was:

> a grand social bargain whereby all sectors of society agreed to open markets, ... but also to contain and share the social adjustment costs that open markets inevitably produce.[25]

It must be pointed out that the embedded liberalism compromise described by Ruggie worked only to sustain the social order within the developed economies of that time, who he described as the regime-givers. Ruggie, noted that the compromise of embedded liberalism was never fully extended to the developing countries.[26]

Despite its usual application to describe actualised or aspirational economic orders in developed societies, the idea of embedded liberalism can be usefully imported into reform debates in developing country contexts. This is because this idea speaks directly to issues of governance reform. At its core, embedded liberalism is concerned with 'governance' and its roots or embeddedness in a given political, social and economic context. Thus, for Ruggie, the social purpose of governance including economic governance must be compatible with the 'collective reality' of the times as to the proper scope of governmental or political authority.[27] Objectives of governance must reflect popular and democratic understandings of appropriate 'state–society relations' relevant to the time's social context. Ruggie explains that the social purpose of governance for a state is forged by the balancing between 'authority' and 'market' in that polity. This balance then defines the 'legitimate social purposes' for which state power can be employed in the domestic economy.[28] In other words, it is through political and social processes in a site for governance, that social compacts are formed or consensus is reached on how far the State ought to interfere with the market in the domestic economy and for what reasons. Embedded liberalism thus denotes a state of affairs where economic governance is properly embedded in the social and political order. This Chapter suggests that this idea of identifying the legitimate social purpose of governance for the state in accordance with a society's collective reality, holds much significance for reform projects in developing countries, and in particular, for democracies like India.

---

[25] JG Ruggie, 'Taking Embedded Liberalism Global: The Corporate Connection', in D Held and M Koenig-Archibugi (eds), *Taming Globalization: Frontiers of Governance* (Polity Press, 2003) 94.

[26] Ruggie, above n 3. See also S Sapra, 'Ideas of Embedded Liberalism and Current and Future Challenges for the WTO', in *WTO Law and Process: Proceedings of the 2005 and 2006 Annual WTO Conferences* (British Inst of Intl & Comparative Law, 2007).

[27] This sense of 'embedded liberalism' is relevant for the current debates about governance, constitutionalisation, and legitimacy that are taking place as part of the larger debates about the future of the WTO.

[28] Ruggie, above n 3, at 386.

The significance of the idea of embedded liberalism for reform in India, becomes clearer once we clarify what reform means. Lewis and Litai define the concept of reform as a 'deliberate and managed process of change.'[29] Samuel Huntington differentiates between reform and what he calls 'consolidation'.[30] The difference between the two lies in the direction of change. For Huntington, a reform is a change 'in the direction of greater social, economic, or political equality, a broadening of participation in society and polity'.[31] Similarly, Hirschman emphasises that in reform the:

> power of hitherto privileged groups is curbed and the economic position and social status of underprivileged groups is correspondingly improved.[32]

Thus there are two kinds of changes in reform, an increase in substantive equality and an improvement in procedural or participatory equality. Since the early 1990s, Indian society has commenced on its own Great Transformation. India's high economic growth rate and growing economic clout are the most visible aspects of this transformation for the outside world. There is however, a dark side to this ongoing transformation. A common theme in commentary upon Indian growth tells a story of 'two Indias'.[33] This story seeks to remind both Indian reformers and outside observers that Indian economic reforms and growth are not necessarily benefiting the vast majority of poor Indians who might become the 'losers' of economic reform programs and globalisation led growth.[34] It is suggested that the ideas of the Great Transformation and embedded liberalism can be useful in generating a discourse about whether the changes being wrought by Indian reforms, are resulting in true 'reform' in the sense in which Huntington and Hirschman define this concept.

---

[29] JW Lewis & L Xue, 'Social Change and Political Reform in China: Meeting the Challenge of Success' (2003) 176 *The China Quarterly* 926, 926.

[30] Huntington, above n 1, at 344. Huntington also distinguishes between reform and revolution. While the former refers to changes to leadership, policy, and political institutions, which are 'limited in scope and moderate in speed'; the latter involves 'rapid, complete, and violent change in values, social structure, political institutions, governmental policies, and social-political leadership'.

[31] Ibid.

[32] See AO Hirschman, *Journeys Towards Progress* (New York, Twentieth Century Fund, 1963) 267.

[33] See S Acharya, *Can India Grow Without Bharat?* (Academic Foundation, 2007). A Google search of 'two Indias' brings up countless stories on the growing disparity between the winners and the losers of economic reforms in India. See *A Tale of Two Indias*, Guardian, 5 April, 2006, available at http://www.guardian.co.uk/india/story/0,,1746948,00.html; *Do not Reinforce Two Indias*, Businessweek, 2 Nov, 2006, available at http://www.businessweek.com/globalbiz/content/nov2006/gb20061102_285971.htm; *A Tale of Two Indias*, Time, 29 Nov, 2006, available at http://www.time.com/time/asia/covers/501041206/story.html.

[34] According to the latest census of the Government of India conducted in 2001, 300 million Indians subsist on less than $1 a day and are unable to access the opportunities offered by economic growth.

In a poor democracy like India, growing economic inequality between social groups not only threatens the future of the economic reform programs,[35] but also provides seed for social conflict and possible violent disruption of the emerging new order. Indian reformers therefore need to ensure that growth and its benefits are more fairly distributed across society. The Chapter suggests that IEL discourse can help conceptualise the objectives of the Indian reform project in a more inclusive manner. For instance, the conceptualisation of reform and development in India as a Great Transformation, positions us at the top of the objectives pyramid and provides an overarching perspective downwards to more specific objectives and agendas. More specifically, it forces agents guiding India's economic reforms programs to acknowledge, respond to and include alternative values from the wider reform discourses in reform agendas. These alternative values of equity, social justice, human rights, solidarity, constitutional guarantees, democracy, pluralism, and egalitarianism can be found in various other existing discourses. Similarly, Indian reformers could more consciously adopt the goal of forging an embedded liberalism compromise for India that embeds economic governance in India within a fair and just social and political order.

As part of its Great Transformation, India too must arrive at an embedded liberalism bargain that creates a stable, balanced, and socially legitimate and just order. Indeed, the very negotiation of this social compromise is a crucial part of the embedding process and requires an inclusive and participatory discourse which not only serves to legitimate outcomes (as a strategy of political mobilisation) but helps craft socially acceptable outcomes in the first place. State–society relations in India are in a state of flux. New objectives of reform and governance in India must themselves be negotiated through participatory political, social and economic processes. An appropriate balance between the market and political authority that respects politically legitimate values and objectives for the social purpose of governance in India must be crafted. Crafting such a compromise will require mediation through the politico-legal structures and values embodied in the Indian Constitution.[36] In using the term embedding liberalism, this Chapter does not imply a greater orientation towards market determined outcomes. Instead, the idea of embedded liberalism is useful because it

---

[35] A recent example is the defeat of the BJP in the most recent Indian parliamentary elections (2004) which they sought to fight on a slogan of 'India Shining'.

[36] These constitutional principles include substantive guarantees like the fundamental rights of all citizens and the Directive Principles of State Policy. The latter can be seen as a constitutional statement reflecting the constituent assembly's consensus on the social purpose of governance in India. Drafted in 1948, this statement on the social purpose of governance in India might require some updating. Reform of Indian governance must also respect procedural and substantive constitutional guarantees that include respect for Indian federalism, local self-governance, and allocation of power between the executive, the legislature and the judiciary.

enables a discourse on how 'governance' or political authority acquires 'purpose' and thereby 'legitimacy' by virtue of its being embedded in the political, social and economic fabric of the site for governance. All stable and legitimate forms of economic governance must necessarily be well embedded in a democratic society. Embedding liberalism in India would require that the scope of economic governance that is eventually negotiated democratically, satisfies social and political constituencies and reflects and accommodates substantive objectives of social justice.

An important contribution of IEL teaching and research to reform in India would therefore be to provide concepts which could frame the domestic discourse on reforms, and provide avenues for contestability of reform objectives and the governance structures that are being installed to deliver these objectives. Besides the ideas of The Great Transformation and embedded liberalism, the IEL epistemic community has been a fertile ground for the development of other ideas. Many of these (for example collective preferences, multi-functionality, subsidiarity, direct effect etc) would also have resonance for Indian reform discourses, concerned as they are with issues of allocation of power, and the negotiation and legitimation of substantive values for multi-layered governance projects. There are also other ways in which IEL teaching or research could contribute to reform. Broadly, we could consider the agendas for IEL teaching in this regard under four functional but interconnected heads. These would be (i) the facilitation of appropriate discourses; (ii) the facilitation of stakeholder participation; (iii) the development of an inward looking focus; and (iv) the creation of appropriate issue linkages. Each of these is discussed further in the following section.

IV. SPECIFIC IMPLICATIONS FOR IEL TEACHING

This Chapter has suggested that in order to define its new agendas, IEL teaching reflect upon its potential contribution to reform in India. In this final section, this Chapter attempts to identify the specific agendas that this might raise for IEL teaching in India. The four specific objectives discussed in this section are not unconnected.

A. Enabling a Mega-Discourse on Reform

IEL teaching could contribute towards creating a mega-discourse or a network of linked discourses on governance reform. Such discourse networks are required to frame, design and execute the Indian reform project. Why is such a mega-discourse necessary? The literature on the political economy of reform in India is instructive in this regard. It unequivocally underlines the urgent need for a broad-based and inclusive discourse in India that would support the case for economic reforms and help legitimate them.[37] The lack of broad-based support for liberalisation in India has been attributed to the government's failure to communicate the need for liberalisation.[38] It has been suggested that the market has not yet become ideologically embedded in India and that in fact the market is competing with other powerful political formations—lower caste assertiveness, Hindu nationalism, and issue-based social activism.[39] Commentators have accused the government of having implemented the first generation of Indian reforms by 'stealth'.[40] Jenkins describes how in implementing the first generation of reforms, political leaders sought to relegate reforms to a secondary political status, and failed to promote, 'at the levels of rhetoric and conviction, the democratic possibilities of various market principles—for instance, the market's ability to threaten status hierarchies.'[41] Others have criticised the Indian reform program for being ad-hoc and for lacking a clear framework.[42] Sachs et al note that:

> though Indian governments since 1991 have demonstrated a pragmatic, 'one-step-here and two-steps-there' approach towards economic reforms, a full-blown, systematic rationale for why India needs reforms has not been boldly articulated in politics.[43]

They argue that:

> [a] discourse and language that can turn ideas about the economic consequences of markets into a political rhetoric of mass welfare are crying out for serious attention in India.[44]

Commentators have argued that the absence of a clear and explicit written statement of a framework for the reforms has limited debate.[45] Further, the

---

[37] See R Jenkins, *Democratic Politics and Economic Reform in India* (Cambridge University Press, 1999); B Debroy & R Mukherji, *India: The Political Economy of Reforms* (Rajiv Gandhi Institute for Contemporary Studies, 2004); P Bardhan, *The Political Economy of Reform in India* (National Council of Applied Economic Research, 1999); FR Frankel, *India's Political Economy 1947–2004: The Gradual Revolution* (Oxford University Press, 2005).

[38] Debroy & Mukherji, above n 37, at 6.

[39] R Jenkins, 'The Ideologically Embedded Market: Political Legitimation and Economic Reform in India', in *Markets in Historical Contexts: Ideas and Politics in the Modern World* (Cambridge University Press, 2004) 206. He regrets that Indian reformers have failed to find 'an idiom through which to "normalize"', through political discourse, market orientated policies'.

[40] Bardhan, above n 37, at 7. 'Like the stealth bomber, reform in India has largely avoided the political radar screen'. The literature differentiates between those reforms which were made early on and were relatively easy to implement (called the first generation reforms) and those still needed to complete the project, which will be more difficult to implement (the second generation reforms).

[41] Jenkins, above n 39, at 206.

[42] See D Nayar, *Democracy and Development: The Indian Experience*, Prem Bhatia Memorial Lecture at University of Delhi (2001).

[43] JDSachs, A Varshney & N Bajpai, 'Introduction', in *India in the Era of Economic Reforms* (Oxford University Press, 1999) 14.

[44] Ibid at 24.

[45] See A Virmani, 'A New Development Paradigm: Employment, Entitlement and Empowerment', in Debroy & Mukherji, above n 37, at 81.

changing nature of the Indian state, also calls for new discourses within India's federal government structures that re-conceptualise the role and purpose of governance itself.[46] Weiner notes:

> The pursuit of market friendly policies by state governments requires a change in the mindset of state politicians, new skills within state bureaucracies, and a different kind of politics. Most fundamentally, it requires rethinking on the part of state politicians, activists in non-governmental organizations, journalists, and politically engaged citizens as to what is the proper role of government, and how and to what end these limited resources should be employed.[47]

These critiques of the manner in which economic reforms have been introduced by the Indian state and the linkages that exist between Indian democracy, federalism, and the changing Indian political economy explain why more discourses on reform are needed. The study of the interaction between the Indian political economy and IEL is only one of these multiple discourses. It is suggested that the IEL epistemic community in India is well placed to reach out to other discourses, and to identify the need for new (presently absent) discourses on reform. This Chapter is not suggesting that IEL teaching can step in and fill these lacunae by itself. However IEL scholarship is one of many discourses and social processes where interventions to this end could be initiated by interested actors, in this case, by IEL academics, researchers, and practitioners. Three specific contributions could be made. IEL teaching could generate new knowledge and discourses by fostering an inward looking focus on the curricula. It could create new issue linkages. And it could empower stakeholders by making available to them the relevant knowledge and new ideas to critically analyse the reform project and devise better solutions to problems. All this would engender more inclusive debates, which are necessary to build consensus on reform and to create legitimacy for actual programs.

B. Facilitation of Stakeholder Participation

India needs more IEL knowledge despite the perception that studying IEL or trade law in law school does not seem to offer increased career opportunities. Academics of course are not responsible for a lack of adequate opportunity to use particular knowledge and skill, yet they must, as part of their social teaching and research functions, help 'create' the space for the use of the knowledge they impart by drawing the necessary connections between such knowledge and the future career of the student, which in most cases would be located in the domestic Indian context. IEL courses in India

---

[46] See M Weiner, 'The Regionalization of Indian Politics and Its Implications for Economic Reform', in Sachs, Varshney & Bajpai, above n 43, at 292–3.
[47] Ibid at 292–3.

must not be oriented towards preparing a student for a possible though extremely unlikely career at the WTO, or in a Brussels or Washington trade law firm, or at UNCTAD. Neither must they be directed only at preparing a student for a career at an Indian anti-dumping firm or IP firm, or in the handful of NGOs in India that are beginning to work on trade matters. Instead, IEL teaching in India must be made relevant for many more students who will end up working for the central, state or local governments, become entrepreneurs, join private business or industry as lawyers or managers, enter politics, or work for the media.

Thus, teaching IEL in India should address not only issues pertaining to the supply of legal knowledge and capacity building, but it should also make the arguments for the usefulness of and demand for such knowledge. Accordingly, IEL educators will need to consider whether they are defining the 'demand' for IEL knowledge in sufficiently broad terms. Thus, the demand part of the argument would not only have to list the possible uses and benefits of such knowledge (for the student and for structural improvements to the domestic political economy), but would also have to engage in a critique of existing systems that govern the economy. Such critiques would need to establish that reform of existing governance systems and political economy structures would gain from perspectives provided by knowledge of IEL, both in making stronger the case for reform but also in imagining new systems and structures that are better able to deliver domestic policy goals. Indeed, the need for IEL knowledge will be increasingly felt within state government structures and within new institutions where it will become necessary to debate, create and implement trade policy at the state levels. More specifically, by broadening the availability of IEL knowledge and demonstrating its usefulness, IEL teaching and research will also contribute towards improvement of the trade policy making process in India by involving greater numbers of stakeholders.[48]

Future planning for IEL teaching in India should thus consider a broader target audience than LLB students. IEL courses could be specifically designed for existing legal practitioners, policy makers (including legislators and bureaucrats), and other stakeholders drawn from business, journalists, consumers, industry associations, civil society, and non-governmental organisations.[49]

---

[48] For discussion of the issues involving trade policy making reform in India see J Sen, *The Importance of Institutionalizing? Structured Consultations in Evaluating Trade Proposals: Lessons from India's Experience and their Wider Relevance*, IPPG Briefing Paper No 11, March 2007, available at http://www.ippg.org.uk/PDF/Importance%20of%20Institutionalising%2011.pdf; J Sen, *Trade Policy Making in India: The Reality Below the Waterline*, June 2003, available at http://www.lse.ac.uk/collections/internationalTradePolicyUnit/events.htm.

[49] A number of governance schools are being established in India. These schools could also offer IEL courses. The MIT School of Government (MIT-SOG), Pune-India, has demonstrated some initiative in this direction. See their website at http://www.mitsog.com/index.htm.

C. Development of an Inward Looking Focus

Courses on IEL in India must draw the necessary connections between IEL and its future evolution, and the current and future challenges for the political economy within India and Asia in general. Thus, while IEL courses in India will need to introduce the student to the WTO, ie what goes on in Geneva, they must lay an equal if not greater emphasis on IEL issues originating in Delhi, in other state capitals and in various institutions, structures and processes across the country, as well as in the broader region surrounding India. There exists a strong case for an inward looking focus for IEL courses. At present, IEL courses in India often do not consider the domestic and international issues that IEL raises from the perspective of the domestic and regional political economy. An inward focus would be useful not only because the domestic environment is where most students will locate their careers, but also because in not doing so, these courses miss out on big substantive questions of how IEL interacts with the domestic political economy of India and on the many fascinating research projects that these questions would offer. In addition, the study of IEL in its interaction with the domestic political economy would also generate the most useful kinds of research, discourse and knowledge-creation in the Indian context, which could contribute in a significant way to the overall national agenda and efforts for reform and development.

A focus on domestic issues in the IEL classroom and research agenda will help in better identification of IEL related concerns for India. Thus, rather than treating the international treaties as their foundational material, and then going on to interpret and respond to Indian problems, the analysis would begin first with the definition of the problem in the light of Indian reform agendas and then move on to consider how IEL contributes to the solution. Looking inwards will enable Indian scholars to externalise and place Indian issues and concerns within the international discourse. Adoption of a deliberate inward looking stance will also result in bringing new issues into the IEL classroom. Many of these issues are not part of IEL curricula in India at present. This is because IEL courses focus on teaching the international law to students. I suggest that new IEL curricula be created that make the study of domestic reform the central concern of these courses. This will call for a more in-depth study of IEL than at present. After gaining familiarity with IEL, such courses will go on to analyse Indian reform issues in the light of this knowledge. Some examples of where this might lead can be mentioned. IEL teaching could facilitate the study of comparative trade law (ie, internal trade law discourse from other jurisdictions) to identify and respond to Indian problems.[50] An inward looking focus would also help

---

[50] For instance, what lessons can Indian legal reformers learn from the study of non-direct effect of WTO treaties in the US and EC legal systems?

create momentum for the adoption of new reform projects like the creation of an internal market in India.[51]

D. Creation of Appropriate Issue Linkages

IEL teaching and research must also draw much needed issue linkages to facilitate more inclusive reform discourses. These linkages need to bring in substantive values and interests other than those of efficiency and growth into the discourse on economic reforms. These linkages must also highlight the link between reform of procedural mechanisms and the delivery of substantive reform outcomes. As Huntington notes, the reformer has to:

> balance changes in social-economic structure against changes in political institutions and to marry the one to the other in such a way that neither is hampered.[52]

Such new linkages between issues, discourses, delivery structures, and stakeholders are the first step towards the generation of new norms. Issue linkages are important to counter a myopic vision of the problem-space of reform.

Once again we can find support for the need for issue linkages in the literature on economic reform in India. Economic reforms have speeded up changes to other constitutional, political, and social structures and institutions in India. In turn, the economic reform process is shaped by changes to these other structures. Thus, economic reform intensifies the need for faster reform of these other structures in order that these other structures can guide the economic reform process and agenda.[53] The official consensus in Indian policy circles that 'gradualism' is the acceptable model of economic reforms in India is also concerned with the need for these multiple and linked reform agendas to develop and evolve in tandem, with different structures and institutions both exerting restraint on the others and pulling along the others when necessary. The ability of the Indian executive to implement reforms is dependent upon the allocation of power within India's federal structures. Thus, reform of the external interface of the Indian economy has been relatively easier than the domestic reform agenda. The reform literature is increasingly focusing on the evolving relationship between Indian federal

---

[51] So far, the domestic market integration project has not moved on to the active reform agenda. For the need for such a project see A Virmani & S Mittal, *Domestic Market Integration* (ICRIER Working Paper No 183, July 2006).

[52] Huntington, above n 1, at 346. See also Lewis and Litai, above n 29 (arguing that similar linkage issues arise in the context of reform in China).

[53] On linkages between reform and Indian democracy, see PB Mehta, *The Burden of Democracy* (Penguin Books, 2003) 134. 'Indian democracy is extraordinarily non-deliberative, especially about policy implications that have a long-run impact.' Also see A Varshney, 'India's Democratic Challenge', (March/April 2007) 86 *Foreign Aff* 93. On linkages between Indian federalism and reform, see below n 54.

governance structures as a result of economic reforms and globalisation.[54] There is a clear trend towards devolution of power as well as functional governance autonomy from the centre towards the states. These changes to Indian governance structures and institutions call for new development strategies and the creation of new institutional links between Indian federal structures. Such changes also create new arenas for the interaction between domestic actors and processes with IEL. Thus, the attainment of substantive reform outcomes depends upon the creation of new institutions, which are necessary to negotiate as well as implement the reforms. IEL discourse, and other law reform discourse can play a role in these projects by creating issue linkages between the competing interests and values of stakeholders and between the establishment and reform of institutions and these substantive outcomes.

It is suggested that IEL teaching and research help link the dissemination and development of IEL knowledge with broader reform issues. This will require development of new curricula that both examines and creates such links. This could involve developing curricula that package different reform discourses alongside the study of IEL.[55] As mentioned before, this might create new and useful knowledge and new discourses. Such packages would for instance, combine the teaching of Indian constitutional law with IEL; or teach the legal and policy issues of law and governance in the Indian context with IEL; or teach the constitutional and legal basis of federalism in India along with IEL. All of these packages would emphasise particular issue linkages. Another useful approach would be to teach a particular issue area of IEL in conjunction with domestic law on the same topic. Thus WTO law on subsidies could be taught along with the constitutional and legal regulation of subsidies in India with an emphasis on the allocation of power and responsibility between India's federal structures. The international regime for agricultural trade could be taught along with the law and regulation of agricultural production and trade in India. Links could also be made to domestic legal regimes for food security, public provision of nutrition, public procurement regimes, public distribution systems and their links to eradication of child labour and to the promotion of education for children including the girl child. The list could go on. The point being made is that curriculum design can play an important role in determining what gets defined as the problem-space and thus as the context for intervention in

---

[54] See Weiner, above n 46; Jenkins, above n 37; L Bhandari and A Khare, 'The Geography of the Post-1991 Indian Economy', in Debroy & Mukherji, above n 37; R Jenkins, 'How Federalism Influences India's Domestic Politics of WTO Engagement (And is Itself Affected in the Process)' (2003) 43 *Asian Survey* 598, 598–621.
[55] A somewhat similar suggestion is made by FA Gevurtz, 'Teaching International Economic Law from a Corporate Perspective', Ch 12 in this volume, where he suggests that that domestic corporate law be considered part of international economic law.

classroom discourse.[56] This discourse will then filter out from the classroom into other discourses including research discourses, political discourses, media discourses and eventually policy discourses.

Such packaging or grouping of IEL knowledge with other discourses will introduce new issues onto the IEL teaching agenda. Thus the issue of how trade policy is or ought to be made in India will raise constitutional law issues. For example, issues relating to the allocation and exercise of trade policy making power, would include discussion of federal structures, parliamentary oversight of treaty making and implementation, and the judicial review of trade policy. Substantive issues concerning the impact of trade policy making on the fundamental rights guaranteed under the Constitution and the social contract embedded in the Constitution in the Directive Principles of State Policy would also arise. Discussions on reform of trade policy making could also take place in a law and governance reform context. The creation of issue linkages might require new IEL courses aimed at different constituencies. Doctoral and other research on such new issue linkages could be encouraged. This section presents very preliminary thoughts on the kinds of issue linkages that could be explored in new IEL curricula. As stated before, these ideas would need to find their concrete shape in specific contexts of curricula design projects.

V. CONCLUSION

In asking what would be new agendas for IEL teaching, this Chapter asks the question: Why teach more IEL in India? An answer must address how IEL courses can be made more useful, not only for the students themselves, but also for their contribution towards the role that academics, lawyers and other epistemic communities need to play in the political, economic and social evolution that is accelerating in India. This Chapter suggests that IEL academics look for their future agendas with an eye on the broader discourses on reform in India. This will require drawing connections between the international law governing economic order and the project of creating a new domestic economic order. The project of domestic economic reform cannot be divorced from social and political reform. This Chapter suggests that IEL discourse in India can help to connect these projects as the Indian polity attempts to negotiate a new social purpose of governance in India in its quest for a domestic compromise of embedded liberalism.

This Chapter has described a very ambitious future agenda for IEL teaching in India. It would be valid to question to what extent are these ideas feasible given the squeeze on resources and that other branches of law would no doubt present their own claims for a greater presence on

---

[56] See Scott, above n 5.

law degree courses. Nevertheless, it is important for academic disciplines to reflect upon their social and political role in a developing society. All the suggestions made in this Chapter will require time and commitment by academics to the development of new courses, curricula and textbooks that use Indian problems, examples, statistics, case-studies, and that incorporate the terms of the reform debates in India. And finally, it is important to note that the new agendas for IEL teaching that this Chapter describes as relevant for India, would also be relevant for other similarly situated countries. Building capacity in IEL knowledge is important for many other developing and least-developed economies. These countries too face similar challenges of development, growth, and reform, and they too must pay much more attention to IEL teaching.

14

Shifting Paradigms of Parochialism: Lessons for Legal Education*

ELIZABETH TRUJILLO

JOHN SEXTON CHARACTERISED the endeavour of teaching globally as an academic calling for the 'global common enterprise.'[1] He explains that the rule of law plays an integral role in integrating a 'global village' and bridging different legal and cultural traditions.[2] It is in this exchange that involved parties may begin to question their own laws, redefine legal applications through comparative inquiry and adapt their legal systems for the sake of a larger common enterprise.

I had the opportunity to reflect on this 'global village' in the context of cross-border legal education through my own experience in developing a transnational course on the North American Free Trade Area (NAFTA). This course, consisting of US, Mexican and Canadian students, became a good forum for inculcating into students that they are members of a larger problem-solving capacity network, larger than the domestic or local one to which they may be accustomed.[3] Whereas much of the study of international private law has focused on exploring differences in legal systems in light of domestic issues or harmonisation,[4] much less attention has focused

---

* Special thanks to Colin Picker, Isabella Bunn, and Doug Arner for their helpful comments on a prior draft and for organising this very intellectually stimulating conference at Bretton Woods. The author would also like to thank Professor Gabriel Cavazos, director of the LLM Program in International Trade Law at the Monterrey Institute of Technology (Instituto Tecnológico de Monterrey) (ITESM) in Mexico for his collaboration on the joint NAFTA course discussed in this paper, as well as the students and other faculty members involved at ITESM and the University of Detroit Mercy School of Law (UDM). A modified version of this Chapter also appears as 'Shifting Paradigms of Parochialism: Lessons for International Trade' (2007) 3 *J Int'l & Int'l Rels* 41.

[1] J Sexton, 'The Academic Calling: To Global Common Enterprise' (2001) 51 *J Legal Educ* 403.

[2] Ibid at 403 (stating that '[t]he rule of law will permeate an emerging global village, touching societies it never has touched. And the success of this new community will depend in large part upon the integration and accommodation of disparate traditions through law.').

[3] See generally below S II A for a description of problem-solving networks.

[4] See MA Drumbl, 'Amalgam in the Americas: A Law School Curriculum for Free Markets and Open Borders' (1998) 35 *San Diego L Rev* 1053 (exploring ways in which to create a NAFTA curriculum that will foster harmonisation within the context of NAFTA); S Zamora,

on accepting these differences as part of the global legal structure and on examining the traditions engendering these differences as a source of understanding parochial interests.[5]

This paper asserts that globalised legal education can explore differences in laws not only as a means for harmonisation or convergence or for finding solutions in domestic law, but also as a means of fostering understanding of domestic parochial interests within a society. Particularly in the context of regionalism, it is in building alliances that extend beyond the parochial network that a new common tradition may form.[6] In exchanging parochial attitudes, students may begin to appreciate that compliance with international principles is driven in part by the recognition that through voluntary cooperation, domestic interests may also be best served.

I. THE CLASSROOM EXCHANGE PROMOTES HYBRIDISATION

While thinking 'globally' appears too vast and amorphous of a concept to translate into practical terms, thinking 'regionally' offers an opportunity for a real exchange by tapping into common regional interests and, in turn, a true exchange in culture, values and social norms.[7] In the context of NAFTA, for example, the US, Canada and Mexico have not only increased trade[8] but also have attempted to find ways of coordinating regulations in order to enhance economic exchange. Furthermore, this coordination has

---

'NAFTA and the Harmonization of Domestic Legal Systems: The Side Effects of Free Trade' (1995) 12 *Ariz J Int'l & Comp L* 401 (stating that NAFTA will encourage harmonisation among the 3 countries at various levels and that University programs can be key to fostering harmonisation); but see A Blackett, 'Globalization and Its Ambiguities: Implications for Law School Curricular Reform' (1998) 37 *Colum J Transnat'l L* 57, 58 (proposing a different starting point for the globalisation in legal education—one that focuses on the 'ambiguities of globalization.'); AM Slaughter, 'Judicial Globalization' (2000) 40 *Va J Int'l L* 1103, 1116 (characterising the influence of judicial applications of various domestic constitutions as an important part of the 'cross-fertilisation' within a domestic legal system).

[5] See HP Glenn, 'Symposium on Continuing Progress in Internationalizing Legal Education—21st Century Global Challenges: Integrating Civil and Common Law Teaching Throughout the Curriculum: The Canadian Experience' (2002) 21 *Penn St Int'l L Rev* 69, 74 (recognising whether while teaching of multiple laws is challenging, 'the object of transnational legal education is not legal unification or even facilitating convergence, but rather understanding of difference and the underlying reasons for difference').

[6] See HP Glenn, *Legal Traditions of the World* 49 (Oxford University Press, 2000) (discussing that globalisation allows for an extension of traditions that are beyond the state).

[7] See HP Glenn, 'Conflicting Laws in a Common Market? The NAFTA Experiment' (2001) 76 *Chi-Kent L Rev* 1789 (explaining that regionalisation is an important factor in the elimination of physical, political and legal borders because 'we define the new regions not so much in terms of geophysical boundaries ... but in terms of new political and legal boundaries that surpass those of the state').

[8] Eg, total US merchandise trade by truck between the US and Canada increased by 113% from 1993 to 2002 and between the US and Mexico, by 319%. See Bureau of Transportation Statistics, available at http://www.bts.gov/cgi-bin/breadcrumbs/PrintVersion.cgi?date=27150819.

emerged not only in the form of harmonisation but also as convergence. NAFTA parties have attempted to find commonalities among their policies rather than purely establish identical regulations or laws.[9] For example, since 2001, regional integration has extended into the energy sector through increased cooperation in setting efficiency and labeling standards under the North American Energy Working Group (NAEWG).[10] Increased investment through cooperative alliances and joint ventures has also contributed to stronger ties among the NAFTA partners.[11]

Economic integration through regionalism may help propel the emergence of new and hybrid cultures.[12] Hybridisation, as characterised by Jagdish Bhagwati, generates cultural, social and economic alliances which can help form larger regional networks.[13] Furthermore, hybridisation can create hybrid legal cultures. One way this can occur is through assimilation of different legal norms and procedural mechanisms. Also, jurisdictional overlaps may emerge when different legal regimes have jurisdiction over a common issue. For example, NAFTA allows disputes arising both under NAFTA and the WTO to be brought under either jurisdiction at the discretion of the involved parties.[14]

What does hybridisation through regionalism say about cross-border legal education and, more specifically, for the future of NAFTA lawyers? It is the axis around which any course in NAFTA may encourage a dialogue among participants whose countries are different and yet are trading partners.

In setting up the framework of a transnational NAFTA course, I worked with my Mexican colleague, Professor Gabriel Cavazos from the ITESM who was teaching a NAFTA course in the LLM Program in International

---

[9] See RD Knutson & RF Ochoa, *Convergence, Harmonization and Compatibility under NAFTA: A 2003 Status Report*, available at http://www.farmfoundation.org/farmpolicy/knutson-ochoa.pdf (last visited 1 Feb, 2007) (distinguishing convergence from harmonisation by explaining that convergence requires 'commonality of policy' rather than the implementation of uniform programs or regulations through harmonization).

[10] S Weil & L Van Wie McGrory, *Regional Cooperation in Energy Efficiency Standard-Setting and Labeling in North America*, available at http://www.osti.gov/bridge/servlets/purl/824274-0MHxDS/native/824274.pdf (last visited 2 Feb, 2007).

[11] See D Sparling & R Cook, *Strategic Alliances and Joint Ventures under NAFTA: Concepts and Evidence*, available at http://www.agecon.ucdavis.edu/aredepart/facultydocs/Cook/rankfoodii/june25final.pdf (last visited 1 Feb, 2007) (stating that strategic alliances and joint ventures are the 'new international business norm').

[12] J Bhagwati, *In Defense of Globalization* (Oxford University Press, 2004) 107 (describing various anti-globalisation forces which the author terms as 'global pessimists' and opining that 'economic globalization is a culturally enriching process.').

[13] Ibid at 109 (illustrating examples of cultural 'hybridisation' resulting from globalisation).

[14] See eg North American Free Trade Agreement, US-Can-Mex, 17 Dec, 1992, 32 ILM 289, 296–456, 605–800 (1993) [NAFTA], art 2005. See P Schiff Berman, 'Global Legal Pluralism' (2007) 80 *S Cal L Rev* 1155 (discussing jurisdictional overlaps). See also Trujillo, *Defining Jurisdictional Overlaps*, below n 39.

Trade Law (*el Instituto Tecnológico de Monterrey, Maestría en Derecho Comercial Internacional*) in Monterrey, Mexico. First, we outlined the objectives of such a course, seeking to provide something that our students would not be able to get in a more traditional NAFTA course. We identified a few key points:

1. Students should achieve a basic understanding of the principles of international trade law generally and of NAFTA more specifically and how these principles pertain to and affect their own local parochial interests and the interests of their future clients.[15]
2. Students should learn basic differences in the political structures and legal systems of their counterparts. But they should also understand where commonalities are, to the extent they exist, including historical, political and economic ones.
3. Finally, students should experience first hand 'an exchange' to help them see for themselves where there are differences and where they may draw on their commonalities. We chose a simulated arbitration as a joint exercise. We used *Corn Products* because it allowed students to work together with an unresolved Chapter 11 NAFTA investor-state arbitration case that also contained issues being adjudicated before a WTO panel. This allowed us to raise many issues pertaining to protectionism more generally and jurisdictional overlaps between the NAFTA and the WTO dispute resolution bodies and their regimes.

Some of the more practical questions we needed to address related to methodology and collaboration, the 'exchange' that should occur, and the role of technology. In teaching transnationally, collaboration first begins with the willingness of the professors as well as that of their institutions. In our case, there had already been some ongoing negotiations between our universities regarding the possibilities for establishing joint programs and faculty exchanges for collaborative research. At the very minimum, the backdrop for such a course should be one characterised by what John Sexton calls a 'minimalist model' in which the faculty members and the institutions themselves act independently, while collaborating under 'an umbrella entity' which facilitates the exchange.[16]

Second, we had to consider what exactly we were exchanging through this course.[17] To the extent that a transnational course is based on an exchange of legal skills and cultural perspectives to resolve common problems,

---

[15] Interestingly, in my experience with this course, students have been primarily from Michigan, Ontario and Nuevo Leon—all regions deeply affected by the implementation of NAFTA. Many of the students had experienced first hand these affects.
[16] See Sexton, above n 1, at 405.
[17] See generally MYK Woo, 'Reflections on International Legal Education and Exchanges' (2001) 51 *J Legal Educ* 449 (discussing the essence of international legal education and exchange).

we also needed to find ways of drawing on our commonalities in order to achieve a cohesive educational experience for our students.[18] This began with the professors sharing outlines and syllabi of the course as if each were to teach it independently of the other. We integrated these into one course syllabus that we then adapted for our own class. Naturally, one of the most obvious obstacles to overcome in such an exchange is the language barrier. In our case, this was a moot point since we had the good fortune that the Mexican LLM students as well as Professor Cavazos were fluent in English.[19] However, the students manifested their linguistic differences in other ways—through syntax and interpretation of legal issues and even in differing analytical approaches to the relevant international law.

Differences in methodological teaching approaches also had to be considered. Whereas US legal education focuses primarily on interactive learning such as the Socratic method or problem-solving approach, Mexican law schools tend to show a preference for lectures rather than cooperative learning (though in some schools like ITESM, other methods are being used as well).[20] Professor Cavazos and I decided that each professor should teach in his or her preferred way the basic principles of NAFTA, but we coordinated the scheduling of the topics being taught, the book being used and outside reading materials. We invited a guest lecturer from the department of economics and business administration from ITESM for the first videoconference session, who lectured on the effects of NAFTA on Mexico. This allowed the UDM students to understand more clearly the impact of NAFTA on our Mexican counterparts.[21]

Third, we had to consider the role of technology in bridging not only geographical distances, but also language barriers. By characterising our course as a *web-based course*, we could facilitate the exchange among the students at both schools and use it as a supplement to learning in the classroom. It was also a means for teaching foreign students while teaching our own.[22] We used the web to communicate with students as if they were all

---

[18] Ibid at 451 (stating that 'exchanges' in the context of international education consist not only of exchanges within substantive law areas, but also an exchange of skills, values and the cultures within the differing legal systems).

[19] Although the author is also fluent in Spanish and some of the American students spoke Spanish as well, the joint portions of the course were conducted in English. Also, the ITESM students were graduates students studying in the LLM program for International Trade ITESM.

[20] See Woo, above n 17, at 453 (discussing different teaching methodologies, some based on a passive approach and others on active learning). See also Drumbl, above n 4, at 1079–99 (comparing the education systems of Canada, the US and Mexico). Several professors at the ITESM were also educated in the US and that influence can be felt in a gradual shift in the traditional Mexican teaching methods.

[21] We did not have a Canadian or US lecturer, but such participation would be useful in the future.

[22] See R Buchanan & S Pahuja, 'Using the Web to Facilitate Active Learning: A Trans-Pacific Seminar on Globalization and the Law' (2003) 53 *J Legal Educ* 578 (discussing the different ways that the Internet may be used to facilitate teaching).

in one classroom. Through video-conferencing, students from both schools presented mock oral arguments on the *Corn Products* investor-state case to a simulated tribunal, consisting of students from both schools. In this way, all participants could appreciate the different styles of advocacy presented by lawyers from the continental and common law traditions.[23] For example, the Mexican students had a more formalist reading of the NAFTA and WTO treaties as normative instruments. In contrast, the tendency of the US students was to attempt to look at precedent, despite the lack of formal *stare decisis* in this area.

In using a simulated arbitration, comparative inquiries can be useful not only for understanding the similarities and differences among legal systems, but also as a backdrop for deciding which aspects of different legal traditions to adopt in resolving the many different problems arising under international trade law. An exercise in the arbitration process offers an opportunity to engage in a dialogical approach to WTO and NAFTA jurisprudence rather than a functionalist one.[24] Ruti Teitel describes the functionalist approach in the constitutional law context as presuming a 'normative constitutional vision across societies'[25] whereas a dialogical discourse allows for a dynamic interpretative that focuses on the judicial processes and interpretation and may draw from various sources of law.[26]

In a similar way, adjudicatory practices of the WTO panels and NAFTA Chapter 11, 19 and 20 tribunals, for example, can be viewed as dynamic and evolving, finding their authority both in normative standards of international trade law, to the extent they exist, and in a more fluid multilateral system that amasses several legal traditions and political cultures.[27]

II. REFLECTIONS ON PAROCHIALISM

A course consisting of students whose different countries share common regional interests raises the question of the role of parochial attitudes. Parochialism generally has a negative connotation for supporters of free trade. Nonetheless, at some level, free trade may itself strengthen internal

---

[23] See Drumbl, above n 4, at 1062–72 (describing differences in the civil law approaches and the common law approaches in all three countries).

[24] R Teitel, 'Comparative Constitutional Law in a Global Age' (2004) 117 *Harv L Rev* 2570, 2584–6 (reviewing N Dorsen, M Rosenfeld, A Sajó & S Baer (eds), *Comparative Constitutionalism: Cases and Materials* (2003)). In a book review, the author compares the functionalist and neofunctionalist approaches in comparative constitutionalism to a more modern one, the 'dialogical approach.'

[25] Ibid at 2576.

[26] Ibid at 2584–6. Professor Teitel states that the dialogical perspective 'theoriz[es] comparative constitutionalism as a dynamic interpretive and discursive practice.' Ibid at 2584–5.

[27] Ibid at 2585. See also below Section II(B).

pressures to establish parochialism through powerful domestic networks. Such networks may form because of a perceived need among network members that if united, they may fight against 'outsiders' who want to dominate them.[28] However counterintuitive it seems, parochial interests are a part of the global structure. Therefore, in teaching international trade law, one should strive to help students understand the relevant parochial interests and the political and economic forces that drive them.

A. Domestic Parochialism

The effect that parochialism has on compliance with international trade agreements lends itself to inquiry into what drives parochial attitudes. The social sciences teach us that parochialism generally arises from the tendency for people to favour groups in which they are members, at the expense of outsiders and even their individual interests. Professors Schwartz-Shea and Simmons describe this tendency as one flowing from a perceived 'self-interest' that in aiding the group that includes themselves, they will promote their individual interests.[29] Jonathan Baron identifies this 'self-interest' as a 'self-interest illusion', which explains why individuals are more willing to sacrifice individual interests for those of certain groups but not for larger-encompassing groups.[30] He explains that a sense of altruism drives parochial attitudes—that individuals may find affinity with groups to which they identify ethnically, culturally, religiously or even politically. As a result, powerful networks may arise domestically. Professors Samuel Bowles and Herbert Gintis define two levels of parochialism in network formations:

1. more obvious network formation based on perceived common traditions in ethnicity, cultural values, politics and religion; and
2. one based on underlying economic advantages within the 'problem solving capacities of networks.'[31]

---

[28] See generally below nn 36–8.
[29] See P Schwartz-Shea & RT Simmons, 'Egoism, Parochialism and Universalism' (1991) 3 *Rationality & Soc'y* 106–32.
[30] See J Baron, *Parochialism as a Result of Cognitive Biases*, 1 Oct, 2005, at 3, available at http://www.econ.ku.dk/tyran/Workshop%20BPE/Baron.pdf.
[31] Samuel Bowles & Herbert Gintis, Persistent Parochialism, July 25, 2003, at 2, available at http://www.umass.edu/preferen/gintis/persist.pdf (stating that '[m]embers, of course, do not normally express their identification with networks in terms of their economic advantages. Rather, they typically invoke religious faith, ethnic purity, or personal loyalty. These sentiments often support exclusion or shunning of outsiders.'). The authors explain that among 'the problem-solving capacities of networks are the powerful contractual enforcement mechanisms made possible by small-scale interactions, notably effective punishing of those who fail to keep promises, facilitated by close social ties, frequent and variegated interactions and the availability of low cost information concerning one's trading partners.' Ibid.

Members may identify with such networks because of these common traditions or advantages. In this context, parochial attitudes may result from a lack of memory that in fact origins have been pluralist in nature.[32]

The strength of these networks remains puzzling in a world of increased globalisation. They resist integration with other networks, especially those outside their geographical borders. One reason for this phenomenon may be that such networks, though insular, may 'solve economic problems that are resistant to market or state-based solutions.'[33] Despite the more obvious cultural, religious, or political affinities that members of such networks seem to share, there is a perceived economic advantage to remaining insular and loyal to the network. However we choose to characterise parochialism, it permeates movements at the domestic level which resist globalisation at the multilateral and even regional levels. For the purposes of this paper, this attitude is characterised as *domestic parochialism*. In discussing parochialism in this context, the focus is on individual attitudes and the way they translate into the larger national scale. There are obvious limitations to applying observations made originally about individuals to a nation consisting of a multitude of special interest groups. However, a full discussion of these limitations is beyond the scope of this paper.

B. NAFTA Parochialism

Assuming the existence of different well-established domestic networks, the question remains of how to coordinate and reconcile the various interests they espouse. The challenge this presents can lead to more division and differentiation among the networks. For some international lawyers, harmonisation may be one solution. However, harmonisation attempts to supplant local norms with universal ones and, in turn, has a hegemonic effect which can just fuel local networks in their resistance to integrate regionally or globally.[34] For the NAFTA partners, harmonisation may not necessarily resolve their cultural, political, economic and legal differences. Perhaps resolving these differences is not the goal at all. Another approach could be one in which parties may draw on their commonalities to create institutions that work toward addressing shared interests. In this way, such institutions would implement procedural and normative

---

[32] HP Glenn, 'Transnational Legal Theory and Practice Essay' (2006) 29 *Fordham Int'l LJ* 457.
[33] Bowles & Gintis, above n 31, at 3.
[34] See Berman, above n 14, at 28 (describing harmonisation as failing to meet the realities of diversity among societies and as potentially being hegemonic). More generally, Professor Berman applies a pluralist framework to international law.

mechanisms that would embrace the pluralist nature of their shared common space.[35]

Despite their differences, NAFTA partners do share some historical and political characteristics. They are all federalist in nature even if the distribution of power and authority may vary from country to country.[36] All three were born out of European colonialism and despite periods of royal or dictatorial dominance, eventually developed into republics with identities separate from their European origins. While each nation has developed distinctively, they share some common traditions that, if fostered, can help form the basis of a quilt of hybridisation. In enhancing these common threads, such hybridisation can lead to the development of a new common tradition that surpasses parochial interests, without necessarily replacing them and in which parochial networks may form alliances. That is, domestic parochialism may be replaced by a *NAFTA parochialism*.

Defining the parameters of regionalism vis à vis the multilateral trade regime is not easy. Trade distortions could emerge as a result of too much emphasis on regional interests or political alliances and these could certainly lead to detrimental effects for the global community more generally. After all, one of the reasons for implementing the GATT was to avoid another World War primarily caused by powerful political military alliances.[37] Regional strength should only exist within a strong multilateral system. In the context of trade, this relationship is continually being tested through WTO decisions that implicate regional partners without clear recognition of the regional issues at play.[38] For example, there are jurisdictional overlaps in the adjudication of disputes concerning anti-dumping and countervailing duty measures as well as alleged national

---

[35] See Berman, above n 14 (arguing that a pluralist framework better manages 'hybrid legal spaces'). For more discussion on reconciling legal pluralism and international trade see generally E Trujillo, 'Shifting Paradigms of Parochialism: Lessons for International Trade Law' (2007) 3 *J Int'l & Int'l Rels* 41.

[36] See Drumbl, above n 4, at 1062–72 (describing generally the differences in political structures and legal systems between the three member states of NAFTA). For more on the Mexican legal and political system, see generally S Zamora, JR Cossio, L Pereznieto, J Roldán-Xopa, & D López, *Mexican Law* (Oxford University Press, 2004). For a comparison of federalism in the United States and Canada, see generally MA Field, 'The Differing Federalism of Canada and the United States' (1992) 55 *Law & Contemp Probs* 107. See also, Trujillo, above n 35.

[37] See JH Jackson, *The Jurisprudence of GATT and the WTO: Insights on Treaty Law and Economic Relations* (Cambridge University Press, 2000) 21 (stating that the goals behind the GATT agreement included 'the prevention of war and the establishment of a just system of economic relations' as well as 'the economic benefits that might derive from international trade and economic stability') . See also C Picker, 'Regional Trade Agreements v The WTO: A Proposal for Reform of Article XXIV to Counter This Institutional Threat' (2005) 26 *U Pa J Int'l Econ L* 267, 280 (discussing interwar concerns regarding regionalism).

[38] See E Trujillo, 'Mission Possible: Reciprocal Deference Between Domestic Regulatory Structures and the WTO' (2007) 40 *Cornell Int'l LJ* 201.

treatment violations.[39] In *Mexico—Tax Measures on Soft Drinks and other Beverages*, for example, the WTO panel and later the appellate body decided that Mexico's tax on soda bottlers using high fructose corn syrup rather than sugar was protectionist.[40] This same issue has been considered in a Chapter 11 foreign investment NAFTA claim by the US investor affected by the tax.[41] Though the issue has not yet been resolved by the NAFTA arbitration tribunal, NAFTA Chapter 11 tribunals have in the past deferred to WTO decisions regarding national treatment violations under Article III of GATT.[42]

More recently, however, the Chapter 11 NAFTA tribunal in *Methanex Corporation v Government of the United States* dealt with a California regulation that, because of alleged health and environmental risks, banned the use of methanol in reformulated gasoline. Here, the Chapter 11 tribunal clearly stated that NAFTA tribunals are not required to look to WTO panel decisions as precedent for their own decisions.[43] Determining which regulatory measures are legitimate (and therefore not in violation of commitments under GATT) is a challenge for international trade adjudicatory bodies. Regulatory measures aimed at placating domestic parochial attitudes can masquerade as legitimate and non-protectionist. Therefore, creating larger capacity networks that incorporate the economic advantages to globalisation is important at the domestic level. In the context of the NAFTA partners, a *NAFTA parochialism* may be the source of power within a multilateral framework.

III. LESSONS REGARDING EDUCATIONAL EXCHANGES AND PAROCHIALISM

In conclusion, several lessons emerged from this legal educational exchange. First, it appears that whether the NAFTA arbitration fosters a functionalist approach or a dialogical one to resolving international trade issues depends,

---

[39] For a discussion of jurisdictional overlaps among domestic, NAFTA and WTO regimes, see E Trujillo, *Defining Jurisdictional Overlaps in the Midst of Regionalism* (draft available with author).

[40] See Appellate Body Report, *Mexico—Tax Measures on Soft Drinks and other Beverages*, WT/DS308/4 (11 Jun, 2004) and WT/DS308/R (7 Oct, 2005) [*Mexico—Tax Measures*]. See also Trujillo, above n 38.

[41] See *Corn Products International v Government of the United Mexican States*, Request for Institution of Arbitration Proceedings, 28 Oct, 2003 [*Corn Products*].

[42] See Trujillo, above n 38, at Pt III for a discussion of NAFTA ch 11 decisions discussing WTO adjudication of national treatment violations.

[43] See *Methanex Corp v United States, Final Award of the Tribunal on Jurisdiction and Merits*, 9 Aug, 2005, pt III, ch B, 37, [*Methanex*] available at http://www.state.gov/documents/organisation/51052.pdf. See also Trujillo, above n 38, at Pts III & IV (discussing the tendency of NAFTA tribunals to defer to WTO decisions and the interesting complexities that these jurisdictional overlaps present. This article also reflects on the impact of Methanex in future NAFTA tribunals and their decisions vis à vis similar WTO decisions).

at some level, on the legal tradition of the interpreter. That is, a civil lawyer may tend to deal with a legal problem from a different perspective than that of a common law attorney. During our simulated arbitration, it was notable that the Mexican students tackled the alleged violations first by using literal treaty interpretations of the NAFTA treaty itself as well as the WTO agreements rather than prior disputes. They focused on the 'correct' understanding of the relevant provisions governing the alleged violations. On the other hand, the US students would begin with the facts themselves, using the rule of law as the guide to better understand relevant facts as they pertained to the relevant provisions.[44] The UDM students looked to prior NAFTA Chapter 11 cases and even WTO decisions in trying to find the best interpretation of the NAFTA provisions, despite being aware that there are no formal *stare decisis* in this context. This illustrates one of the big differences between the two legal systems—the role of the judiciary. In Mexico, the primary sources of law do not include case law and the legislatures and national agencies have a more authoritative role in creating new law than the courts do. By contrast, the role of the US judiciary is much more pronounced; courts can set precedent and create new law.[45] Interestingly, as the discussions among the students from both schools developed over time, the Mexican students also began to look to precedent. The UDM students, on the other hand, began trying to understand the 'plain meaning' of the relevant provisions of NAFTA and were concerned about the arbitrators creating expansive interpretations that were beyond their scope.

Second, despite the occasional comment regarding general disillusionment with compliance in international agreements, the students treated each other with respect. Their willingness to learn from one another was evident. This willingness and interest to learn from their foreign counterparts ultimately created a forum for healthy discourse. No one side dominated the discussion and no one legal tradition supplanted the other. The students even recognised moments of differences in legal approaches and adapted their own way of thinking to better understand their counterparts. In this way, the simulated arbitration was dynamic and pluralist in nature, leaving room for multiple interpretations.

Finally, there were lessons about the effect of parochial attitudes on international adjudicatory processes. We saw that it is important for us as international lawyers and educators to recognise not only that parochialism

---

[44] See Drumbl, above n 4, at 1066–69 (explaining differences in approaches to legal problems between a common law attorney and a civil law attorney). Generally speaking, civilian lawyers will as an initial matter focus on the 'plain meaning' of the text and interpretation of code provisions are taken out of their historical context and applied according to 'the current sense of justice and ... to its purpose.' See Ibid at 1067.

[45] Ibid at 1066, 1070. Professor Drumbl emphasises that the important role of the 'common law judge creates a need for some consistency in how judges exercise their power.' See Ibid at 1070.

exists, but also that it serves a perceived purpose for those benefiting from being a member of a problem-solving capacity network. In *Mexico—Tax Measures*, for example, the Mexican government argued before the WTO panel and Appellate Body that Mexico had a special interest in protecting its sugar industry, especially in the context of a larger sugar dispute between the United States and Mexico. Whether placing a tax on soda bottlers using high fructose corn syrup is the most efficient means of aiding the Mexican sugar industry is arguable and best left to the economists.[46] However, at a more individual level, NAFTA students studying this case, though from different countries, did in fact sympathise with Mexico and the challenges of adapting a traditionally protected sugar industry, deeply drenched in local politics, to free market principles. They understood first hand the difficulties of transitioning regulated markets and adapting them for free trade as well as the challenges for foreign investors in those markets. Students were able to set aside their own parochial attitudes and perceptions of their counterparts and debate common issues arising out of a shared sphere of regionalism.

Such an exercise presents an opportunity for creating a shift in parochialism paradigms, one from domestic parochialism to one that incorporates several regional exchange networks and may help to generate a new common tradition.[47] This new common tradition may be one that invokes cultural, political and economic ties, leading to hybridisation. In doing this, domestic parochialism will be only one part of a quilt consisting of a patchwork of parochial interests. Such regional parochialism should not be the basis for diverging from the multilateral regime, but rather, should ground itself within the multilateral framework. Strengthening and defining this framework is also necessary. However, at a more individual level, students of NAFTA participating in a joint course, though from different countries, can in fact set aside their own parochial attitudes and participate in shared hybrid regional space. In doing so, legal education can play an important role in helping to engender a new common tradition for all parties involved.

---

[46] See eg A Sykes, 'Regulatory Protectionism and the Law of International Trade' (1999) 66 *Univ Chi L Rev* 1. See generally, AO Kreuger, *Economic Policies at Cross Purposes: the United States and Developing Countries* (Brookings Institution Press, 1993) 251.

[47] See also Zamora, above n 4, at 401 (explaining that NAFTA creates not only economic ties but also 'brings three disparate societies into closer contact' through 'formal and informal transactions between citizens of the NAFTA countries' in a phenomenon he describes as the 'NAFTA exercise.').

15

Corporate Social Responsibility of Multinational Enterprises and the International Business Law Curriculum

CONSTANCE Z WAGNER

I. INTRODUCTION

THE THESIS OF this Chapter is that corporate social responsibility (CSR) of multinational enterprises (MNEs) should be given more emphasis in the international business law curriculum in US law schools. CSR, the notion that businesses have a broad set of obligations for ethical and socially responsible conduct, has become an important topic in recent years. It is receiving increased attention in the business world, in governmental and intergovernmental organisations, in non-governmental organisations, and in academic circles.

Traditionally, CSR has been thought to be synonymous with legal compliance and corporate philanthropy. However, in today's world, the notion of CSR goes beyond this limited view and requires that corporations take into account the impact of their operations on a broad range of stakeholders, including not only shareholders, but also employees, customers, suppliers, community organisations, and local neighbourhoods, as well as on the environment. It requires corporations to balance the needs of these stakeholders with their primary goal of generating profits for their shareholders. This topic has particular resonance in the international community with respect to the operations of MNEs, which have sometimes operated outside of the strictures of effective government control in areas such as labour and environmental regulation. CSR will remain an important topic in the years ahead as companies increasingly move across national borders to conduct their business operations, and its coverage in the US law school curriculum should be expanded.

This Chapter is organised as follows. Section II will discuss the increasing significance of CSR in the context of international business operations of MNEs. Section III will discuss the current coverage of this topic in the curriculum in US law schools. Section IV will discuss the arguments supporting expanded coverage of CSR in the law school curriculum. Section V will propose a framework for a law school course or seminar on CSR. Section VI will conclude with some recommendations on improving current approaches to CSR in the law school curriculum.

II. THE GROWING SIGNIFICANCE OF CSR FOR MNES

CSR is a concept that has attracted the attention of just about everybody who has a stake in what business enterprises do: corporate managers and their legal counsel, national governments, intergovernmental organisations (IGOs), business watch dog groups and other non-governmental organisations (NGOs), the media, investors, labour, and consumers. Since CSR has been taken up by so many different constituencies, there is no consensus on what the concept means. One widely accepted definition, used by the World Business Council for Sustainable Development, states that:

> CSR is the continuing commitment by business to behave ethically and contribute to economic development while improving the quality of life of the workforce and their families as well as of the local community and society at large.[1]

A number of commentators have adopted the definition used by the International Chamber of Commerce, which provides that CSR is 'the voluntary commitment by business to manage its role in society in a responsible way.'[2]

The rationale for CSR is the notion that business and society are interwoven and that growing societal expectations about appropriate business behaviours and outcomes are legitimate. Some theorists have grounded arguments for the enhanced social responsibilities of business on the concept of a 'social contract' between a corporation and its host society. This social contract extends beyond the legal charter that permits a corporation to operate within a system of laws and regulations, and encompasses additional obligations that extend beyond legal obligations to include those reflecting changing social norms that are not currently mandatory.[3] A complementary theory is stakeholder analysis, which posits that corporations

---

[1] The World Bank, *What is CSR All About?* http://worldbank.org/wbi/governance/CSR/Topic%201/whatiscsrabout.htm (last visited 1 Mar, 2007).
[2] R Mullerat, 'The Global Responsibility of Business', in R Mullerat (ed), *Corporate Social Responsibility: The Corporate Governance of the 21st Century* (Kluwer, 2005) 1 (quoting the International Chamber of Commerce).
[3] UN Conference on Trade and Development [UNCTAD], *The Social Responsibility of Transnational Corporations*, 5, UNCTAD/ITE/IITMisc. (Oct 1999) 21 (prepared by JM Kline and L Odenthal) http://www.unctad.org/en/docs/poiteiitm21_en.pdf (last visited 20 Feb, 2007) [UNCTAD Report].

have a broad set of responsibilities to groups or interests that impact or are impacted by a corporation's actions.[4] This contrasts with the traditional notion of shareholder primacy in US corporate law, which focuses on the responsibilities of corporate management in enhancing shareholder value.

The expanding interest in CSR is especially strong in the area of international business. This is due to a number of factors, including the rapid increase of foreign investment and cross-border trade that has occurred in recent years. CSR can be viewed as part of a more general effort to link social justice issues to international economic developments, and finds parallels in efforts made to address the social impacts of international trade law and policy and the social responsibility of international economic institutions.

In the arena of international business, it has become obvious that national laws and regulatory regimes do not provide sufficient protection against adverse social impacts caused by the operations of MNEs. One well-publicised case involving the 1984 Bhopal gas plant disaster highlighted the problem of safety standards and the regulation of hazardous materials.[5] Other prominent cases involving the use of child labour in the supply chain of the garment and sporting goods industries focused public attention on the need for regulation of core labour practices.[6] More broadly, such cases highlighted the need for a layer of regulation at the international level stemming from the recognition that the operations of MNEs may fall within a gray area that is not reached by either home country or host country regulation. The laws of a MNE's home country typically do not apply to the MNE's operations abroad, due to reservations about the extraterritorial application of home country laws and corporate structuring to minimise liability. The failure of a host country to effectively regulate the operations of MNEs within its borders may be a result of weak laws, lax enforcement, or lack of political will. While some have argued in favour of a binding international legal code for the operations of MNEs, a consensus on this issue has never been achieved.[7] Since many of the worst cases have involved investment by MNEs from developed countries in developing countries, one might assume that the lack of consensus is due to the so-called North-South

---

[4] A Winkler, 'Corporate Law or the Law of Business? Stakeholders and Corporate Governance at the End of History' (2004) 67 *Law & Contemp Probs* 109.

[5] For a description of the accident, see *In re Union Carbide Corp Gas Plant Disaster* at Bhopal, India in Dec 1984, 809 F.2d 195, 197 (2d Cir 1987).

[6] For a description of the use of child labour by Reebok International and Levi Strauss & Co, see K Schoenberger, *Levi's Children* (Grove Press, 2000) 133–140.

[7] The UN Centre on Transnational Corporations was established in 1974 as the organisational focal point for matters related to MNEs and foreign direct investment. The Centre drafted a code of conduct for MNEs but this effort resulted in failure and the Centre was disbanded in 1992. Since 1993, UNCTAD has been responsible for the UN's Program on Transnational Corporations. See UNCTAD, The United Nations Centre on Transnational Corporations, http://unctc.unctad.org/aspx/index.aspx (last visited 6 Mar, 2007).

split between the interests of rich and poor countries. In fact, the situation is far more complex, especially in today's globalised economy with national competition for foreign investment. The goals and priorities of developing countries may themselves diverge, prompting the governments of developing countries to resist enhanced CSR standards in light of their national interests.[8] Whatever the root cause of this failure to achieve international consensus on such issues, currently there are no binding international standards on CSR applicable to MNEs.

However, IGOs, NGOs, and the business sector have responded to the felt need for a principled approach to the conduct of international business by promulgating voluntary codes of conduct and guidelines for operations of MNEs. The most prominent examples of codes of conduct developed by international organisations covering a wide range of MNE activities include the United Nations (UN) Global Compact (Global Compact) championed by former UN Secretary-General Kofi Annan, the Organization for Economic Cooperation and Development (OECD) Guidelines for Multinational Enterprises (OECD Guidelines), and the draft UN Norms on the Responsibilities of Transnational Corporations on Human Rights (UN Norms).[9] Each of these three instruments sets forth non-binding guidelines for the conduct of MNEs in areas such as core labour standards, environmental protection, bribery of foreign government officials, and human rights. These guidelines are intended to form a baseline for the ethical business conduct of MNEs.

Both the Global Compact and the OECD Guidelines have gained wide acceptance in the business community. The Global Compact is designed as a network-based initiative that brings together companies, UN agencies, labour groups and civil society to support its principles and currently includes some 2,900 businesses located in 100 countries among its participants.[10] The OECD Guidelines are aimed at MNEs operating in or from the territories of member states, and have been described as the only multilateral, comprehensive code of conduct that governments are committed to promoting.[11] They have been accepted by the 30 OECD member

[8] See UNCTAD Report, above n 3, at 10.
[9] UN Global Compact, http://www.unglobalcompact.org/index.html (last visited 6 Mar, 2007) [Global Compact]; OECD Guidelines for Multinational Enterprises, 27 Jun, 2000, 40 ILM 237 (2001) [OECD Guidelines]; UN Econ & Soc Council [ECOSOC], Sub-Comm. on the Promotion & Protection of Human Rights, Norms on the Responsibilities of Transnational Corporations and Other Business Enterprises with Regard to Human Rights, UN Doc E/CN.4/Sub.2/2003/12/Rev.2 (13 Aug, 2003), http://www.unhchr.ch/Huridocda/Huridoca.nsf/0/64155e7e8141b38cc1256d63002c55e8?Opendocument (last visited 6 Mar, 2007) [UN Norms].
[10] UN Global Compact, *What is the Global Compact?* http://www.unglobalcompact.org/AbouttheGC/index.html (last visited 6 Mar, 2007); The Global Compact Network, http://www.unglobalcompact.org/ParticipantsandStakeholders/index.html (last visited 6 Mar, 2007).
[11] United Kingdom National Contact Point, OECD Guidelines for Multinational Enterprises, http://www.dti.gov.uk/europeanandtrade-policy/oecd-multinat-guidelines (last visited 6 Mar, 2007).

countries, which represent the headquarters for most of the largest MNEs, along with seven other countries.[12] The UN Norms are still in draft form, but if finalised would become the strongest comprehensive statement by the international community on the social responsibilities of MNEs.[13]

In addition to these codes, there are a number of more specialised instruments that cover particular areas of concern. These codes have been developed by IGOs, NGOs, and the business community. For example, the International Labour Organization (ILO) promulgated the ILO Tripartite Declaration of Principles Concerning Multinational Enterprises, which, among other matters, urges both ILO Member States and MNEs to respect the four core labour standards (freedom of association and the right to organise and bargain collectively, the elimination of forced labour, the abolition of child labour, and non-discriminatory treatment in matters related to industrial relations), as well as international human rights instruments.[14] In the area of environmental protection, a group of environmental organisations and institutional investors introduced the CERES Principles, which call on companies to act as stewards of the environment in conducting their business operations, including by protecting the biosphere, sustaining natural resources, and reducing the volume of waste.[15] Finally, the Global Sullivan Principles of Corporate Social Responsibility were developed by a coalition of US companies under the leadership of the Reverend Leon Sullivan, a clergyman and civil rights activist, and were directed at improving the workplace and social conditions of blacks in South Africa during the period of apartheid.[16] Each of these codes has been influential in shaping corporate conduct on relevant CSR issues.

---

[12] Ibid. See also OECD, The OECD Guidelines for Multinational Enterprises, http://www.itcilo.ir/english/actrav/telearn/global/ilo/guide/oecd.html (last visited 6 Mar, 2007).

[13] D Kinley & R Chambers, 'The UN Human Rights Norms for Corporations: The Private Implications of Public International Law' (2006) 6 *Hum Rts L Rev* 447, 493. For recent developments on efforts to develop such standards, see, UN Hum Rts Coun, 'Business and Human Rights: Mapping International Standards of Responsibility and Accountability for Corporate Acts', Report of the Special Representative of the Secretary-General on the Issue of Human Rights and Transnational Corporations and Other Business Enterprises, UN Doc A/HRC/4/035 (9 Feb, 2007), http://www.business-humanrights.org/Documents/RuggieHRC2007 (last visited 14 Jun, 2007).

[14] Int'l Labour Org [ILO], Tripartite Declaration of Principles Concerning Multinational Enterprises, 8, 22, 37, 41, 48 (2000), http://www.ilo.org/public/english/employment/multi/download/english.pdf (last visited 2 Mar, 2007) [ILO Tripartite Declaration]. Revisions to the Tripartite Declaration in 2000 incorporated the ILO Declaration on Fundamental Principles and Rights at Work and urged the ratification of the ILO Convention on Minimum Age and the ILO Convention on the Worst Forms of Child Labor. See, ILO, Report of the Subcommittee on Multinational Enterprises, GB279/12 (Nov. 2000), http://www.ilo.org/public/english/standards/relm/gb/docs/gb279/pdf/gb-12.pdf (last visited 28 Feb, 2007).

[15] CERES Principles, http://www.ceres.org/coalitionandcompanies/principles.php (last visited 2 Mar, 2007).

[16] The Global Sullivan Principles of Social Responsibility, http://www.globalsullivanprinciples.org/principles.htm (last visited 2 Mar, 2007).

In addition to these developments, individual companies are beginning to adopt their own codes of conduct to govern their business operations, which are keyed to the developing international standards. Use of such codes is increasing in frequency among a wide range of companies involved in a variety of different industries. Some companies have had a historical commitment to CSR, which is reflected in their operating procedures and frequently embodied in a code of conduct. An example is the Body Shop, whose corporate values centre on those of its founder, Dame Anita Roddick. Its policies promote social and environmental change, including the defence of human rights, protection of the environment, and support of community trade.[17] Other companies have had the harsh light of media and NGO criticism focused on their business operations due to problems with their labour or environmental records, and adopted codes of conduct in response to public pressure to correct such problems. For example, US companies in the apparel, footwear, and sporting goods industry experienced consumer backlash when it was discovered that their subcontractors in foreign countries were using child labour in their manufacturing operations.[18] Well-known companies such as Reebok, Nike and Levi Strauss took remedial action to address the issue of child labour, including the adoption of codes of conduct that required their subcontractors to refrain from employing children younger than a specified minimum age in their factories.[19]

Other companies have acknowledged the importance of CSR in their business operations, even though they may not have a historical record of commitment to CSR or have experienced scandals involving their supply chain or other aspects of their business operations. CSR programs have become part of the 'best practices' of many Fortune 500 companies, and supporting information is frequently posted on company web sites. Some companies have CSR officers or divisions devoted to the task of mainstreaming CSR throughout the organisation. Consulting services for companies interested in designing CSR programs are also being offered. Business for Social Responsibility, based in San Francisco, California, is an example of such development. It describes itself as an association of companies that helps its members 'achieve viable, sustainable growth that benefits stakeholders as well as stockholders. By providing tools, training and custom advisory

---

[17] The Body Shop, Our Values, http://www.thebodyshopinternational.com/Values+and+Campaigns/Our+Values/ (last visited 2 Mar, 2007).

[18] Schoenberger, above n 6.

[19] University of Minnesota Human Rights Library, Reebok International Ltd, Human Rights Production Standards, http://www1.umn.edu/humanrts/links/reebokcode.html (last visited 2 Mar, 2007); Nike's Code of Conduct, http://www.itcilo.it/english/actrav/telearn/global/ilo/code/nike2.htm (last visited 2 Mar, 2007); and http://www1.umn.edu/humanrts/links/leviguidelines.html (visited 27 Feb, 2007).

services, BSR enables its members to leverage corporate social responsibility as a competitive advantage.'[20]

There are a number of reasons that MNEs and other corporations are taking CSR seriously, although there are very few legally binding norms that require them to do so.[21] Some investors view attention to CSR as a proxy for good corporate governance and value corporations following best practices on CSR more highly than those that do not. Some consumers are more willing to buy products from companies that can demonstrate they follow good labour and environmental standards than from those that cannot. NGOs and the media have frequently focused on some of the more egregious examples of socially irresponsible conduct by corporations, prompting increased attention to CSR. A further impetus for observing voluntary guidelines comes from corporate concern that national governments will impose greater regulatory requirements. Since businesses prefer the flexibility that voluntary guidelines permit them, this may be a powerful motivating factor to follow voluntary codes of conduct. Whatever the reasons for upholding CSR principles, MNEs in particular will find CSR an increasingly important topic.

There are also areas of legal liability involving CSR principles that are emerging as a result of national regulatory developments. The OECD Convention on Combating Bribery of Foreign Public Officials in International Business Transactions requires signatories to adopt laws criminalising bribery in connection with the conduct of international business.[22] The United States was in the forefront of this development, passing the 1977 Foreign Corrupt Practices Act prohibiting the payment of bribes to foreign government officials in order to obtain or retain business many years before the OECD Convention was adopted.[23] In the United States, MNEs have been named as defendants in law suits alleging that their complicity in violations of human rights by foreign governments is actionable under the federal Alien Tort Claims Act.[24] On the regional level, the

---

[20] See Business for Social Responsibility, BSR Details, http://www.bsr.org/Meta/about/bsrdetails.cfm (last visited 2 Mar, 2007).

[21] See generally, Business for Social Responsibility, Overview of Corporate Social Responsibility: Business Importance, http://www.bsr.org/CSRResources/IssueBriefDetail.cfm?DocumentID=48809 (last visited 2 Mar, 2007).

[22] Organisation for Economic Cooperation and Development [OECD], Committee on International Investment and Multilateral Enterprises, Convention on Combating Bribery of Foreign Public Officials in International Business Transactions, OECD Doc. DAFFE/IME/BR(97)20 (1 Nov, 1997) [OECD Bribery Convention].

[23] Foreign Corrupt Practices Act of 1977, Pub L 95–213, 91 Stat 1494 (1977), amended by International Anti-Bribery & Fair Competition Act, Pub L 100–415, 102 Stat 1107 (1988).

[24] Alien Tort Claims Act of 1789, 28 USC. §1350. See, *Doe v Unocal Corp*, 395 F.3d 932 (9th Cir 2002) (reversing the grant of summary judgment by the district court on plaintiffs' Alien Tort Act claims based on allegations of forced labour, murder, and rape). The case was settled in Dec 2004. Center for Constitutional Rights, Docket: *Doe v Unocal*, http://www.ccrny.org/v2/legal/corporate_accountability/corporateArticle.asp?ObjID=lrRSFKnmmm&Content=45

European Union Modernisation Directive mandates disclosure by certain companies located in Member States of their record on environmental and social issues and some countries have passed legislation requiring such disclosure by companies.[25]

III. COVERAGE OF CSR IN THE US LAW SCHOOL CURRICULUM

Currently, CSR is rarely referred to in the curriculum of US law schools. Most law schools offer a number of courses where CSR is potentially relevant and might be discussed, including corporate law, international business transactions, international human rights, and international environmental law. This section will focus on the coverage of this topic in courses on corporate law and international business transactions.

In the typical corporate law course, CSR is not discussed at all. The phrase CSR is not even mentioned in most corporate law casebooks. Many corporate law courses cover the nature and purpose of the modern business corporation by discussing only the shareholder primacy model of corporate governance as the prevailing view. Shareholder primacy is the view that corporate managers are constrained in their decision-making by the requirement that they act in the best interests of the corporation, which is interpreted by courts to mean shareholder wealth maximisation. Many casebooks use *Dodge Brothers v Ford Motor Company*, dating from 1919, to illustrate this principle.[26] In *Dodge v Ford*, the Michigan Supreme Court declared that the board of directors of Ford Motor Company had abused its discretion and showed a lack of good faith when it failed to continue a long standing practice of declaring large special dividends in a year when the company earned huge profits. The board's decision to use

---

(last visited 18 Jun, 2007) (reporting that the settlement consisted of compensation for the plaintiffs and funds to improve living conditions, health care, and education in the community where plaintiffs live).

[25] Council Directive 2003/51/EC, art 1, §14 (a)(1)(a), 2003 OJ (L178) 16, 18 (EU). France enacted legislation in 2001 as part of its New Economic Regulations requiring detailed reporting by all companies traded on the French stock exchange of environmental, labour, community engagement, and health and safety matters in annual reports. Law No. 2001-420, art 116, of 15 May, 2001, JO, 16 May, 2001, p 7776. See, C Williams & J Conley, 'An Emerging Third Way? The Erosion of the Anglo-American Shareholder Value Construct' (2005) 38 *Cornell Int'l LJ* 493, 504. The UK Parliament enacted a statute in 2005 that required certain British companies to disclose social and environmental risks as part of an annual Operating and Financial Review and Directors Report. The Companies Act 1985 Regulations 2005, SI 2005/1011 (UK). This legislation was later rescinded. However, the UK Parliament revised UK company law in 2006 and British companies are now required to include reporting on social and environmental issues as part of a business review that must conform to the European Union Modernisation Directive. The Companies Act 2006, ch 46, §§172, 417. See, C Williams and J Conley, 'Triumph or Tragedy? The Curious Path of Corporate Disclosure Reform in the UK' (2005) 31 *Wm & Mary Envtl L & Pol'y Rev* 317, 317–18, 320–1.

[26] *Dodge Brothers v Ford Motor Company*, 170 NW 668 (Mich 1919).

the company's profits to reduce the selling prices of its cars, pay increased wages to its employees, and expand its productive capacity by building an ore smelter was held not entitled to the protection of the business judgment rule. According to the court, a board of directors may not change the primary purpose of the business corporation from making money for the shareholders to focus on the interests of other stakeholders such as employees, consumers, or the general public.[27]

While it is true that the notion of shareholder primacy is a powerful force in US corporate law, it would be an overstatement to claim that it is the only valid viewpoint.[28] A competing school of thought, the stakeholder theory, has been part of the landscape of US corporate law at least since the 1930s when, in a series of articles in the Harvard Law Review, Professors Merrick Dodd and AA Berle, Jr debated the question of whether corporate managers should consider only the interests of shareholders or whether they also should consider the interests of other constituencies as well.[29] A prominent legal commentator has remarked that these two views have continued to coexist within US corporate law and that neither side has prevailed.[30] US corporate law scholarship has continued to debate this point in recent years.[31]

Notwithstanding this dichotomy within the legal community, the usual corporate law course does not explore the stakeholder theory in any depth. Rather, most courses discuss corporate philanthropy as a limited exception to the norm of shareholder primacy. Typically, this is accomplished through a discussion of statutes that include charitable giving as a permissible corporate power and case law that upholds such gifts against claims that they are ultra vires subject to the condition that the gifts confer a corporate benefit and are reasonable in amount.[32] This conveys to the students the impression that corporate philanthropy is the sole instance in which managers may, or should, take the interests of other corporate constituencies into account in their corporate decision-making.

---

[27] Ibid at 670.
[28] See H Hansmann and R Kraakman, 'The End of History for Corporate Law' (2001) 89 *Geo LJ* 439, 439. ('There is no longer any serious competitor to the view that corporate law should principally strive to increase long-term shareholder value'.)
[29] This academic exchange between Professors Dodd and Berle has been cited often as a classic statement of the 2 opposing viewpoints in this debate. See AA Berle, Jr, 'Corporate Powers as Powers in Trust' (1931) 44 *Harv L Rev* 1049; EM Dodd, 'For Whom are Corporate Managers Trustees?' (1932) 45 *Harv L Rev* 1145; AA Berle, Jr, 'For Whom Corporate Managers Are Trustees: A Note' (1932) 45 *Harv L Rev* 1365.
[30] WT Allen, 'Our Schizophrenic Conception of the Business Corporation' (1992) 14 *Cardozo L Rev* 261, 264.
[31] For 2 examples of this continuing debate, see Hansmann and Kraakman, above n 28 (defending the shareholder primacy view) and C Williams, 'Corporate Social Responsibility in an Era of Economic Globalization' (2002) 35 *UC Davis L Rev* 705 (advocating a more progressive view of corporate powers based on the stakeholder theory in light of the globalisation of business).
[32] See Del Code Ann title 8, §122; *AP Smith Mfg Co v Barlow*, 98 A.2d 581 (NJ 1953).

Most law students complete their course in corporate law without understanding the increased importance that CSR plays in the corporate world. They are left with the impression that the shareholder primacy model is the guiding light for US corporations. They learn nothing about countervailing trends. In this sense, US corporate law pedagogy has failed to stay in touch with developments in the modern business corporation and its operating environment. Shareholder primacy is no longer the predominant form of thinking among business people. Most corporations acknowledge the stakeholder theory of governance and proclaim publicly in their annual reports and in other promotional material, including their websites, that they are concerned with a wide range of corporate constituencies, including their employees, consumers, the environment, and the community in which they operate, in addition to their investors.

Courses on international business transactions (IBT) give more coverage to CSR, but such coverage is still rather limited. For example, one of the leading IBT casebooks covers two areas in US law where legal liability may attach to US companies doing business abroad, namely for bribery of foreign government officials under the Foreign Corrupt Practices Act and for alleged violations of human rights under the Alien Tort Claims Act.[33] Two other IBT casebooks currently on the market cover not only these two topics, but also include discussions regarding liability for environmental damage and voluntary corporate codes of conduct.[34] Although this represents a good start for instructors interested in integrating CSR into the standard IBT course, it should be noted that these topics as presented form a relatively small part of the content of the IBT course, which tends to focus primarily on technical legal aspects of transactions. Some IBT casebooks on the market fail to include any mention of these topics and one may therefore conclude that CSR is not discussed at all in many IBT courses. One may also reasonably conclude from reviewing available commercial materials that even where CSR is addressed, the emphasis is on the potential for legal liability under existing regulations. Areas of growing importance are omitted, including the comprehensive scope of the international voluntary guidelines for MNEs that have been developed by IGOs and NGOs, voluntary company codes of conduct on labour and environmental issues, risk disclosure in the area of environmental and social concerns, and the significance of CSR as part of the best practices of MNEs.

To summarise, although CSR is a topic of growing importance for business, especially international business, discussion of it forms a small part of the standard curriculum in both corporate law and IBT courses. This

---

[33] RH Folsom, MW Gordon, JA Spanogle, Jr & PL Fitzgerald, *International Business Transactions*, 9th edn (West, 2006) 732–62, 1091–151.

[34] See DCK Chow & TJ Schoenbaum, *International Business Transactions* (Aspen, 2005); D Frisch & R Bhala, *Global Business Law* (Carolina Academic Press, 1999).

highlights the need for increased coverage of the topic either in the standard IBT course or in a more specialised course or seminar devoted to the subject. Currently, specialised courses on CSR in US law schools are uncommon, although there may be a handful of schools that include such an offering in their curriculum.

IV. REASONS FOR EXPANDING COVERAGE IN THE LAW SCHOOL CURRICULUM

There are at least two distinct reasons supporting the argument that current coverage of CSR in the international business transactions curriculum is inadequate and should be expanded. Both stem from the concern that law students are not being adequately prepared to represent clients in meeting the challenges of our current business environment. One is that the current approach does not reflect the growing importance of CSR in business, especially in international business. The other is that the current approach does not train law students to identify and analyse ethical and social issues that arise in the context of international business transactions and operations.

First, lawyers should be equipped to counsel their clients on emerging CSR norms, including potential legal liability related to such norms. Since very few law students are exposed to CSR during their law school careers under the current system, they may be ill-prepared to counsel clients in identifying and responding to CSR issues in an appropriate manner, whether in a business planning or litigation context. One commentator has argued that lawyers and law firms should be prepared not only to react to litigation or the threat of litigation based on claims of human rights violations by corporations, but also to advise clients in a proactive manner on practicing CSR and avoiding the conflicts that lead to litigation in the first place.[35] Both aspects of the lawyer's role will play a part in the future legal landscape that is developing alongside the increased emphasis on CSR in the business world.

The faculties in US business schools are further along the learning curve in understanding the importance of CSR than US law faculties. Business schools in the United States are increasingly focusing on ethical issues in the curriculum and frequently require a core course on business ethics. Some business schools curricula also include courses on CSR in the context of their international business offerings.[36] There should be a similar emphasis on the legal aspects of CSR in US law schools so that new lawyers will be prepared to meet the challenges faced by their business clients.

---

[35] D Kinley, 'Lawyers, Corporations and International Human Rights Law' (2004) 25 *The Company Lawyer* 298.

[36] GH Iyer, *Teaching International Business: Ethics and Corporate Social Responsibility* (Haworth Press, 2000).

Second, lawyers should be educated in the fundamental skills and values of the legal profession, which should include the value of striving to promote justice, fairness, and morality. This was the position taken by the 1992 McCrate Report prepared under the auspices of the American Bar Association, Section of Legal Education and Admissions to the Bar.[37] Such training should include the professional value of:

> contributing to the profession's fulfillment of its responsibility to enhance the capacity of law and legal institutions to do justice.[38]

Legal training in CSR contributes to this goal by addressing issues related to many aspects of social justice.

For some law schools, incorporating CSR into the curriculum will further their special mission of social justice. While all US law schools strive to train students in the technical legal skills needed to pursue a successful career, some schools also seek to foster an awareness of social justice among their students through their curricular offerings and in the extracurricular projects they support. This is the case with Saint Louis University School of Law, which includes the following goal in its mission statement: '[s]ensitize students to ethical standards and norms, including the traditional obligation to engage in public service.'[39] Training lawyers on the social responsibility of MNEs and other businesses falls within this broader goal of social justice.

V. FRAMEWORK FOR A LAW SCHOOL COURSE OR SEMINAR ON CSR

Ideally, law schools should offer a course or seminar on the corporate social responsibility of multinational enterprises as part of the IBT curriculum.[40] This section describes a proposed structure for such a course, including suggestions on the topics that might be covered and the types of course materials that might be appropriate.

Starting from the assumption that most students do not have training in any area of corporate law or IBT other than what is currently offered in the standard courses on that subject, a separate course devoted to CSR of MNEs should attempt to fill the gap in student's knowledge and to train

---

[37] American Bar Association, Section of Legal Education and Admissions to the Bar, Report of the Task Force on Law Schools and the Profession: Narrowing the Gap (1992) at 140–141, available at http://www.abanet.org/legaled/publications/onlinepubs/maccrate.html (last visited 8 Mar, 2007) [McCrate Report].

[38] Ibid at 141 (Value 2).

[39] Saint Louis University School of Law, Mission Statement, http://law.slu.edu/curriculum/planning.html (last visited 6 Mar, 2007).

[40] This author's concern about the absence of a meaningful treatment of CSR in the IBT curriculum led her to design and teach a course devoted specifically to that topic as part of a summer study abroad program offered in Madrid, Spain by Saint Louis University School of Law. She has subsequently offered a seminar on the topic during the regular academic year.

them to identify issues and analyse problems from the perspective of a lawyer representing a business. One way to structure such a course would be to devote separate units to each of the following topics: US corporate law on the nature and purpose of the modern business corporation, including the stakeholder theory; the reasons for the rise of CSR and the meaning of CSR; the development of international codes of conduct for MNEs and environmental and social reporting as a means to encourage greater CSR; and the main areas of concern in CSR as they relate to MNEs, namely bribery and corruption, core labour standards, human rights, and the environment; and the relevance of CSR to the practice of corporate law.

A. US Corporate Law: The Nature and Purpose of the Modern Business Corporation

In order to set the stage for an understanding of the extent to which CSR is pursued by US corporations, a course on CSR should begin by revisiting the theory and law on the nature and purpose of the modern business corporation. Many students will have already taken the basic corporate law course and will be familiar with the shareholder primacy theory. However, very few students, if any, will be familiar with the stakeholder theory. It would be useful to present both sides of the issue, starting with the historical background of the Berle-Means debate and updating with more recent discussions of the two competing theories.[41] It would also be useful to refer to case law and statutes that illustrate the unresolved nature of the debate and to make the point that there seems to be some tolerance in US law for corporate decision-making that may benefit stakeholders other than shareholders.[42]

A second topic that should be explored is corporate philanthropy. This, along with compliance with laws, forms the historical bedrock of socially responsible business behaviour in the United States. While current developments in CSR theory and practice would seek to expand the social obligations of businesses beyond this historical understanding, it is still useful to examine this topic since it has gained wide acceptance in the United States and is viewed by the public as a form of CSR. While some students may have been exposed to corporate charitable giving in their basic corporate law course, no student will have an in-depth knowledge of the state law limitations on charitable giving or the practices of US corporations in terms of types of charitable gifts and amounts of charitable gifts. Including a discussion on international philanthropy as practiced by some US companies will serve as a bridge to a discussion of the CSR responsibilities of MNEs.

---

[41] Berle and Dodd, above n 29; Hansmann and Kraakman, above n 28; Williams, above n 31.
[42] Allen, above n 30.

B. The Rise of CSR and the Current Definition of CSR

Prior to discussing substantive CSR norms and their current legal status, it is useful background to analyse the reasons for the rise of CSR and its meaning. Students will benefit from a discussion of the rapid rise in foreign direct investment and cross-border trade, which has led to a rise in the operations of MNEs. Incorporating a discussion of some of the literature on globalisation and its social implications and recent case studies on the negative consequences of MNE activity in host countries will help to focus the students' attention on the reasons for the heightened interest in the international community on developing CSR norms. Another topic that should be covered is the lack of effective national regulation to constrain the negative social consequences of MNE activities and the options for developing more effective control mechanisms. The choice of voluntary norms, which MNEs would prefer, versus legally binding rules is an important subject to explore with students.

C. International Codes of Conduct for MNEs; Environmental and Social Reporting

The failed attempt by the UN Centre on Transnational Corporations to regulate MNE conduct through adoption of international standards might be explored as a means to understand the difficulties of achieving consensus on CSR issues.[43] More recent attempts to promulgate voluntary codes of conduct through IGOs and NGOs should then be covered, with a special emphasis on those that have broad scope and have achieved wide acceptance, namely the Global Compact and the OECD Guidelines.[44] It is worthwhile to compare these initiatives to the draft UN Norms, which would impose more stringent social standards for MNEs than any of the extant voluntary codes of conduct.[45] Another important area to explore is the development of international and national standards for corporate reporting on environmental and social issues arising in business operations.[46]

D. Substantive CSR Norms

There are four primary areas of concern in international instruments addressing CSR: bribery and corruption, core labour standards, human rights, and environmental impacts. Each of these topics merits a discussion in its own right. The use of case studies helps to focus student attention on the problems in each area and facilitates discussion of the appropriate standards that might be adopted to address these issues.

---

[43] Above n 7.
[44] Above n 9.
[45] Above nn 9 & 13.
[46] Above n 25 and accompanying text.

In the area of bribery and corruption, a discussion of the historical background surrounding the adoption of the Foreign Corrupt Practices Act can provide a focus for class discussion on the reasons for the US prohibition on bribery of foreign government officials in order to obtain or retain foreign business.[47] A study of the Foreign Corrupt Practices highlights one of the areas of CSR in which legally binding national norms constrain MNE activity. It can also be used to provide training on a significant litigation issue that may arise in practice when representing MNEs. The subsequent recognition by the international community of the social costs of bribery and corruption in international business and the development of the OECD Bribery Convention provides an interesting case study on the process of achieving consensus on a CSR issue at the international level.[48]

Regarding core labour standards, a case study focusing on the use of child labour by host country contractors for companies in the sporting goods or apparel industry, such as Reebok or Levi Strauss, is a good starting point. This will lead naturally into a discussion of the remedial efforts of such companies to address the problem of child labour and other violations of core labour standards through voluntary codes of conduct at the company level. It is also useful to explore the concept of core labour standards as they apply to MNEs through a study of the ILO Tripartite Declaration.[49]

Human rights violations by MNEs have been addressed through litigation in the US federal courts under the Alien Torts Claims Act.[50] A study of one of the litigated cases in this area, such as the Unocal litigation eventually brought before the Ninth Circuit Court of Appeals, can provide a focal point for this discussion.[51] This is another area in which the course can provide training for US law students on a litigation issue that they may encounter in practice. Finally, reference should be made to the proliferation of human rights standards on the international level and the approach adopted in the draft UN Norms on these issues.[52]

The topic of environmental impacts of MNE operations might be approached by reference to the litigation stemming from the Union Carbide gas plant disaster at Bhopal, India.[53] A discussion of the litigation and its resolution in US and Indian courts will illustrate for students some of the impediments to securing remedies for environmental damage caused by MNE operations in foreign countries. This case will also provide an opportunity to explore the development of international standards on

---

[47] Above n 23.
[48] Above n 22.
[49] Above n 14.
[50] Above n 24.
[51] *Doe v Unocal*, 395 F.3d 932 (9th Cir 2002).
[52] Above n 9.
[53] In *re Union Carbide Corp Gas Plant Disaster* at Bhopal, India in Dec 1984, 809 F.2d 195, 197 (2d Cir1987).

environmental issues, such as the CERES Principles, and whether they provide adequate protection for host countries and their citizens.[54]

E. CSR as Part of the Practice of Law

A good way to conclude a specialised course on CSR and to integrate the themes outlined above is to provide students with a case study that raises several CSR issues. There are numerous examples that could be used as the basis for such a final class exercise, including those that have arisen in extractive industries, such as gold mining or oil exploration. Such an exercise will train students to identify CSR issues that may arise in corporate legal practice representing MNEs and to respond by, for example, drafting a voluntary code of conduct for the company involved. This type of training prepares students to be proactive lawyers in the area of CSR.

VI. CONCLUSION: IMPROVING CURRENT APPROACHES TO CSR IN THE US LAW SCHOOL CURRICULUM

The US law school curriculum has seen a proliferation in the number of courses offered in recent years. It may not be possible to incorporate yet another specialised course in the IBT curriculum in every law school. However, it is possible to address some of the concerns raised by this Chapter within the context of the standard IBT course offered in many US law schools. At a minimum, the content of the standard IBT course should be expanded to incorporate a discussion of the relevance of CSR to MNEs, including the importance of CSR as part of the best practices of many US companies and the development of voluntary codes of conduct by IGOs, NGOs, and companies themselves as a means of regulation. Further, the practice of some IBT instructors of focusing on legally enforceable CSR norms in the areas of bribery of foreign government officials under the Foreign Corrupt Practices Act and human rights violations under the Alien Torts Claims Act should be continued. In this way, the best interests of students will be served because they will receive some training in both the reactive and proactive aspects of CSR practice. This change will better prepare students for representing MNEs in the business environment in which such companies currently operate. Such training will have the added benefit of introducing ethical considerations into the study of international business transactions. Issues of justice, fairness and morality have proven troubling in the current discussions over globalisation and we must recognise that students will need to face such issues and find solutions to them in the years ahead.

---

[54] Above n 13.

Part III

The State & Future of International Economic Law Practice in the Bretton Woods Era

16

The Future of International Economic Law Practice

AMELIA PORGES

THE PARTICIPANTS AT the IELG's Bretton Woods Conference spanned academia, government, international organisations and private legal practice. All expressed the desire to see better links between and among all of these spheres; the practitioners wished for academic writing to be more relevant for the issues they face, the academics wished for more contact with and feedback from the world of practice, and both sides aspired to enhanced two-way information flows. This report focuses on the interaction between practice and academic public international economic law, and where this interaction is headed as we move forward in the twenty-first century.[1] It focuses on key recent events and trends in the world at large, which have had a profound effect on the practice of international economic law, in government, in international organisations and in the private sector.

I. EXPANDED SCOPE OF INTERNATIONAL ECONOMIC LAW

The scope of public international economic law is wider and deeper now than it has ever been before. Until the 1970s, private practice in this area consisted essentially of customs law (including trade remedies) and export controls. In the General Agreement on Tariffs and Trade (GATT) Secretariat and in government, international trade law was largely steered by non-lawyer negotiators. The Trade Act of 1974,[2] which set the agenda for the Tokyo Round, included the well-known Section 301[3] but its provisions simply authorised discretionary action by government. The 1979 Trade Agreements

---

[1] By 'public international economic law' I mean economic law concerned with government interventions of various types in trade and investment flows.
[2] Trade Act of 1974, 19 USC § 2101.
[3] § 301 of the Trade Act of 1974 (19 USC 2411 et seq); see, eg, J Bhagwati & HT Patrick (eds), *Aggressive Unilateralism: America's 301 Policy and the World Trading System* (University of Michigan Press, 1990).

Act then prompted an expansion in the US trade remedies bar, by creating a new antidumping and countervailing duty statute with more judicial review and more due process. The 1979 Act also amended Section 301 to refocus it on enforcement of treaty rights and institutionalise stakeholder input—creating another type of public international economic law practice.

In 1995, the WTO Agreement widened the domain of trade law enormously. It included the new Agreement on Trade-Related Aspects of Intellectual Property Rights (TRIPS Agreement) and the General Agreement on Trade in Services (GATS). It reincorporated agriculture and textiles into the standard trade law regime; set out entirely new disciplines on sanitary and phytosanitary measures, trade-related investment measures and safeguard measures; and revamped the existing rules on antidumping, subsidies, and technical barriers to trade. At the insistence of the United States and its major trading partners, the multilateral package was enhanced by a system for enforcement of all of these rights through binding dispute settlement.

In addition, the period since the 1990s has seen a great expansion in regional trade agreements including customs unions and free trade area (FTA) agreements. Here again, there is more law to master, and more scope for the practice of law. The European Community (EC) has expanded the network of its cooperation agreements and FTAs. Since the North American Free Trade Area (NAFTA), the United States has negotiated a string of other FTAs, bundling together trade in goods and services, investment, e-commerce, intellectual property rights protection and other provisions on behind-the-border barriers to market access. The WTO now counts close to 400 regional trade agreements in force or due to be implemented by 2010, including all WTO Members but one.[4] This ever-denser network of FTAs with conflicting, complex rules of origin has lowered trade barriers, but greatly complicated business decision making about plant location and sourcing of inputs. During the same period, bilateral investment treaties (BITs—including investment chapters in FTAs) have also mushroomed, growing from 385 in 1989 to 2,495 as of December 2005.[5]

II. CHANGING GLOBAL ECONOMIC AND BUSINESS STRUCTURES

This great expansion of trade and investment agreement rights is both the effect and cause of a shift in the world economy, of a move in Europe and in

---

[4] Figures and link to spreadsheet on notified regional trade agreements, available at http://www.wto.org/english/tratop_e/region_e/region_e.htm (the sole exception as of Jul 2007 was Mongolia).
[5] For analysis, see UNCTAD, http://www.unctad.org/Templates/WebFlyer.asp?intItemID=3150&lang=1; and UNCTAD, World Investment Report 2006 – FDI from Developing and Transition Economies: Implications for Development, UNCTAD/WIR/2006, at 26, http://www.unctad.org/en/docs/wir2006_en.pdf.

the United States toward globalised production and trade, and of the increased importance of services within economic activity. Trade flows today have grown to many times their level in 1948. As of 1970, only 15 per cent of US manufactured goods production was exported; in 2000, the share of exports had grown to 43 per cent.[6] Investment flows are still larger, reaching $1.2 trillion in 2006.[7] FDI is now the largest source of external finance for developing countries.[8] Services (often delivered by investing and being present in the target market) now account for over 64 per cent of world GDP, 79 per cent of US GDP and 76 per cent of US employment, and over 90 per cent of GDP in the most service-based economy of the world, Hong Kong.[9] Inclusion of rules on services within the WTO reflected these new realities.

Companies now do business very differently compared to the world of the 1940s, and even the world of the 1970s—and this has affected the demand for trade law. Even those US manufacturers who in the 1970s bought all of their inputs domestically and sold to the domestic market now source their inputs globally, compete with imports, distribute both imported and domestic products, and export to global markets. A company's global positioning, including its supplier and distribution networks, may matter more to it than defending the US market by using trade remedies. The ownership of US basic industries, which have been the major domestic users of trade remedies, has also become more diverse. The largest US steel producer is now Mittal Steel, which has joined the many other steel companies worldwide owned by the Indian-European global steel company Arcelor Mittal. Trade remedies law has always been a counter-cyclical business, because injury to domestic industry from imports is more difficult to prove when the economy is booming; however, some commentators argue that these structural changes in business may lead to a permanent downtrend in US trade remedy investigations.[10]

Globalised trade has also faced new regulatory challenges which again affect the demand for international economic law. Post-9/11 cargo security rules and concerns about import compliance with food and drug safety rules have led to increased regulatory enforcement at borders. And the

---

[6] US DOT Bureau of Transportation Statistics, Merchandise Export Trade and Goods Production in the US Economy 1970–2000, available at http://www.bts.gov/publications/us_international_trade_and_freight_transportation_trends/2003/index.html.

[7] UNCTAD Investment Brief, *Foreign Direct Investment Rose by 34% in 2006*, UNCTAD/PRESS/PR/001, 9 Jan, 2007, available at http://www.unctad.org/Templates/webflyer.asp?docid=7993&intItemID=1634&lang=1.

[8] World Bank, World Development Indicators 2006, item 6b, available at http://devdata.worldbank.org/wdi2006/contents/Section6_1.htm#f2.

[9] Estimates for 2006, see CIA World Factbook, available at https://www.cia.gov/library/publications/the-world-factbook/index.html.

[10] *ITC Commissioner Says Drop in AD Cases Due to Changing Business Realities*, Inside US Trade, 20 Apr, 2007.

Sarbanes-Oxley Act,[11] with its emphasis on corporate governance and accountability, encourages companies to undertake improved compliance and reporting procedures in these and other areas—including customs procedures, export controls, trade and financial sanctions and anti-bribery laws.

III. DIVERSIFICATION OF DISPUTE SETTLEMENT

Wider access to various forms of international economic dispute settlement has obviously affected international economic law practice—as has the increased transparency of dispute settlement. In the era of the GATT, almost all complaints concerning GATT violations were brought by and against the United States and other developed countries. A GATT case could reach decision within a few months, or could take years; until the panel report became public, the exact nature of the complaint could be unknown. The lack of transparency prevented meaningful stakeholder participation in disputes; hardly anyone knew GATT law, other than diplomats or negotiators who had learned the GATT on the job. The lack of stakeholder participation, and resource limitations in governments and the GATT Secretariat, meant that disputes tended to be simple and almost never involved panel evaluation of factual evidence. There were limits to what a panel was able to do and to the kinds of disputes with which it could cope.

The advent of the WTO has changed all that. In the WTO, use of dispute settlement procedures is no longer limited to the US-European dyad. In the period since January 1995, the United States and the EC have brought less than half of all complaints and have been the targets of slightly over 40 per cent of complaints by others.[12] Many cases have not involved the EU or the United States at all: a series of aircraft disputes between Canada and Brazil; a case by Poland against Thai antidumping measures on steel; a complaint by Mexico against Chinese subsidies; and the many complaints brought by one developing country about access to another developing country's market. In the Tokyo and Uruguay Rounds, the United States used GATT dispute settlement to advance its negotiating agenda and satisfy the demands of exporting stakeholders; a quarter century later in the Doha Round, Brazil has advanced its agricultural agenda with WTO actions brought on behalf of its cotton and sugar exporters.

What has led to this diversification of actors? To begin with, wider knowledge about WTO dispute settlement—fed by the instant availability of WTO complaints, panel reports and Appellate Body reports on the

---

[11] Public Company Accounting Reform and Investor Protection Act of 2002, Pub L No 107–204, 116 Stat 745 (2002).
[12] For statistics, see www.worldtradelaw.net.

Internet, the vast expansion in academic programs teaching international economic law throughout the world, and the large volume of academic and student work analysing and reanalysing the WTO's written output. Law schools are graduating ever-increasing numbers of lawyers familiar with WTO and trade law rules. There is more lawyering in disputes, and more access to justice in the WTO. The Geneva-based Advisory Centre for WTO Law, founded in 2000, advises developing countries about their legal rights and helps represent them in WTO disputes. Governments have also increased the use of specialist lawyers in their WTO missions or in their trade ministries. Governments also work with private counsel in their countries, the Advisory Centre or international law firms specialised in WTO law.

Increased professionalisation of dispute settlement has also strengthened the system's ability to deal with fact-intensive disputes. The limits on panel capacity during the GATT era meant that rules involving an assessment of economic facts—such as those on actionable subsidies, or de facto discrimination—were unenforceable in practice. But in the WTO era, panels have been able to draw on party submissions of economic data and arguments, to finally realise the potential of these rules as negotiated.[13]

Governments are still the only direct participants in WTO dispute settlement, and stakeholders still can only participate to the extent that governments will let them. But developing country stakeholders have emerged with global ambitions, like the Brazilian aircraft, cotton and sugar industries or the Ecuadorian banana industry. Stakeholders from developed countries and stakeholders from developing countries can equally ask their governments to bring WTO actions, and then assist their governments and work with them during the dispute settlement process. After 364 complaints, 111 panel reports, 67 Appellate Body reports and 29 compliance proceedings,[14] the WTO has proven itself as a viable option for governments and stakeholders to use to address their foreign market access and other problems. WTO rights have also become a significant factor in international business planning—for instance, in China, where the government has tied the extent of licences for foreign investment in services to its GATS commitments in China's WTO accession package.

The same story applies for foreign investment, investment arbitration and investment planning under the widening network of BITs. Global businesses have realised that they can use BIT rights in planning and structuring investments so as to reduce their level of business risk, and in addressing

---

[13] Compare the rudimentary evidence and analysis in *Japan—Restrictions on Imports of Certain Agricultural Products*, BISD 35S/163 (1988) with economic evidence presented by the parties in *US—Subsidies to Upland Cotton*, WT/DS267/R, WT/DS267/AB/R (2005); and *Korea—Taxes on Alcoholic Beverages*, WT/DS75/R, WT/DS75/AB/R (1999).

[14] As of July 2007.

problems as they arise. Moreover, as UNCTAD's 2006 World Investment Report points out, developing country multinationals are emerging as major regional and global players, and account for a significant share of inward FDI in some countries.[15] In treaty-based investment arbitration, increasingly the claimants may be investors from another developing country. These stakeholders too are a source of demand for international economic legal services.

These economic developments, driving the development of international economic law, have opened the way for a new type of international economic law practice, applying treaty rights under the WTO, BITs and FTAs. Counsel can help stakeholders and governments use these treaty rights and domestic trade and investment rules—to address market access problems; to remedy discrimination or takings of property; to negotiate to open markets; and to shape legislative proposals that do not run afoul of international obligations. And although governments must ultimately resolve competing values in the public interest, governments may also find it useful to call on the assistance that stakeholders can provide.

At the Bretton Woods conference, the discussion explored these phenomena and focused on steps that could be taken in this connection to strengthen the practice and discipline of international economic law. The participants agreed that international economic law as a discipline would benefit substantially from better contact between the academic world and the practitioner world; better current information on practice would help produce research and writing that would be more widely read, and would more directly shape the development of WTO law.

The practitioners present expressed their keen interest in seeing more academic writing that addresses head-on the issues that come up in their practice of law. The best arguments made in the WTO or other public international legal proceedings are those that combine highly persuasive writing, mastery of doctrine and past precedent, a sense of where the desired result fits within the context of mainstream trade policy and ongoing negotiations, and a steady focus on achieving results that will be useful to the client. Old-fashioned doctrinal analysis that makes sense of a series of past analyses of national treatment, for instance, can be helpful when framing an argument about the meaning of national treatment and how the panel should apply national treatment principles in a consistent manner to the facts in a current case. Yet formalism alone will not do the job. The data points in public international economic law are still so few that to understand past cases, it

---

[15] UNCTAD, World Investment Report 2006, above n 5, at 5–9, available at http://www.unctad.org/wir; Press Release, UNCTAD, Firms Based in Developing Countries Joining Ranks of World's Largest Transnational Corporations, UNCTAD/PRESS/PR/2006/034 (16 Oct, 2006), available at http://www.unctad.org/Templates/webflyer.asp?docid=7466&intItemID=1528&lang=1.

is crucial to appreciate their idiosyncrasies, as well as the factual and policy problems that the litigants and decision-makers faced at the time.

The academics wanted to have more contact with practitioners to better understand which issues are the most relevant for their research. Since they are training future practitioners, they wanted a better understanding of what kind of substantive knowledge and skills their students will need to be effective practitioners of international economic law. The conference participants discussed at length the use of moot courts in international economic law as a means to integrate international economic law teaching with practice. They commented on moots held in recent years on WTO law, as well as the Vis moot court on international commercial arbitration. They recognised that organising a moot involves significant demands on the time and resources of the hosting school, and that the need to mobilise knowledgeable panelists limits the feasible moot sites in North America to a few cities. Participants hoped that a North American round of the WTO Moot Court organised by the European Law Students Association (ELSA) could be held in the next few years.

All agreed on the need to mobilise greater efforts by practitioners and academics to provide service to the public and to developing countries in particular. Conference participants urged a greater attention to pro bono work in trade and investment law, to improve access to justice for the poorest developing countries.

Conference participants agreed that since its formation in the early 1980s, the ASIL International Economic Law Interest Group has served as an effective bridge between practitioners and academics. They urged the Group to continue on in that role, and agreed that the new Society of International Economic Law should complement these missions of the Interest Group, and take them to a global level reaching practitioners and academics worldwide.

17

The Developing Discipline of International Financial Law

DOUGLAS W ARNER[*]

I. INTRODUCTION

IN 1944, AT the conclusion of the Second World War, the allied powers under the leadership of the United States and the United Kingdom agreed on a design for the redevelopment and reintegration of the world economy following three decades of crisis and conflict. That design, the Bretton Woods international economic system, was based on the premise of trade liberalisation, closed domestic financial systems and fixed exchange rates.

While international finance began to re-emerge, due to the Bretton Woods focus on fixed exchange rates and closed domestic financial systems, there were no corresponding efforts directed towards its regulation, leaving finance to domestic law. The first change occurred in the 1970s, when the collapse of Bankhaus Herstatt in Germany and Penn Central Bank in the United States highlighted that not only was international finance of increasing importance, but also that there were significant interlinkages between domestic financial intermediaries and systems that raised real cross-border risks. The result was a series of discussions among the major jurisdictions involved, hosted by the Bank for International Settlements (BIS) in Basel, Switzerland, and later formalised as the Basel Committee on Banking Supervision, the Committee on the Global Financial System and the Committee on Payment and Settlement Systems—all hosted today by the BIS.

As international finance developed and globalised, it has faced a number of crises, with each resulting in international efforts to prevent similar situations through financial regulatory cooperation.

Today, after 35 years of further evolution, international financial law focuses not only on the Bretton Woods institutions and the BIS, but also

---

[*] Special thanks to Prof Rolf H Weber of the University of Zurich for his comments and suggestions.

on an ever-increasing number of international financial organisations (such as the Basel Committee and the International Organization of Securities Commissions) of varying levels of formality involved in the development, implementation and monitoring of international financial standards.

This Chapter argues that while this system of international financial standards is a significant development in response to the risks of financial globalisation, it in fact merits a higher level of attention, design and formalisation. Section II discusses the emergence of international financial law since the Second World War; and Section III contains an overview of the current system of international financial cooperation and standards. From this basis, in Section IV it is suggested that the current system deserves a thorough re-design, focusing on financial globalisation and the twin objectives of financial stability and financial development. Finally, Section V presents ideas for creating an appropriate regime.

II. THE INTERNATIONAL ECONOMIC SYSTEM

By the mid-1990s, both the theoretical understanding of finance and the actual nature of international and domestic financial systems had changed radically from those at the end of the Second World War.

A. The Bretton Woods System and Globalisation of Financial Markets

In August 1941, Franklin D Roosevelt and Winston Churchill met on a battleship near Nova Scotia in the Atlantic Ocean and laid down their vision of a peaceful world order after World War II in the Atlantic Charter.[1] This document was essentially based on three pillars: peace, financial stability and trade between equal nations. The second and third pillars (discussed in 1944 under the auspices of the United States and the United Kingdom) focused on preventing international economic instability of the sort seen in the interwar period (1914–1944) and supporting economic development through reintegration of domestic economies. The design encompassed three elements: First, its structure was formal and institutional, based on an interlinked set of international treaties and institutions. Second, it assumed closed national financial markets, with limited capital flows, but open markets for trade in goods. Third, relationships among closed national systems were structured through an international institutional framework.[2] Institutionally, the Bretton Woods system was to include three interlinked international organisations: the International

---

[1] See SI Rosenman (ed), *The Public Papers and Addresses of Franklin D Roosevelt* (Random House, New York, 1938–1950) (1941) 314.
[2] See Proceedings and Documents of the United Nations Monetary and Financial Conference Bretton Woods, New Hampshire, 1–22 Jul, 1944 (US Governmental Printing Office, 1948).

Monetary Fund (IMF), the World Bank and the International Trade Organization (ITO).

However, the Bretton Woods system as designed never actually functioned: the ITO was still-born[3] (though ultimately reincarnated as the World Trade Organization [WTO] in 1994 after 50 years in the limbo of the General Agreement on Tariffs and Trade [GATT]). Likewise, the role of the World Bank was quickly usurped in many ways first by the bilateral efforts of the United States through the Marshall Plan and related reconstruction initiatives, complemented later by the European Community with its aid programs for Southern and Eastern European countries. This left the World Bank to focus on developing (often post-colonial) countries—the role it continues to play today. Nonetheless, the design for monetary relations, with the IMF at the centre of a system of fixed exchange rates based on the US dollar and its link to gold, did function—arguably quite well—until the early 1970s.

Since the end of the Bretton Woods international monetary system in 1973, financial markets have changed dramatically through a process of liberalisation, internationalisation and globalisation, undergirded by incredible technological changes. In the 1990s, the deficiencies of the existing international institutions and arrangements (the 'international financial architecture') to deal with these changes came dramatically to light through the Mexican, East Asian and other financial crises which followed. Since that time, the IMF, World Bank and WTO gradually have been forced to come to grips with the increasingly globalised nature of finance. Discussions both in these institutions and elsewhere have focused on whether there is a need to reform the existing international institutional arrangements—whether there is a need for a 'new international financial architecture.'[4]

B. Bretton Woods as Designed

The Bretton Woods system as designed was largely the result of the work of two economists and civil servants, one British, one American: John Maynard Keynes and Harry Dexter White. Both approaches reflected the need to support the future development of the international economy following the end of the Second World War. In the light of the much stronger bargaining position of the United States, White's ideas were taken up to a greater extent than those of Keynes during the negotiations in Bretton Woods in 1944 and the institutions were subsequently located in Washington, DC.

---

[3] See JH Jackson, *The Jurisprudence of GATT and the WTO: Insights on Treaty Law and Economic Relations* (Cambridge University Press, 2000) 21–22.

[4] For an overview, see RH Weber, 'Challenges for the New Financial Architecture' (2001) 31 *Hong Kong LJ* 241; M Giovanoli, 'A New Architecture for the Global Financial Market: Legal Aspects of International Financial Standard Setting', in M Giovanoli (ed), *International Monetary Law: Issues for the New Millennium* (Oxford University Press, 2000) 3; JJ Norton, 'Qualified Self-Regulation in the New Financial Architecture' (Jul 2000) *J Int'l Bnkg Reg* 9.

The essential underlying theory of both approaches and the final structure adopted was based, first, on a system of stable exchange rates. All negotiators involved felt that, while it was impossible to return to the gold standard as it existed prior to the First World War it was important to return to a parallel system, with money circulating on the basis of a fixed relationship to gold, rather than on the basis of pure paper currencies ('fiat money'). This design was intended to provide a stable base for finance, investment and trade—the other central pillars of the structure—and to avoid the sorts of monetary instabilities seen during the period from 1914–1944. Capital movements would be largely controlled through domestic restrictions, with the IMF supporting the system through monitoring of capital flows and facilitating orderly exchange readjustments when necessary.

Underpinned by this international system of fixed exchange rates and limited capital mobility, the system then addressed the need to re-establish international trade linkages,[5] based around the ITO, which was intended to serve a formal role both in reducing trade barriers and in policing the agreements. However, due to US and French political concerns, this institution was not established. Rather, trade relationships were addressed through a system of negotiations, formalised as the GATT. Despite not being of the same magnitude as the ITO system, the GATT—over the next 50 years—gradually and successfully reduced trade barriers around the world, especially among developed economies. In 1994, the WTO, an institution in many ways paralleling the ITO, was established, though by this time, the system of fixed exchange rates with which it was meant to operate in tandem had long ceased to exist.

C. Bretton Woods in Practice: 1944–94

In practice, the Bretton Woods international economic system never came into existence as intended, as the ITO was not formed and the central role of the World Bank in post-war reconstruction was quickly displaced by bilateral efforts such as the Marshall Plan.

(i) The IMF and the International Monetary System

Nonetheless, the international monetary system, centred on the IMF, came into life: The system of fixed exchange rates in fact functioned rather well from 1945–73,[6] at which time the United States finally abandoned the fixed link between the US dollar and gold. Despite the abandonment of the fundamental link to gold, many economies continued to maintain fixed

---

[5] By 1944, due to economic nationalism and the needs and results of war, the system of free trade which had existed in the 1870–1914 period had been completely destroyed.

[6] With some exceptions, see AF Lowenfeld, *International Economic Law* (Oxford University Press, 2003) 526–27.

relationships between their currencies and the US dollar (though subject to periodic, often painful adjustments) and capital flows remained largely restricted during this period (with the exception of the development of the euromarkets, laying the foundation of today's global financial system). During this period, the role of the IMF mainly focused on the relationship between the developed economies and exchange rate adjustments.[7]

During the 1970s, the IMF, having partially lost its role after the abandonment of the gold standard, sought to replicate this link through the creation of a new synthetic currency, the special drawing rights (SDR); however, this never really worked as intended. Nonetheless, the IMF continued to maintain a certain role in the process of exchange rate adjustment. Additionally, two amendments to the IMF Articles of Agreement reflected its new role in the international monetary system,[8] allowing the IMF to increasingly focus on lending to support economies dealing with periodic exchange crises, including a range of conditions for such support, IMF 'conditionality.'

In the early 1990s, the IMF argued for a further amendment to its Articles to formalise its role in encouraging and supporting capital liberalisation, especially in developing, emerging and transition economies. In addition, with the collapse of the Soviet Bloc, the IMF began to focus on monetary aspects of the economic transition process. By 1994, the 50th anniversary of the Bretton Woods conference, it appeared that the IMF largely understood its role—and the mechanisms through which to achieve its goals—as centred on the policy-focused ideas of the Washington Consensus.[9]

(ii) Finance and the World Bank

With the onset of the Cold War in the late 1940s, the United States realised the need to build allies, even on the foundations of former enemies,

---

[7] Especially as the economic importance of Germany and Japan increased and that of the United Kingdom decreased.

[8] The IMF Articles were adopted at the United Nations Monetary and Financial Conference, Bretton Woods, New Hampshire on 22 Jul, 1944 and entered into force 27 Dec, 1945. They have subsequently been amended 3 times: (1) Board of Governors Resolution No 23–5, adopted 31 May, 1968 and effective 28 Jul, 1969; (2) Board of Governors Resolution No 31–4, adopted 30 Apr, 1976 and amended effective 11 Nov 1992; and (3) Board of Governors Resolution No 45–3, adopted 28 Jun, 1990 and effective 11 Nov, 1992.

[9] See P Krugman, 'Dutch Tulips and Emerging Markets' (Jul/Aug 1995) 74 *Foreign Aff* 28. Krugman describes the so-called 'Washington Consensus' regarding economic policies that developed in the early 1990s as: Liberalize trade, privatize state enterprises, balance the budget, peg the exchange rate, and one will have laid the foundations for an economic takeoff; find a country that has done these things, and there one may confidently expect to realize high returns on investments. Ibid at 29. J Williamson (ed), *Latin American Adjustment: How Much Has Happened?* (Institute for International Economics, 1990); World Bank, World Development Report 1991: *The Challenge of Development* (1991); S Fischer, 'ABCDE: Past Ten Years, Next Ten Years. Annual World Bank Conference on Development Economics 1998', in Stanley Fischer (ed), *IMF Essays from a Time of Crisis: The International Financial System, Stabilization and Development* (MIT Press, 2004).

and initiated a number of bilateral programs to support reconstruction, especially in Europe and Japan. As a result, in a very short period following its creation, the primary role and mission of the World Bank had been directed elsewhere.

Therefore, the World Bank was forced to search for a new role, almost from the beginning; its attention turned increasingly to the needs of developing countries around the world, rather than post-war reconstruction of the developed countries. This role received a significant boost as the former colonial powers lost their empires, whether through emancipation, revolt or abandonment. The World Bank sought to step in and assist these new countries in developing infrastructure and building their economies. During its initial decades, the World Bank focused on loans to governments for both specific projects and increasingly, through the 1970s, for general budgetary support. Lending was supplemented by the provision of grants to the least developed countries, generally through the International Development Agency (IDA) created in 1960.

With the onset of the developing country debt crisis in the early 1980s, the World Bank was faced with a challenge to its program of state lending, as it became obvious that resources lent for general purposes and even for specific projects had often been squandered and in some cases even caused more harm than benefit. As a result, in addition to state lending and grants, the World Bank began to focus to a greater extent on providing private sector assistance through the International Finance Corporation (IFC) and Multilateral Investment Guarantee Agency (MIGA), established in 1956 and 1988, respectively. By the end of the 1980s, the World Bank Group included the World Bank, IFC, IDA and MIGA, dealing with (respectively) state lending and technical assistance, private sector projects, grants to developing countries and investment guarantees.[10] With the collapse of the Soviet Bloc, like the IMF, the World Bank also added the transition economies to its development assistance portfolio. Nonetheless, unlike the IMF, the World Bank was facing many questions about its role and future at the time of the 50th anniversary of the Bretton Woods conference in 1994, leading it to focus on the overall objective of poverty reduction.

(iii) Trade, the GATT and the WTO

As noted above, international trade relationships were structured through a series of rounds of negotiations, formalised through the GATT (established in 1948). Even with a narrower focus than planned, the GATT was, in fact, quite effective in gradually reducing trade barriers, especially among

---

[10] In addition, it also serves as a host for the International Centre for Settlement of Investment Disputes (ICSID), founded in 1966 (which along with MIGA, supports the development of international investment).

the developed countries. In 1994 the GATT members agreed to the establishment of the WTO, reflecting a general consensus in support of greater trade liberalisation. Therefore, by the 50th anniversary of the Bretton Woods conference in 1994, the successor to the ITO had finally emerged, to much fanfare and high expectations.

(iv) Coordination and Linkage

Because the ITO was never formed, the planned coordinating committee likewise never was formed. Perhaps as a result, the IMF and the World Bank often have been accused of failing to coordinate their activities—despite the fact that they sit on opposite sides of the same street in central Washington, DC Only a few efforts have been made in this direction following problems arising in the context of the 1980s debt crisis (ie, the creation of the 'Interim' Committee to coordinate activities), but this remains a continuing concern.[11]

III. GLOBALISATION OF FINANCE AND THE IMPERATIVES OF FINANCIAL CRISES

Following the Asian financial crisis, the discussions on the IMF's role in transparency and liquidity increased, with new questions about whether there was a need to reform the existing international financial architecture.[12] These discussions first looked to the changed nature of international finance and the implications of these changes. Two specific areas received the greatest attention: crisis prevention and crisis resolution. Both of these issues largely arose due to the transformation of the international financial system through the process of globalisation.

A. Globalisation of Finance

A number of factors underlie the process of financial market globalisation (or re-globalisation), namely the liberalisation of money, finance and investment, as well as trade; the process of disintermediation (sometimes labeled as securitisation); technological innovation; financial innovation; and privatisation. The elements can be identified as the following:[13] First, there has been a progressive and comprehensive liberalisation of capital

---

[11] See JE Stiglitz, *Globalization and Its Discontents* (Norton, 2002); AH Meltzer, 'The Report of the International Financial Institution Advisory Commission: Comments on the Critics', in D Vines & CL Gilbert (eds), *The IMF and its Critics: Reform of Global Financial Architecture* (Cambridge University Press, 2004).
[12] For an overview see Weber, above n 4, at 250.
[13] See D Arner, *Financial Stability, Economic Growth and the Role of Law* (Cambridge University Press, 2007).

flows and financial systems from the original closed and fixed structure established under the Bretton Woods system. Second, finance both internationally and domestically has undergone a process of disintermediation, as financial flows have moved from banks to capital markets. Third, technological innovation has increased the speed with which information is transferred around the world, reinforcing interlinkages between formerly isolated financial systems and markets. Fourth, financial innovations have sought to meet the challenges of changing financial markets and their participants, with constant development of new intermediaries and products to deal with the increased volatility and flexibility inherent in international finance. Fifth, there has been a reduction in the role of centralised economic decision-making, evidenced by the spread of privatisation around the world since the early 1980s, supporting both the development of international markets as funding sources and reducing government influence and control over domestic markets.

By the beginning of the 1990s, these trends had fundamentally altered the financial landscape, both internationally and domestically. As the decade progressed, a clear feature of international finance was a succession of financial crises, often with international or global implications—exactly the sort of crises that the Bretton Woods system was designed to prevent. These crises brought increasing attention to their causes, resolution and possible future prevention, often discussed in the context of a 'new' international financial architecture.[14]

Today's financial markets exhibit a number of characteristics:[15] First, the nature of the markets is largely global at the wholesale level, but at best international at the retail level (even in the context of the European Union). Second, the dominant international monetary system is one based on floating rates between major currencies, with many other currencies linked to the major currencies through a variety of systems. Third, capital flows are largely unrestricted. Fourth, significant financial crises have once again become more frequent. Fifth, international financial cooperation is shaped both by the continued development of the existing international financial architecture and by the creation of the WTO. Sixth, international financial institution innovations include the EU Single Market Financial Market project, WTO, Financial Stability Forum, and a proliferation of international financial organisations of various characters and forms. Seventh, major financial innovations and developments include the massive growth of derivatives instruments and markets (especially the over-the-counter-market), as well as the on-going process of transition from central planning, state ownership and control to regulated market economies,

---

[14] See B Eichengreen, *Toward a New International Financial Architecture* (Peterson Institute, 1999), *Appendix B*.
[15] See Arner, above n 13.

alongside technological developments, especially in communications and computing. Eighth, the dominant economic philosophy has been integration, with a continued role of the Washington Consensus, modified by a new focus on incentives and institutions. Ninth, regulatory developments include increasing attention to risk-based regulation, especially in the context of discussions of capital adequacy and legal infrastructure. Finally, fragmentation continues among more than 200 different national jurisdictions, including different currencies, different supervisory authorities, different tax systems, different laws and regulations, and different courts.

What does this mean for the future of both individual countries and the international financial system? According to Michel Camdessus, then IMF Managing Director, speaking in 1998, seven areas of the 'architecture of the international financial system' needed to be strengthened in the wake of the Asian and Mexican financial crises.[16] First, more effective surveillance over countries' economic policies, coupled with fuller disclosure of all relevant economic and financial data, was needed, given that in each situation market responses were aggravated by a significant lack of proper information.[17] Second, regional surveillance efforts needed to be improved in order to encourage neighboring countries to put pressure on one another to prevent contagion. While little has yet developed in this respect outside of the context of the European Union, discussions continue in regional fora world-wide. Third, financial sector reform grounded in improved prudential regulation and supervision is necessary; this reform is based on on-going efforts to develop 'best practices' through the activities of the various organisations and institutions in order to transfer lessons learned as broadly and quickly as possible. Fourth, more effective structures needed to be developed in regard to debt workouts, both on a national level through bankruptcy laws and at the international level through on-going efforts[18] such as those of the Group of Ten (G-10).[19] Fifth, capital account liberalisation should continue but needs to be based on prudence and proper sequencing to increase the orderliness of and access to international capital markets. Sixth, world-wide efforts must be increased to promote good governance and to fight against corruption. Seventh, multilateral financial

---

[16] M Camdessus, *The Role of the IMF: Past, Present, and Future*, IMF Speech 98/4, Remarks at the Annual Meeting of the Bretton Woods Committee, Washington, DC (13 Feb, 1998).

[17] In this regard, the IMF developed the Special Data Dissemination Standard (SDDS) (and General Data Dissemination Standard [GDDS]) and promoted disclosure through its programs and policy advice.

[18] Crisis resolution and workout issues are beyond the scope of the present Chapter. For more detailed discussion, see Arner, above n 13.

[19] The G-10 includes Belgium, Canada, France, Germany, Italy, Japan, Luxembourg, the Netherlands, Spain, Sweden, Switzerland, the United Kingdom and the United States. Therefore, it actually includes 13 countries.

institutions need to be strengthened, both in terms of resources and authority and in terms of equitable representation.[20]

B. Financial Crises and the International Response

Following the Asian financial crisis, a number of actions were taken to address these issues and to build on the initiatives undertaken after the Mexican financial crisis, centring on the IMF (transparency and liquidity), the World Bank (technical assistance) and international financial standards.

First, the IMF acted to further enhance its role both in the provision of international liquidity and in encouraging transparency. In regard to additional liquidity, the IMF approved the Supplemental Reserve Facility (SRF) and a general capital increase. In addition, the IMF initially continued to attempt to expand its mandate to include capital account liberalisation, though this was largely abandoned by the end of 1998.

The focus of the World Bank and the regional development banks[21] (collectively 'multilateral development banks') is somewhat different from that of the IMF. In general terms, the IMF can be compared to the fire brigade while the World Bank is more of a construction agency.[22] While these institutions are increasingly working together (especially the IMF and World Bank), a number of differences can be discerned. First, the multilateral development banks' focus is structural and sectoral, as compared with the IMF's traditional focus on macroeconomic aggregates. Second, the multilateral development banks' focus is more on long-term restructuring as opposed to short-term adjustment. Third, the multilateral development banks focus not solely on economic and financial issues, but often on a broad array of development issues (especially poverty reduction).

Overall, the division of responsibilities among these various international institutions remained (and remains) still somewhat tentative. Nonetheless, following the Mexican and Asian financial crises, the multilateral development banks increasingly focused on efforts to strengthen domestic financial systems of their member countries, especially given the potential of financial crisis to negatively impact development and the quality of the multilateral institutions' own loan portfolios. These initial steps, aimed at strengthening the financial resources of the IMF and on increasing transparency of financial markets, were useful. However, more was required.

---

[20] M Camdessus, *Reflections on the Crisis in Asia*, IMF Speech 98/3, Address to the Extraordinary Ministerial Meeting of the Group of 24, Caracas, Venezuela (7 Feb, 1998).

[21] Multilateral regional development banks include the Inter-American Development Bank, African Development Bank, Asian Development Bank, European Bank for Reconstruction and Development, and Islamic Development Bank.

[22] S Sandström, *The East Asia Crisis and the Role of the World Bank*, Statement to the Bretton Woods Committee (13 Feb, 1998), 5–6.

IV. THE 'NEW' INTERNATIONAL FINANCIAL ARCHITECTURE

In addition to liquidity and transparency issues, the third major area of concern is prevention of financial crises through enhancement of the quality of individual financial systems. In response to an initiative at the Lyon summit of the Group of Seven (G-7)[23] in June 1996, representatives of the G-10 countries and of emerging and transition economies jointly sought to develop a strategy for fostering financial stability through the analysis of experiences in previous crises and to elucidate basic standards and principles to guide individual economies in the development of stronger financial systems.[24] The primary conclusion to emerge from this study was that a robust financial system is less susceptible to the risk of a crisis in the wake of real economic disturbances and is more resilient in the face of crises that do occur.

As noted, financial crises can have serious repercussions for economies in terms of heightened macroeconomic instability, reduced economic growth and a less efficient allocation of savings and investment.[25] In its report, the G-10 focused on three central elements necessary to the development of a robust financial system: (1) creation of an institutional setting and financial infrastructure necessary for a sound credit culture and effective market functioning; (2) promotion of functioning of markets so that owners, directors, investors and other actual and potential stakeholders exercise adequate discipline over financial intermediaries; and (3) creation of regulatory and supervisory arrangements that complement and support market discipline.[26] The World Bank and regional development banks were given a leading role in providing technical assistance to countries seeking to build robust financial systems.

A. Financial Stability

Since the Mexican financial crisis, the concept of 'financial stability' has become the primary target in preventing financial crises and reducing the severe risks of financial problems which do occur from time to time.

---

[23] The G-7 includes Canada, France, Germany, Italy, Japan, the United Kingdom, and the United States. The Group of Eight (G-8) also includes Russia. The European Union is also a member of both the G-7 and the G-8. For the best resource on the G-7/8, see http://www.g7.utoronto.ca/.

[24] G-10, Report of the Group of Ten (G-10) Working Party on Financial Stability in Emerging Markets, Financial Stability in Emerging Market Economies: A Strategy for the Formulation, Adoption and Implementation of Sound Principles and Practices to Strengthen Financial Systems (Apr 1997), available at http://www.bis.org/publ/gten02.pdf [G-10 Strategy (1997)]. This framework was developed further in Group of 22 Systemically Significant Countries (G-22), Reports on the International Financial Architecture, Oct 1998.

[25] G-10 Strategy (1997), above n 24, at 1.

[26] Ibid at 3–4.

Financial stability, however, is not a clearly defined term. In fact, financial stability is usually described by what it is not than by what it is: the absence of a major financial crisis.[27] According to Garry Schinasi discussing the term in literature and practice,[28] financial stability may be defined as the joint stability of the key financial intermediaries operating within the financial system and the stability of the constituent markets.[29] For financial intermediaries, this generally means that they are sound, ie they have sufficient capital to absorb normal, and at times abnormal, losses and sufficient liquidity to manage operations and volatility in normal periods of time. Market stability generally means the absence of the kind of volatility that could have severe real economic consequences (ie, systemic risk).

Financial stability is therefore both the absence of financial crisis and the normal operation of financial intermediaries and markets. Marc Quintyn and Michael Taylor go one step further, suggesting that the financial sector plays a special and unique role in an economy, and that as a result, 'the achievement of *financial stability* ... is now generally considered a *public good*'.[30] With financial stability the agreed international objective, a system has been developed to assist countries to achieve this goal.

B. Structure and Process

The emerging international strategy for the development of financial stability can be described as a system of international financial standards. The system has the following primary characteristics: (1) development of an international consensus on the key elements of a sound financial and regulatory system by representatives of the relevant economies; (2) formulation of sound principles and practices by international groupings of technocratic authorities with relevant expertise and experience, such as the Basel Committee, IOSCO, the International Accounting Standards Board, the International Association of Insurance Supervisors (IAIS) and the Joint Forum on Financial Conglomerates; (3) use of market discipline and market access channels to provide incentives for the adoption of sound supervisory systems, better corporate governance and other key elements of a robust financial system; and (4) promotion by multilateral institutions such as the IMF and the

---

[27] See U Das, M Quintyn & K Chenard, *Does Regulatory Governance Matter for Financial System Stability? An Empirical Analysis*, 5–6 (IMF Working Paper WP/04/89, May 2004). As a result, they use a definition of 'financial system soundness' rather than 'financial stability.'

[28] See GJ Schinasi, *Responsibility of Central Banks for Stability in Financial Markets* (IMF Working Paper WP/03/121, Jun 2003); for further discussions see A Crockett, *The Theory and Practice of Financial Stability* (GEI Newsletter Issue No 6) 1997; DS Bieri, *The Basel Process and Financial Stability* (Social Research Science Network Working Paper, 8 Nov, 2004).

[29] See Schinasi, above n 28, at 4.

[30] M Quintyn & MW Taylor, *Regulatory and Supervisory Independence and Financial Stability*, (IMF Working Paper WP/02/46, Mar 2002) 8.

multilateral development banks of the adoption and implementation of sound principles and practices.[31] Importantly, however, the ultimate responsibility for policies to strengthen financial systems lies with the governments and financial authorities in the economies concerned.

Most generally, this system can be described as having four levels, incorporating both existing and new international institutions and organisations. At the first level, there is a structure which has mainly been established through political processes. The second level is international standard-setting, largely of a technocratic nature. At the third level is implementation of standards—in principle a domestic process but with technical assistance through a variety of international, regional and bilateral sources. The fourth level focuses on monitoring implementation of standards.[32]

C. International Financial Standards and Standard-setting Organisations

International standards and their development are the the only truly new element of the international financial architecture to emerge from the series of financial crises over the past 15 years. Given that a safe and efficient financial system is crucial for the functioning of any economy, the G-7 at their Lyon Summit in 1996 directed the international financial institutions and international financial organisations—especially the IMF, World Bank and Basel Committee—to set standards for financial regulation to be implemented in developed, developing, emerging and transition economies, as well as to seek solutions for domestic crises with international implications. As a result, a wide range of institutions and organisations have been producing standards in an increasing range of areas.

The only new institution to emerge from discussions of the international financial architecture is the Financial Stability Forum (FSF).[33] The FSF was established to serve the role of the coordinator in the system of international standards and to promote standards. In addition to coordination and standard-setting through the FSF, the established international financial institutions such as the IMF, World Bank and BIS, adhere to their mandate of standard-setting, as well as implementation and monitoring. In addition to the international financial institutions, other formal international organisations such as the Organisation for Economic Cooperation and Development (OECD) are of importance. However, the WTO is not formally included—a potential weakness in the existing framework. Finally,

---

[31] See G-10 Strategy (1997), above n 24, at 49.
[32] This essential structure was affirmed by the G-7 Finance Ministers in the Communiqué from their Köln summit in 1999, see G-7 Finance Ministers, Report of the G7 Finance Ministers to the Köln Economic Summit, Cologne, Germany (18–20 Jun 1999).
[33] See http://www.fsfforum.org.

much standard-setting takes place through various international financial organisations of varying levels of formality.[34]

At the political level, the G-7 industrialised countries have taken the lead in establishing an operating framework for the process. In addition, the G-10 initiated efforts to elaborate the details. Finally, other groups such as the Group of Twenty (G-20)[35] are also involved in various aspects. Today, the process has largely been formalised.

(i) Coordination

The FSF and the BIS currently serve the primary role in coordination of the process of standard-setting. As noted, the FSF was established under the auspices of a G-7 mandate in February 1999, with a threefold purpose: (1) promote international financial stability; (2) improve the functioning of markets; and (3) reduce systemic risk through enhanced information exchange and international cooperation in financial market supervision and surveillance.

The FSF includes five different types of members: national authorities,[36] international financial institutions,[37] other international organisations,[38] international financial organisations[39] and committees of central bank experts.[40] In addition, the FSF has created a number of ad hoc working groups to develop recommendations on specific issues. These include: highly leveraged institutions, capital flows, offshore financial centres, implementation of standards, incentives to foster implementation of standards, deposit insurance, and e-finance.

In addition to the FSF, the BIS plays an important role in coordination. It provides the secretariat for the FSF, as well as the Basel Committee, Committee on Payment and Settlement Systems, Committee on the Global Financial System, G-10 and IAIS.

---

[34] D Zaring, 'International Law by Other Means: The Twilight Existence of International Financial Regulatory Organizations' (1998) 33 *Tex Int'l LJ* 281.

[35] The G-20 includes the finance ministers and central bank governors of 19 countries: Argentina, Australia, Brazil, Canada, China, France, Germany, India, Indonesia, Italy, Japan, Mexico, Russia, Saudi Arabia, South Africa, South Korea, Turkey, the United Kingdom and the United States. It also includes the European Union (Council President) and the European Central Bank (ECB), as well as (on an ex officio basis) the Managing Director of the IMF, the President of the World Bank, and the chairs of the International Monetary and Financial Committee and Development Committee of the IMF and World Bank.

[36] National authorities are the G-7 plus the ECB plus 4 economies, therefore: Australia, Canada, France, Germany, Hong Kong, Italy, Japan, Netherlands, Singapore, Switzerland, United Kingdom, United States, and the ECB.

[37] BIS, IMF, World Bank.

[38] Organisation for Economic Cooperation and Development (OECD).

[39] Basel Committee on Banking Supervision, the International Association of Insurance Supervisors (IAIS), and the International Organization of Securities Commissions (IOSCO).

[40] Committee on the Global Financial System (CGFS) and the Committee on Payment and Settlement Systems (CPSS).

The Developing Discipline of Int'l Financial Law 259

(ii) Key Standards for Sound Financial Systems

The FSF has agreed upon 12 key standards areas,[41] including a total of 15 standards, which are considered as the quintessential minimum requirements for good practice.[42] They are grouped into three main categories encompassing several different aspects. The intention is that each set of key standards will be supported by a methodology for assessment and implementation and a variety of related principles, practices and guidelines.

(iii) Process of Standard-Setting

As noted, standard-setting takes place through a range of different bodies. These can largely be grouped into international financial institutions,[43] other formal international organisations[44] and international financial organisations. The international finanical organisations include a range of different forms, including regulators,[45] central banks,[46] professional groups,[47] market associations,[48] expert groups,[49] and legal groups.[50]

To date, the exact processes of selecting standard areas, designating standard areas and standards as 'key,' selecting appropriate standard-setting organisations, and developing standards themselves are all unclear—despite the extended emphasis on transparency. Selection and designation seems to have been something of a bottom-up process, with standard setters choosing to address and promote their respective standards to the political groupings such as the G-7 and the international financial institutions for adoption and support. Nonetheless, a sort of standardised process for standard-setting does appear to be developing. In addition, more recent processes

---

[41] Some of the key standards are relevant for more than 1 policy area, eg sections of the Code of Good Practices on Transparency in Monetary and Financial Policies have relevance for aspects of payment and settlement as well as financial regulation and supervision.

[42] See http://www.fsforum.org/compendium/key_standards_for_sound_financial_system.html.

[43] The international financial institutions include the IMF, World Bank and BIS.

[44] At present, the OECD. The WTO is not officially represented.

[45] Basel Committee, IAIS and IOSCO. The Financial Action Taskforce (FATF) can also be included in this category.

[46] CPSS and CGFS.

[47] These include the International Accounting Standards Board (IASB) and the International Federation of Accountants (IFAC).

[48] Market associations include the International Swaps and Derivatives Association (ISDA), the International Capital Markets Association (ICMA) and the Loan Market Association.

[49] Expert groups include the Institute of International Finance, the Group of Thirty, the Institute for International Economics and a plethora of domestic and academic research and policy institutes.

[50] Legal groups include the International Law Association, International Bar Association, the UN Commission on International Trade Law (UNCITRAL), the International Institute for the Unification of Private Law (UNIDROIT), the Hague Conference on Private International Law, and the Council of Europe.

have included an increasing amount of public consultation and input, enhancing the quality of and support for resulting standards.

Standard-setting processes now appear to follow a similar pattern, with the basic elements (for both initial development and revision) appearing to be as follows: (1) networking and lobbying by potential standard setters for mandates to develop standards in various areas; (2) support through the G-7, FSF and/or other bodies for a standard development process to proceed; (3) an international process of awareness building and discussion of issues; (4) multilateral technocratic cooperation in drafting; (5) support from the governing body of the standard-setting organisation; (6) testing the use of standards in monitoring and implementation; (7) finalisation of guidance and supporting materials; and (8) approval by the governing body of the standard-setting organisation(s) and referral to other bodies such as the G-7 and/or FSF. Revisions (recently completed in some areas and on-going in others) appear to be following a similar path.

D. Implementation and Monitoring

An important element of the standard-setting process involves monitoring the implementation of international standards. While primarily a domestic process; implementation is supported by a range of assistance mechanisms. Monitoring mainly takes place at the international level through the international financial institutions, especially the IMF and World Bank. Specifically, the IMF works through its annual Article IV consultations. The IMF and the World Bank collaborate through Reports on the Observance of Standards and Codes (ROSCs) and Financial Sector Assessment Programs (FSAPs). The OECD and the Financial Action Task Force on Money Laundering (FATF) also engage in monitoring, with the FATF playing quite an influential role in the context of money laundering and terrorism financing. At a regional level, the regional development banks[51] encourage implementation through their respective projects and reviews. In addition, regional economic associations[52] may have a role—in some cases (eg, the European Union) a very important one. At the bilateral level, some countries (especially the United States) are keen to support the implementation of certain standards—for example, those of the FATF. Finally, at the market level, the rating agencies have shown some interest in monitoring standards, though not to the extent of policy makers' hopes.

---

[51] Chiefly, the African Development Bank, Asian Development Bank, European Bank for Reconstruction and Development, and Inter-American Development Bank.
[52] Chiefly, the European Union (EU), Association of Southeast Asian Nations (ASEAN), Mercosur, North American Free Trade Agreement (NAFTA), and Southern African Development Community (SADC).

E. Financial Liberalisation and the WTO

In addition to the various organisations discussed above, foreign participation in domestic financial services is dealt with largely through bilateral, regional and international negotiations, with the latter centred on the WTO. Specifically, on 1 January, 1995, the Marrakesh Agreement Establishing the WTO (WTO Agreement) entered into force, with its annexes, including, inter alia, the General Agreement on Tariffs and Trade 1994 (GATT), and the General Agreement on Trade in Services (GATS). The main legal components affecting international trade in financial services include: (1) GATS,[53] (2) Annex on Financial Services, (3) Second Annex on Financial Services, (4) Understanding on Commitments in Financial Services, (5) Second Protocol to the GATS, (5) Fifth Protocol to the GATS, (6) Decisions, and (7) Understanding on Rules and Procedures Governing the Settlement of Disputes (DSU).

These components contain a number of general obligations respecting trade and financial services contained in the various agreements, including most-favoured nation (MFN) treatment,[54] transparency, and the effect of domestic regulation, discussed further in the following Section. The GATS covers all sectors of services,[55] including financial services. In addition, the Annex on Financial Services and the Second Annex on Financial Services, as part of the GATS, directly relate to financial services.[56] The Understanding on Commitments in Financial Services, as part of the Final Act, stipulates higher requirements for financial liberalisation for those members that have adopted it. The so-called Financial Services Agreement and its scheduled commitments, in contrast to the financial services commitments undertaken in the Uruguay Round and in the 1995 interim agreement, are not temporary, but permanent, until the WTO members conclude a new agreement through negotiations. The Fifth Protocol to the GATS entered into force on 1 March, 1999, and at the same time, those schedules of specific commitments and lists of MFN exemptions annexed to the Fifth Protocol replaced those undertaken in the 1995 interim agreement or in the Uruguay Round. These commitments form the basis for future financial services negotiations.

---

[53] According to the Results of the Uruguay Round of Multilateral Trade Negotiation, the GATS is composed of 4 parts: (1) the main text of the Agreement (The General Agreement on Trade in Services), (2) 8 Annexes, (3) Schedules of specific commitments (4) List of Art II Exemptions. The GATS Text refers to only the 1st part.

[54] GATS Article II (Most-Favoured-Nation Treatment) is composed of 3 paragraphs, applicable to all services sectors. Para 1 is the core rule identifying the MFN obligation with respect to trade in services. It requires that each member accord to services and service suppliers of any other member treatment no less favourable than that it accords to like services and service suppliers of any other country.

[55] GATS Art I: 3(b): '"services" includes any service in any sector except services supplied in the exercise of governmental authority.'

[56] For a general overview, see W Dobson & P Jacquet, *Financial Services Liberalization in the WTO* (Institute for International Economics, 1998).

The WTO provides the international framework for foreign participation in financial services. However, unlike areas such as trade in goods, in the area of financial services, commitments made by members are exclusive rather than inclusive. Therefore liberalisation is at the discretion of individual WTO members and remains quite limited in most cases. The framework is an important starting point in supporting foreign competition in financial services, but needs to be extended through further negotiations in order to provide greater benefits. It also should be explicitly incorporated into the system of international financial standards. At the same time, it needs to be carefully considered in the context of the relationship between financial liberalisation and financial stability.

V. A GLOBAL FINANCIAL REGIME?

The previous Sections reviewed the development and role of the international financial architecture. Based on the preceding Sections, it can be said that international financial regulation today is an accretion of institutions, organisations, international standards and domestic laws and rules in many ways not designed to address the requirements of the continuing integration of domestic economies into an increasingly globalised financial system. While the original Bretton Woods design was for a coherent global economic governance structure, today's matrix of actors lacks any coherent overarching economic, institutional or legal framework. Rather, international financial regulation has developed in reaction to the globalisation of finance. In fact, today's 'system' of international financial regulation is more of a non-system.

While the development of international financial standards is definitely a major step in the development of the international financial architecture, certain issues remain unaddressed. The existing framework focuses on financial stability, but it should also tackle financial development in the context of the on-going process of globalisation. In addition to including certain other specific areas, in order to better address the needs of emerging, transition and developing economies, both the standards themselves and the supporting framework for implementation and monitoring should incorporate development issues explicitly. This probably has the greatest relevance for the multilateral development banks. Furthermore, international financial standards should also include guidance on competition in the financial sector, both domestic and foreign (notwithstanding the fact that foreign competition is addressed by the WTO financial services framework, which as noted above should be further integrated with other actors and standards).

On the basis of the preceding discussion, this Section asks whether the existing structures are appropriate to the changed needs of the international financial system. As noted above, the international financial architecture as it currently exists does not yet deal with the issue of crisis resolution.[57] In addition, the international financial architecture, as designed, does not integrate its various components in such a coherent manner as the Bretton Woods design. In looking forward, the international financial architecture should focus on the issue of integration into the global financial markets and related sequencing.

As originally structured, the Bretton Woods system was designed to establish a framework to support the reconstruction of the international economy on the basis of monetary stability, trade liberalisation and finance for reconstruction and development. Since agreement on the original design and subsequent partial implementation, the nature of the international economy has changed fundamentally in many respects, most notably as a result of liberalisation, deregulation and globalisation. In many ways, the series of financial crises around the world over the past fifteen year has reflected these changes and the weaknesses of the existing international economic arrangements.

While much has been said and written about a need for a 'new international financial architecture' as a result of the series of crises, little reform has actually taken place. The major exception has been the development of a system of international financial standards, standard-setting organisations, and monitoring and implementation arrangements centred around the Bretton Woods institutions, the BIS and the FSF.

This system of standards, although based on soft law arrangements, is having a significant impact on financial law, including scholarship, teaching and practice. Likewise, it has the potential to shape the future roles of the IMF and the World Bank. However, while this system is an incremental means to address issues of financial stability, it is not yet complete, especially in regard to its integration with financial development and trade in financial services.

---

[57] This is an area which merits further attention but which is beyond the scope of the present Chapter.

18

Investment Treaty Arbitral Decisions as Jurisprudence Constante

ANDREA K BJORKLUND

DECISIONS BY ARBITRAL tribunals in investment treaty cases do not have formal precedential status. Yet certain issues recur, and prior decisions at the least provide guidance to later tribunals as to the scope of the obligations states have undertaken in investment treaties. The content of the most frequently invoked substantive treaty provisions— the obligations to accord national treatment and fair and equitable treatment to foreign investors, and to expropriate the property of foreign investors only in accordance with international law and on payment of due compensation— is far from clear. Furthermore, procedural matters, such as decisions regarding the place of arbitration or the allocation of costs, play an increasingly important role in investment arbitrations but are also not addressed thoroughly in the treaties themselves.

Given those limitations, it seems inevitable that arbitral decisions, as they accumulate, will help to flesh out the extent of state parties' obligations and investors' legitimate expectations when their relationship is governed by an investment treaty. The informal and dispersed regime of investment treaty arbitrations is not well suited to developing a system of formal precedent. Eventually, however, an accretion of decisions will likely develop a *jurisprudence constante*—a 'persisting jurisprudence' that secures 'unification and stability of judicial activity.'[1] Furthermore, organisations such as the Organisation for Economic Cooperation and Development (OECD), the United Nations Conference on Trade and Development (UNCTAD), and the International Law Association's (ILA) Committee on International Law on Foreign Investment have undertaken projects to describe, and in some cases offer normative comment, on the law of international investment. In large part these projects draw on arbitral case law. Case law thus plays a fundamental role in developing the scope of treaty obligations and the

---

[1] M Troper and C Grzegorczyk, *Precedent in France*, in *Interpreting Precedents*, DN MacCormick & RS Summers (eds), (Ashgate/Dartmouth, 1997) 103, 137.

procedural rules tribunals need to employ as they hear increasingly complex cases.

The development of arbitral case law is desirable in that it increases predictability for both states and investors. Nonetheless, developing law under the aegis of ad hoc arbitral tribunals poses practical problems. First, the desired predictability is only enhanced to the extent that decisions are widely available so that arbitrators and counsel know of them. Second, arbitrators need to take prior decisions into account, explaining both agreement and disagreement with them. Third, the sheer number of decisions will soon make it difficult for arbitrators to canvass all relevant prior cases.

These problems are not insurmountable: so long as the movement towards transparency continues, and so long as there is a vibrant discourse about the content of international law, proponents of the international investment regime will be able to point to the development of a jurisprudence that elaborates on the obligations states have undertaken by treaty. Arbitrators will face informal and formal pressures to review, explain, and often harmonise the treaty and customary international law provisions they apply and seek to interpret. Scholars, intergovernmental organisations, members of civil society, arbitrators, arbitration counsel—in short, the entire arbitral community—will help to establish a hierarchy of cases, and the scope and meaning of the law itself, as they both criticise and praise arbitral decisions in the development of a *jurisprudence constante*.

I. USING ARBITRAL DECISIONS TO DEVELOP APPLICABLE LAW

Formally speaking, the awards in cases decided by international tribunals, including investment treaty tribunals, are discrete; each award reports only the decision of the tribunal in the specific case presented. Moreover, international tribunals do not in themselves create law in the manner of common-law courts. Judicial decisions are but a subsidiary means for determining the rules of law under the widely accepted hierarchy of the sources of international law set forth in the Statute of the International Court of Justice.[2]

Practically speaking, however, the reality is rather different. International tribunals are not only aware of but also regularly rely on the decisions of

---

[2] Statute of the International Court of Justice, 26 Jun, 1945, 59 Stat 1055 [ICJ Statute]. Art 38(1) states:

> The Court, whose function is to decide in accordance with international law such disputes as are submitted to it, shall apply: (a) international conventions, whether general or particular, establishing rules expressly recognized by the contesting states; (b) international custom, as evidence of a general practice accepted as law; (c) the general principles of law recognized by civilized nations; (d) subject to the provisions of Article 59, judicial decisions and the teachings of the most highly qualified publicists of the various nations, as subsidiary means for the determination of rules of law.

previous tribunals in similar cases. This is true of investment treaty tribunals, and is also true of the World Trade Organization (WTO) Dispute Settlement Body and the International Court of Justice, notwithstanding the fact that the governing rules of those bodies do not appear to endorse that option.[3] For example, while the ICJ Statute, in Article 38, places judicial decisions below the other sources of international law that it applies, that placement has been less important in practice than might be expected. First, even on a conservative reading, Article 38 has often been interpreted simply as a directive to look to jurisprudence and doctrine for evidence of the existence of the rights and obligations of states, without particular reference to the hierarchy set forth in the ICJ Statute.[4] Second, and less conservatively, most agree that case law plays a more important function than just pointing to other sources of law. Cases decided by international tribunals, including the International Court of Justice, do in fact contain 'a law-creating element':

> If a judgment, especially of the highest court, has pronounced legal rules and principles, legal certainty requires adherence to these rules and principles in other cases, unless compelling reasons militate in favour of changing the case law.[5]

Furthermore, while the language of the ICJ Statute refers to 'judicial' decisions, in practice decisions of international arbitral tribunals have also been used as jurisprudential sources.[6]

Each of these practical considerations is clearly visible in the many decisions of the tribunals that have been convened to hear claims under the increasingly significant network of investment treaties. Investment treaty arbitration is burgeoning; as of the end of 2006, at least 255 investment treaty cases had been filed.[7] The number of awards is also growing rapidly.

---

[3] See, eg, M Shahabuddeen, *Precedent in the World Court* (Cambridge University Press, 1996) 107–10 (noting that the exclusion of stare decisis does not exclude decisions of the ICJ from having precedential force); R Bhala, 'The Myth About Stare Decisis and International Trade Law (Part One of a Trilogy)' (1999) 14 *Am U Int'l L Rev* 845, 849–932 (discussing the de facto precedential value accorded to General Agreement on Tariffs and Trade panels and WTO panel and appellate body decisions).

[4] See, eg, S Rosenne, III *The Law and Practice of the International Court 1920–2005*, (M Nijhoff Publishers, 2006) 1550–51. The subsidiary means are 'the store-house from which the rules of heads (a), (b) and (c) can be extracted'. Ibid at 1551.

[5] *The Statute of the International Court of Justice: A Commentary* 1244–45 (A Zimmermann, C Tomuschat, & K Oellers-Frahm (eds)), (Oxford University Press, 2006) [ICJ Statute Commentary].

[6] Ibid at 785–8 (recognising that the ICJ has referred to arbitral decisions, albeit less frequently than to decisions of the ICJ or its predecessor, the Permanent Court of International Justice).

[7] UN Conference on Trade & Dev (UNCTAD), *Latest Developments in Investor-State Dispute Settlement*, 2, UNCTAD/WEB/ITE/IIA/2006/11 (2006). 156 of these disputes were filed under the ICSID Convention or ICSID Additional Facility Rules and 65 were filed under the UNCITRAL rules. The remainder were filed at the Stockholm Chamber of Commerce, the International Chamber of Commerce, the Cairo Regional Centre for International Commercial Arbitration, or in ad hoc arbitration. In 7 cases the exact venue was unknown. Ibid.

Thus, the status of those awards is becoming more and more important as arbitrators, and counsel, decide new cases against the backdrop of several, perhaps dozens, of recently decided cases that are on-point.

Despite these realities, the standard view of these tribunal decisions is that they are not precedential, but are at most merely persuasive.[8] This view is usually supported by treaty language. For example, NAFTA chapter 11 states:

> An award made by a Tribunal shall have no binding force except between the disputing parties and in respect of the particular case.[9]

This position is similar to that formally taken in other international fora.[10] In fact, the NAFTA language is remarkably like that in the Statute of the International Court of Justice:

> The decision of the Court has no binding force except between the parties and in respect of that particular case.[11]

Yet, after noting the treaty language, tribunals can and do refer to decisions of other tribunals. They do so both to find evidence of the existence of certain rights and obligations and to identify the content of those rights and obligations. They do not do so, however, in the guise of looking to previous decisions as binding precedent, and indeed they jealously guard their autonomy. Thus, tribunals frequently disavow any formal obligation to review prior case law, even as they express their willingness to do so:

> An identity of the basis of jurisdiction of these tribunals, even when it meets with very similar if not even identical facts at the origin of the disputes, does not suffice to apply systematically to the present case positions or solutions already adopted in these cases. Each tribunal remains sovereign and may retain, as it is confirmed by ICSID practice, a different solution for resolving the same problem; but decisions on jurisdiction dealing with the same or very similar issues may at least indicate some lines of reasoning of real interest; this Tribunal may consider them in order to compare its own position with those already adopted by its predecessors and, if it shares the views already expressed by one or more of these tribunals on a specific point of law, it is free to adopt the same solution.[12]

---

[8] See eg, G Kaufmann-Kohler, 'The 2006 Freshfields Lecture—Arbitral Precedent: Dream, Necessity, or Excuse?' 23 *Arb Int'l* (forthcoming 2007) (manuscript at 1).

[9] North American Free Trade Agreement, US–Can–Mex., Art 1136, 17 Dec, 1992, 32 ILM 605 (1993) [NAFTA].

[10] Art 53(1) of the ICSID Convention states 'The award shall be binding on the parties', a statement usually read as 'excluding the applicability of the principle of binding precedent to successive ICSID cases.' Convention on the Settlement of Investment Disputes Between States and Nationals of Other States, Art 53(1), 18 Mar, 1965, 17 UST 1270, 575 UNTS 159 [ICSID Convention]; C Schreuer, *The ICSID Convention: A Commentary* (Cambridge University Press, 2001) 1082 (citation omitted).

[11] ICJ Statute, above n 2, Art 59.

[12] AES Corp. (US) v Argentina, ICSID (W Bank) Case No ARB/02/17, 30 (Decision on Jurisdiction) (26 Apr, 2005).

After making this pronouncement, the tribunal 'actually proceeded to examine and rely on previous decisions by other tribunals.'[13]

This practice is so common as to be almost taken for granted. For example, Christoph Schreuer has noted:

> In actual fact, tribunals in investment disputes, including ICSID tribunals, rely on previous decisions of other tribunals whenever they can.[14]

An empirical analysis of the cases cited in ICSID awards suggests significant upward movement in the number of awards referred to by arbitrators in deciding the case before them, with the average number of awards cited rising from 3 in 2002 to 15.5 in 2006.[15]

The importance of awards, and the notion that each one has resonance beyond the parties to the dispute, is not unknown to the treaty drafters. That awareness is illustrated by the existence of the mechanism in NAFTA chapter 11 that permits the Free Trade Commission (the Trade Ministers of the respective governments) to issue Notes of Interpretation of the NAFTA. It is confirmed by the fact that in the aftermath of the *Pope & Talbot* and *Metalclad* awards, in particular, the Free Trade Commission issued a Note of Interpretation 'clarifying' the scope of NAFTA Article 1105.[16]

Even as they may disavow the ability of the tribunals to create precedent, the states signing investment treaties may be said to have effectively set up this system of arbitral case law in which tribunals develop the details of investment policy and investment standards. The content of the obligations established by investment treaties is often far from clear. For example, many treaties include obligations to afford treatment in accordance with the minimum standard of treatment in customary international law, including obligations to accord 'fair and equitable treatment' and 'full protection and security.'[17] The fair and equitable treatment standard in particular is vague, and it is inevitable that cases deciding disputes alleging

---

[13] C Schreuer, 'Diversity and Harmonization of Treaty Interpretation in Investment Arbitration' (Apr 2006) 3 *Transnat'l Disp Mgmt* at 14 (noting paras in which the AES tribunal did so).

[14] Ibid at 11.

[15] JP Commission, 'Precedent in Investment Treaty Arbitration: A Citation Analysis of a Developing Jurisprudence' 24 *J Int'l Arb* (forthcoming 2007) (manuscript at 31–2).

[16] NAFTA Free Trade Commission, Note of Interpretation of Certain Chapter 11 Provisions (31 Jul, 2001). This process is not without flaws. This Note of Interpretation has caused significant controversy in that many argued that it was an amendment of NAFTA, rather than merely an explanation of previously-agreed-upon text. See generally CH Brower, II, 'Why the FTC Notes of Interpretation Constitute a Partial Amendment of Article 1105' (2006) 46 *Va J Int'l L* 347.

[17] Canada's Model FIPA provides that: 'Each Party shall accord to covered investments treatment in accordance with the customary international law minimum standard of treatment of aliens, including fair and equitable treatment and full protection and security.' Ibid Art 5(1).

breaches of it will contribute to a general understanding of its breadth and its meaning.[18]

II. PERSUASION, PRECEDENT, AND *JURISPRUDENCE CONSTANTE*

Assuming that the trends described in the preceding section continue, the question raised is how to treat the decisions to maximise their potential for creating predictable and widely accepted principles of investment law, while minimising any potential harm that might ensue from such a system of de facto precedent. At this time, establishing an appellate body that would be charged with creating a harmonious body of investment law is not a viable option.[19] Indeed, establishing such a precedential system would be difficult given the decentralised nature of investment treaty arbitration. Given the lack of hierarchy and potentially divergent treaty language and ensuing obligations, the de facto precedent system arguably holding sway in the WTO is not an apt model for investment treaty arbitration.

Investment treaty arbitration is not well suited to establishing a formal system of precedent. First, it is perhaps overreaching to suggest there is a 'system' of investment treaty arbitration at all. While many investment treaties have similar or even identical provisions, many do not. The various arbitral tribunals are not, in general, construing the same treaty. Differences in the scope and language of a treaty provision should (and often do) lead to differing outcomes.[20] Though it would be possible for 'mini-systems' to grow up around individual treaties, no such structure has yet coalesced. The many tribunals that have considered cases under NAFTA chapter 11 have been construing the same rights spelled out in the same treaty, but they have not always followed each other's lead.[21] Similarly, in the aftermath of the

---

[18] See generally Kaufmann-Kohler, above n 8, at 26–9; R Dolzer, 'Fair and Equitable Treatment: A Key Standard in Investment Treaties' (2005) 39 *Int'l Law* 87; CH Schreuer, 'Fair and Equitable Treatment in Arbitral Practice' (2005) 6 *J World Invest & Trade* 357.

[19] ICSID proposed establishing such a body when it suggested amending its rules in 2004. ICSID Secretariat, Discussion Paper: Possible Improvements of the Framework for ICSID Arbitration (22 Oct, 2004), available at www.worldbank.org/icsid/improvearb.htm. Commentary on the idea was largely unfavourable, however, and the proposal was not included in the rule change that eventually occurred. The idea may yet regain currency, but significant movement is unlikely in the near future.

[20] Certain cases have been celebrated in recent years because tribunals came to divergent outcomes in very similar cases. In at least a few instances, however, those differences in outcome can be attributed to different constructions stemming from slightly different language formulations. Eg, cases have diverged on the question of whether most-favoured-nation clauses in investment treaties apply only to substantive rights or also to procedural requirements in the dispute settlement systems set forth in the treaties. See M Kinnear, AK Bjorklund & JFG Hannaford, *Investment Disputes Under NAFTA: An Annotated Guide to NAFTA Chapter 11* (Kluwer Law International, 2006) 1103–12 to 22.

[21] See, eg, Kinnear et al, above n 20 (discussing different approaches of the NAFTA tribunals to the various obligations under the treaty, including Arts 1102, 1105, and 1110).

Argentine financial crisis, several cases based on the same Argentina—US Bilateral Investment Treaty have been brought, but they have not always come to consistent conclusions.[22]

Moreover, there is no clear hierarchy in the tribunals. In systems of government using stare decisis, there are formal rules or understandings about which decisions are binding and which are merely persuasive. In the United States, for example, a federal district court will be bound by decisions of the appeals court in its circuit, and by decisions of the US Supreme Court. Decisions of other US district courts are advisory only, and even decisions of federal appeals courts outside the circuit in which the district court sits have merely persuasive authority. In contrast, there are no such hierarchies for investment treaty arbitration. There is, in some circumstances, the possibility that an arbitral decision can be corrected. For example, arbitrations that occur under the ICSID Convention give rise to the possibility of an annulment tribunal. These tribunals, however, may annul awards on only limited grounds; they lack the authority to review the merits of the first tribunal decisions and therefore could not be looked to as authoritative arbiters of the content or application of the law.[23] The same objection could be made with respect to national courts that recognise or enforce awards under the New York Convention; the grounds on which they may review the awards are limited.[24] In addition, the previous objection would apply as well—those national courts from different states do not form a coherent system in which a hierarchy of authority could be established.

The fact that as a formal matter arbitration decisions are not precedential is important, but it is worth noting that there is a fine line between precedent and the persuasive role this Chapter is suggesting for arbitration decisions. While it is true that treating prior decisions as precedent contributes to the establishment of consistency and predictability in a system of law, and that *stare decisis et quieta non movere* ('to stand by things decided and not disturb settled points')[25] is the official doctrine in courts in the United States and England, even in those systems precedent is not quite so simple. When decisions have formal precedential value under

---

[22] See AK Bjorklund, 'Emergency Exceptions and Safeguards: State of Necessity and Force Majeure as Circumstances Precluding Wrongfulness', in P Muchlinski, F Ortino & C Schreuer (eds), *Oxford Handbook of International Investment Law* (Oxford University Press, forthcoming 2008) (discussing differences in the holdings in *LG&E v Argentina* and *CMS v Argentina*).

[23] ICSID Convention, above n 10, Art 52. Under Art 52, an annulment request may be based on the following grounds: '(a) that the Tribunal was not properly constituted; (b) that the Tribunal has manifestly exceeded its powers; (c) that there was corruption on the part of a member of the Tribunal; (d) that there has been a serious departure from a fundamental rule of procedure; or (e) that the award has failed to state the reasons on which it is based'.

[24] New York Convention on the Recognition and Enforcement of Arbitral Awards, Art 5, 10 Jun, 1958, 21 UST 2517, 330 UNTS 38.

[25] BA Garner, *A Dictionary of Modern Legal Usage*, 2nd edn (Oxford University Press, 1995) 827.

a regime of stare decisis, prior decisions are sometimes not as controlling as one might think. One of the first things common law students learn is how to distinguish cases, whether on factual or legal bases. Common law judges, too, often parse the decisions in prior authoritative cases finely in order to avoid being limited by those holdings. Moreover, even strong proponents of the common law would acknowledge that prior precedents can and should be overruled when warranted. In the words of Chancellor Kent:

> But I wish not to be understood to press too strongly the doctrine of *stare decisis*, when I recollect that there are one thousand cases to be pointed out in the English and American books of reports, which have been overruled, doubted, or limited in their application. It is probable that the records of many of the courts in this country are replete with hasty and crude decisions; and such cases ought to be examined without fear, and revised without reluctance, rather than to have the character of our law impaired, and the beauty and harmony of the system destroyed by the perpetuity of error.[26]

The absence of stare decisis need not be fatal to the establishment of a coherent and respected body of jurisprudence. But then simply noting that some awards will be more persuasive than others does not quite go far enough in bringing order to a system characterised by disorder. A better analogy is to the '*jurisprudence constante*' of the French civil law tradition.

Jurisprudence constante is an appealing analogy. In the French tradition, the starting point for any analysis is the language of the code, but judicial decisions construing the code will have an influence on other courts as representing an accepted interpretation of the statute.[27] Similarly, in an investment treaty case, the starting point for tribunal analysis should be the language of the treaty in question. Secondarily, but not insignificantly, tribunals would next turn to the decisions of other tribunals construing identical or similar treaty language. Also, in France, precedent is used with two different meanings: it refers to the decision of a higher court which, while not binding, for practical purposes ought to be followed by lower courts; and it refers to the decision of even a lower or equal court which, while not binding, can serve as a positive (or negative) model for the case under consideration.[28] This latter description fits most neatly within the investment treaty context of dispersed tribunals of equal authority. Thus, decisions of other tribunals construing identical or similar treaty provisions would be viewed as persuasive to the extent they were well reasoned. Moreover, one of the distinguishing features of *jurisprudence constante* is the development

---

[26] J Kent, *I Commentaries on American Law*, 4th edn (ES Clayton Printer, 1840) (1826) 477.
[27] MG Algero, 'The Sources of Law and the Value of Precedent: A Comparative and Empirical Study of a Civil Law State in a Common Law Nation' (2005) 65 *La L Rev* 775, 789.
[28] Troper & Grzegorczyk, above n 1, at 111.

of doctrine through the accretion of a consistent line of cases, rather than the establishment of a rule by an individual case.[29]

Jurisprudence constante is not a perfect model in all respects. Often French courts will be interpreting a single code provision, rather than potentially differing treaty provisions. Moreover, there is a hierarchical court system in which superior courts can directly affect the decisions of other courts, even if they theoretically do so only for individual cases and without establishing broader precedent. The career advancement of lower-court judges may hinge on their following the direction of senior judges.[30] Nonetheless, a *jurisprudence constante* approach preserves the primacy of the code provision as a source of law, but recognises the evolution of code-based law through interpretation:

> [P]recedent is very rarely an isolated decision. It is the result of an evolution. Once the principle has been accepted, the Cour de Cassation will proceed by way of continuous formulation of rules, related together and gradually forming a coherent system. This is what practising lawyers call the method of small paces.[31]

In the context of investment treaty arbitration, the development of a *jurisprudence constante* would perform two primary functions: law development and law harmonisation. Taking a parsimonious stance towards the citation of previous decisions would leave the obligations undertaken by states party to investment treaties with little or no explanation of what they mean. Tribunals can and should set forth their reasoning, and place it in the context of other cases, thereby contributing to the development of the law in this field. Law development will not come overnight, but will be part of a process of accretion and criticism, of judgment and explanation. Resolution may come easier in areas in which standards are malleable and tribunals have leeway to interpret them in any given case. For example, Professor Kaufmann-Kohler suggests that resolution of the proper interpretation of the umbrella clause, which requires a 'yes' or 'no' decision, will be more difficult than developing a coherent approach to an issue such as fair and equitable treatment.[32] Furthermore, decisions that gain wide acceptance

---

[29] See Kaufmann-Kohler, above n 8, at 5–6. This is not dissimilar to the role that international judicial and arbitral decisions have in practice played in the formation of customary international law under the ICJ statute; repetition of a principle, particularly by the Court itself, can assist in the establishment of customary international law. Nonetheless, the rules of law referred to by the Statute do not directly address the relationship between tribunal decisions and the elucidation or elaboration of the meaning or content of treaty provisions. See above nn 2–6 and accompanying text.

[30] Arbitrators might also feel a similar, though less institutionalised, pressure. Arbitrators who wish to obtain repeat appointments might feel some pressure to take into account earlier decisions, or decisions authored by tribunals whose members are exceptionally well-regarded. See below discussion in S III.

[31] Troper & Grzegorczyk, above n 1, at 137–8.

[32] Kaufmann-Kohler, above n 8, at 29.

will lead by degrees to a general harmonisation of the legal obligations in question:

> Arbitral jurisprudence can be compared to a competitive market: various solutions to arising interpretative challenges compete for attention and acceptance; there is experimentation going on. The most persuasive solutions will generate a momentum that leads to *'jurisprudence constante'*.[33]

The fact that decisions will not always agree is an inevitable component of the process and should not prove fatal to law development and overall harmonisation. Those in common law jurisdictions, particularly in the United States, are used to divergent decisions in courts of equal weight in the hierarchy. In US federal courts the so-called circuit split, in which the law is decided one way in one circuit and the other way in another, is a fact of life. This split only gets resolved if one of the circuits convenes itself 'en banc' and reverses the decision of one of its constituent panels, or if the Supreme Court decides to hear one of the cases. It does not always do so, but the United States manages nonetheless to have a reasonably cohesive system of justice. In contrast, it will be the market place of ideas, and not a higher court or tribunal or the concept of binding precedent, that will serve to resolve such splits among tribunals, as the best solutions tend to be cited and employed.

Thus, there are significant advantages with respect to predictability and legitimacy in establishing, over time, an effective and persuasive *jurisprudence constante* that would serve the development and harmonisation of the laws at issue:

> Drawing on the experience of past decisions plays an important role in securing the necessary uniformity and stability of the law. The need for a coherent case law is evident. It strengthens the predictability of decisions and enhances their authority.[34]

III. ENHANCING THE LEGITIMACY OF A JURISPRUDENCE CONSTANTE

Certain factors are key to ensuring the development of a jurisprudence commanding the respect of the international community. A foundational requirement is the continued development of a transparency norm in the arbitration of international investment disputes. If the awards are not in the public domain their influence is necessarily limited. Public availability

---

[33] TW Wälde, 'The Present State of Research', in *New Aspects of International Investment Law 2004* (Brill, 2006).

[34] Schreuer, above n 13, at 10; see also KM Meessen, *Economic Law in Globalizing Markets* (Kluwer Law International, 2004) 296–317 (discussing ways in which international arbitration has established and can continue to enhance its legitimacy as an alternative to municipal court dispute resolution).

of the awards also strengthens pressures placed on arbitrators to rely on, or distinguish their decisions from, prior arbitral awards. Finally, public availability is necessary for publicists and international organisations to use the awards in their own law-harmonising projects. Arbitrators and publicists will engage in a dialogue about the persuasiveness of certain decisions, thereby ensuring the eventual emergence of a *jurisprudence constante*.

The public availability of the decisions in investment treaty arbitrations is crucial to the development of a *jurisprudence constante*. The decisions serve a variety of constituencies, both before and after litigation. States entering into investment treaties in which they bind themselves to afford full protection and security or fair and equitable treatment need to know what kinds of obligations they are undertaking. Investors seeking to gauge the breadth and effectiveness of the protections offered by an investment treaty need to know how such protections have been interpreted in the past. Once a case has commenced, counsel to both investors and states need access to the cases to formulate their arguments. And finally the arbitrators need access to the decisions in order to ascertain previous practice and determine whether and how the case before them fits in to the line of cases that have gone before. More and more arbitral decisions are available as the public interest in investor-state arbitration is recognised and as the internet permits the broad dissemination of information with a minimum of effort and cost. With respect to published awards, there are no barriers of confidentiality or privilege preventing the award from being used in subsequent cases.

Despite the benefits of such increased transparency, the greater availability of cases leads to certain problems. There are beginning to be so many cases that a thorough analysis and reconciliation of all cases on any given point would force tribunals to write extremely long decisions.[35] There has to be some room for arbitrators to ignore or summarily treat tangential decisions, or those of poor quality that have been found unpersuasive by other tribunals. In time, some decisions will establish their position as important, path-breaking decisions—one thinks of *Erie Railroad Co v Tompkins*[36] in the United States, the *Mareva*[37] decision in England, the *Reparation*,[38] *Genocide*,[39] *Fisheries*,[40] and *Nottebohm*[41] cases in the International Court

---

[35] Decisions are already not short, by any means. Eg, the *Methanex* decision on the merits runs to some 300 pgs. *Methanex Corp (Can) v United States*, (UNCITRAL) (Final Award of the Tribunal on Jurisdiction and Merits) (7 Aug, 2005).
[36] *Erie RR Co v Tompkins*, 304 US 64 (1938).
[37] *Mareva Compania Naviera SA v International Bulk Carriers SA*, [1975] 2 Lloyd's L Rep 509 (UK Ct of Appeal).
[38] *Reparation for Injuries Suffered in the Service of the United Nations*, 1949 ICJ 173 (11 Apr).
[39] *Reservations to the Convention on the Prevention and Punishment of the Crime of Genocide*, 1951 ICJ 14 (28 May).
[40] *Fisheries (UK v Nor)*, 1951 ICJ 115 (18 Dec).
[41] *Nottebohm (Liech v Guat.)*, 1955 ICJ 3 (6 Apr).

of Justice[42]—while other less notable decisions, as Jan Paulsson has remarked, 'will also doubtless turn out to be subject to the same Darwinian reality: the unfit will perish.'[43] If the unfit do not perish, a further problem will be the ability of arbitrators to pick and choose from among existing decisions those that support virtually any proposition, thereby undermining the development of a coherent and consistent jurisprudence and undermining the legitimacy of international arbitral tribunals.

Already a few decisions of 'modern' investment treaty tribunals have been cited repeatedly as setting forth the standard for other tribunals to follow. One example is the *Mondev* case, in which the tribunal set forth an updated description of denial of justice, a subset of the international minimum standard of treatment, that has found favour in other tribunals as well.[44] The *Tecmed* tribunal has been frequently followed in its approach to regulatory expropriation.[45] On the procedural side, a good example is the decision by the *Methanex* tribunal holding that the tribunal had the authority to permit interested parties to participate as *amici curiae*,[46] a determination followed by the tribunals in *UPS v Canada*[47] and *Aguas Argentinas SA v Argentina*.[48] In what might be denominated an example of inter-systemic use of persuasive authority, the *Methanex* tribunal relied on its authority under the UNCITRAL Rules, but referred for support to similar practice by the Iran–US Claims Tribunal and the WTO Appellate Body.[49]

Informal and formal pressures on the arbitrators will likely ensure that they take prior decisions into account. Informal pressure will arise from

---

[42] These International Court of Justice cases were selected by Professor Ian Brownlie. I Brownlie, *Principles of Public International Law*, 6th edn (Oxford University Press, 2003) 20.

[43] J Paulsson, 'International Arbitration and the Generation of Legal Norms: Treaty Arbitration and International Law', *Transnat'l Disp Mgmt* (Provisional Issue Sep 2006).

[44] *Mondev Int'l Ltd v United States*, ICSID (W Bank) Case No ARB(AF)/99/2, 127 (Award) (11 Oct, 2002) ('In the end the question is whether, at an international level and having regard to generally accepted standards of the administration of justice, a tribunal can conclude in the light of all the available facts that the impugned decision was clearly improper and discreditable, with the result that the investment has been subjected to unfair and inequitable treatment.'). This standard was cited in *The Loewen Group Int'l (Can) v United States*, ICSID (W Bank) Case No ARB(AF)/98/3, 133 (Award) (26 Jun, 2003); and *Waste Management (US) v Mexico*, ICSID (W Bank) Case No ARB(AF)/00/3, 95, 30 (Award) (30 Apr, 2004).

[45] See *Técnicas Medioambientales Tecmed, SA (Spain) v Mexico*, ICSID (W Bank) Case No ARB(AF)/00/2 (Award) (29 May, 2003); Kaufmann-Kohler, above n 8, at 26.

[46] *Methanex Corp. (Can) v United States*, (UNCITRAL) (Decision of the Tribunal on Petitions of Third Persons to Participate as 'Amici Curiae') (15 Jan, 2001) [*Methanex Decision on Amicus Curiae*].

[47] *United Parcel Svc of Am Inc (US) v Canada*, (UNCITRAL) (Decision of the Tribunal on Petitions for Intervention and Participation as Amici Curiae) (17 Oct, 2001).

[48] *Aguas Argentinas SA v Argentina*, ICSID (W Bank) Case No ARB/03/19 (Order in Response to a Petition for Transparency and Participation as Amicus Curiae) (19 May, 2005).

[49] *Methanex Decision on Amicus Curiae*, above n 46, 33.

arbitrators' interests in protecting their reputations for expertise, and hence future engagements as arbitrators. Clients might reasonably expect arbitrators to know how cases involving similar factual issues, or similar legal doctrines, have been decided. Given the imprecision in many of the treaty obligations, and the dearth of sources aside from arbitral case law to look to for guidance, an arbitrator might have difficulty explaining why she did not look to a decision interpreting a similar provision, even if the reference were only to differ from the analysis set forth by the other tribunal. The most evident way an arbitral tribunal can demonstrate its knowledge of the prior cases is to cite them in the decision. Including bare references to similar cases might demonstrate an acquaintance with the cases and might be adequate in some instances. Yet unadorned references without even short parenthetical descriptions would not demonstrate how or why an arbitrator followed, or did not follow, a particular case. This imperative would become more acute once several tribunals had indeed followed a case. How would a later tribunal then explain ignoring it? Arbitrators understandably guard their right to depart from previous decisions if they are demonstrably wrong, but a tribunal enhances its credibility by recognising a case and, if it disagrees with the reasoning, explaining its disagreement, or distinguishing the case from the matter at hand. This process is essential, especially for international adjudicators, whose authority derives from convincing their constituencies that their decisions are correct, rather than on the enforcement power of the state.[50]

Other informal pressure may stem from the arbitrators' ethical sense. Professor Kaufmann-Kohler suggests that arbitrators, as decision makers, have a moral obligation to follow precedents 'so as to foster a normative environment that is predictable.'[51] She notes that this obligation is heightened when a nascent legal system is struggling to develop rules, which is the case with investment arbitration.[52]

As Professor Schreuer and others have noted, tribunals have indeed been citing the decisions of prior tribunals. This practice in and of itself will likely operate as a kind of ratchet mechanism. Once people start expecting tribunal decisions to cite awards in other cases, tribunals will have increasing incentives to pay them greater attention. The same phenomenon has occurred in the WTO context. Once people started to expect existing decisions to have some degree of authority, their legitimate expectations required later tribunals to act in a consistent manner.[53]

---

[50] See TM Franck, *Fairness in International Law and Institutions* (Oxford University Press, 1995) 26–46; D Palmeter & PC Mavroidis, 'The WTO Legal System: Sources of Law' (1998) 92 *Am J Int'l L* 398, 402; Commission, above n 15.
[51] Kaufmann-Kohler, above n 8, at 31.
[52] Ibid at 32–3.
[53] Palmeter & Mavroidis, above n 50, at 402–07.

Additional formal pressures stem from the demands of the arbitral rules, which often require arbitrators to decide all questions put to them.[54] Counsel will usually rely on arbitral awards in making arguments before the tribunal; the tribunal would thus be obligated to consider those arguments and explain the points on which they agreed or disagreed with counsel. As a *jurisprudence constante* emerges, the number of awards to which counsel need refer should diminish as well; over-citation is a problem among advocates as well as adjudicators, and exists even in a system with stare decisis.[55] Moreover, depending on the arbitral regime, another requirement is often that arbitrators give adequate reasons for their awards.[56] Thus, an arbitral tribunal that does not take into account prior decisions risks its decision being set-aside, vacated, or not enforced.[57]

Arbitral tribunals faced with investment treaty cases must decide them on the basis of applicable law. Usually the applicable law will be international law, and will be composed of a mix of treaty-based standards and international custom. Arbitrators must take due account of the treaty applicable to the case before them; their authority derives from that treaty by virtue of the defendant state's consent to arbitration, and failure to follow that treaty's directives could vitiate state consent and tribunal authority. To the extent that the tribunal needs to apply inchoate customary international law, the decisions of prior tribunals might be relevant insofar as they identify those international obligations. To the extent that the decisions themselves comprise and give content to those obligations, ignoring such cases would equate to a failure to apply the applicable rule of substantive international law. Investment treaty arbitral decisions are establishing a law of foreign investment notwithstanding the status of international decisions as subsidiary sources of international law.[58] A significant question beyond the scope

---

[54] See, eg, ICSID Convention, above n 10, Art 48(1)(3) ('The award shall deal with every question submitted to the Tribunal, and shall state the reasons upon which it is based').

[55] Eg, the House of Lords has recently issued a practice direction that attempts to limit such citation. See The Lord Chief Justice of England and Wales, *Practice Direction on the Citation of Authorities* (9 Apr, 2001), available at http://www.hmcourts-service.gov.uk/cms/814.htm.

[56] Ibid; see also the UNCITRAL Arbitration Rules ('The arbitral tribunal shall state the reasons upon which the award is based, unless the parties have agreed that no reasons are to be given.'), UN Comm'n on Int'l Trade L [UNCITRAL], UNCITRAL Arbitration Rules, GA Res 31/98, Art 32(3), UN GAOR, 31st Sess, UN Doc 31/98 (15 Dec, 1976).

[57] See, eg, TH Webster, 'Review of Substantive Reasoning of International Arbitral Awards by National Courts: Ensuring One-Stop Adjudication' (2006) 22 *Arb Int'l* 431 (noting that the English Arbitration Act requires arbitrators to give reasons in their awards, but also concluding that set-aside of awards is most likely to be based on jurisdictional or procedural grounds, rather than on substantive legal reasoning). In Australia, the Victoria Supreme Court recently set aside an arbitral award that did not provide adequate reasons. *BHP Billiton Ltd v Oil Basins Ltd*, 2006 VS Ct 402.

[58] See, eg, Kaufmann-Kohler, above n 8, at 35 ('[T]here are recurring issues in investment arbitration as well, which must be resolved by the application of one and the same rule of law.').

of this paper is whether those decisions are establishing a customary international law applicable beyond the confines of investment treaty arbitration.

The increasing obligation of arbitrators to address prior decisions is having an interesting and not yet fully developed effect on the conflict-of-interests norms applied to international arbitrators. Many practicing counsel sit as arbitrators as well. Those dual roles, combined with the recurrence of certain issues in arbitration, have led to an increase in the number of so-called 'issue' conflicts. One example is the situation of an arbitration in which counsel argue that the arbitral tribunal should treat as authoritative a decision in another case, but one of the arbitrators turns out to have acted as counsel in that other case, or turns out to be actively engaged in getting that case annulled or set aside. Is that arbitrator suddenly faced with a conflict that would support a challenge to his independence or impartiality? These issues and others will require attention, but are not likely to slow the trend towards reliance on arbitral awards.

The legitimacy, and hence subsequent use, of the decisions of arbitral tribunals will be enhanced also by the writings and commentary of publicists. The writings of the most eminent publicists are of course included in the ICJ Statute as one of the subsidiary sources of law, along with judicial decisions.[59] The publicists affect the perceptions of various arbitral decisions as in their writings they collect, criticise, and praise the decisions of arbitrators in particular cases. Professor Paulsson notes:

> The intense attention of the international community of scholars and practitioners will undoubtedly have a salutary effect: good awards will chase the bad, and set standards which will contribute to a higher level of consistent quality.[60]

Other potential sources for judging the legitimacy and staying power of individual awards are projects undertaken by intergovernmental and international organisations, often under the direction of influential publicists, to opine on the current state of the law, frequently through examination of arbitral decisions. The International Law Commission's recent adoption of articles on State Responsibility is one example of such an endeavor.[61] The International Law Association's Committee on International Law on Foreign Investment is writing a report detailing the status of foreign investment law and also a publication compiling the individual papers from which the report is derived.[62] UNCTAD has published several monographs

---

[59] ICJ Statute, above n 2, Art 38(1)(d).
[60] Ibid at 13.
[61] The Commission adopted the text of the articles and submitted them to the General Assembly with the recommendation that it take note of the draft articles in a resolution and that it annex the articles to the resolution. Report of the Commission At Its Fifty-third Session, ¶ 11, UN Doc. A/56/10 (2001).
[62] An interim report is available at the ILA website. http://www.ila-hq.org/. The publication will be the *Oxford Handbook of International Investment Law*, above n 22.

on different subjects, including fair and equitable treatment and the most-favoured-nation clause.[63] The OECD, too, has a series of working papers on varied foreign investment topics, also including most-favoured-nation clauses.[64] These projects all look to arbitral cases as sources of law and hence reinforce the use of these decisions by later tribunals.

CONCLUSION

The decisions of investment treaty arbitral tribunals are proving to be essential in establishing the modern international law of investment. Given the paucity of detail in the international investment treaties to which states have adhered, it is inevitable that the meaning and contours of the legal standards in those treaties will be defined and clarified in arbitral decisions. The actual compilation of a generally accepted set of standards will be an accretive process developed little by little as tribunals make decisions in individual cases, and as those decisions are tested by other tribunals, by publicists and international organisations, and by the states themselves. Gradually one may expect the institution of a *jurisprudence constante*, and the emergence of key decisions that are judged to be the influential starting points from which further analysis should flow.

---

[63] UN Conference on Trade & Dev (UNCTAD), Fair and Equitable Treatment, UN Doc UNCTAD/ITE/IIT/11 (Vol III), UN Sales No E.99.II.D.15 (1999); UN Conference on Trade & Dev (UNCTAD), Most-Favoured-Nation Treatment, UN Doc UNCTAD/ITE/IIT/10 (Vol III), UN Sales No E.99.II.D.11 (1999).

[64] OECD, *Most-Favoured-Nation Treatment in International Investment Law* (2004).

19

The Role of Law and Lawyers in Vietnam's WTO Accession

DAVID A GANTZ

THE ENTHUSIASTICALLY COMMUNIST/socialist state that was Vietnam from the departure of US troops in 1974 to about 1985 was what Carol Rose terms a 'command economy'[1]. It had no use and little respect for attorneys, whether in the very limited domestic private sector, in government or from overseas. While a few United States and French-trained attorneys remained after 1974, mostly in the Saigon area, most Vietnamese who had been trained in the law left after the Communist takeover in 1975. During this period (1974–1985), few lawyers were educated at law schools in Vietnam—probably no more than 200–500 per year. A limited number were sent overseas, usually to the USSR, where 'legal' education tended to focus on socialist ideology.

However, by the early 1980s, first in the agricultural sector, and then more broadly, it was becoming painfully obvious that the collectivisation of agricultural production and the virtual prohibitions on private business were damaging what was left of the post-war economy.[2] In addition, that economic model was making it virtually impossible for the nation to generate foreign or domestic investment related jobs for the estimated one million Vietnamese entering the work force each year. Of course, there were other important causes of the severe economic problems at that time, including disastrous wars with Cambodia's Pol Pot regime beginning in 1978[3] and with China in 1979.

The end result of these challenges was the so-called 'Doi Moi' (renovation) policy officially adopted by the Vietnamese Communist Party in 1986, after several years of debate, discussion and more than a little dissent from those in the government that feared an economic opening would threaten

---

[1] CV Rose, 'The "New" Law and Development Movement in the Post-Cold War Era: A Vietnam Case Study' (1998) 32 *Law & Soc'y Rev* 93, 97.
[2] R Templer, *Shadows and Wind: A View of Modern Vietnam* (Penguin Books, 1999) 57–9.
[3] S Karnow, *Vietnam: A History* (Penguin Books, 1997) 54–6.

the stability of the regime. The essence of Doi Moi as originally enacted was political and social renewal through rapid industrial growth and development.[4] The most important aspects of Doi Moi were the initiation of policies aimed at encouraging foreign investment, stimulating exports and increasing the competitiveness of the local economic structure (both state-owned and private). This meant legal reform (more slowly than in retrospect was desirable and with more than a little backsliding), which in turn necessarily meant a resurgence of the legal profession and legal education. Furthermore, Doi Moi was the beginning of a 20 year period that culminated in normalisation of political and economic relations with the United States, initially through the US—Vietnam Bilateral Trade Agreements (VBTA) in 1995 and 2001, respectively,[5] and in entry to the World Trade Organization in January 2007.[6]

Part I of this chapter summarises the economic and political developments from 1974 to 1986. Part II views the development of the Doi Moi policies from 1986 to about 1995. Part III discusses developments in the 1995–2000 period, focusing on the negotiation and conclusion of the US—VBTA. Part IV discusses the WTO accession process, completed with Vietnam's formal accession to membership in January 2007. Finally, Part V discusses recent plans for far-reaching reforms in the legislative process and the functions of the judiciary, as well as the role of lawyers in society.

In each section, much of the emphasis is on the growing role and importance of the legal profession. That role initially was taken on by indigenous Vietnamese attorneys staffing the Trade, Justice and other ministries. These attorneys were and continue to be responsible for negotiating and drafting the trade agreements, preparing the implementing legislation and presenting those laws for enactment to the National Assembly, and assuring that the implementing process (including myriad regulations) continues at the ministry and sub-ministry levels. However, at least three other groups of attorneys played a significant role. First, the Australian, French, British, American and other foreign attorneys who staffed law firm branch offices in Saigon and/or Hanoi beginning in the late 1980s. Second, the even larger number of 'legal consultants' from those nations, plus Canada, Singapore, Sweden and other European Union nations (usually funded by bilateral aid agencies or the international financial institutions) who provided technical assistance (no doubt of varying quality and relevance) to government ministries, the National Assembly and various law faculties,

---

[4] L Aloysius McGrath, 'Vietnam's Struggle to Balance Sovereignty, Centralization and Foreign Investment Under Doi Moi' (1995) 18 *Fordham Int'l LJ* 2095, 2096.

[5] Agreement Between the United States of America and the Socialist Republic of Vietnam on Trade Relations, 13 Jul, 2000, available at http://www1.mot.gov.vn/en/Agreements/wwwfbta.pdf.

[6] Press Release, WTO, General Council Approves Viet Nam's Membership (7 Nov, 2006), available at http://www.wto.org/english/news_e/pres06_e/pr455_e.htm.

among others.[7] Finally, one should not underestimate the legal 'education' provided to a very bright, very dedicated group of Vietnamese government lawyers by the lawyers (and other negotiators) at the Office of the US Trade Representative (USTR), the Department of State and other US government agencies, and by delegations of foreign governments negotiating other trade and investment agreements with the Government of Vietnam during this period.

I. CREATING AN ECONOMIC CRISIS, 1975–1985

From the late 1940s to at least 1979, the policy of Vietnam, first in the north and then in the south after its fall, was one of collectivisation. Post-1975, the emphasis was on land redistribution, both in the north and the south. When the state entered into rice purchasing and distribution, yields decreased and much of the stockpiled rice spoiled. Food imports increased with an impact that went beyond the rice market per se, to the point where cooperatives were again authorised. However, continuing state intervention, along with heavy taxation, reduced many of the gains of the late 1970s, and ultimately produced famine in some parts of the country.

The collectivisation was not, of course, limited to land under the Communist regime. Industry that was already in place was also brought under state ownership and control, as Vietnam embraced a Soviet style economic system. The impact on Vietnam's then existing legal system was predictable. Vietnam's legal system has historically reflected elements from various invading powers, including Chinese (neo-Confucian), French (parallel to the system at the end of the Nineteenth Century) and American, with all of these overlaying Vietnam's own 'ancient tradition of law.' An 'Indochina Law School' operating between 1920–1950 in Hanoi trained many Vietnamese lawyers in the French system, while during the US period (1960 to 1975) some Vietnamese lawyers were trained by visiting American lawyers and law professors, or in the United States.

Much changed in this period, in the south as well as the north, especially after the withdrawal of US forces and the Communist takeover of the entire country. There was, understandably, both an anti-legal and anti-colonialist attitude within the Vietnamese government. In a process that was not unique to Vietnam, the government ruled by decree, no objection to administrative orders was permitted, legality became at best a formality, and even the Ministry of Justice was eliminated from 1961–1981.[8] When

---

[7] By way of example, the author has made 6 trips to Vietnam to consult with the Ministry of Justice, the National Assembly and a large group of actual or hopeful international trade law professors.

[8] Rose, above n 1, at 95–9.

Vietnamese lawyers were sent abroad to train in the late 1970s and early 1980s, it was usually to the Soviet Union (or Eastern Europe); many of today's most important upper middle level legal bureaucrats were in fact trained at places such as Patrice Lumuba University in Moscow (training which in the author's view nevertheless produced a number of first-rate lawyers). The climate for traditional members of the legal profession was thus not a favourable one.

Re-evaluation of these policies was stimulated by the obvious concerns of that time: an agricultural production crisis, an absence of foreign investment and insufficient domestic financial resources for economic development and job creation. There were shortages of common goods, the annual inflation rate was more than 100 per cent, and the Soviet Union had reduced economic assistance during the period. '[T]he Vietnamese economy was dysfunctional,' with the failure of heavy industry to develop production, the bureaucracy blocking all market forces, and the emergence of a black market.[9] Ultimately, the result of these factors was the adoption of a limited market-based system, and policies to encourage foreign investment and stimulate the economy. These changes were formally launched at the Sixth Communist Party Congress in 1986.

II. DOI MOI AND THE ECONOMIC OPENING, 1986–1995

The steps taken under Doi Moi included substantial limits on the extent of central planning, with price controls lifted on many commodities and decollectivisation of agricultural land. There was not, however, an elimination of state enterprises, or even a reduction of their substantial role in the economy. Efforts to 'equitise' (privatise) state enterprises in the early and mid-1990s were official policy, but lagged in practice.[10]

A major goal of Doi Moi was to stimulate an increase in foreign investment, and that necessarily required an improved legal structure and lawyers competent to interpret and apply it. Such reform, however imperfect, began to take place. During the period 1987–1995, a new constitution was adopted (1992) and over 100 laws, including a Civil Code, were enacted. Doi Moi was expanded in 1991 to explicitly include legal reform, with the predictable references to 'running the nation by law.' Legislation alone, of course, did not resolve potential problems for foreign investors. There was a lack of regulations and other guidelines; a lack of effective dispute settlement mechanisms and other ways of forcing national and local officials

---

[9] P Tran, 'Vietnam's Economic Liberalization and Outreach: Legal Reform' (2003) 9 *L & Bus Rev Am* 139, 142.
[10] WAW Nielsen, 'Asia's Economic Crisis Poses Challenges for Vietnam as Doi Moi Enters Second Decade' (1998) 20 No 2 *E Asian Executive Rep* 9.

(including the Party members who staffed 'peoples' courts') to comply with the laws; and perhaps most significantly, a continuing lack of competition in many sectors of the economy.

The success of the Doi Moi in stimulating investment was mixed at best, with a falling off of investment experienced in the mid-1990s, well before the broader Asian financial crisis in 1997. This was probably a result of the continued influence of (and favouritism toward) the state sector, and the fact that the initial package of business legislation was more a control mechanism than one focused on economic growth. The Vietnamese Communist Party remained subject to criticism for mismanagement, corruption, muzzling of the press and over-rigidity; it was said to be out of touch with the 'real situation in the country.' Under key laws—on private enterprises and companies, for example—various restrictions remained, including: onerous state approval requirements; high costs of incorporation; high minimum capital requirements; a variety of special licenses and limits on access of foreign investors to some sectors; and the general frustrations of dealing with the government.[11]

However, it was significant that this shift under Doi Moi to some semblance of a nation of laws implied that lawmakers, both in the National Assembly and in the government, would have to improve their legal skills. The Ministry of Justice, which had been back in business since 1981, increased its influence in the government hierarchy, and by the end of the first 10 years of Doi Moi, the total available law school student enrollments had increased to 2,000, fourfold from a decade earlier.

Furthermore, it was in the early 1990s that foreign legal assistance, with visiting foreign lawyers and academics, grew in volume. By 1996, various donors, including governments, NGOs, foundations and law firms, had pledged or spent over $13 million in such legal assistance, often described as supporting Vietnam's movement toward freer markets. The major players included the United Nations Development Programme (UNDP), the World Bank and the Asian Development Bank, as well as the governments of Denmark, Sweden, Canada, France, Japan and Australia, all of which are still active in Vietnam today. Although US efforts remained very limited until 1988, they later blossomed.

More or less at the same time, no doubt encouraged by the increase in foreign investment, foreign law firms began operations in earnest in Vietnam. These law firms were primarily from Europe, Australia, Hong Kong and the United States. As in many other developing countries, foreign legal professionals served private foreign clients (primarily in foreign investment and establishment areas), hired and trained Vietnamese attorneys and from time to time assisted Vietnamese government agencies in reviewing

---

[11] P Tran, above n 9, at 150, 152–3.

drafts of proposed laws and ordinances.[12] However, these foreign legal activities were viewed with suspicion by the Vietnamese government, which reacted with onerous licensing requirements, restrictions on the hiring of local attorneys, restricting legal advice to international law, and occasionally interfering with basic law firm functions such as renting office space and obtaining telephone lines. (This changed significantly with the advent of the VBTA.)

III. NEGOTIATING THE US—VIETNAM BILATERAL TRADE AGREEMENT, 1996–2000

The mixed success of Doi Moi and the remnants of the failed economic policies for attracting foreign investment and improving living standards, combined with the demise of the Soviet Union, the Asian financial crisis, the increased export success of China, along with the normalisation of political relations with the United States in 1995, provided Vietnam with both challenges and opportunities. Interestingly, the Chinese and American influences, though in different ways, were likely the most important factors in convincing Vietnamese officials at the highest levels to conclude the VBTA.

The importance of China in influencing Vietnamese economic policies during the 1990s can not be overemphasised. China, even before its WTO accession in November 2001, was highly successful in attracting foreign investment, far outperforming Vietnam and other South-East Asian Nations. Vietnam accordingly had to find some way to keep up. Similarly, Doi Moi and its related legal reforms continued throughout the 1990s, as they were also influenced by the same pressures that ultimately led to the VBTA—and to WTO accession. These pressures encouraged continuing efforts with regard to new incentives (or removal of disincentives) to foreign investment, through further amendment of relevant legislation.[13] However, it was becoming obvious that Doi Moi alone was not enough.

In 1995, Vietnam joined the Association of South-East Asian Nations (ASEAN) and became a party to the Asean Free Trade Agreement (AFTA), no doubt hoping that AFTA membership would result in an increase of Vietnam's exports to other ASEAN/AFTA members, particularly Singapore and neighboring Thailand. Vietnam also became a member of the Asian Pacific Economic Cooperation group (APEC) in 1998, in the midst of the VBTA negotiations.

There were obvious practical reasons for Vietnam to improve diplomatic and economic relations at that time. Unlike other members of ASEAN and China, after 1951 (for Communist-controlled areas) and then for the entire

---

[12] Rose, above n 1, at 119–20.
[13] P Tran, above n 9, at 154.

country between 1975 and 2001, Vietnam had only limited access to the highly lucrative US market. Until 2001, the United States did not accord 'most favoured nation' (MFN) tariff treatment to Vietnam for its exports to the United States, thus making those exports prohibitively expensive to US consumers. Unconditional MFN status is typically conferred only by GATT/WTO membership; even then, other WTO Members can exercise an initial right of non-application under the Marrakech Agreement.[14] Otherwise MFN is available only through the conclusion of a bilateral trade agreement, such as the United States and China concluded in 1979.[15] In the second half of the 1990s, the prospect of increased exports to and investment from the United States must have seemed very attractive to Vietnamese officials. Additionally, concluding a trade agreement with the United States may also have been important for political reasons, as a part of continuing efforts to 'balance' its relations between China and the United States.[16]

According to the principal US negotiator of the VBTA, both President Clinton and Secretary of State Warren Christopher expected the opening of diplomatic relations in 1995 to be followed with a process of economic normalisation. Rather than follow the approach taken with China in 1978, under which China obtained MFN trading status on the basis of a narrow commercial agreement, USTR was intent on negotiating a comprehensive accord. As a potentially effective tool to open up the still largely closed Vietnamese market, it would include not only trade in goods, but trade in services, protection of intellectual property and possibly investment. The VBTA thus ended up looking more like the North American Free Trade Agreement (NAFTA) in terms of its scope than the typical commercial agreements concluded by the United States in the past.

The comprehensive trade agreement approach required some four-and-a-half years of difficult negotiations, and an additional year, from mid-1999 to mid-2000, while the Vietnamese Government agonised over whether the completed agreement should be formally concluded. Even at the end, in the months before signature in July 2000, there was apparently within the highest levels of the Vietnamese government 'an intensive period of analysis and soul-searching' in which the defenders of inefficient state-owned enterprises and those concerned with 'security' clashed with the freer traders. [There

---

[14] Marrakech Agreement Establishing the World Trade Organization, 14 Apr, 1994, art XIII, available at http://www.wto.org/English/docs_e/legal_e/04-wto.pdf.

[15] Agreement on Trade Relations between the United States and the People's Republic of China, 7 Jul, 1979, available at http://www.fas.usda.gov/itp/agreements/chintra.html.

[16] See JM Damond, *Give Trade a Chance: The Negotiation of the US Vietnam Trade Agreement*, 65 (2004; unpublished manuscript, on file with author) [Damond]; MR Gordon, *Rumsfeld, Visiting Vietnam, Seals Accord to Deepen Military Cooperation*, NY Times, 6 Jun, 2006, at 8 (positing that the bilateral decision to increase military contacts resulted in part from Vietnam's efforts to 'establish more balance with its neighbor to the North'). Former USTR negotiator Damond's manuscript is the principal source for this discussion of the VBTA negotiations.

were no free traders, just freer traders!] Ultimately, the agreement was approved by both the Vietnamese National Assembly and the US Congress, and became effective 10 December, 2001.

The US negotiators had taken the position that the size of the Vietnamese economy was such that its economic development, if it were to follow the paths of Japan, Korea, Taiwan, China and other countries in Southeast Asia, would be successful only if Vietnam were willing to accept in the VBTA such WTO-type disciplines as national treatment/nondiscrimination and the avoidance of non-tariff barriers such as import quotas and government subsidies. US negotiators saw the VBTA as a step toward WTO accession, a process in which additional market opening concessions would be demanded, even though in principle the US negotiators (in good faith) assured Vietnamese officials that they supported Vietnam's WTO accession. But Vietnamese officials were concerned that some of the VBTA obligations went well beyond WTO rules, and wanted the United States to treat the VBTA commitments as the 'basis' for later WTO accession.

Equally significant for Vietnam, the VBTA negotiations, and the subsequent efforts to implement the agreed obligations under Vietnamese law, became a difficult but vitally important educational process in the legal requirements of the world trading system. This proved to be an important step toward WTO membership. The VBTA inevitably also generated a major reform of the legal system as a result of the rewriting of many laws in order to implement the agreement, a consideration that became obvious to the Vietnamese negotiators early on.

The educational process was not, however, primarily driven by the lawyers. Neither side used attorneys as their chief negotiators, and the principal non-governmental facilitator was another non-lawyer, US–Vietnam Trade Council (USVTC) President Virginia Foote. However, USTR and other US and Vietnamese government attorneys played a critical role at virtually all stages of the negotiations and drafting processes. Furthermore, a former USTR attorney and official, providing 'technical assistance' to the Vietnamese through the good offices of the USVTC, apparently played a key role in helping the Vietnamese negotiators understand the implications of what the United States was demanding, particularly in the area of protecting foreign investment.[17] Also, private foreign attorneys, many practicing law in Vietnam, provided important feedback both to the US negotiators and to their Vietnamese counterparts, again through the good offices of the USVTC.

During the negotiations, Vietnam also continued to benefit from a variety of foreign government and institutionally funded foreign legal assistance

---

[17] Daniel Price, by the mid-1990s a partner in a private law firm, had been one of the principal negotiators of the NAFTA investment chapter.

projects. These included, for example, those sponsored by the UNDP and headed by then regional legal adviser John Bentley, an American attorney who had worked for over 30 years on legal and institutional reform before moving to Vietnam in the mid-1990s. Additionally, beginning around 1995, USAID expanded its technical assistance on legal and commercial reform issues. This was initially in support of the VBTA negotiations and later was provided to assist in the implementation process. USAID created, just before entry into force of the VBTA in late 2001, the 'Star-Vietnam' program. This program provided legal and economic analysis and recommendations, as well as a variety of training workshops, study tours and publication and translation of reference materials. In the view of the US negotiators, this combination of 'educational' activities throughout the process led to a 'much greater level of sophistication with respect to the [VBTA] issues,'[18] on the part of the Vietnamese negotiators than had been evident at the outset.

The end result of this process was the completion of a comprehensive agreement—the VBTA. It was not designed to be a free trade agreement or customs union as those terms are used in the GATT/WTO context, because it does not eliminate 'duties and other restrictive regulations of commerce' on substantially all trade within a reasonable period of time.[19] It is more accurately a 'freer' trade agreement, in that it reduces Vietnamese tariffs and grants Vietnam MFN access to the US market. However, in the most basic measure—increased trade—it has been wildly successful. In the period 2000–2004, Vietnamese exports to the United States increased, from $822 million to $5,275 million, while US exports to Vietnam increased from $368 million to $1,163 million.[20] This trend has continued and total trade between the United States and Vietnam reached $10 billion in 2006, mostly in shrimp, textiles and footwear exports to the United States.[21]

The VBTA includes chapters on trade in goods (reducing tariffs and tariff barriers on the part of Vietnam, and providing MFN treatment on the part of the United States); intellectual property rights (similar to WTO obligations under TRIPS); trade in services (incorporating most of the WTO GATS disciplines, the US GATS schedules and an extensive series of Vietnam services market access obligations, including hotly-debated rights

---

[18] Damond, above n 16, at 112.
[19] GATT, art XXIV(5)(c), XXIV(8)(b) (1947), available at http://www.wto.org/english/docs_e/legal_e/gatt47_02_e.htm#articleXXIV.
[20] US Census Bureau: Foreign Trade Statistics, available at http://www.census.gov/foreign-trade/balance/c5520.html.
[21] J Perlez, *US Competes with China for Vietnam's Allegiance*, NY Times, 19 Jun, 2006, at 3; Office of the US Trade Representative, Vietnam—Trade News and Trade Facts, available at http://www.ustr.gov/World_Regions/Southeast_Asia_Pacific/Vietnam/Section_Index.html (US exports to Vietnam include industrial goods such as information technology products, civil aircraft equipment, chemicals, cosmetics and pharmaceuticals).

relating to financial and telecommunications services); investment relations (a sort of 'BIT- Lite,' but including the basic investor protection obligations and international arbitration of investor-state disputes); various business facilitation measures; extensive transparency obligations (including publication of laws and administrative or judicial review of administrative decisions); and a series of exceptions and general provisions.

In terms of the impact on lawyers and on legal system reform, the intellectual property chapter is likely to be one of the most difficult to implement. Article 11 provides that:

> Each Party shall ensure that its enforcement procedures are fair and equitable, are not unnecessarily complicated or costly, and do not entail unreasonable time limits or unwarranted delays

along with the specific legal and procedural obligations. Such provisions have proved difficult to achieve in practice for most LDCs, even those with Western-style legal systems. The VBTA also provides detailed requirements for judicial enforcement procedures, and for 'provisional measures.'

Other provisions that have required significant changes in laws and regulations include those on business facilitation and transparency, which are designed to create a more open economic and commercial system for Vietnam, similar in many ways to Article X of GATT, but with much more detail. The objective is a legal and administrative process that avoids unpleasant surprises to business and provides an opportunity for interested parties (whether foreign or domestic) to comment on regulations that will affect them *before* the regulations go into force. Additionally, administrative and judicial tribunals for review and correction of administrative actions must be maintained.

Not surprisingly, the VBTA constituted a massive implementation challenge. As one expert suggested in late 2001:

> It is an open question whether the Vietnamese government has the will or the wherewithal to implement the pervasive reforms required by the US-Vietnam bilateral trade agreement.[22]

The answer, with the benefit of five years' hindsight, is emphatically 'yes.' In 2002, after a review of existing laws, the Vietnamese government began to amend dozens of legal instruments (laws, ordinances, regulations, etc) as required for compliance with the VBTA's provisions.[23] Most such changes have been enacted, although not always in ideal form.

Interestingly, Vietnam ultimately agreed to open up its legal services market to a significantly greater degree than has been the case in many other Asian nations (with the exception of Singapore). Apparently the

---

[22] ME Manyin, *The Vietnam-US Bilateral Trade Agreement, Congressional Research Service*, 11 Dec. 2001, at 15, available at http://www.usvtc.org/info/crs/bta-dec01.pdf.

[23] US—Vietnam Trade Council, Catalog of Legal Updates: Vietnam Trade Policy Regime (Sep 2006), at 11, available at http://www.usvtc.org/updates/legal/Catalog/CatalogSep06.pdf.

sector was liberalised because foreign attorneys, both private and within the US government, persuaded Vietnamese officials that the presence of foreign lawyers would facilitate foreign investment. Today, foreign law firms may establish 100 per cent equity ownership in legal firms, joint ventures and branches (on a 5-year renewable license). While foreign lawyers may not appear in Vietnamese courts, their firms may advise on Vietnamese law if they hire Vietnamese lawyers qualified for practice in Vietnam.[24] Implementing regulations have been issued, although some law firms believe that in the absence of the right of Vietnamese lawyers to hold equity interests in the foreign firms, retaining Vietnamese lawyers on staff will continue to be difficult.

IV. VIETNAM'S ACCESSION TO THE WTO, 2001–2007

The WTO Agreement provides no detailed guidance on the admission of new members. It simply provides that 'Any state ... may accede to this Agreement, on terms to be agreed between it and the WTO.'[25] Decisions on accession are taken by the 'Ministerial Conference' (the trade ministers of the Member nations), specifying a two-thirds vote. In practice, however, accession decisions have always been taken by consensus, as with virtually all other decisions under the WTO Agreement.

The accession process normally begins with the candidate providing detailed information on its trade and economic policies to a 'working party' of interested Members. At the request of individual Members, this is followed by a series of parallel bilateral talks with the candidate on tariff rates, access commitments, and other goods and services policies:

> The talks can be highly complicated. It can be said that in some cases the negotiations are almost as large as an entire round of multilateral trade negotiations.[26]

Once the bilateral negotiations have all been concluded, the working party finalises the terms of accession, in effect combining the bilateral agreements into a single package, since under the principle of non-discrimination the benefits garnered by any Member in its bilateral agreement with the candidate are applied to all other WTO Members. In most cases, including Vietnam's, the prospective member is providing information to and negotiating with the Working Party simultaneously with its efforts to conclude bilateral agreements with those Members that have requested such negotiations.

---

[24] US-Vietnam Bilateral Trade Agreement: Vietnam's Services Annex, at G4, available at http://www.usvtc.org/trade/bta/text/annexG_VN.PDF.
[25] Marrakech Agreement, above n 14, at art XII.
[26] See WTO, How to Join the WTO: The Accession Process, http://www.wto.org/english/thewto_e/whatis_e/tif_e/org3_e.htm (last visited 4 Jul, 2007). See also WTO, Viet Nam Accession, http://www.wto.org/english/thewto_e/acc_e/a1_vietnam_e.htm (giving detailed information on Vietnam's WTO accession process) (last visited 4 Jul, 2007).

Vietnam's process of accession—as for China, Saudi Arabia and Russia—was long, complex and frustrating. While application was initially made in 1995, little progress occurred until 2001, after the Vietnamese government at the highest levels made the political decisions necessary to open the market, initially by concluding the VBTA. That decision itself was likely motivated in part by the fact that by late 2000, it had become increasingly obvious that China's 20-year quest for WTO membership was close to completion. This would likely make it even more difficult for Vietnam to compete with China for foreign investment and trade opportunities. Another likely factor was US antidumping cases against imports of Vietnamese tri and basa (catfish) and shrimp, which provided inter alia an excellent lesson as to why it could be useful for Vietnam to have access to the WTO's Dispute Settlement Body. As WTO members they would then be able to challenge national administrative decisions imposing trade remedies.

The increased pace of progress during the 2004–2006 period likely reflects an important political point realised by the Vietnamese political elites: China's WTO accession, with the accompanying opening of competition and markets, confirmed earlier indications that the requirements of accession had not in any significant way threatened the 'stability' of the Communist regime there. Also, some Vietnamese policymakers may have realised that WTO membership would make Vietnam an attractive investment location for companies that wished to hedge their bets by not placing all of their manufacturing assets in China (or in any other single nation). The anecdotal evidence supports this realisation, suggesting that some Chinese factories are relocating to Vietnam.

Nevertheless, Vietnam missed its initial target date for admission, at the Hong Kong WTO Ministerial Meeting in December 2005. It had to settle instead for entry into the WTO in early 2007. The delay is not surprising in light of the fact that Vietnam did not submit important new documentation (including tariff schedules with reduced tariff commitments, a new services offer and an 'action plan' for implementing legislation) to the Working Party, until October 2003. Furthermore, Working Party negotiations were only held periodically, once or twice a year. At each session, Vietnam would make a range of major or minor concessions, while the Working Party would essentially make further demands, deeming the offer on the table to be insufficient.

At the same time as the Working Party negotiations, some 30 WTO Members, including the United States, the EU, Japan, China, Korea, Australia, New Zealand, Brazil and Mexico, were negotiating and concluding bilateral agreements. The last of those were concluded with the United States in May 2006 and Mexico in April, 2006. The bilateral process represents, for most WTO Members, the final and best opportunity they will have for ensuring that an existing or potential world trading power opens its own market for goods and services to outside competition. Moreover, WTO members appreciate that the terms of a WTO accession agreement constitute binding

The Role of Law and Lawyers in Vietnam's WTO Accession 293

treaty obligations; as such, the economic and legal reforms agreed to by the candidate nation will effectively become irreversible.

For the United States, in its bilateral negotiations, the sticking points included reduction of most Vietnamese non-agricultural tariffs to 15 per cent or less *ad valorem*; significant reduction of agricultural tariffs, many to 15 per cent or less; and improved market access for the financial, telecom, distribution, courier and energy services. The United States also required that it be able to treat Vietnam (as it does China under its accession agreement) as a 'non-market economy' for the purposes of antidumping actions for up to 12 more years. In practice, this will likely lead to the imposition of a higher level of anti-dumping duties. The United States, for its part, agreed to drop its bilateral textile and apparel quota agreement, in return for a one-year 'safeguards' mechanism in the event of surges in exports to the United States, as well as in return for Vietnam's undertaking to end immediately all WTO-illegal subsidies related to those products. This was an important victory for Vietnam, although it was potentially undermined later by a unilateral Bush Administration decision to consider self-initiation of anti-dumping cases against Vietnamese textiles[27]. The United States also agreed to modify the so-called 'Jackson–Vanik' legislation so as to be able to provide 'permanent normal trade relations' treatment (ie, MFN) without the need for annual action by the President. This process was finally completed in early December 2006.[28]

The eventual accession package included, inter alia, in addition to the requirements of the US bilateral agreement (incorporated into the WTO accession agreement), bound duty rates in the 0–35 per cent range; elimination of all but a handful of tariff quotas; signature by Vietnam of the WTO Information Technology Agreement (allowing the importation of products covered by the ITA duty-free no later than 2014); and elimination of agricultural export subsidies and limitation of other trade-distorting domestic subsidies to about US$246 annually. Major commitments in services, particularly telecommunications and financial services were also made, along with extension of trading (export/import) rights to all duly registered persons, including foreign firms and individuals.[29] Vietnam also agreed immediately to comply with WTO disciplines under the agreements on customs valuation, rules of origin, pre-shipment inspection, anti-dumping safeguards, subsidies and trade-related investment measures, technical

---

[27] *Inside U.S. Trade, Textile Interests Fight over Interpretation of Vietnam Deal*, 6 Oct, 2006 (An Inside Washington Publication) (discussing the circumstances under which the Commerce Department would self-initiate).

[28] See Press Release, *United States Trade Representative, US Trade Representative Susan Schwab Welcomes Bipartisan Senate Vote Approving Key Trade Legislation* (9 Dec, 2006) (noting, inter alia, the enactment of PNTR for Vietnam).

[29] Press Release, *WTO, General Council Approves Viet Nam's Membership* (7 Nov, 2006), available at http://www.wto.org/english/news_e/pres06_e/pr455_e.htm (referencing that the specific commitments are contained in the accession agreement and in the working party report).

barriers to trade, sanitary and phytosanitary measures and trade-related intellectual property. In most of these areas, Vietnam's commitments go somewhat beyond what was agreed in the VBTA.

During this period, and as a result of the demands of WTO accession, there was thus tremendous pressure on the Vietnamese legal system and the lawyers involved in it. By 2004 the focus of implementation had changed from the VBTA to the enactment of national laws, ordinances and regulations that would be necessary for Vietnam to comply with the parallel and additional obligations it was in the process of accepting with WTO accession. The Working Party had insisted that Vietnam enact essentially *all* the legislation that the Working Party deemed necessary for implementing its accession obligations, *before* accession was granted, for review (in English translation) by the Working Party. (Presumably, this reflected dissatisfaction with the rapidity with which China had issued implementing laws and regulations in the period since China's WTO accession in November 2001.) As a result, Vietnam enacted changes in hundreds of laws, decrees and regulations, beginning in 2004[30], primarily through the efforts of the Ministries of Justice and Trade, and the National Assembly. These included key statutes such as the Law on Enterprise, Law on Investment, Law on Conclusion of International Treaties and various tax laws.

It is apparent that not only in the negotiations, but perhaps even more in the legislative drafting and enactment process, the role of the government attorneys—led by the Ministry of Justice which is principally responsible for the VBTA and WTO implementation—has been most significant. The same relatively small group of 25–35 Vietnamese attorneys involved in the VBTA were, by the time of the WTO negotiations, quite well prepared for that process. However, the growing level of international trade expertise has now extended beyond the governmental sector. By 2006, reflecting the increased role of trade law in Vietnam's legal system, the two leading law faculties in Vietnam (the Ho Chi Minh City Law University and the Hanoi Law University) were both in the process of incorporating *required* international trade law courses in their first (undergraduate) law degree curriculum, and many others were expected to follow.[31]

V. LEGAL AND JUDICIAL REFORM

The Government of Vietnam is continuing its efforts to regularise the practice of law and improve the functioning of the judiciary and legal system. This reform process is key for WTO compliance and for maintaining

---

[30] See US—Vietnam Trade Council, Catalog of Legal Updates: Vietnam Trade Policy Regime (Jan 2007) available at http://www.usvtc.org/updates/legal/Catalog/CatalogJan07.pdf.

[31] Based on the author's discussions with law professors in Hanoi in Aug 2004 and at various times with Virginia Foote of the US—Vietnam Trade Council.

Vietnam's international competitiveness for foreign investment. It will also enable ordinary Vietnamese citizens to benefit more fully from Vietnam's embrace of globalisation. As part of that reform, in June 2006, a 'Law on Lawyers' was enacted, which governs, inter alia, the practice of law by both Vietnamese citizens and foreign law firms and foreign lawyers operating in Vietnam. The restrictions on foreign lawyers, in particular, were substantially relaxed, probably going beyond the requirements of the VBTA discussed earlier. This included the right of foreign lawyers to consult on Vietnamese law if they had obtained a Vietnamese law degree. However, a foreign lawyer may not:

> participate in legal proceedings as a defense counsel . . . or as the representative of a client before the bodies conducting legal proceedings in Vietnam.[32]

Under these and the other circumstances discussed in this article, it is not surprising that the number of new lawyers in Vietnam is skyrocketing. By 2005, lawyers were emerging from the major Vietnamese law faculties, and from the 'legal institution training course,' at a rate of 4,000 to 4,500 persons per year, a far cry from the numbers in the early 1970s.

More significantly, a long-term judicial reform strategy has been developed and is now in the process of implementation. The stated objective is to build 'an ethical, healthy, strong, democratic, strict, fair and justice-protecting judiciary, as well as [to ensure] that the judiciary will be modernised on a step-by-step basis to serve the Socialist Fatherland of Vietnam and its people and that judicial activities, among which adjudication plays the key role, will be highly efficient and effective.'[33]

In parallel developments, the Politboro recognised, despite some years of reforms, that broader problems in the legal system remain:

> The system is still not comprehensive and consistent; its viability is still low, and its implementation in practice remains slow. The mechanism for making and amending laws has many deficiencies and is still not properly observed. The speed of law-making activities is slow. The quality of the laws is not high. There is lack of attention paid to the research and implementation of international treaties to which Vietnam is a party. The effectiveness of legal dissemination and education is limited. Institutions for law implementation are still inadequate and weak.[34]

The reform plans, if successfully implemented, could greatly improve the functioning of the legal and judicial systems, and increase the level of confidence which Vietnamese and foreigners have in both.

---

[32] Law on Lawyers, 29 Jun, 2006, No 65/2006/QH11, 11th Legis, 9th sess, arts 1, 70, passim, available at http://www.usvtc.org. (visited 18 Sep, 2006) (translation).

[33] Communist Party Central Committee, Resolution of the Politburo on the Judicial Reform Strategy to 2020, No 49-NQ/TW, 2 Jun, 2005, at 1 (translation).

[34] Communist Party Central Committee, Resolution of the Politburo on The Strategy for the Development and Improvement of Vietnam's Legal System to the Year 2010 and Direction for the Period up to 2020, No 48-NQ/TW, 24 May, 2005, at 1 (translation).

CONCLUSION

The completion of a two decade-long process, from Doi Moi to the VBTA to WTO membership for Vietnam, reflects a long and difficult movement of the nation toward a market-oriented economy and the rule of law, while still maintaining its Communist system largely intact. Despite the fits and starts, the nation has, in the view of World Bank officials, effectively climbed from being poor to being middle-income in about 15 years, with per capita incomes expected to exceed $1,000 by 2010, compared to $180 in 1993.[35] The process has benefited from, and helped to generate, a thriving domestic legal community. This perhaps sets the stage for a situation 3–5 years from now, when the understanding of the international trading system by lawyers and other professionals will be more profound in Vietnam than in many other developing countries.

However, WTO accession is perhaps best viewed as an analogy to a university graduation, a 'commencement' of a long-term process toward a truly open economy and the widespread rule of law. The implementation of VBTA and WTO obligations is not finished and transition to a fully-functioning rule of law society is still some distance from completion. The amendment (and, hopefully, improvement) of key laws and regulations, with the help of the legal profession, is likely to continue *sua sponte* and in some instances under pressure from other WTO Members or even from the WTO's Dispute Settlement Body. Government lawyers, judges and members of the legal profession in Vietnam will continue for some years to struggle with all that is required from such a system, though the tremendous progress of recent years provides great hope for their success.

---

[35] Perlez, above n 21, at 3.

20
Exercising Quasi-Judicial Review Through a World Bank Appellate Body

RUMU SARKAR

INTRODUCTION

THIS CRITICAL ESSAY examines the enduring legacy of the Bretton Woods system with a view towards suggesting specific means for improving the operation and viability of both Bretton Woods institutions (ie, the International Monetary Fund and the World Bank) in the 21st century.

In particular, this essay will explore certain administrative law aspects stemming from the creation of the World Bank Inspection Panel (WBIP) in 1993. The following discussion will examine: (1) the relative merits of a general protocol by the World Bank and its members setting forth the principles underlying the Bank's formal lending practices; and (2) the establishment of a World Bank appellate body to render legal opinions on: (a) whether WBIP recommendations to reject a request for inspection for failing to meet the required eligibility criteria are legally sustainable; and, (b) whether the WBIP's report to the President and Executive Directors of the World Bank containing its factual conclusions and recommendations is legally sufficient, if the report is appealed by the complaining party. The discussion will draw on lessons from the World Trade Organization (WTO).

It is worth noting that the creation of three multilateral institutions was contemplated in 1940s. At the seminal conference held in Bretton Woods from 1–22 July, 1944, towards the end of World War II, two institutions were established. The International Bank for Reconstruction and Development, commonly referred to as the World Bank, was created to facilitate post-war reconstruction and development. The International Monetary Fund (IMF) was designed to promote international monetary cooperation, exchange stability, orderly exchange arrangements and, more importantly, to provide temporary financial assistance to countries to help ease balance of payments adjustments.

After several years of separate negotiations, a charter for an International Trade Organization was proposed in Havana, Cuba, in 1948. Such a charter was not adopted, but elements of a trade agreement survived in a truncated form known as the General Agreement on Tariffs and Trade (GATT). The GATT eventually evolved into a forum for sovereign member nations to discuss and resolve international trade issues and disputes. However, it was not until the adoption of the 'Final Act Embodying the Results of the Uruguay Round of Multilateral Trade Negotiations,' in Marrakesh on 15 April, 1994, that a new organisation called the WTO was finally established in January 1995.

I. INTERNATIONAL PROTOCOLS AND DISPUTE RESOLUTION: THE WTO EXAMPLE

Although the WTO may be viewed as a relative latecomer to the international scene, it has outpaced both the World Bank and the IMF in certain key aspects. There is relative symmetry among all three institutions insofar as none of them provides any means of formal legal redress or adjudication of disputes that may arise between a sovereign member and the respective institution. However, there are two critical respects in which the WTO has adopted a different course of action that clearly distinguishes it from its two 'sister' counterparts.

First, the WTO provides a mechanism for promulgating and formalising international protocols that permits its members to negotiate and agree to principles of, inter alia, trade law, intellectual property, technology and environmental-related matters, trade-related investment measures, subsidies and countervailing measures, agriculture, textiles, anti-dumping, customs valuation, import licensing procedures, electronic commerce, government procurement, and even ways to achieve greater coherency in global economic policy-making. The process of mutually agreeing to these principles continually creates fresh new public international law on substantive trade-related topics.

Second, the WTO provides a forum for adjudicating disputes that arise among its members for breaching such WTO agreements. Thus, the WTO has established a rules-based system that is enforced, first, by consultative means on a bilateral basis between the countries in dispute or as mediated by a third party, and then by consensual means through the formal operation of law. In a nutshell, the WTO's Dispute Settlement Body (DSB) sets up a panel to hear the dispute between its members with clearly demarcated, time-restricted stages for the administrative proceedings. The final report issued by the panel indicates whether a WTO agreement or obligation has been violated and, if so, the measures that may be taken to encourage the offending member to comply with those requirements. The report becomes the final ruling within 60 days *unless* the WTO members reject it by consensus. Further, the DSB is empowered to monitor compliance with the panel's rulings and recommendations, and is empowered to authorise retaliatory measures in instances of non-compliance by a member.

One or both parties to the dispute may appeal the final ruling. However appeals are made strictly on the basis of the interpretation of points of law, and do not re-examine existing evidence or hear new issues. Appeals are heard by the WTO's Appellate Body (AB), which can uphold, modify or reverse the panel's legal findings and conclusions, and generally issues its ruling within 90 days of the filing of the appeal. The DSB has 30 days in which to accept or reject the AB's findings, and rejection must be by consensus only.

The DSB is thus empowered to resolve legal disputes arising among WTO members based on applicable international agreements, understandings and protocols. The DSB functions as a neutral adjudicatory body that addresses compliance with substantive legal principles that the WTO has adopted as a body, and which its individual members have ratified, and adjudicates disputes arising therefrom among its members.[1] In the WTO's own opinion, '[d]ispute resolution is the central pillar of the multilateral trading system, and the WTO's unique contribution to the stability of the global economy.'[2]

Appeals of the DSB's panel's decisions are heard by a specially constituted permanent appellate body that renders its legal opinion solely on issues of law arising from the original panel ruling. This, in effect, creates new public international law arising from the administrative (ie, appellate) legal proceedings of the WTO. It may be fairly argued that these administrative legal proceedings add to the transparency, predictability and enforceability of an international trade regime. In sum, the WTO provides its members with a highly structured and timely dispute resolution process for alleged violations of internationally-agreed WTO protocols and understandings.

In contrast, while the World Bank's Operational Manual sets forth its policies and procedures for financing projects in support of the economic development of the borrowing member, this is an internal document, not a multilateral agreement. Although alleged deviations from the procedures described in the Operational Manual may be set forth in a complaint by a private (non-state) party affected by the project supported by the World Bank and submitted to the World Bank Inspection Panel in a process described more fully below, it is important to keep in mind that this manual

---

[1] See generally, RB Stewart, 'US Administrative Law: A Model for Global Administrative Law?' (2005) 68 *Law & Contemp Probs* 63, 93. 'The WTO Dispute Settlement Body, and especially its Appellate Body, increasingly function as a regulatory administrative body with the aim of constructing a fully articulated trade regulatory system and supervising its implementation by member states.' Further, 'the Appellate Body has sought to use the resolution of particular disputes regarding member state compliance to develop systemic norms and procedures to govern the trade regulatory regime, including the development of a global administrative law for member state authorities whose decisions are regulated by WTO law'. Ibid at 102.

[2] See the WTO's official website at http://www.wto.org/english/thewto_e/whatis_e/tif_e/disp1_e.htm (last visited on 17 May, 2007).

is an internal document, and not a multilateral agreement of the members of the World Bank. Thus, it may be argued, that neither the World Bank (nor the IMF) have agreements, understandings or protocols that set forth their underlying principles—supporting economic development in the case of the World Bank, or structural adjustment and balance of payments support in the case of the IMF. Although the World Bank may enter into specific loan, grant, guarantee or hedging agreements and related documentation with the individual member requiring assistance, there is no overarching protocol entered into by all members of the World Bank that describes that manner in which such financing is arranged.

Similarly, the IMF may enter into an 'arrangement' for financing with one of its members. However, rather than entering into a mutual agreement, it is customary for the sovereign member to submit a Letter of Intent to the Executive Board of the IMF outlining a general description of the need for and the uses to which the IMF's financing shall be dedicated, along with policy changes to be undertaken by the host government. There is no single protocol to which all IMF members are party that describes the core principles of such lending practices.

In the case of the World Bank, the Inspection Panel will only review requests for inspection that allege a material adverse effect affecting the private complainant that stems from the failure of the Bank (and *not* the member state where the complainant is located) to follow its own operational policies and procedures as set forth, in effect, in its Operational Manual.[3] However, this restricts the claim to being solely administrative in nature, based on the alleged failure of the Bank to follow its own internal policies and procedures. This is unlike the WTO's dispute system where, in effect, one member state is alleging that another member state has breached public international law by failing to meet the terms of a WTO agreement, understanding or rule.

Moreover, commentators have argued that the official lending practices of the World Bank, and especially of the IMF, have created a layer of unregulated 'extra-governance' that is shielded from participation in or review by the affected populations of the member country.[4] This criticism has been especially harsh where painful adjustment programs imposed by the IMF have

---

[3] See Resolution No IBRD 93–10; Resolution No IDA 93–6, The World Bank Inspection Panel (22 Sep, 1993), 12 available at http://web.worldbank.org/WBSITE/EXTERNAL/EXTINSPECTIONPANEL/0,,contentMDK:20173262~menuPK:64129254~pagePK: 64129751~piPK:64128378~theSitePK:380794,00.html (last visited on 17 May, 2007).

[4] Stewart, above n 1, at 70. 'Regarding procedure, treaty-based regimes like the WTO and the IMF have been widely attacked for imposing measures generated by secret processes without opportunity for participation and review by affected domestic interests.' Further, '[p]rocess-based criticism tends to focus on the secrecy of international and transnational regulatory decisional processes and the lack of adequate opportunity for effective access to information, participation and input in global regulatory decision-making on the part of affected global or domestic publics, including the interest of environmentalists, workers, consumers, developing countries, and indigenous peoples.' Ibid at 71.

required the reduction of social safety net protections in health, education, pension plans and other poverty reduction programs in affected member countries.

While this critique cannot be addressed here, it may be worthwhile to suggest that by entering into a general lending practices protocol with their respective members, both Bretton Woods institutions may add to the transparency and the accountability of their lending practices. This could also strengthen the operations and viability of both institutions in the future. Further, it could mature the World Bank process of dispute resolution from being solely administrative in nature and raise it to the level of being a question of public international law. This could effectively move it from the realm of international administrative proceedings into the arena of public international law. (Naturally, some may view this as worsening rather than improving the current state of affairs.)

Now, turning to the second point, the WTO provides the right to redress a purported trade violation between its members, thus giving rise to the DSB system of dispute resolution. This is a system of rights and relationships that is decidedly state-centric in its focus as private parties do not have an independent right of action. They may, in effect, 'lobby' their host governments to take action to redress perceived trade violations by another state party. But as far as the World Bank and the IMF are concerned, there does not seem to be any need, as far as the author can ascertain, to resolve conflicts among the members themselves. In other words, there does not seem to be a demonstrable need, for example, for Russia to challenge a World Bank loan made to Kenya. Neither Bretton Woods institution provides for or seemingly has any need for resolving conflicts between or among its sovereign members.

In contrast, however, the World Bank has created a right of legal recourse that is truly far-reaching and even revolutionary in a sense. By creating the Inspection Panel, the World Bank has established a legal nexus between the end-user of the development project or undertaking and the Executive Directors of the World Bank.[5] In this author's view, this new legal relationship is almost breath-taking in its impact. By giving a private party a legal right of action, the World Bank has effectively exited the state-centric world of public international law—and entered a new, privately enforceable dimension of public international administrative law. Perhaps it is more accurate to say that the World Bank has actually created that new dimension of law by recognising and giving legal legitimacy to the claims of private end-users of a World Bank project.[6]

---

[5] DD Bradlow, 'A Test Case for the World Bank' (1996) 11 *Am U J Int'l L & Pol'y* 247, 247. 'The [Inspection] Panel is the first forum in which private parties can seek to hold international organizations directly accountable for their actions.'

[6] 'Professor Bradlow heralds the creation of the [Inspection] Panel as "the first formal acknowledgement that international organizations have a legally significant non-contractual relationship with private parties that is independent of either the organization's or the private actor's relationship with a member state"'. JN Weidner, 'Note, World Bank Study' (2001) 7 *Buff Hum Rts L Rev* 193, 215.

The World Bank Inspection Panel was created by a resolution of its Executive Directors dated 22 September, 1993, to ensure that the Bank adheres to its operational policies and procedures during the design, preparation, appraisal and implementation phases of its projects.[7] The Panel is authorised to accept requests for inspection filed by an affected party (who is not an individual but an organisation, society or grouping of individuals) in the territory of the borrowing country. The Chairperson of the Inspection Panel then informs the President and the Executive Directors of the World Bank that a request for inspection has been received. Within 21 days of notification by the Chairperson of the Inspection, the Management of the Bank is required to provide a statement on whether it has complied or intends to comply with the Bank's operational policies and procedures that allegedly have been breached.

Within 21 days of receiving the Management's response, the World Bank Inspection Panel must recommend to the Executive Directors whether the matter meets the eligibility criteria as set forth in the resolution establishing the Panel,[8] and should be investigated. The World Bank Executive Directors then decide whether to accept the Panel's recommendation. If accepted for investigation, the Panel may consult with the Bank's Legal Department[9] and the Bank's staff as appropriate, and may visit the borrower country. Upon completion of its investigation, the Panel is required to issue its report to the President and the Executive Directors, setting forth its findings and conclusions of all relevant facts. The Bank's Management has six weeks to respond to the Panel's report. Information concerning the Executive Board's final decision as well as the Panel's report and the Management's response are posted on the Panel's official World Bank-hosted website.

While it may seem that my analogies to the WTO system of dispute resolution have come to an end, I will argue that there is more to be learned from the WTO example. The discussion above addresses the merits of the World Bank and the IMF promulgating, and having their members ratify, general accords regarding their official lending practices thus following the WTO's lead in creating new public international law on substantive trade-related topics. I would also suggest that the WTO's lead should be followed in another respect. The dispute resolution process, including the appellate procedures of the WTO, has the effect of creating new public international

---

[7] See above n 3.
[8] See above n 3.
[9] Bradlow, above n 5, at 292. 'With regard to matters related to the Panel, the Legal Department's advice to the Board, at least from the perspective of the requester and other outside observers, has the appearance of a conflict of interest. The conflict arises because the Legal Department is providing advice to the decision-maker about a matter in which some of the issues to be determined by the decision-maker are likely to relate to the Legal Department's prior advice to Bank Management and staff or to decisions in which the Legal Department participated.'

law through the administrative process of an international organisation. Likewise, the World Bank should consider establishing an appellate procedure within the Bank itself as part of the Inspection Panel dispute resolution process. This will have the desired effect of producing appellate rulings that will be legal conclusions.

Why is this important and desirable? The WBIP issues findings and conclusions of fact, not law.[10] These findings are accepted by, modified or rejected by the World Bank's Executive Directors. Any recommendation or finding issued by the Executive Directors is also a statement of fact, not law. Moreover, neither the findings of the WBIP nor of the Executive Directors are subject to legal scrutiny at any stage.

Inevitably, this means that the WBIP's reports, while helpful in sustaining the remarkable legal nexus established between the end-user and the Executive Directors, are not actually creating law. The findings and conclusions of the WBIP cannot be considered administrative law, public international law, or even legal conclusions, in effect.[11] Consequently, this means that these findings cannot legitimately be assigned any real legal precedent or legally binding value. Thus, regrettably, the factual findings and conclusions of the WBIP do not create actual legal principles, and arguably do not measurably add to the transparency or predictability of the official lending practices and their downstream impact on the end-users in a strictly legal sense.

However, it is clear that this system of reviewing the claims filed by private claimants before the WBIP does add to the accountability of the World Bank in adhering to its own rules and procedures. Nevertheless, this jurisdictional territory is very narrow. A multilateral protocol that actually describes the general principles pursuant to which official lending by the World Bank may take place would be far more effective in setting the ground rules supporting the official lending practices promulgated by the World Bank. Moreover, such a protocol would help in the practical and legal determination of potential breaches or violations.

---

[10] From a US legal practitioner's standpoint, it may have been preferable to have given the WBIP the authority to issue conclusions of law along with findings of fact, mirroring US administrative law practice where Administrative Law Judges are empowered to do exactly that. Thus, appellate review of the administrative trial level decision may be more clearly focused on the legal questions raised by the proceeding below. (However, in many instances, federal district courts with jurisdiction over the dispute have de novo review authority to both try the facts and decide the law.)

[11] B Kingsbury, N Krisch & RB Stewart, 'The Emergence of Global Administrative Law' (2005) 68 *Law & Contemp Probs* 15, 34. 'The [Inspection] Panel only has the power of issuing reports and recommendations, and cannot halt or modify non-conforming projects. Moreover, the grounds for such challenges are limited to allegations of non-compliance with the World Bank's own policies and thus do not extend to international law in general; but this limitation has frayed on occasion, and might turn out not to be sustainable.'

Indeed, it seems unlikely that the Bank's staff would deliberately fail to follow the operational policies and procedures of the Bank.[12] As of July 2006, the WBIP has only received 40 requests for inspection, several of which are still under investigation. The Executive Board has rejected the WBIP's recommendation to investigate the claim in only three reported instances.[13]

In sum, it may be worth exploring the possibility of instituting an appellate procedure as part of the WBIP administrative process. If quasi-judicial review were made possible by establishing an appellate body by resolution of the World Bank's Executive Directors, then this appellate body could be legally authorised to review certain administrative decisions made at the following points in the administrative process:

— If the WBIP recommends that the request for investigation be rejected.
— If the Executive Board rejects the WBIP's recommendation that the request for inspection be accepted.
— If the WBIP's report to the Executive Board does not meet the complainant's satisfaction on substantive grounds.
— If the Executive Board rejects the WBIP's report after the World Bank Management has filed its response.

Like the WTO AB, the quasi-judicial review of a World Bank appellate body should be limited to legal questions, and should not be permitted to extend to questions of fact, the sufficiency of the evidence presented to the WBIP, or to issues not presented for review in the proceeding below. Of course, it is likely that the second and fourth grounds for appeal described above (that question the final judgment of the Executive Directors) may be limited to whether there has been an abuse of discretion, thus, making the appeal very difficult to sustain as a matter of law.

Nevertheless, the issuance of a legal opinion (as opposed to simply issuing findings and conclusions of fact) by an appellate body will produce international administrative law. Moreover, if an international protocol is adopted by World Bank members, legal decisions by a World Bank appellate body regarding such a protocol will create a body of public international law in the end. It may be argued that creating a new genre of public international law will add to the transparency and predictability of the administrative process. Legal principles would guide, for example, the application of eligibility criteria by the WBIP in accepting or rejecting requests for inspection

---

[12] In fact, there is some evidence of the 'phenomenon of "Panel proofing" projects in the World Bank. "Panel proofing" refers to enhanced efforts by Bank staff to ensure that their activities are in compliance with the World Bank's operational policies and procedures.' See DD Bradlow, 'Private Complainants and International Organizations: A Comparative Study of the Independent Inspection Mechanisms in International Financial Institutions' (2005) 36 Geo J Int'l L 403, 463.

[13] See the Summary of Requests document, available at http://web.worldbank.org/WBSITE/EXTERNAL/EXTINSPECTIONPANEL/0,,contentMDK:20221606~menuPK:64129250~pagePK:64129751~piPK:64128378~theSitePK:380794,00.html (last visited on 17 May, 2007).

and the legal sufficiency of the factual conclusions and recommendations made by the WBIP.

It may be further argued that instituting a system of quasi-judicial review at the World Bank may also support its anti-corruption mandate. The Bank's efforts to tackle corruption are directed at the country and project levels, and through partnerships with civil society, the private sector, borrowing countries and other multilateral development banks.[14] Thus, the creation of *international administrative law* within the context of a multilateral institution may itself be a worthwhile endeavor since it creates principles of legal review that ultimately will be of persuasive authority. This, in turn, will encourage the standardisation, predictability, transparency and accountability of the World Bank's internal operating procedures.

Of course, this level of review can be significantly enlarged in scope if the Bank actually entered into a legal protocol with its members setting forth its lending principles that could form the underlying substantive basis for legal review. As discussed above, this would move the level of legal scrutiny by the World Bank appellate body from the arena of international administrative law to the realm of public international law. In fact, for World Bank decision-makers, the threshold question is deciding whether the establishment of such an appellate body is desirable and secondarily, whether it is politically feasible. Since this creates a new office and function within the World Bank institution, the immediate decision is to ascertain the political viability of such a proposal.

If the threshold question is answered in the affirmative, and a World Bank appellate body is established, then a second level of decision-making follows. The World Bank officials deciding this matter will need to define the goals of creating such an appellate body. In other words, does the World Bank wish to continue to simply enforce its own operational rules and procedures, and create a legal means of such enforcement? This means that the appellate body, if established, would create international administrative law.

Alternatively, does the World Bank wish to have its members enter into a legal protocol that clearly defines its official lending principles? Such an agreement may mirror the existing Bank operational rules and procedures, but rather than being an internal document, it would be an international agreement. If the World Bank appellate body enforced such a legal protocol, its rulings would be considered public international law. In fact, the World Bank could follow the first option, and once an international protocol is entered into by its members, follow the second option.

---

[14] See P Wolfowitz, *Good Governance and Development: A Time for Action* (11 Apr, 2006), available at http://web.worldbank.org/WBSITE/EXTERNAL/EXTABOUTUS/ORGANIZATION/EXTOFFICEPRESIDENT/0,,contentMDK:20883752~menuPK:64343258~pagePK:51174171~piPK:64258873~theSitePK:1014541,00.html (last visited on 17 May, 2007).

Entering into an underlying international protocol that defines official lending practices of the World Bank would also close the gap on another issue. At present, it is only possible to bring private complaints against the World Bank for its purported failure to follow its own operational procedures. These complaints are *not* directed against the state in which the complaint originated. However, as signatories to an international protocol, individual members of the World Bank could agree to undertake certain duties and responsibilities, thereby increasing the scope of potential legal review to extend beyond the World Bank as an institution to the conduct of its individual members as well. This is a controversial matter, and may fail as a political question, but it should be considered in this discussion.

As a final matter, the World Bank appellate body, if established, may also be empowered by the World Bank Executive Directors to monitor World Bank compliance with WBIP rulings and recommendations. The appellate body could facilitate compliance with its rulings by, for example, issuing 'declaratory' relief-type measures.[15] This also somewhat follows the lead established by the WTO which has empowered the DSB to monitor and enforce the compliance of its affected member state(s) with the rulings and recommendations issued by the panel on a specific dispute.[16] This may be a welcome change since monitoring compliance with WBIP rulings is uneven, and is a responsibility that generally falls to the Executive Directors. This has led to somewhat mixed results.[17]

Hopefully, appeals will be filed rarely. Nevertheless, making limited quasi-judicial review on an 'interlocutory' basis available during the course of the administrative process of the WBIP's proceedings may yield interesting results.

---

[15] 'By contrast, the accountability concept for which the Inspection Panel stands, is essentially not a remedy concept. [Footnote omitted.] It does not give a right to remedial measures and it also does not provide for a correspondingly enforceable judgment.' See International Law Weekend Proceedings: S Schlemmer-Schulte, 'The Impact of Civil Society on the World Bank, the International Monetary Fund and the World Trade Organization: The Case of the World Bank' (2001) 7 *ILSA Int'l & Comp L* 399, 409.

[16] See Art 21.6 of the WTO's Understanding on Rules and Procedures Governing the Settlement of Disputes stating '[t]he DSB shall keep under surveillance the implementation of adopted recommendations or rulings. The issue of implementation of the recommendations or rulings may be raised at the DSB by any Member at any time following their adoption. Unless the DSB decides otherwise, the issue of implementation of the recommendations or rulings shall be placed on the agenda of the DSB meeting after six months following the date of establishment of the reasonable period of time pursuant to paragraph 3 and shall remain on the DSB's agenda until the issue is resolved. At least 10 days prior to each such DSB meeting, the Member concerned shall provide the DSB with a status report in writing of its progress in the implementation of the recommendations or rulings.' Available at http://www.wto.org/english/docs_e/legal_e/28-dsu.pdf (last visited on 17 May, 2007).

[17] 'After some uncertainty, the Board [of World Bank Executive Directors] decided that the Panel should not play any role in monitoring implementation of the final decision. This has caused problems because it means that there is no entity in the World Bank that can give the Board an independent assessment of whether its final decision is actually being implemented as intended. According to some observers, in a number of cases the Board's decisions have not actually been implemented and the original complainants have not seen improvements in their conditions promised by the Board's decision, Bradlow, above n 12, at 419.

II. A TABULAR SUMMATION

The following table sets forth in more graphic form a summation of the discussion above.

	Int'l Protocols	State vs Int'l Org.	State vs State	State vs End-User	Dispute Resolution	Appellate Process
WTO	YES	NO	YES	NO	YES (DSB)	YES (AB)
World Bank	NO	NO	NO	YES	YES (WBIP)	NO
IMF	NO	NO	NO	NO	NO	NO

As indicated by the highlighted areas, it may be useful to consider making certain institutional reforms by the World Bank in terms of entering into a general protocol for its official lending practices, and creating an appellate body.

The IMF, as always, seems impervious to outside scrutiny or internal controls.[18] Nevertheless, as a first step, the IMF may wish to consider entering into a general protocol describing the principles of its lending practices. It is only when the IMF decides to establish a legal connection with the member state itself (Column 2) or with the end-user of IMF-financed assistance (Column 4) that establishing an Inspection Panel, or appellate procedures related thereto, becomes relevant. If it decides to follow this course of action, the IMF would be following clear precedent established by the World Bank (and other multilateral development banks)[19] as well as the WTO.

III. A NEW PROTOCOL

To emphasise the practical aspects of any reform initiatives to be considered by the World Bank or the IMF, the following proposal for a protocol addresses the ideas and suggestions discussed above in concrete form.

A DRAFT PROTOCOL ESTABLISHING AN APPELLATE BOARD

ARTICLE I
ESTABLISHMENT OF THE ORGANIZATION

The World Bank Appellate Board (hereinafter referred to as the 'AB' or the 'Board') is hereby jointly established by the Executive Directors of the International Bank for Reconstruction and Development (IBRD) and

---

[18] Apparently, the reason for a lack of an internal quasi-judicial function within the IMF and, '[o]ne reason why the IMF Executive Board was given the power of authoritative interpretation was because the original drafters of the Bretton Woods Agreement could not agree on the composition of the tribunal.' EJ Pan, 'Recent Development: Authoritative Interpretation of Agreements: Developing More Responsive International Administrative Regimes' (1997) 38 *Harv Int'l LJ* 503, 514–15.

[19] See Bradlow, above n 12, at 409.

the International Development Association (IDA) as an independent, permanent body.

ARTICLE II
MEMBERSHIP

1. All members of the IBRD and the IDA (the 'Members') automatically accede to this agreement (the 'Agreement').
2. No reservations may be made with respect to any provision of this Agreement.

ARTICLE III
FUNCTIONS

1. The AB shall be authorised to hear the following appeals (the 'Appeals') submitted by an affected party who has previously lodged a request for inspection with the World Bank Inspection Panel (the 'Panel') where:
    (a) The Panel has recommended to the Executive Directors that the request for inspection be rejected;
    (b) Where the Executive Directors have rejected the Panel's recommendation that the request for inspection be accepted;
    (c) Where the affected party disagrees on substantive grounds with the report filed by the Panel with the Executive Directors following the completion of the Panel's investigation into the matter;
    (d) Where the Executive Directors have rejected the Panel's final report containing its factual conclusions and recommendations; or
    (e) Where a recommendation of the Executive Directors to address the matter complained of by the affected party has not been complied with in a legally sufficient manner by the party from whom an action or an omission is required.
2. (a) The following bases for an Appeal must be demonstrated by an affected party bringing a matter for consideration or review by the AB:
    (1) that the Panel's recommendation is legally insufficient or not adequately supported by its findings of fact or, that in making or implementing its recommendation, the Panel failed to follow its respective policies or procedures;
    (2) that the Executive Directors, in making or implementing its recommendation, exercised an abuse of discretion or otherwise failed to follow its own rules, policies or procedures;
    (3) that any act or omission the Executive Directors recommend be undertaken to remedy the matter alleged by the affected party has not been sufficiently complied with by the party to whom the recommendation is directed.

(b) In filing an Appeal, the affected party must certify in writing, and demonstrate to the satisfaction of the AB, that the following options have been exhausted or cannot be exercised:
  (1) negotiation with the respective institution; and,
  (2) cancellation of the underlying commitment, financing, loan or provision of assistance with the respective institution.

If the affected party fails to do so, the Appeal may be dismissed by the AB.

ARTICLE IV
POWERS

1. The AB shall be empowered to adjudicate Appeals, and, on a limited basis, issue declaratory judgments.
2. If, in the judgment of the AB, the information is presented during the course of an Appeal is insufficient or inadequate to reach a decision, then it may stay the appellate proceedings until such time as such information is presented to the AB sufficient for it to render judgment. The AB shall also be authorized to direct the Panel to conduct an independent investigation of the Appeal under the direction of the AB while the stay is in effect. The stay shall be terminated within a reasonable time, as shall be determined by the AB.
3. The AB shall issue decisions on an expedited basis of not more than forty-five (45) days from when an Appeal is received or from when an additional investigation is completed, whichever is later, such a decision being final and binding on the parties with no further right of appeal. These decisions shall be of public record, and made available to the public at a *de minimis* cost. Upon the request of a Member, the AB shall provide adequate protection of non-public, classified or other sensitive information contained in such decisions, as appropriate.
4. The AB shall be authorized to issue declaratory judgments holding certain acts or omissions of a Member or of the IBRD and IDA; statements or provisions set forth in loan, or other, agreements by or between the parties; or undertakings expressly undertaken or agreed to by a member to be null and void. The AB shall make provision for an oral hearing in such cases, as deemed necessary. If a provision contained in a document is declared to be a nullity by the AB, such provision shall be stricken from said document while the remainder of the document shall continue to be in force. A declaratory judgment issued by the AB shall not affect the financing agreed to by the Member and the respective institution which may be the subject of the Appeal, unless so recommended by the AB, and subsequently approved by the Executive Directors.

ARTICLE V
SCOPE OF POWERS

The AB shall be empowered to hear Appeals of any decision or recommendation issued by the Executive Directors with respect to the matter alleged by the affected party, without limitation as to the nature of the decision or recommendation, and without regard to the nature of the underlying financing provided by the IBRD or IDA.

ARTICLE VI
STRUCTURE

1. The AB shall be composed of five (5) members who shall serve in staggered terms for not more than two terms of three (3) years each. The members of the AB shall be nominated and elected by the Executive Directors.
2. The Executive Directors shall appoint a Chairperson of the AB who shall be empowered to hire staff, experts and consultants, as necessary, to support the AB's function.
3. The AB shall be funded by the IBRD, and shall make an annual budgetary submission for the approval by the Executive Directors.

ARTICLE VII
LEGAL STATUS

1. The AB shall have legal, juridical personality, and shall be empowered with such legal capacity as may be necessary in order for it to perform its functions.
2. The AB, its members and staff, shall be accorded such privileges and immunities as may be necessary for it to perform its functions.
3. The privileges and immunities which shall be accorded to the AB, its members and staff shall be similar in nature to the privileges and immunities stipulated in the Convention on the Privileges and Immunities of the Specialized Agencies, approved by the General Assembly of the United Nations on 21 November 1947.
4. The AB may conclude a headquarters agreement, as necessary.
5. The AB may issue internal regulations governing its conduct, and may issue rules and procedures concerning Appeals brought before it for adjudication.

ARTICLE VIII
MISCELLANEOUS PROVISIONS

1. This Agreement may be amended, from time to time, upon the unanimous, mutual written agreement of the Executive Directors.
2. This Memorandum of Agreement shall enter into full force and effect upon signature below by the duly authorized representative of the Executive Directors.

IN WITNESS WHEREOF, the Executive Directors, acting through their duly authorized representative, have caused this Protocol to be signed in their name and delivered as of the date written below.

INTERNATIONAL DEVELOPMENT ASSOCIATION

By: _____
Name: _____
Title: _____
Date: _____

INTERNATIONAL BANK FOR RECONSTRUCTION AND DEVELOPMENT

By: _____
Name: _____
Title: _____
Date: _____

IV. CONCLUSION

This essay is offered in the spirit of moving the WBIP process to the next step in its evolution. Introducing an element of limited legal review along the lines suggested above is designed to facilitate the transformation of the inspection panel process from simply issuing findings of fact by the WBIP to issuing actual legal conclusions by a newly created World Bank Appellate Board. The legal conclusions of the AB will not only be binding on the parties but will also facilitate establishing persuasive legal precedence in this area. Moreover, this proposal, if accepted, will move what now are internal administrative proceedings of the World Bank into the arena of international administrative law, and perhaps ultimately into the realm of public international law. The relative merits of the World Bank entering the arena of international law in this fashion and for this purpose remain to be seen. Nevertheless, it is my hope that this foregoing discussion will create a new dialogue that is both constructive and innovative.

21

Jurisdiction to Prescribe and the IMF

ANDREAS F LOWENFELD*

I. INTRODUCTION: REASONABLENESS AND JURISDICTION

MY TITLE—JURISDICTION to Prescribe and the IMF—may strike some readers as odd. We have come to think of jurisdiction to prescribe as a way to analyse the efforts by sovereign states, and most particularly the United States, to assert its law beyond its borders. The American Law Institute's Restatement (Third) of Foreign Relations Law has set out under this heading the principle of reasonableness, based on the proposition that for a state to apply its law to persons or activity located outside the state's territory a link of territoriality or nationality is a necessary, but not a sufficient basis for jurisdiction, that is for legitimacy under international law. Exercise of jurisdiction must also pass a test of reasonableness.[1]

'Reasonableness' is not easy to define—indeed we have preferred the phrase 'not unreasonable.' Different observers have placed different emphasis on the listed factors designed to illustrate reasonableness in different situations. But I believe the fundamental concept has been accepted that it is useful—I would say necessary—to have some guidelines against which to test the reach of a state's jurisdiction into what might (to borrow from the UN Charter) be called 'matters which are *essentially* within the domestic jurisdiction' of another state, but not *exclusively* so. My effort—I should say my experiment—in this Chapter is to see whether something like the Restatement's guidelines for states can be developed for the International Monetary Fund which finds itself involved—inevitably but uncertainly—in matters that are essentially, but not exclusively within the domestic jurisdiction of member states. For the Fund, the key concept is 'conditionality.'

---

* Portions of this paper are adapted from my 'Essay in Honor of Cynthia Lichtenstein' published in 25 B C Int'l & Comp L Rev (2002), 257.

[1] American Law Institute, *Restatement (Third) of the Foreign Relations Law of the United States*, §§ 402, 403 (1987). The present author served as one of the Associate Reporters of the Restatement, with principal responsibility for the sections on jurisdiction.

II. DEFINING DRAWING RIGHTS: STAND-BY ARRANGEMENTS AND LETTERS OF INTENT

When the delegates to the founding conference of the IMF (as well as the World Bank) met at Bretton Woods in the summer of 1944 to draft the Articles of Agreement of the Fund, they were quite vague—I think deliberately—about the subject I address in this Chapter. It was understood that the Fund—meaning both the organisation to be created and the pool of resources to be contributed by member states—would be available for purchase of reserve currencies (principally US dollars) by member states with their own currencies, subject to an obligation of repurchase. In fact, though not in name, the Fund would make loans for specified periods to central banks of member states. The question that remained open was whether member states could draw on the Fund whenever they considered it necessary, or whether the managers of the Fund (and ultimately the Executive Directors) could ask questions about the member state's needs or impose conditions on the use of the assets that it sought to borrow.

Some people, including Lord Keynes, thought no questions should be asked at all. If I go to Bloomingdales or Harrods and express an interest in an expensive carpet, I do not have to explain why I want the carpet, whether I can truly afford it, whether the money would not better be used to pay my children's tuition, or whether it will fit in my house. If I go to the perfume counter, I will not be asked whether I am looking for a gift for my wife, for a girlfriend, or for some actress whose eye I would like to catch. At most, the credit card company—Visa, Master Card, or American Express—will check whether the purchase comes within my allowed credit, and whether I am current on my minimum monthly payment. Keynes thought that the same should apply to countries drawing on the Fund—ie, purchasing dollars or other convertible currencies with their own currencies. He wrote to Professor Viner (half a year before the Conference):

> Our view has been very strongly that if countries are to be given sufficient confidence, they must be able to rely in all normal circumstances on drawing a substantial part of their quota without policing or facing unforeseen obstacles.[2]

The US position was that:

> discretion on the part of the Fund was essential if the Fund's resources were to be conserved for the purposes for which the Fund was established and if the Fund were to be influential in promoting what it considers to be appropriate financial policies.[3]

---

[2] Letter from Lord Keynes to Prof Jacob Viner (18 Oct, 1943), quoted in JK Horsefield, de Vries, et al, *The International Monetary Fund 1945–65*, (Croom Helm, 1969) 75.

[3] JP Young, 'Developing Plans for an International Monetary Fund and a World Bank' (1950), 23 *Dep't St Bull* 778, 783, quoted in RN Gardner, *Sterling-Dollar Diplomacy*, 3rd edn (McGraw Hill, 1980) 113.

Both views could be supported by the text of the Articles of Agreement of the IMF as they emerged from the Bretton Woods conference.[4] Article V(3) read:

> A member shall be entitled to buy the currency of another member ... [if it] *represents* that [the currency] is presently needed for making in that currency payments which are consistent with the provisions of this Agreement. (emphasis added).

That seemed to support Keynes. But according to Article V(5), the Fund could limit or deny access to the Fund's resources if it was:

> of the opinion that any member is using the resources ... in a manner contrary to the purposes of the Fund

What did that mean?

In their first interpretation in 1946, on request of the United States, the Executive Directors said authority to use the resources of the Fund is:

> limited to use in accordance with its purposes to give temporary assistance in financing balance of payments deficits on current account for monetary stabilization purposes.[5]

That was not very illuminating, but at least it suggested that requests for drawings were subject to some scrutiny. Then the question arose how to understand the phrase 'the member ... *represents*' in Article V(3). Did the Fund have to take the member's word that it needed the Fund's resources for a purpose consistent with the Agreement? Or could an independent examination be undertaken to see whether the representation was correct?

In 1948, the Executive Directors said that if the member applying to use the Fund's resources made the representation set out in Article V(3), it had fulfilled the requirement. But, the decision went on, the Fund may, 'for good reasons' challenge the correctness of the member's declaration on the grounds that the currency is not 'presently needed,' or because the currency is not needed for payment 'in that currency,' or because the payments will not be 'consistent with the provisions of this Agreement.'[6]

What did that mean?

Four years later, the Managing Director said 'a body of particular criteria will have to be built up,' but even at the outset:

---

[4] For an interesting discussion on whether the text as it emerged constituted a retreat by Keynes or simply a concession to the United States, see Horsefield et al, above n 2, at 72–77. The official record of the Conference does not contain any debate on the issue.

[5] Ex Bd Decision No 1–2, 26 Sep, 1946, Selected Decisions of the International Monetary Fund, 249 (31st Issue 2006).

[6] Ex Bd Decision No 284-4, 10 Mar, 1948, Selected Decisions of the International Monetary Fund, 243 (31st Issue 2006).

it must be clear that access to the Fund should not be denied because a member is in difficulty ... . The Fund's attitude ... should turn on whether the problem to be met is of a temporary nature and whether the policies the member will pursue will be adequate to overcome the problem within such a period. The policies, above all, should determine the Fund's attitude.[7]

That seemed to mean that if the member's problem did not fit the Managing Director's standard, that is if the problem could not be met within a period of one to three years, then the issue was one of 'fundamental disequilibrium' (an undefined term in the Articles of Agreement), and the member might be authorised—in the age of fixed exchange rates—to devalue its currency. Still, when the Managing Director said 'The policies, above all, should determine the Fund's attitude,'[8] the question remained 'what policies.'

I think the prevailing view at the time—the 1950s—looked to the member's balance of payments and management of its international reserves—perhaps to borrowing from other sources, and to surplus or deficit in the national budget—all in gross terms, and within the obligation to maintain fixed exchange rates. But there was a kind of jurisdictional barrier between the international organisation and sovereign states that could not be breached, even in the context of extending financial assistance. Thus, for instance, the Fund might say to Patria, you must keep your budgetary deficit within 5 per cent of your GDP; but the Fund could not decide or even advise on whether this prescription would be carried out through a reduction in veterans' benefits, farm subsidies, or road building. The Fund could not prescribe—much less condition aid on—say, privatising electric power production or opening telecommunications up to foreign investment. Such matters were 'essentially within the domestic jurisdiction of the member state', or to put it another way, outside the purposes of the IMF:

> to promote exchange stability, to maintain orderly exchange arrangements among members, and to avoid competitive exchange depreciation.[9]

III. INTERNAL AND EXTERNAL POLICIES: THE JURISDICTIONAL BARRIER IS BREACHED

Gradually, the understanding—a truism today—hit home that a state's international economic policies, including the balance of payments and the value of its currency, could not be separated from its internal economic policies. A striking example came in connection with the devaluation of the

---

[7] Ex Bd Decision No 102–(52/11), 13 Feb, 1952, Selected Decisions of the International Monetary Fund, 211 (28th Issue 2003) (not published in subsequent issues).
[8] Ibid.
[9] International Monetary Fund, Articles of Agreement, art I (iii) (1994), unchanged in the Amended Articles of Agreement, effective 1 Apr, 1978.

British pound sterling in 1967. Britain, which had been 'living on tick,' in the language of the London streets, that is by financing its deficits rather than undertaking fundamental reforms, found that its credit was exhausted, and that only a substantial devaluation of the pound would open up the opportunity for new borrowing, including for the first time, drawing under the General Arrangements to Borrow. The conditions for the grant of a stand-by arrangement would be contained in a Letter of Intent, nominally a letter from the Finance Minister or comparable official to the Managing Director of the Fund but in fact a negotiated document. In those days the Fund was more committed to confidentiality than it is today, and it did not make public the conditions for the stand-by arrangement. But political pressure forced the British government to publish its Letter of Intent—for Parliament, and all the world, to see what commitments the government had had to make to obtain its loan.[10]

Some of the commitments—or rather stated 'policies and intentions'—of the government fit well within the traditional scope of concern of the IMF. 'My Dear Mr. Schweitzer,' Jim Callaghan, the Chancellor of the Exchequer, wrote to the IMF's Managing Director:

> I am setting out in this letter a statement of the policies and intentions of the Government of the United Kingdom ...
> so far as the balance of payments is concerned, the Government's aim ... is an improvement of at least £500 million a year. ...
> The Government ... intends to abolish all remaining restrictions on current transfers and payments as soon as the balance of payments allows.

But also:

> it will be the Government's intention to maintain the policy under which there is no entitlement to a 'norm' or standard increase in pay ... [and there] is no criterion for pay increases related to changes in the cost of living.

The Chancellor promised that the government would not borrow from domestic sources more than £1 billion; that vetting arrangements would be strengthened in order to ensure that the rise in wages and salaries does not exceed what the economy can afford over the next twelve months; and that it would be 'happy to consult' with the Managing Director on the results of its devaluation and accompanying measures within three months and twice more in the coming year, as well as whenever the Managing Director thought it appropriate, as long as the United Kingdom remained a substantial debtor to the Fund.

One could not quite say that the jurisdictional barrier had crumbled—at least not without knowing what went on in the consultations to which the government had committed itself. For instance, would the Fund

---

[10] Letter of Intent, 23 Nov, 1967, 755 Parl Deb, HC (5th Ser) 648–65 (1967).

tell—or urge—the British government to take back the policy under which prescriptions under the National Health Service were free? Or how many troops Britain should maintain in Germany? But at least there was a breach in the barrier—an acknowledgment, if not an articulation, that countries were subject not only to the forces of nature—the laws of economics—but to a considerable extent to the judgments of the international community, represented not by the gnomes of Zurich but by the International Monetary Fund.

IV. DEVELOPING COUNTRY DEBT AND THE ROLE OF THE FUND

In the 1970s, the original understanding reached at Bretton Woods—fixed exchange rates, measured by an unchanging US dollar linked to gold—collapsed. But contrary to what some economists had expected, the need for reserves remained, and the balance of payments turned out not to be irrelevant. The Fund retained its role as supplier to member states of resources, subject to an obligation to repay, and subject to conditions concerning the state's behaviour during the period of a stand-by arrangement. Even when there were coordinated efforts to assist a country in trouble—including assistance from, say, the United States, Germany, and Japan—it would be the IMF that made the demands (ie, required promises set out in a Letter of Intent) concerning particular measures that the borrower would take, such as reducing subsidies, improving tax collection, and curtailing government spending.

When the Articles of Agreement were amended at Jamaica in 1976, Article V(3) was amended to confirm that the Fund could—and indeed shall—place conditions on all requests for drawings beyond the reserve tranche—ie, beyond the member states' own gold or hard currency contributions.[11] But as the conditions for drawings or stand-by arrangements became more refined and more detailed—with phased drawings and performance criteria, the time had come to make explicit what had hitherto been merely implied—that there was a jurisdictional barrier beyond which the conditions prescribed by the Fund could not extend.

In 1979 the Executive Directors issued *Guidelines on Conditionality* calling for phasing and performance clauses beyond the first credit tranche, but stating:

> In helping members to devise adjustment programs, the Fund will pay due regard to the domestic social and political objectives, the economic priorities, and the circumstances of members, including the causes of their balance of payments problems ...

---

[11] International Monetary Fund, Amended Articles of Agreement, art V(3)(b) and (c).

Performance criteria will normally be confined to (i) macroeconomic variables, and (ii) those necessary to implement specific provisions of the [Articles of Agreement] or policies adopted under them. Performance criteria may relate to other variables only in exceptional cases when they are essential for the effectiveness of the member's program because of their macroeconomic impact.[12]

By this time—the end of the 1970s—two things had become clear, at least to those who paid careful attention. First, the clients of the Fund, that is the countries that sought to draw on the Fund's resources, were now entirely developing countries, so that the issue here focused on became essentially a North–South issue, until the 1990s, when Russia and some of the other states that once made up the Second World, became members of the Fund and then clients.[13]

Second, a number of countries, particularly in Latin America, had figured out how to get around the intrusiveness of the IMF—which was threatening even if the new performance criteria were limited to 'macroeconomic variables.' The major money-centre banks (and some not so major banks as well) were flush with the deposits from the newly rich oil producers for which they had agreed to pay high interest rates, and they were only too glad to re-lend these funds to developing countries, with no questions (or at least not many questions) asked—certainly not questions about internal policies.

Shortly after the beginning of the next decade, the first crisis of developing country debt broke out, set off by Mexico's announcement in August 1982 that it could not make the payments due on its external debt, followed not very long thereafter by Brazil, Venezuela, Argentina, and others.

The causes of the defaults—carelessness by the lender banks, recklessness by the borrowing states, shifts in interest rates to the detriment of the borrowers, inadequacy of the surveillance supposed to be undertaken by the IMF—are outside the topic of this essay, though of course everything is related to everything else. What brings me back to my topic is that at this point private lenders were no longer available as an alternative to the IMF and those who relied on the IMF to set the conditions. A massive rescue effort was arranged for Mexico by the United States, the Group of Ten countries, the commercial banks and the Fund, which then became the model for rescue of the other countries in trouble. Each participant depended on the others before a deal could be struck, and all counted on the Fund to ask the necessary questions and secure the necessary commitments from the countries in distress. Among the many documents, the critical one was an IMF stand-by arrangement granted on the basis

---

[12] Ex Bd Decision No 6056–(79/38), 2 Mar, 1979, 4, 9, Selected Decisions of the International Monetary Fund, 228 (25th Issue), repealed by Decision No 12864, below n 26.
[13] Italy was the last 'First World' country to draw on the Fund, in 1977. See MG de Vries, *The International Monetary Fund 1972–1978*, vol 1, (International Monetary Fund, 1985) ch 23–4.

of a Letter of Intent. Though technically the commitment was only to the IMF, and the Fund always maintained that stand-by arrangements are not international agreements,[14] in fact the commitment extended to the entire international financial community. Funds were to be made available periodically, and if the IMF turned off its tap, it was very likely that the other participants would do so as well, as indeed happened more than once.

Amid various rumours of a sell-out, the government of Mexico made its Letter of Intent public promptly, as the British government had done 15 years earlier, but it did not attach a 'Technical Memorandum of Understanding.' Once this also became public, it contributed to the perception, as one of Mexico's newspapers wrote, that 'the IMF runs Mexico even according to the calendar.'[15]

I do not share the accusation of 'sell-out' or surrender. And indeed a good case can be made that what the international community demanded, with the IMF out front, came within 'macroeconomic variables,' and thus within the jurisdictional barrier with which we started. But now the Fund was not content to negotiate about gross targets—for reduction in fiscal deficits, limits on public debt, increased tax collection, and so on. As the press pointed out, the government's commitments came with detailed performance requirements, linked, at least by implication, to dates for phased disbursements. And the critical demand, designed to bring down the rate of inflation, was an 'incomes policy,' ie, the opposite of a rise in wages to keep up with a rise in prices due to the devaluation of the peso. The Letter of Intent contained a vague paragraph about 'protecting the standard of living of the popular classes'; the IMF's own press release spoke of a reduction in inflation from 90–100 per cent in 1982 to about 55 per cent in succeeding years, and said 'incomes policy, was of central importance in the adjustment program.'[16]

The issue of incomes policy became even more critical at year-end 1982 with respect to Brazil, which was just emerging from two decades of military rule, and had held its first election since 1964—for the Chamber of Deputies and state governors, not yet for the presidency—in November 1982, just before its cash ran out.

Brazil also received first a rescue package to prevent default, followed by a massive credit and postponement of maturities of existing credits built around negotiation of a Letter of Intent. Brazil agreed, among other measures, to reduction in agricultural subsidies, and increases in specified taxes on income, sales, and exports. The commitments extended well

---

[14] See Guidelines on Conditionality, above n 12, 3; see also J Gold, *Stand-by Arrangements of the International Monetary Fund* (International Monetary Fund, 1970) 44–5.
[15] Proceso, 29 Nov, 1982.
[16] Press Release, International Monetary Fund, No 82/72 (23 Dec, 1982), reprinted in 12 IMF Survey 1 (1 Jan, 1983).

beyond macroeconomic variables, but one could say that here was an 'exceptional case' when the conditions are 'essential for the effectiveness of the member's program because of their macroeconomic impact.' I do not—a generation later—quarrel with the specific conditions; I point out only that 'exceptional' or not, by now the Fund was deep in the internal affairs of a country just beginning, after a two-decade hiatus, to come once again to terms with democracy.

The key was inflation, which the Brazilian government promised to reduce from 100 per cent in 1982 to 80 per cent in 1983, 40 per cent in 1984 and so on, to be accomplished by interrupting the cycle of wage increases reflected in, and at least partly caused by, the practice of indexing practically everything, that is making wages, interest rates, tax rates and currency values move in paralleL. The government was reluctant to force visible give-backs by the population, and in fact did not meet its targets for the first quarter of 1983.

If the Fund now refused to permit the next scheduled disbursement to go forward, and the other lenders followed suit, as was likely, Brazil might be forced into default, with all kinds of consequences not only for Brazil but for the international financial system generally. If, on the other hand, the Fund granted a waiver, what would become of the credibility of conditionality? The Fund decided to send another mission, with a view to renegotiating the Letter of Intent.

The negotiations involved a decree-law to be issued by the President limiting wage increases to 80 per cent of price increases, with some relaxation by the Fund of the targets for reduction of the public sector deficit. But under the newly revived Brazilian Constitution a decree-law could remain in effect only for 60 days without approval of the Congress, and when the Congress voted, the decree-law was defeated. With the revised financial package not yet signed in Washington, President Figueredo issued another decree-law, still designed to meet the IMF's demand to reduce the inflation rate to 80 per cent but with the lowest paid workers—roughly two-thirds of the work force—retaining their right to increases equal to 100 per cent of the inflation rate. Subsequently the President issued still another decree, and after an all-night session including a seven-hour filibuster, the Chamber of Deputies approved it by a vote of 245 to 3, with 231 members abstaining. Eventually a US$6.5 billion credit package that had been tentatively announced in September was signed in January 1984, with 550 banks participating.[17]

I tell this story not to bring up details over 20 years old, but to point out that when democracy itself hangs in the balance, the focus on 'macroeconomic variables' cannot be the whole story, for the IMF or for the international financial community as a whole.

---

[17] See NY Times, 28 Jan, 1984, at 39.

V. THE SOUTH-EAST ASIA CRISES AND EXPANSION OF THE FUND'S AGENDA

I want to move ahead about 15 years to the Southeast Asian financial crisis, which flared up in the summer of 1997. It is still not clear—and may never be—what combination of factors caused the crisis, which started in Thailand and spread with surprising speed to the Philippines, South Korea, Indonesia, and elsewhere in the region. What seemed to be different this time, however, was the absence of macroeconomic imbalances. In contrast to Mexico, Brazil, and other states of Latin America, the countries of Southeast Asia had experienced low budget deficits, relatively low public debt, inflation in single digits, rapid economic growth, and high savings and investment rates. If these indicators looked healthy, what could have caused the sudden capital flight, sharp drop in currency values, bankruptcies and massive layoffs?

The answer, as it seemed to the IMF and other outsiders, must be in internal management.

For the first time in the IMF dialogues, one hears of nepotism, corruption, the need on the one hand for more regulation of weak banking systems, on the other hand for deregulation of economic sectors with sheltered inefficient monopolies.

'Crony Capitalism' entered the vocabulary. The *chaebols* in Korea—the large conglomerates with cross-holdings linking banking, steel, automobiles, and electronics, which had once been looked up to as propelling Korea almost into the First World (it had become the 11th largest economy in the world)—were now seen as a major cause of collapse.

There were, of course, other factors, of the kind the IMF and the G-10 countries lining up with it were more familiar. For instance, as the Japanese economy stagnated and the yen lost value in relation to the dollar, economies whose currencies were tied to the US dollar found it harder to compete with Japan in export markets. Certainly the IMF did not forget all that it had learned over half a century, nor totally discard its form books. But there was a new approach, as commitments of a different kind were now required from the applicant countries. The new buzz word was 'structural adjustment.'

I focus here on Korea—which is interesting also because there was an election in the middle of the negotiations with the Fund—but the same point could be made with respect to Thailand, Indonesia, or the Philippines. The Fund—prodded by the United States—was looking closely at the private sector, and securing commitments related specifically to private activity. For instance, the deal with Korea was held up for 10 hours in its final stages before the Korean government agreed to require GAAP—generally accepted accounting practices, American style.[18] Korea

---

[18] See NY Times, 8 Dec, 1997, at A-1.

also agreed for the first time to acquisitions by foreign companies of Korean companies—not hostile take-overs but friendly mergers, and it agreed to permit companies to lay off workers, which had previously been close to impossible.[19]

A few excerpts from Korea's ten-page Letter of Intent to the IMF of 7 February, 1998, will serve to illustrate the new limits, or rather lack of limits, of international concern.[20]

In addition to commitment to targets concerning such macroeconomic indicators as growth in Gross Domestic Product and increase in usable foreign exchange reserves, the government now undertook to issue regulations on:

— mark-to-market accounting for all financial institutions;
— loan classification criteria;
— external audits of specialised and development banks by internationally recognised accounting firms;

and about a dozen similar subjects related to management of the internal financial market. Further, the government undertook (where necessary by legislative amendment) to:

— clarify the circumstances and procedures for layoffs;
— relax restrictive legal provisions relating to private job placement and manpower leasing services;
— triple budgetary resources for an employment insurance fund, including more training support and employment stabilisation;
— expand unemployment benefits to cover firms with more than 10 employees (in contrast to the previous minimum of 30 employees), and to increase the minimum benefit level to 70 per cent of the minimum wage (compared to the prior level of 50 per cent);

and so on.

---

[19] For a look back at the response of the international community to the East Asian crisis by the US Secretary of the Treasury at the time—on the whole satisfied with the results, see RE Rubin, *In an Uncertain World: Tough Choices From Wall Street to Washington* (Random House, 2003) 212–65. For a detailed analysis and critique of the Korean situation from several points of view, see DT Coe and S Kim (eds), *Korean Crisis and Recovery* (IMF and Korea Institute for International Economic Policy, 2002).

[20] In accordance with the IMF's new policy of encouraging Member States to make their Letters of Intent and associated documents public, Korea's Letter of Intent and 6 accompanying Memoranda on Economic Program, 1998, appear on the IMF Web Site at http://www.imf.org/external/np/loi/020798.htm. A footnote to the Memorandum on Macroeconomic Policies states 'It is the government's intention to seek approval of the National Assembly for the measures that require the enactment or amendment of laws.' Footnotes to 2 other Memoranda stated that the details of the measures there outlined would be included in the World Bank Structural Adjustment Loan negotiated at the same time.

Corporate governance became a major subject of discussion, and commitment. Korea committed to requiring:

— financial statements of listed companies to be prepared and audited in accordance with international standards;
— publication of combined financial statements for associated companies;
— reduction in use of mutual guarantees by corporate affiliates and subsidiaries;
— at least one outside director for companies listed on the Korea Stock Exchange;
— strengthened rights of minority shareholders; and
— believe it or not, reviewing the possibility of allowing for class action suits against corporate executives and auditors.

One would expect the Fund to call for trade liberalisation, and phasing out trade-related subsidies, linked to commitments under the rules of the World Trade Organization. But Korea now undertook as well a series of commitments on foreign direct and portfolio investment:

— foreign banks and brokerage houses were to be permitted to establish subsidiaries in Korea;
— ceilings on foreign investment in Korean equities were to be eliminated; and
— transparent guidelines would govern foreign investment in domestic financial institutions.

Each of these commitments carried a target date in calendar year 1998. In March 1999 Korea and the IMF negotiated a further Letter of Intent covering many of the same subjects plus details on privatisation of specified state-owned enterprises, regulation of insurance companies, and restructuring of *chaebol*.[21]

Most of the reforms appear sound to an outside observer. I do not even want to make the point that they seem to impose (if that is the right word) Western and largely American practices. My point here is only that the boundary between international and internal concern seems to have largely disappeared. The 'exceptional' seemed to have become routine. There were debates within the IMF, within the United States Treasury Department, and among the G-7 about many of the conditions, but so far as appears those debates were about whether a given measure would work, whether it could

---

[21] Letter of Intent of 10 Mar, 1999, reproduced on IMF Web Site, available at http://www.imf.org/external/np/loi/1999/031099.htm. Similar Letters of Intent were negotiated with Thailand and Indonesia, differing in detail but not in the scope of the subjects covered.

be enforced, whether it would be inconsistent with another measure, and how the new administration in South Korea would react to negotiations begun with the outgoing administration.

There were, of course, critics, and some of the economists who believed that particular measures urged (or imposed) on the countries in crisis were the wrong ones sought to strengthen their arguments by criticising the whole approach of the United States and the IMF. Some critics in the United States and elsewhere thought that the new IMF was over-stepping its bounds. Professor Martin Feldstein, for example, contended that the legitimate political institutions of the country, not the Fund, should determine the nation's economic structure. 'A nation's desperate need for short-term financial help,' he wrote:

> does not give the IMF the moral right to substitute its technical judgments for the outcome of the nation's political process.[22]

Joseph Stiglitz argued that structural economic issues were irrelevant, none of the Fund's business, and were reminiscent of colonialism.[23] For the Fund, however, and the US Treasury, the key task was restoration of the confidence of the market, and that required attention to underlying causes, whether internal or external. Michel Camdessus, then the Fund's Managing Director, said:

> The centerpiece of each program is not a set of austerity measures to restore macroeconomic balance, but a set of forceful, far-reaching structural reforms, to strengthen financial systems, increase transparency, open markets, and in so doing, restore market confidence.[24]

Stanley Fischer, the Fund's Deputy Managing Director and the official most intimately involved in the Southeast Asia crisis, replying directly to Professor Feldstein, wrote:

> Interesting as they are, Feldstein's three criteria [for deciding whether any particular measure should be included in a program] omit the most important question that should be asked. Does this program address the underlying causes of the crisis?[25]

If that meant that the Guidelines on Conditionality would have to be changed, so be it.

And in fact, in due course the Guidelines were changed.

---

[22] M Feldstein, 'Reforming the IMF', 78 *Foreign Aff* (1998), 20, 27.
[23] See, eg, JE Stiglitz, *Globalization and Its Discontents* (Norton, 2003) 40–5.
[24] M Camdessus, *Remarks at the Council on Foreign Relations* (6 Feb, 1998), 27 IMF Survey 49, 50 (23 Feb, 1998), available at http://www.imf.org/external/np/speeches/1998/020698.htm. To the same effect, see Rubin, above n 19, at 253.
[25] S Fischer, *The IMF and the Asian Crisis*, Address at UCLA (20 Mar, 1998), available at http://www.imf.org/external/np/speeches/1998/032098.htm.

VI. THE FUND'S NEW GUIDELINES ON CONDITIONALITY

After several years of study, consultation and negotiation, the Fund published a new set of *Guidelines on Conditionality*.[26] Macroeconomic variables still mattered, but the focus was on program goals:

> Program-related conditions governing the provision of Fund resources will be applied parsimoniously. (para 7)

In other words, if I understand correctly, when a condition is proposed, the burden is on the proponents to justify the need for the condition in accordance with the revised Guidelines. The new buzzword, used repeatedly in speeches of successive Managing Directors is *ownership*. It is an odd word, especially as applied to a borrower, but the concept is clear. The Guidelines say:

> In responding to members' requests to use Fund resources and in setting program-related conditions, the Fund will be guided by the principle that the member has primary responsibility for the selection, design, and implementation of its economic and financial policies. The Fund will encourage members to seek to broaden and deepen the base of support for sound policies in order to enhance the likelihood of successful implementation. (para 3)

In general, the new Guidelines say, all variables or measures that meet the criteria will be established as conditions (para 7(a)).

As in the 1979 Guidelines:

> Conditions will normally consist of macroeconomic variables and structural measures that are within the Fund's core areas of responsibility.

But the references to one-year normal periods for stand-by arrangements and a three-year maximum, which had long disappeared from the practice of the Fund, are gone in the text as well. Variables and measures outside the Fund's core areas of responsibility may also be established as conditions, 'but may require more detailed explanation of their critical importance.' The definition of the Fund's core areas of responsibility in this context has expanded to comprise not only the traditional monetary, fiscal, and exchange rate policies, but to include the 'underlying institutional arrangements and closely related structural measures' and financial system issues related to the functioning of both domestic and international financial markets. (para 7(b)).

The Guidelines distinguish between 'outcomes-based conditionality', ie, meeting particular targets, and 'actions-based conditionality' in which, presumably, performance will be judged by whether the government in question did the best it could, for example in collecting taxes or seeking

---

[26] Guidelines on Conditionality, Ex Bd Decision No 12864—(02/102), 25 Sep, 2002; Selected Decisions, above n 5, at 250.

legislation to eliminate disfavoured subsidies. Moreover, whereas under the 1979 Guidelines performance criteria relating to other than macroeconomic variables were to be applied only in 'exceptional cases', in the intervening years such performance criteria were extended to cases that could not fairly be described as exceptional. The 2002 Guidelines, accordingly, provide:

> Performance criteria will apply to clearly-specified variables or measures that can be objectively monitored by the staff and are so critical for the achievement of the program goals or monitoring implementation that purchases or disbursements under the arrangement should be interrupted in cases of nonobservance. (para 11(b))

By the time the new Guidelines were issued in final form, Argentina had massively defaulted on its sovereign debt. Some people blamed the Argentine crisis on the Fund for 'pulling the plug' in late 2001 on the country that it had supported for a decade. Others blamed the Fund for its long-standing support of Argentina's currency board and tight link to the dollar, although economic analyses for several years had indicated that that policy was unsustainable. The Fund's answer to the latter point, as emerged at the time and later, was that the currency board and convertibility were so essential to successive Argentine governments that to withhold its support at several instances before the crash would have constituted an unacceptable intervention in Argentina's political as well as economic affairs. Putting it in the Fund's current idiom, the Argentine government, first under President Menem and then under his successors, would not have accepted 'ownership' of a Fund program that insisted on ending convertibility of the peso and dismantling of the currency board.

The Guidelines said:

> The Fund will grant a waiver for nonobservance of a performance criterion only if satisfied that, notwithstanding the nonobservance, the program will be successfully implemented, either because of the minor or temporary nature of the nonobservance or because of corrective actions taken by the authorities. (para 12)

In fact the Fund granted successive waivers to Argentina throughout 2000 and most of 2001, though the respective performance criteria—structural as well as fiscal—were never met. But that is the subject for another paper. For present purposes, I want to come back to what I think is missing from the Guidelines, and more important, from the overall approach of the Fund: the approach of international law.

VII. SOME SUGGESTED PRINCIPLES

I invited readers at the beginning of this essay to consider the analogy between the International Monetary Fund, attempting to impose its views on member states engaged in the international economy, and individual states—typically the United States—attempting to impose its views on other states engaged in the international economy. My analogy, certainly not perfect, was based on the perception that in both scenarios one keeps bumping up against ill-defined concepts of sovereignty, or better, of supposedly exclusive jurisdiction over internal affairs.

Having taken you through the evolution of the IMF's efforts to put its views into effect through the technique of conditionality—I almost said 'money talks'[27]—I want to try to offer some principles to be considered by the IMF, suggesting on the one hand restraint, but offering on the other hand legitimacy. I suggest these as legal principles—not quite as neutral principles, but distinct from particularistic views about interest rates, exchange rates, or appropriate ratios between gross domestic product and fiscal deficit.

A. The Territorial Principle

The more a proposed measure addresses external relations, such as exchange controls, export subsidies, or import restraints, the less problematic it is from the perspective of jurisdiction by an international organisation to which the target state belongs, such as the IMF. *The more a measure would address essentially internal activity, even if it could be shown to have international effects, for example risk assessments by banks making domestic loans, or governance requirements for domestic corporations, the less justification there is to break the jurisdictional barrier and to prescribe it as a condition.*

B. The Mirror Principle

The international organisation contemplating prescribing a given measure or set of measures should ask how we—by which I mean first world nations such as the United States, Japan, the United Kingdom, the European Union or one of its prickly member states—would feel if some outside institution told us to take a given measure, for instance to open up foreign direct investment, permit class actions, or change accounting rules on stock options. *The more we would regard such an prescription as excessively intrusive, the less justification there is to break the jurisdictional barrier and prescribe it as a condition.*

C. Probability of Conflict

Suppose Patria has just had an election—as South Korea did in the middle of its crisis—in which a major platform of the party that prevailed was

---

[27] For a recent book with just that title, see ER Gould, *Money Talks: The International Monetary Fund, Conditionality, and Supplemental Financiers* (Stanford University Press, 2006).

raising the minimum wage. Now comes the IMF offering a loan not available elsewhere, coupled with the prospect of additional support from the United States, the World Bank, and others, but subject to a condition that the minimum wage not be raised, or that it be raised by no more than 5 per cent. Or take the reverse situation: the election has not been held, but the minimum wage, or the formula for indexation, is a major issue. Either way, *the greater the likelihood of conflict between the IMF and the government or its electorate, the less justification there is to break the jurisdictional barrier and prescribe the measure in question as a condition.*

D. International Consensus

There has been a good deal of talk about the 'Washington Consensus.' But are Sarbanes-Oxley reforms accepted world-wide? There may be almost universal opposition to price-fixing cartels, though it seems they are never completely stamped out. But is there consensus about other aspects of antitrust law—mergers, abuse of market power, reciprocal dealing? One could ask comparable questions about risk assessment for banks, safety and environmental controls, maximum or minimum working hours, and so on. *The less consensus prevails on the desirability of a proposed measure, the less justification there is to break the jurisdictional barrier and prescribe it as a condition.*

Note that each of the principles that I have suggested is stated in terms of a sliding scale—an issue to be considered by the directors of the IMF or other international organisation apart from or in addition to the economic pros and cons in a given situation. All the situations I have posited raise an amber light, an issue of reasonableness.[28]

There are red light issues, where no matter what the economic justification for a measure, no other country or international organisation would dare to tread:

— It might be economically sound, for instance, for women to be permitted to work, but no outside authority would think of ordering, or pressuring a country to change its laws on that issue as a condition for financial support.
— Fair and free elections are a good thing, and probably desirable for an economy looking to participate in the world market. But making electoral reform a condition for a loan from the international community, would, I believe, be beyond the jurisdiction of the IMF and similar organisations.

---

[28] A Summing Up by the Acting Chair of the Fund of a meeting in 2002 on Access Policy in Capital Account Crises reports that Directors discussed the possibility of requiring a supermajority of Board votes to approve exceptional access. 'They generally agreed that such a fundamental change to the governance structure of the Fund—which would necessitate a change in the Articles of Agreement—should not be pursued at this time.' Selected Decisions, above n 5, at 351.

Reasonable people can differ on some other issues that on the one hand touch sovereign nerves, on the other hand threaten programs of economic adjustment and assistance—for instance, arms budgets, commitment to suppression of the narcotics trade, corruption of public officials. My instinct is that these subjects belong outside the scope of Fund conditionality, ie, that they are beyond the Fund's jurisdiction to prescribe. Perhaps they could be addressed indirectly. For instance, a strict target for reduction of fiscal deficits might have an impact on the amount devoted to purchases of military equipment. But whether the country seeking support from the Fund reduces old age pensions or arms purchases ought not, as I see it, be the Fund's business.[29]

I do not, evidently, claim to have found the answer to the inevitable dilemma of conditionality. But I hope that I have introduced another way—not an alternative but an additional way—for the IMF and its patrons to look how it addresses its member states in need, substituting flexible concepts of jurisdiction for intractable notions of sovereignty.

---

[29] I do not, of course, suggest that the Fund ignore all non-strictly economic misbehaviour by states. But for countries engaged in genocide, or in breach of international peace, drawing on the Fund is not an option in any case. I am addressing situations in which the Fund, alone or as leader of a consortium, is negotiating a stand-by arrangement and Letter of Intent.

Index

acculturation 74–5
AFTA (Asean Free Trade Agreement) 286
Alien Tort Claims Act (US) 225, 234
American Law Institute, Restatement (Third) of Foreign Relations Law 313
American Society of International Law (ASIL), International Economic Law Interest Group 2–4, 243
Annan, Kofi 222
Archilochus 113–14
Argentina-US Bilateral Investment Treatment 271
asbestos case 178
ASEAN (Association of South-East Asian Nations) 286
Asean Free Trade Agreement (AFTA) 286
ASIL *see* American Society of International Law
Association of American Law Schools (AALS), Associate Deans 136–7
  survey 138–42
Association of South-East Asian Nations (ASEAN) 286

Bank for International Settlements (BIS) 245–6, 258
banking (global), prudential regulation 99–102
Barnett, MN 80, 81
Baron, J 213
Basel Committee on Banking Supervision 100–2, 113, 256
Baum, L Frank 17
Bentley, John 289
Berle, AA 227
Berlin, I 113–16
Bhagwati, J 209
Bhopal gas plant disaster 221, 233
bilateral investment treaties (BITs)
  practice 241–3
  purpose 22–3
BIS (Bank for International Settlements) 245–6, 258
BITs *see* bilateral investment treaties
Bourneuff, Alice 162
Bowles, S 213
Braithwaite, J 34
Brazil, developing country debt 320–1
Bretton Woods
  IELG conference (2006) 1–2, 135–6
  original conference 121–2, 162

  system 246–51
    coordination/linkage 251
    design 247–8
    development finance 249–50
    establishment 246–7
    trade relationships 250–2
bribery 225, 233
Broude, T 25
Brunée, J 86
Business for Social Responsibility (BSR) 224–5

Callaghan, Jim 317
Camdessus, Michel 253, 325
Carruthers, B 40–1
Cavazos, G 209–11
chaebols 322–5
Charnovitz, S 58
China 286–7
Christopher, Warren 287
Clinton, President 287
cognitive-cultural control 79–81
Cold War 131, 249
collaboration, interdisciplinary *see under* interdisciplinary research
corporate law 171–83
  doctrine of piercing corporate veil 178
  domestic doctrines and IEL 175–7
  and European economic integration 176–7
  and global trade 173–4
  incorporation doctrine 175
  internal affairs rule 175–6
  and legal education 171–3, 182–3
  limited liability 177–8
  managers and social obligations 179–82
  seat theory 175
corporate social responsibility (CSR) 219–34
  codes of conduct 222–4, 232
  and corporate governance 225–6
  and corporate law, US 231
  definitions 219–20, 232
  environmental and social reporting 232
  and legal education, US 226–9, 234
    course/seminar framework 230–4
    expansion of coverage 229–30
  and MNEs 219, 220–6
  national regulatory developments 225–6
  and practice of law 234
  rationale 220–1

shareholder primacy model 226–8
stakeholder theory 228, 231
substantive norms 232–4
courses *see under* legal education, US
critical legal studies 48–9
cross-border economic activities, private law regulation 97–9
CSR *see* corporate social responsibility

Dezalay, Y 34
Dietrich, Ethel 161
Dimand, RW 160–1
Dispute Settlement Body (WTO) 298–9, 301–2, 306
dispute settlement, diversification 240–3
doctrinal analysis/description 30, 45–7
Dodd, EM 231
Dodge Brothers v Ford Motor Company 226
Doi Moi policy 281–3, 284–6
Drahos, P 34
DSB (Dispute Settlement Body (WTO)) 298–9, 301–2, 306
Dulles, Eleanor Lansing 161, 162
Dunoff, J 32

economic law approach 89–106
  see also international economic law
  background 89–91
  case studies *see* global economy law
  concept 92–5
  conclusion 106
  and international economic law 95–6
  and international law *see* international law
economics *see* international economics
Edelman, LB 79, 86
education *see* legal education
Emani, Z 165
empiricism 33–7
  consequentialist 43–4, 49–51
environmental and social reporting 232
Erie Railroad Co v Tompkins 275
Erler, G 90
Escobar, A 81
European economic integration 176–7
European Union Modernisation Directive 226

FATF (Financial Action Task Force on Money Laundering) 260
Feldstein, M 325
feminism *see* women's contributions
Financial Action Task Force on Money Laundering (FATF) 260
financial crises, international responses 254
financial markets, globalisation 246–7, 251–4

financial stability 255–6
Financial Stability Forum (FSF) 257–8, 259
financial system *see* international financial system
Finnemore, M 75, 80, 81, 85
Fischer, Stanley 325
Foote, Virginia 288
Foreign Corrupt Practices Act (US) 225, 233, 234
foreign investment, international law 102–6
  intergovernmental economic/social development disciplines 103–4
  national administrative/transnational commercial disciplines 104–6
French jurisprudence 272–4
Friedman, L 33
FSF (Financial Stability Forum) 257–8, 259

G-7 (Group of Seven)/G-10 (Group of Ten) 255, 258
GAAP (generally accepted accounting practices) 322–3
Garth, B 34, 35
gateway courses 151–2
GATT *see* General Agreement on Tariffs and Trade
gender impacts *see* women's contributions
General Agreement on Tariffs and Trade (GATT) 127–8, 130, 237–8, 247
  see also sociological institutionalism, trade regime
  creation 298
  dispute settlement 240
  and financial liberalisation 261
  and trade liberalisation 250–1
generally accepted accounting practices (GAAP) 322–3
Gintis, H 213
global banking, prudential regulation 99–102
global common enterprise, and legal education 207–8
Global Compact (UN) 222
global economy law 96–7
  international law of foreign investment *see* foreign investment, international law
  private law regulation, cross-border economic activities 97–9
  prudential regulation of global banking 99–102
global trade
  regulation
    abstraction effect 70–1
    as legal discipline 59–62
  structures 238–9
globalisation of finance 251–4
Goldstein, J 76
Goodman, R 33, 74

Index   333

Great Transformation 192–7
Group of Seven (G-7)/Ten (G-10) 255, 258
Grundnorm 112

Halliday, T 34, 40–1
Hirschman, AO 195
Hudec, RE 33–4, 48
Huntington, S 195, 202
hybridisation, and legal education 208–12

ICJ (International Court of Justice) 266–7
ICSID (International Centre for the Settlement of Investment Disputes) 269
IEL *see* international economic law
IFC (International Finance Corporation) 250
ILO Tripartite Declaration of Principles Concerning Multinational Enterprises 223, 233
IMF *see* International Monetary Fund
incorporation doctrine 175
India *see* legal education, India
Indochina Law School 283
institutional theories *see* sociological institutionalism
integrationism 109–13
interdisciplinary research 121–31
   background 121–2
   collaboration 122–3
   combined fields 123–30
   conclusion 130–1
intergovernmental economic/social development disciplines 103–4
internal affairs rule 175–6
international business transactions (IBT) courses
   and CSR 228–9
   professors 136–7, 144–5
International Centre for the Settlement of Investment Disputes (ICSID) 269
International Court of Justice (ICJ) 266–7
international economic law
   see also economic law approach
   characteristics 126
   and economic law 95–6
   and international law 92
   as liberal project 17–19
   meaning/importance 158–9
   post-war reality 19–21
   transactional/regulatory processes 127
   uncertain environment 16–17
International Economic Law Interest Group (IELG) (ASIL) 2–4, 243
international economics
   and international law 126–7
   and international relations 127–30
International Finance Corporation (IFC) 250

international financial system 255–63
   background 245–6
   Bretton Woods *see* Bretton Woods, system
   financial crises, international responses 254
   financial markets, globalisation 246–7, 251–4
   financial stability 255–6
   financial system *see* international financial system
   global regime prospect 262–3
   standard-setting 257–60
      coordination 258
      implementation/monitoring 260
      key standards 259
      process 259–60
   structure/processes 256–7
international labour mobility, regulation 23–4
international law
   definition 91–2
   and international economic law 92
   and international economics 126–7
   and international relations 123–5
   separatism *see* separatism
International Law Association, Committee on International Law on Foreign Investment 279
International Law Commission
   Articles on State Responsibility 279
   Study Group on the fragmentation of international law 110–12
international law of foreign investment *see* foreign investment, international law
International Monetary Fund (IMF) 121, 130, 247–8
   creation 297
   developing roles 249, 251
   financial crises, responses 254
   financial monitoring 260
   procedures 300
   underlying principles, promulgation 300, 302, 307
International Monetary Fund (IMF), and jurisdiction to prescribe
   Articles of Agreement 315, 318
   background 313
   conditionality 313
      Guidelines on 318–19, 325, 326–7
   developing country debt 318–21
   drawing rights, redefinition 314–16
   expansion of agenda 322–5
   internal external policies 316–18
   international consensus 329–30
   mirror principle 328
   probability of conflict 328–9
   reasonableness 313
   suggested principles 327–30
   territorial principle 328

international relations
  and international economics 127–30
  and international law 123–5
International Trade Organization 121, 247
internships 142
investment
  foreign *see* foreign investment, international law
  protection treaties, purpose 22–3
investment treaty arbitration, and case law 265–80
  see also jurisprudence constante, and investment treaty arbitration
  applicable law 278–9
  background 265–6
  conclusion 280
  in hierarchy of sources 266–7, 270–1
  legitimacy 279–80
  persuasive role 271–2
  precedent
    importance 267–70
    problems 270–1

Jackson, JH 19, 158
Janow, Merit 162
Jenkins, R 198
Jinks, D 33, 74
jurisprudence constante, and investment treaty arbitration 265, 273–8
  see also investment treaty arbitration, and case law
  basic approach 272–4
  formal/informal pressures 276–8
  international development 274–5
  tangential decisions 275–6
  transparency 275

Kant, I 111–12, 117
Kaufmann-Kohler, G 273, 277
Kelsen, H 111–12, 117
Keynes, John Maynard 247, 314
Keynesian approach 18–19
Kindleberger, CP 76
Koch, Karin 161
Koh, HH 85
Korea, and IMF 322–5
Koskenniemi, M 20, 110
Krueger, AO 76

labour mobility, international, regulation 23–4
Lamy, Pascal 71
law, international *see* international law
law schools (US) *see* legal education, US
legal education, India 185–205
  background 185–8
  conclusion 204–5
  and embedded liberalism 192–7
  governance reform discourses 197–9

inward looking focus 201–2
issue linkages 202–4
law schools 188–9
specific teaching 189–91
stakeholder participation 199–200
work opportunities 192
legal education, US 135–56
  additional coverage of IEL 140
  background 135–7
  conclusion 156
  courses
    depth/breadth 152–3
    gateway 151–2
    importance to Law School curricula 140–1
    individual subject areas 145–7
    offerings/frequency 139–40, 143–4
    as preparation for practice 141
    professors' own 144–5
  curricular changes 154–5
  fundamental competences 148–9
  institutional coverage 149
  gateway courses 151–2
  institutional support 151, 153–4
  internships 142
  moot competitions 141–2, 155–6
  non-traditional methodologies 149–50
  opportunities outside classroom 141–2
  student participation 154
  study abroad programs 142
  suggestions 150–1
  surveys
    Associate Deans 138–42
    Law Professors 142–51
    methodology 136–7
  and technology advances 155
legal formalism 30
legal realism 37, 48
  see also new legal realism
lex mercatoria 99
liberalism, pragmatic 17–19, 20–1
limited liability 177–8
Lindroos, A 110
Lyon summit (G-7) 255

MacKinnon, C 70
managers and social obligations 179–82
Marcet, Jane 161, 162
March, JG 74
Marrakesh Agreement Establishing the WTO 261
Martineau, Harriet 161
Mehling, M 110
Methanex tribunal 276
Mexico, developing country debt 319–20, 320–1
MIGA (Multilateral Investment Guarantee Agency) 250

MNEs (multinational enterprises) *see under* corporate social responsibility
Mondev case 276
moot competitions 141–2, 155–6
Multilateral Investment Guarantee Agency (MIGA) 250
multilateral trading system
  and development 22
  and international trade 21
multinational enterprises (MNEs) *see under* corporate social responsibility

NAEWG (North American Energy Working Group) 209
NAFTA (North American Free Trade Agreement) 67–8, 208–12, 268, 270
  parochialism 214–16
national administrative disciplines 104–6
neo-functionalism 128–9, 131
New Haven school 32
new legal realism 29–42
  analytic approach 37–8
  background 29
  conclusion 41–2
  examples 40–1
  law/fact constructions 38–9
  and recursive interactions 39–40
  scholarship categories *see* research typologies
  top-down/bottom-up approach 39
Newcomer, Mabel 162
Nielsen, LB 35
normative advocacy 31
normativity 111–12, 114
North American Energy Working Group (NAEWG) 209
North American Free Trade Agreement (NAFTA) 67–8, 208–12, 268, 270

OECD
  Convention on Combating Bribery of Foreign Public Officials 225, 233
  on foreign investment 280
  Guidelines for Multinational Enterprises 222
Ohlson, PI 165
Olsen, JP 74
Ostry, Sylvia 162

parochialism 212–18
  background 212–13
  domestic 213–14
  and legal education exchange 216–18
  NAFTA 214–16
Paulsson, Professor 279
pedagogy *see* legal education, US
Polanyi, K 186, 193
Porges, A 48

practice developments
  background 237
  dispute settlement, diversification 240–3
  global structures 238–9
  scope 237–8
pragmatic liberalism 17–19, 20–1
prescription 48
private law regulation, cross-border economic activities 97–9
problem-space concept 187
prudential regulation of global banking 99–102
public choice scholarship 49

Quintyn, M 256

Rawls, J 18
realism 124–5, 131
refugee status 81
regime theory 125, 131
regional trade agreements 238
  regulation 23
regionalism *see* hybridisation; parochialism
regulatory processes 127
research typologies 15–28, 29–37, 43–51
  background 15–17, 43–4
  common law consistency 47–8
  complementarity 26–8
  critical legal studies 48–9
  description and prescription 48
  doctrinal analysis/description 30, 45–7
  empirical *see* empiricism
  interdisciplinary research *see* interdisciplinary research
  new legal realism *see* new legal realism
  normative advocacy 31
  policy issues 21–4
  post-war reality 19–21
  pragmatic liberalism 17–19, 20–1
  public choice scholarship 49
  qualitative work 34–6
  quantitative work 34
  relevance 24–6
  theory *see* theoretical exposition
Ricardian-Smithian traditions 17–18
Risse, T 74, 75
Rose, CV 281
Rose, A 21, 24
Ruggie, JG 19, 186, 193

Samuelson, Marion Crawford 161
Schinasi, G 256
scholarship categories *see* research typologies
Schreuer, C 269
Schwartz-Shea, P 213
Schweitzer, Mr. 317
Scott, WR 80
SDR (special drawing rights) 249

seat theory 175
separatism 107–19
  background 107–8
  definition 108–9
  and integrationism 109–13
  and legality 118–19
  and substantive values 117–18
  as value pluralism 113–17
Sexton, J 207
shareholder primacy model 226–8
SIEL (Society of International Economic Law) 9–11
Simmons, RT 213
Society of International Economic Law (SIEL) 9–11
sociological institutionalism 73–88
  background 73
  cognitive-cultural control 79–81
  and compliance 83–4
  conclusion 87–8
  judicialisation effects 84–5
  normative systems 73–5
    and legal processes 85–6
  and trade lawyers 83–7
  and trade regime 75–9, 81–3
South-East Asia crises 322–5
special drawing rights (SDR) 249
stakeholders
  emerging 241–2
  theory 228, 231
standards, financial see international financial system, standard-setting
stare decisis 271–2
Stiglitz, J 22, 24
study abroad programs 142
Study Group on the fragmentation of international law (International Law Commission) 110–12
Suchman, MC 79, 86
Summers, Larry 68–9
Sutherland, Peter 71

Tarullo, DK 85
Taylor, M 256
teaching disciplines see legal education
theoretical exposition 31–3
  and methodology 44–5
Toope, SJ 85, 86
Torrens, Robert 161
TPRM (Trade Policy Review Mechanism) 78
Trachtman, JP 32, 54, 58–9
Trade Act 1974 (US) 237
Trade Agreements Act 1979 (US) 237–8
trade agreements, purpose 22
trade barrier concept 81–3
Trade Policy Review Mechanism (TPRM) 78
transactional processes 127
transnational commercial disciplines 104–6

United Nations (UN) 123–4
  Global Compact 222
US law schools see legal education, US

value pluralism 113–17
VBTA (Vietnam bilateral trade agreement with US) 286–91
Vietnam 281–96
  background 281–3
  bilateral trade agreement with US (VBTA) 286–91
  Chinese influence 286–7
  conclusion 296
  economic crisis 283, 284
  economic opening 284–6
  legal system 283–4, 284–6, 288, 290–1
  legal/judical reform 294–5
  WTO accession 288, 289, 291–4
Viner, J 314

Washington Consensus 249
WBIP see World Bank Inspection Panel
Weiler, JHH 76–7
Weiner, M 199
White, Harry Dexter 247
Wilkinson, R 77
Williams, B 116
women's contributions 157–70
  background 157–8
  celebration 160–2
  conclusion 169–70
  enrolment numbers 163–4
  feminist perspectives 159–60, 169
  ghettoisation concerns 166–7
  interview approach 165–6
  journal articles 164–5, 168
  quantification 162–5
  teaching/scholarships 162–3
World Bank 81, 121, 130, 247
  creation 297
  developing roles 249–50, 251
  and international financial system 255
World Bank Inspection Panel (WBIP) 297–311
  background 297–8
  conclusion 311
  creation 302
  procedures 299–300
  requests for inspection 300–1
    appellate body proposal 304–6, 307–11
  findings/conclusions 303
  tabular comparison 307
World Business Council for Sustainable Development 220
World Trade Organisation (WTO) 40, 53–72, 127–8, 130, 247, 251
  agreement 238, 261
  corporate opportunism 63–5

creation 54–5, 298
dispute settlement
  Body (DSB) 240–1, 298–303, 306
  precedents 267
  tabular comparison 307
and financial liberalism 261–2
and financial standards 257
and global financial markets 252–3
global trade regulation, and legal education 59–62
institutional issues *see* sociological institutionalism
and integrationism 109–10
and international agreements 298
and legal education 209, 212
legal/conceptual structure 65–6
legitimacy debates 55–7
  post 2001 57
opportunism 53–4
  corporate 63–5, 68–70
prospects 71–2
role of participating states 66–8
scholarship limitations 62–3
separatism *see* separatism
Vietnam's accession 288, 289, 291–4